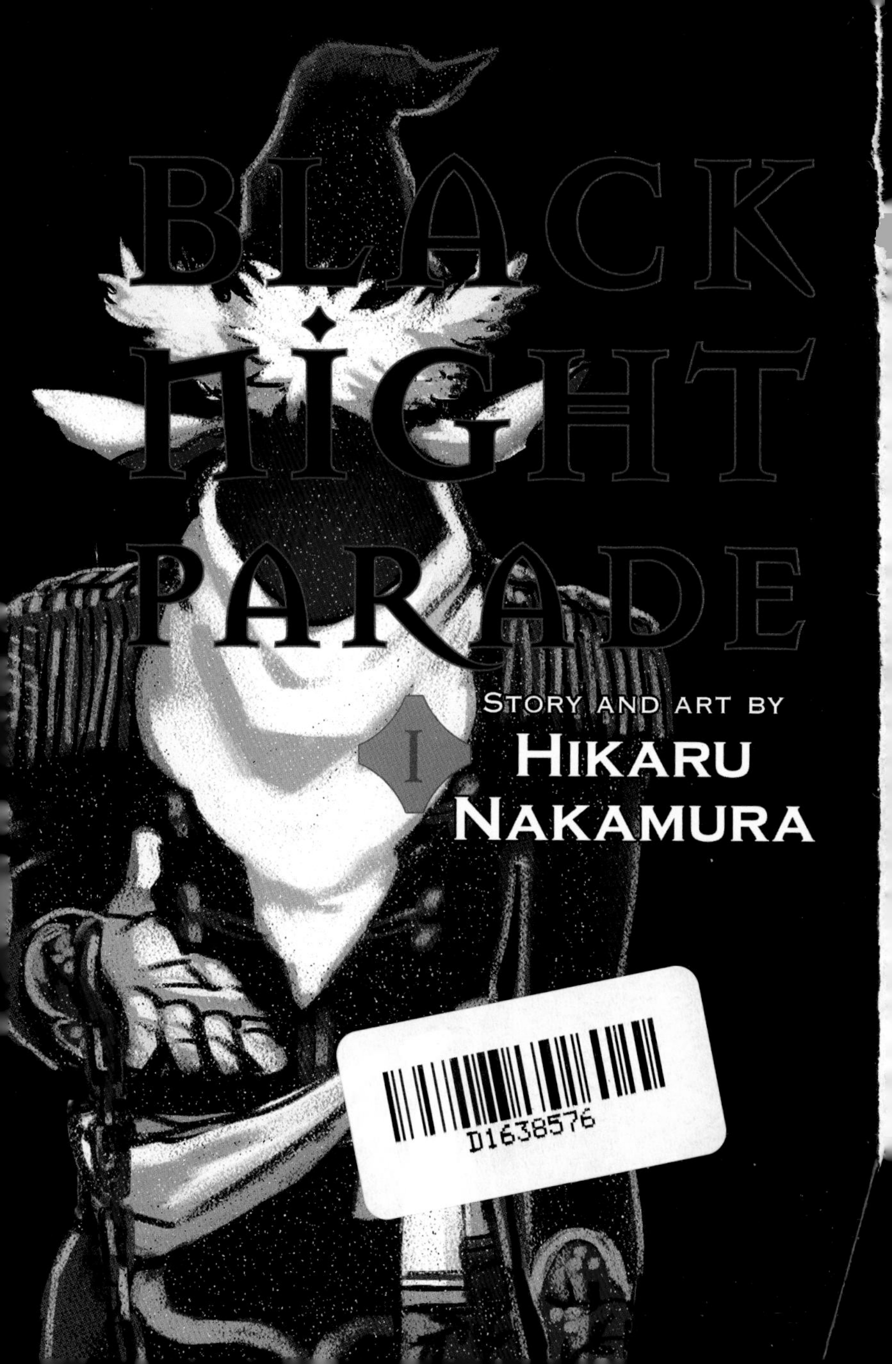
BLACK NIGHT PARADE
I
STORY AND ART BY
HIKARU NAKAMURA

BLACK NIGHT PARADE

CONTENTS

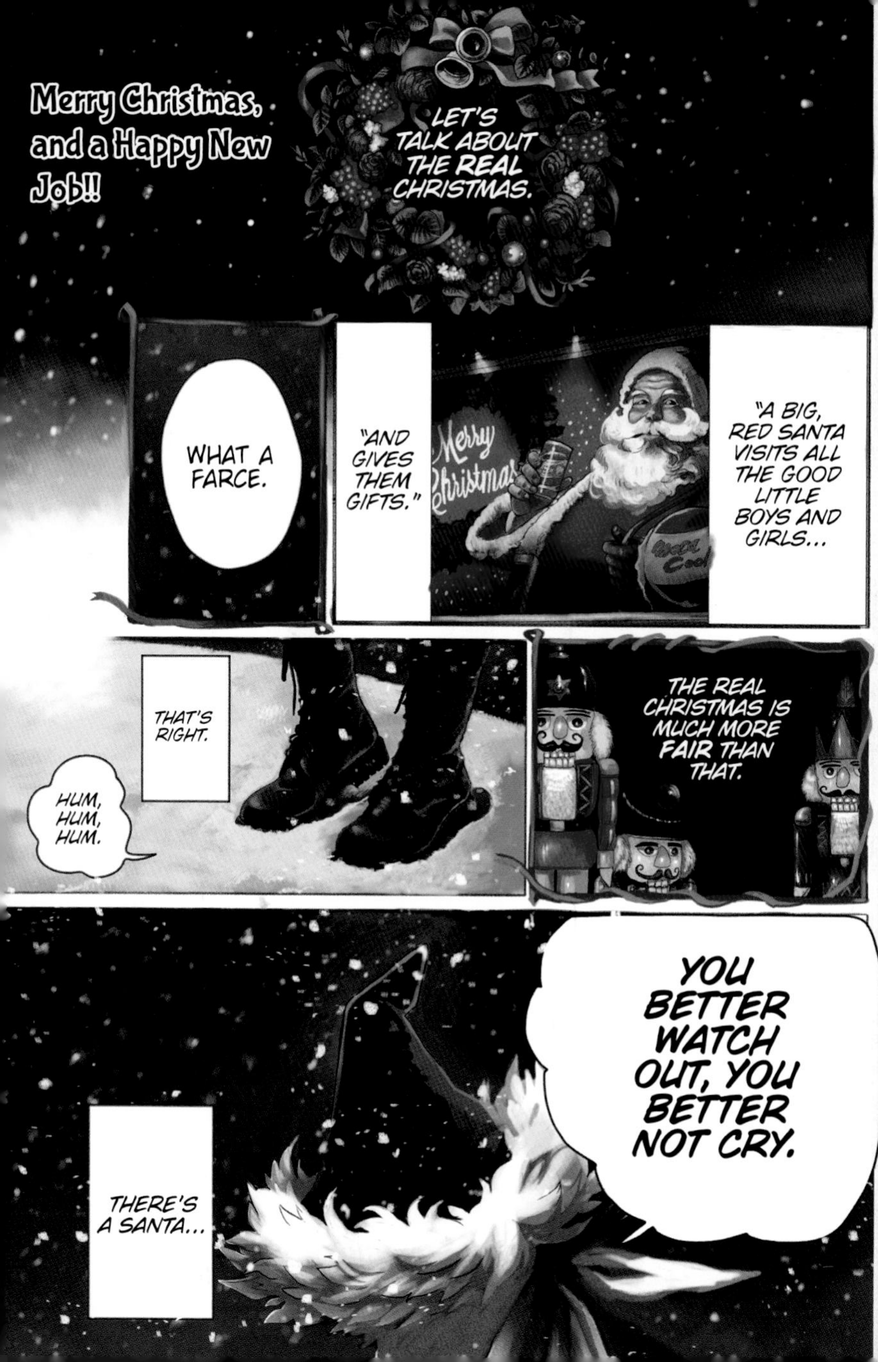
LET'S TALK ABOUT THE REAL CHRISTMAS.
Merry Christmas, and a Happy New Job!!
"A BIG, RED SANTA VISITS ALL THE GOOD LITTLE BOYS AND GIRLS...
"AND GIVES THEM GIFTS."
Merry Christmas
WHAT A FARCE.
THE REAL CHRISTMAS IS MUCH MORE FAIR THAN THAT.
THAT'S RIGHT.
HUM, HUM, HUM.
YOU BETTER WATCH OUT, YOU BETTER NOT CRY.
THERE'S A SANTA...

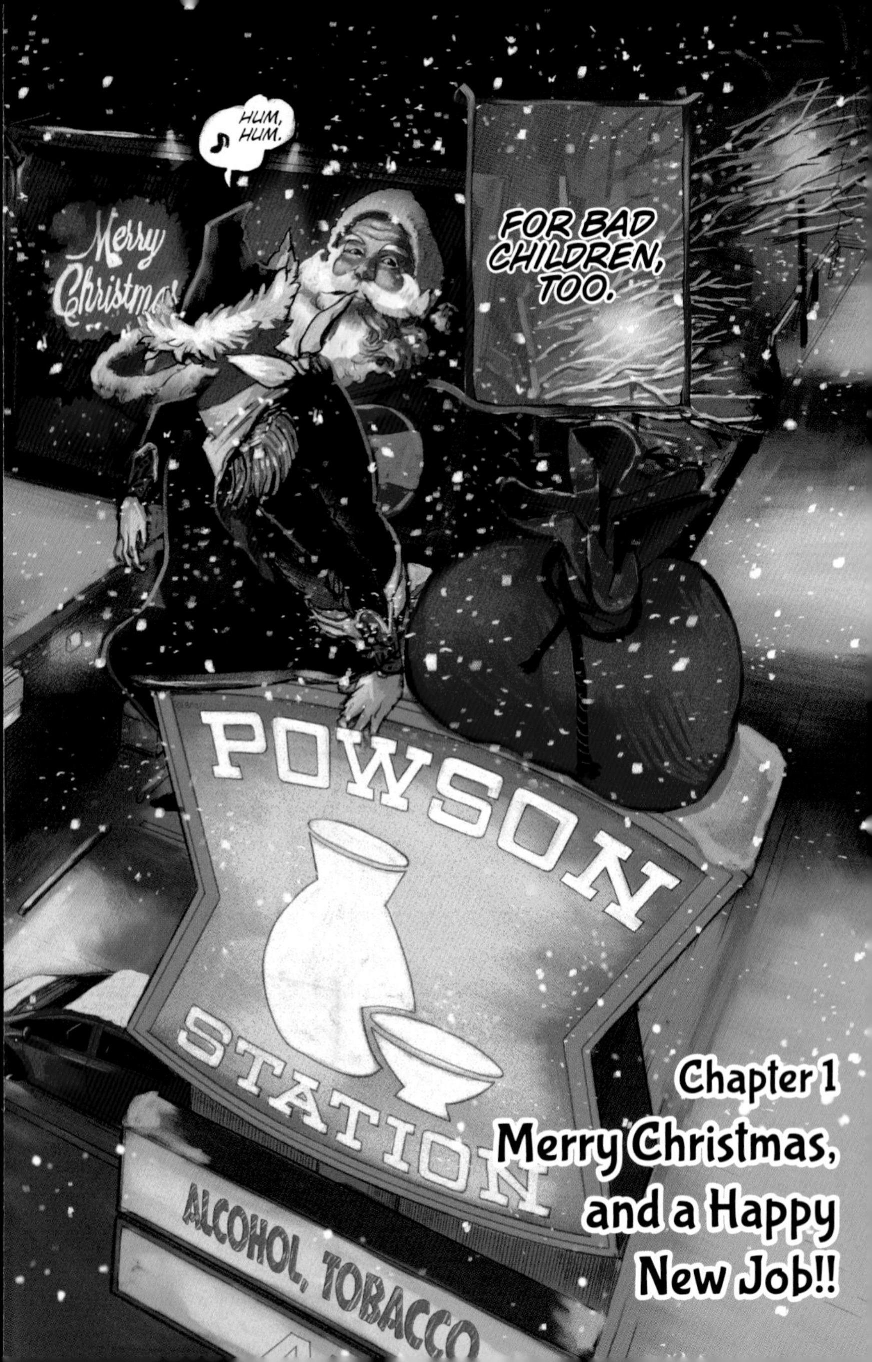
HUM, HUM.
Merry Christmas
FOR BAD CHILDREN, TOO.
POWSON STATION
ALCOHOL, TOBACCO

Chapter 1
Merry Christmas, and a Happy New Job!!

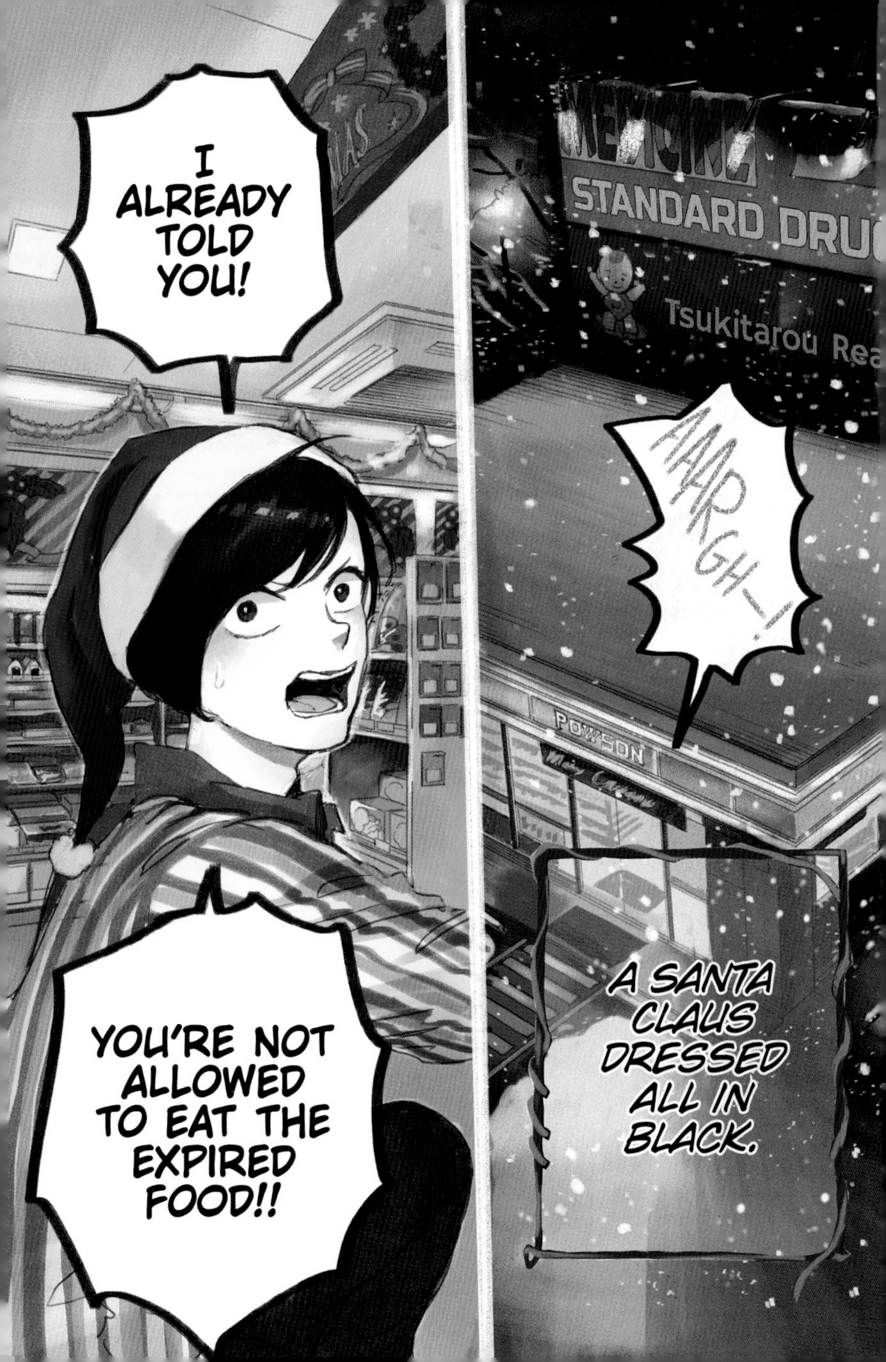
STANDARD DRU
Tsukitarou Rea
AAARGH—!
POWSON
A SANTA CLAUS DRESSED ALL IN BLACK.
I ALREADY TOLD YOU!
YOU'RE NOT ALLOWED TO EAT THE EXPIRED FOOD!!

BLACK
NIGHT
PARADE

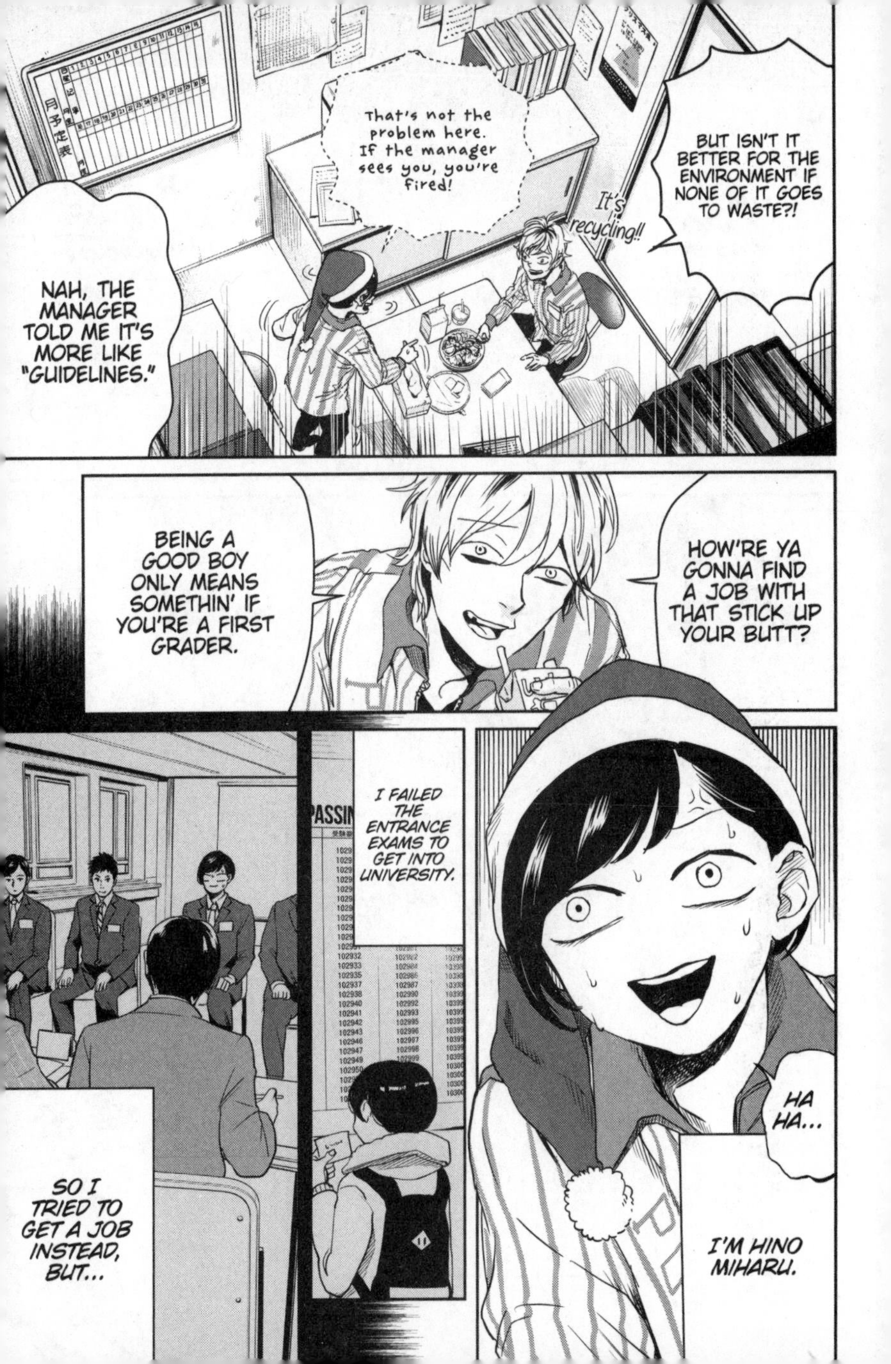
BUT ISN'T IT BETTER FOR THE ENVIRONMENT IF NONE OF IT GOES TO WASTE?!
It's recycling!!
That's not the problem here. If the manager sees you, you're fired!
NAH, THE MANAGER TOLD ME IT'S MORE LIKE "GUIDELINES."
HOW'RE YA GONNA FIND A JOB WITH THAT STICK UP YOUR BUTT?
BEING A GOOD BOY ONLY MEANS SOMETHIN' IF YOU'RE A FIRST GRADER.
HA HA...
I'M HINO MIHARU.
I FAILED THE ENTRANCE EXAMS TO GET INTO UNIVERSITY.
SO I TRIED TO GET A JOB INSTEAD, BUT...

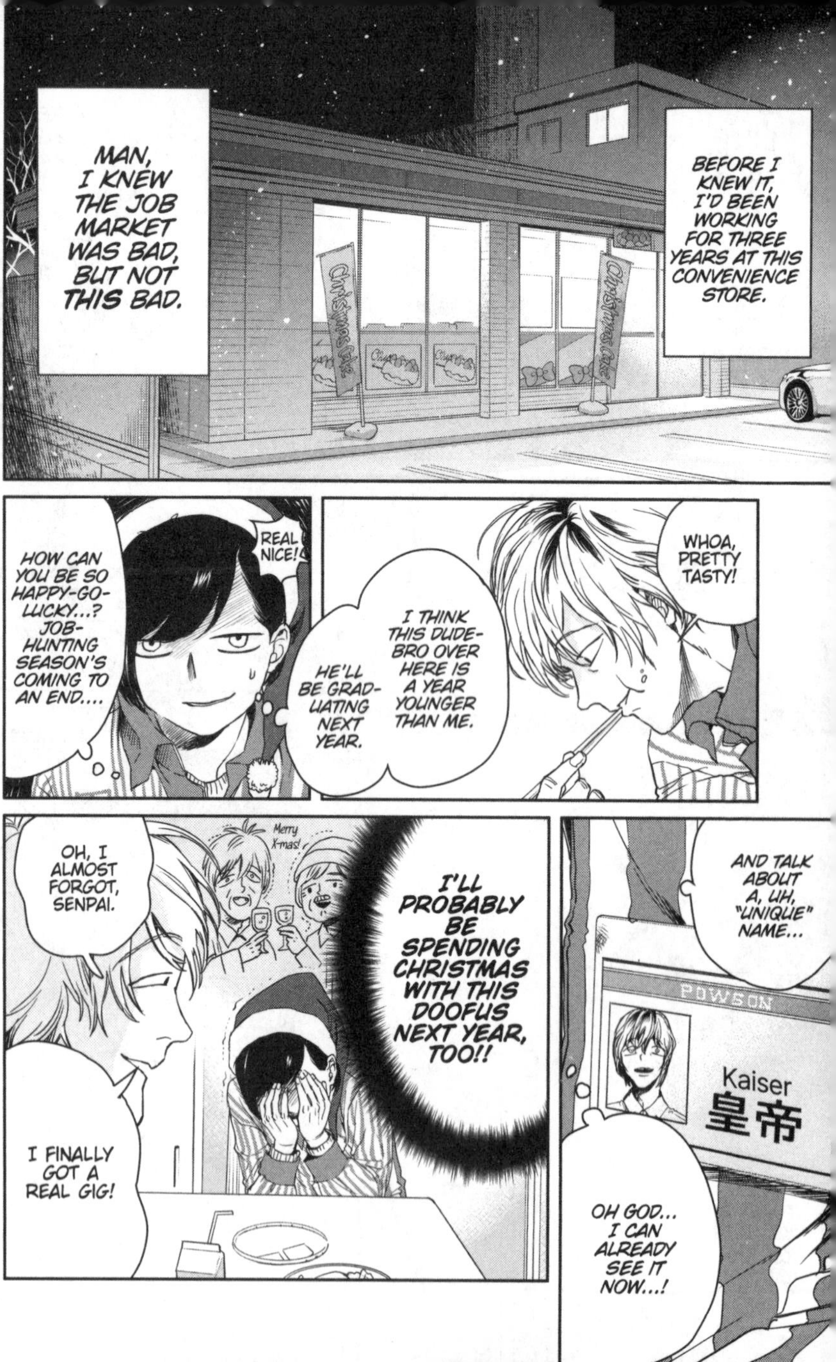
BEFORE I KNEW IT, I'D BEEN WORKING FOR THREE YEARS AT THIS CONVENIENCE STORE.
MAN, I KNEW THE JOB MARKET WAS BAD, BUT NOT THIS BAD.
Christmas Cake
Christmas Cake
WHOA, PRETTY TASTY!
I THINK THIS DUDE-BRO OVER HERE IS A YEAR YOUNGER THAN ME.
HE'LL BE GRADUATING NEXT YEAR.
REAL NICE!
HOW CAN YOU BE SO HAPPY-GO-LUCKY...? JOB-HUNTING SEASON'S COMING TO AN END....
AND TALK ABOUT A, UH, "UNIQUE" NAME...
POWSON
Kaiser
皇帝
OH GOD... I CAN ALREADY SEE IT NOW...!
Merry X-mas!
I'LL PROBABLY BE SPENDING CHRISTMAS WITH THIS DOOFUS NEXT YEAR, TOO!!
OH, I ALMOST FORGOT, SENPAI.
I FINALLY GOT A REAL GIG!

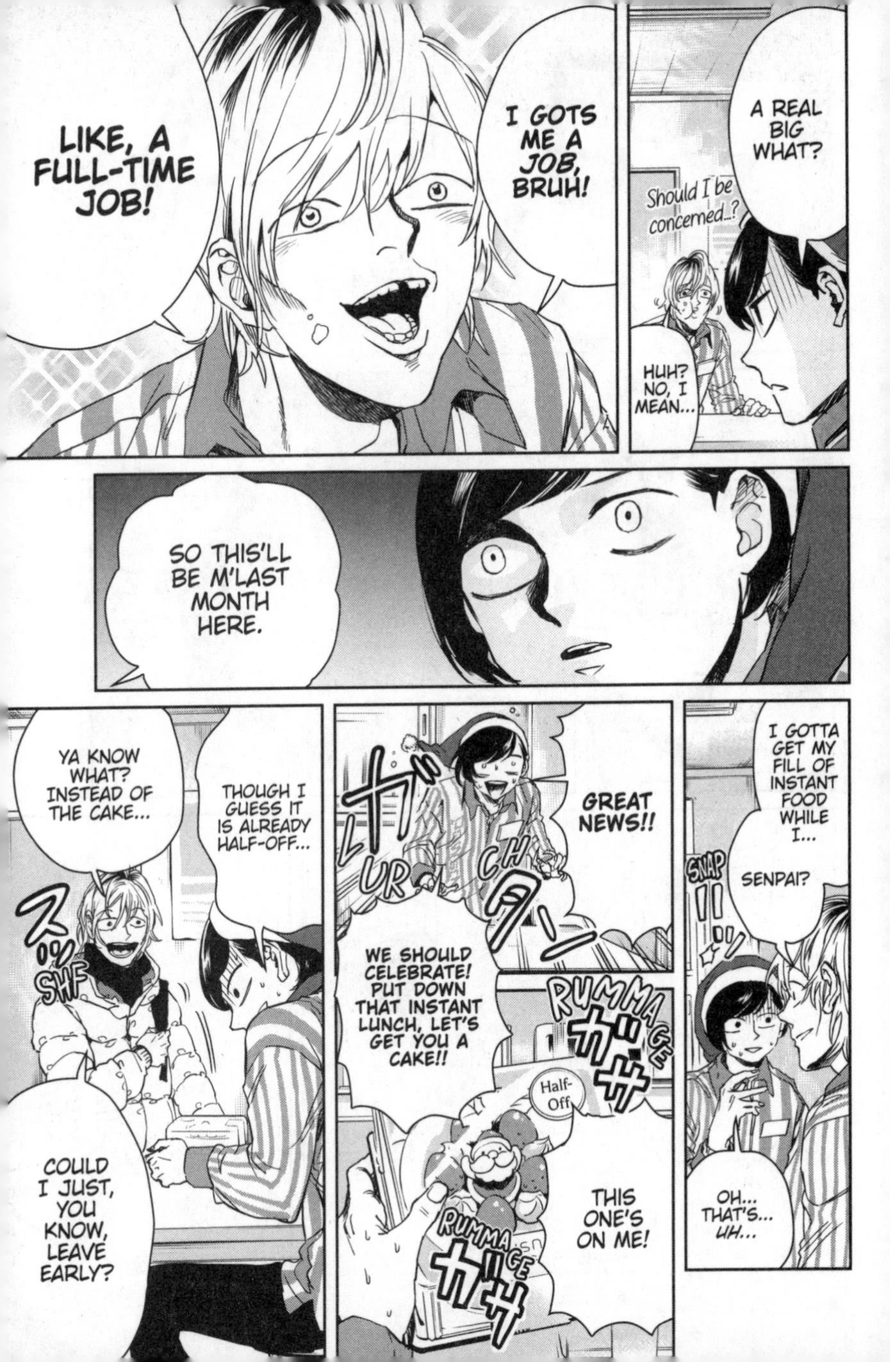
A REAL BIG WHAT?
Should I be concerned..?
HUH? NO, I MEAN...
I GOTS ME A JOB, BRUH!
LIKE, A FULL-TIME JOB!
SO THIS'LL BE M'LAST MONTH HERE.
I GOTTA GET MY FILL OF INSTANT FOOD WHILE I...
SNAP
SENPAI?
OH... THAT'S... UH...
GREAT NEWS!!
LURCH
WE SHOULD CELEBRATE! PUT DOWN THAT INSTANT LUNCH, LET'S GET YOU A CAKE!!
RUMMAGE
Half-Off
THIS ONE'S ON ME!
RUMMAGE
THOUGH I GUESS IT IS ALREADY HALF-OFF...
YA KNOW WHAT? INSTEAD OF THE CAKE...
SHF
COULD I JUST, YOU KNOW, LEAVE EARLY?

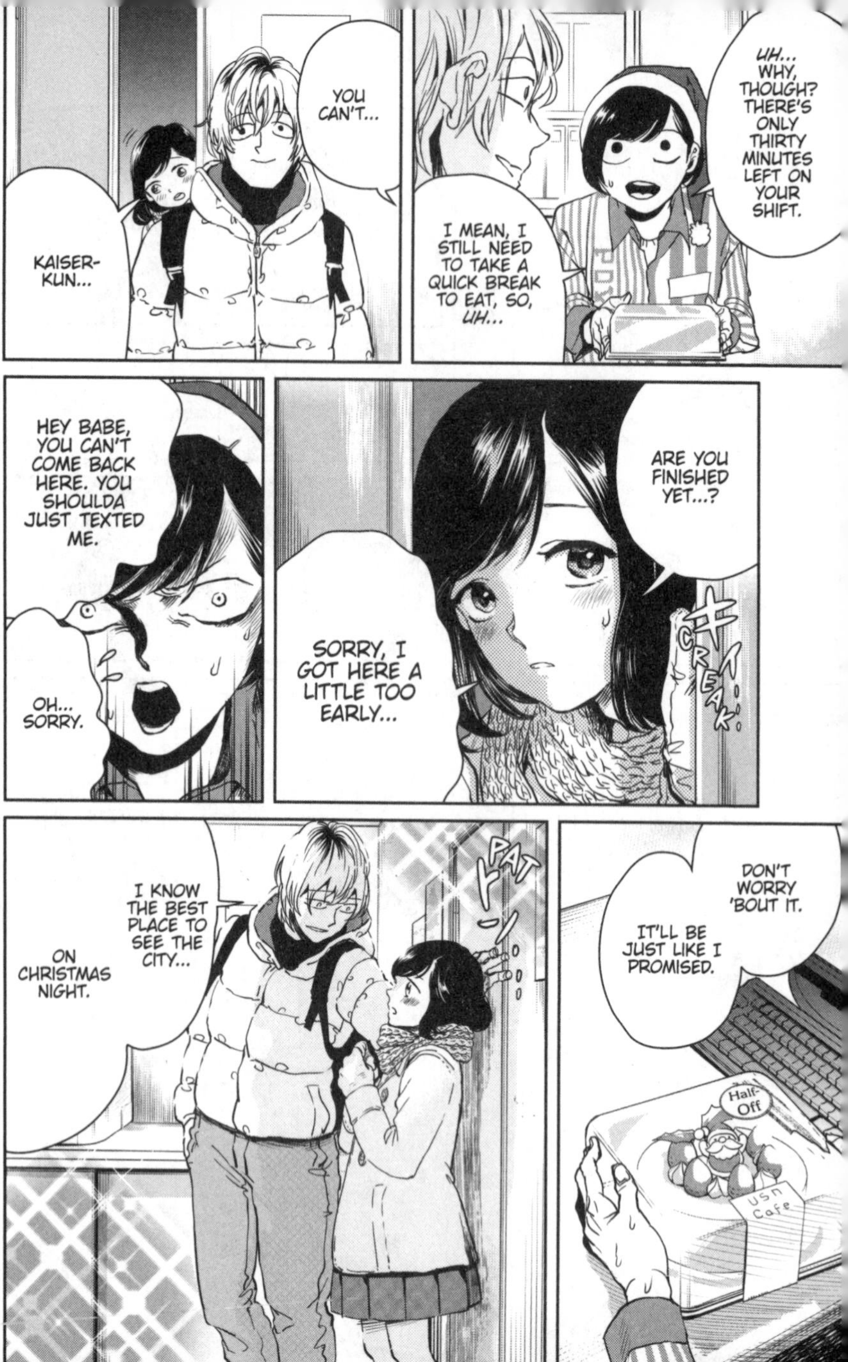
UH... WHY, THOUGH? THERE'S ONLY THIRTY MINUTES LEFT ON YOUR SHIFT.
I MEAN, I STILL NEED TO TAKE A QUICK BREAK TO EAT, SO, UH...
YOU CAN'T...
KAISER-KUN...
ARE YOU FINISHED YET...?
CREAK
SORRY, I GOT HERE A LITTLE TOO EARLY...
HEY BABE, YOU CAN'T COME BACK HERE. YOU SHOULDA JUST TEXTED ME.
OH... SORRY.
DON'T WORRY 'BOUT IT.
IT'LL BE JUST LIKE I PROMISED.
Half-Off
USn Cafe
PAT
I KNOW THE BEST PLACE TO SEE THE CITY...
ON CHRISTMAS NIGHT.

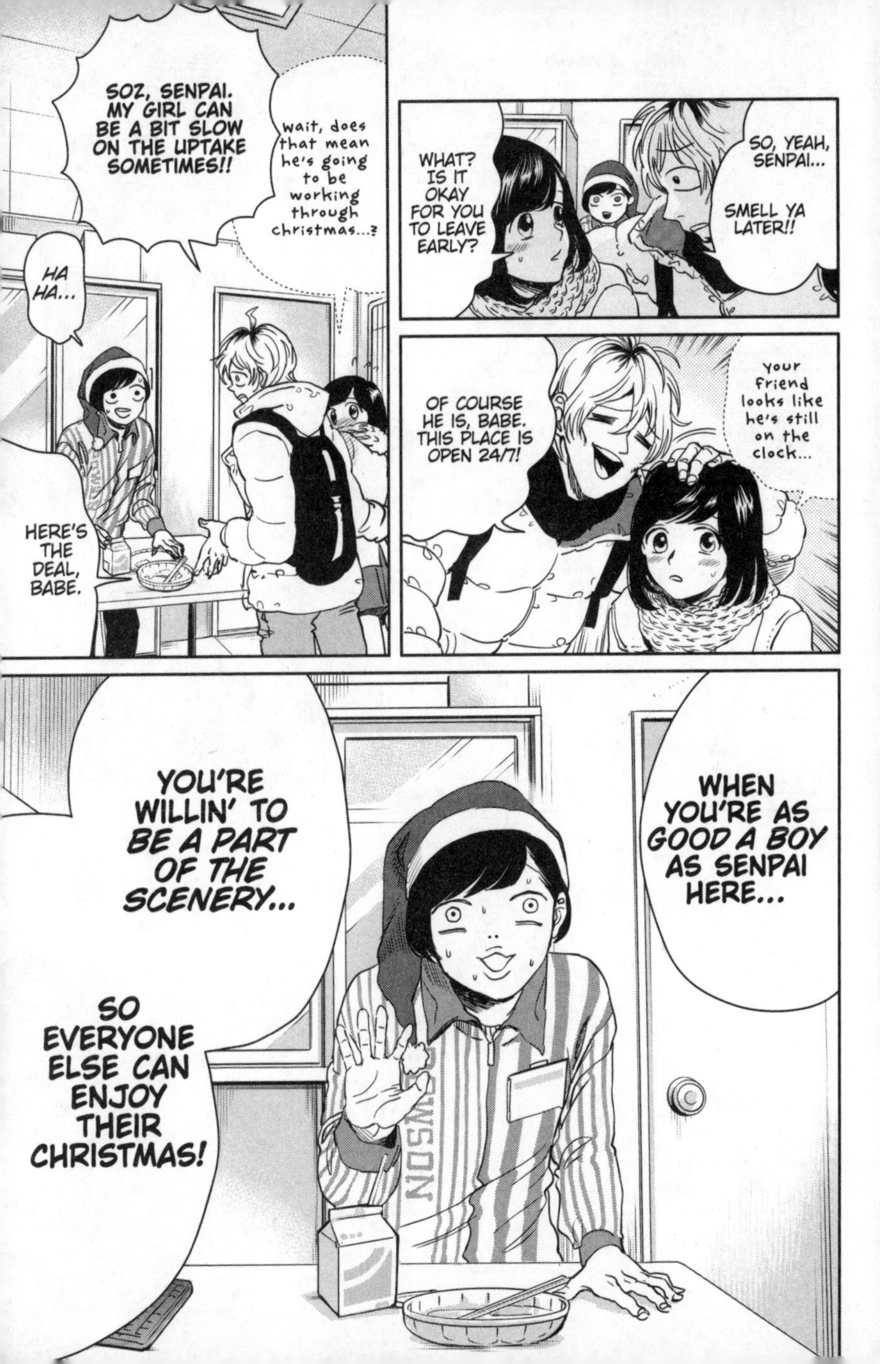
SO, YEAH, SENPAI...
SMELL YA LATER!!
WHAT? IS IT OKAY FOR YOU TO LEAVE EARLY?
Your friend looks like he's still on the clock...
OF COURSE HE IS, BABE. THIS PLACE IS OPEN 24/7!
wait, does that mean he's going to be working through christmas...?
SOZ, SENPAI. MY GIRL CAN BE A BIT SLOW ON THE UPTAKE SOMETIMES!!
HA HA...
HERE'S THE DEAL, BABE.
WHEN YOU'RE AS GOOD A BOY AS SENPAI HERE...
YOU'RE WILLIN' TO BE A PART OF THE SCENERY...
SO EVERYONE ELSE CAN ENJOY THEIR CHRISTMAS!

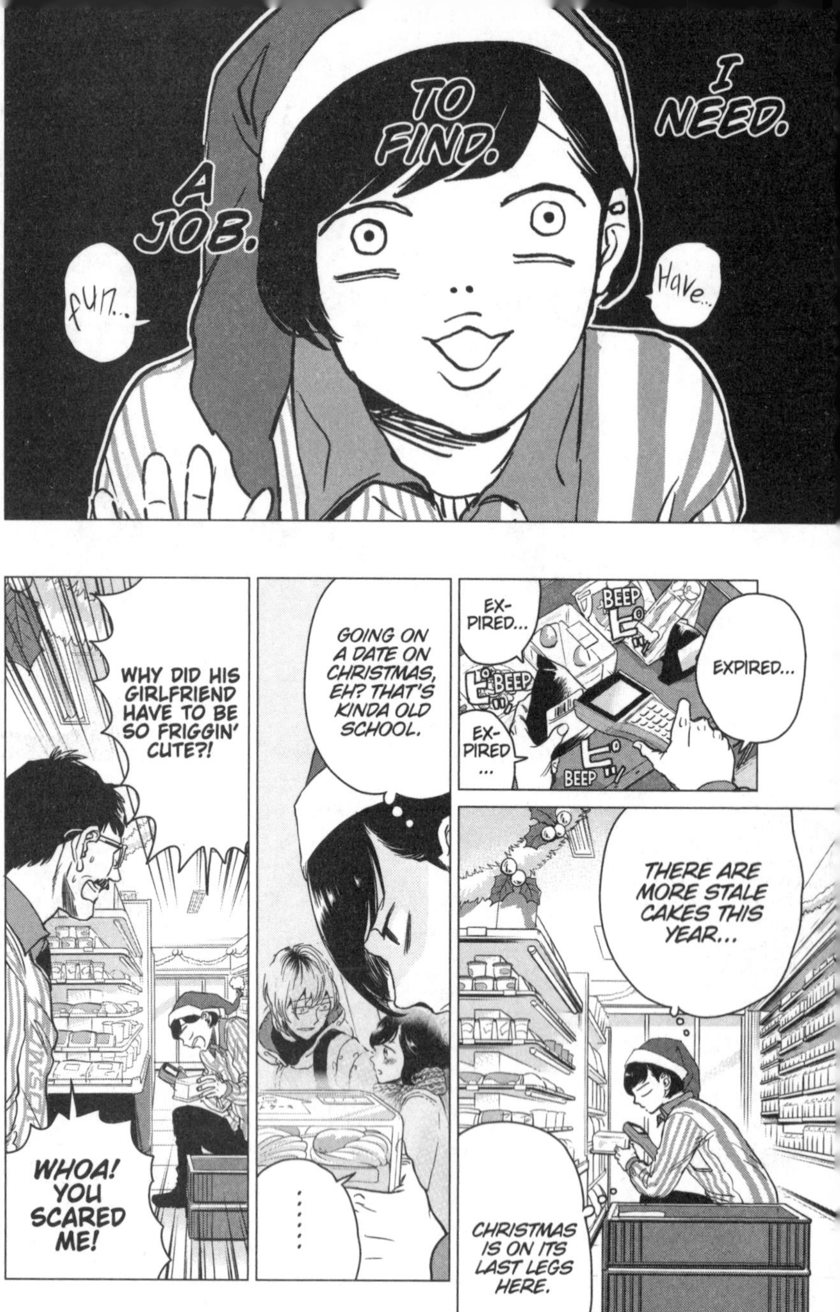
I NEED.
TO FIND.
A JOB.
Have...
fun...
BEEP
EXPIRED...
EX-PIRED...
BEEP
EX-PIRED ...
BEEP
THERE ARE MORE STALE CAKES THIS YEAR...
CHRISTMAS IS ON ITS LAST LEGS HERE.
GOING ON A DATE ON CHRISTMAS, EH? THAT'S KINDA OLD SCHOOL.
......
WHY DID HIS GIRLFRIEND HAVE TO BE SO FRIGGIN' CUTE?!
WHOA! YOU SCARED ME!

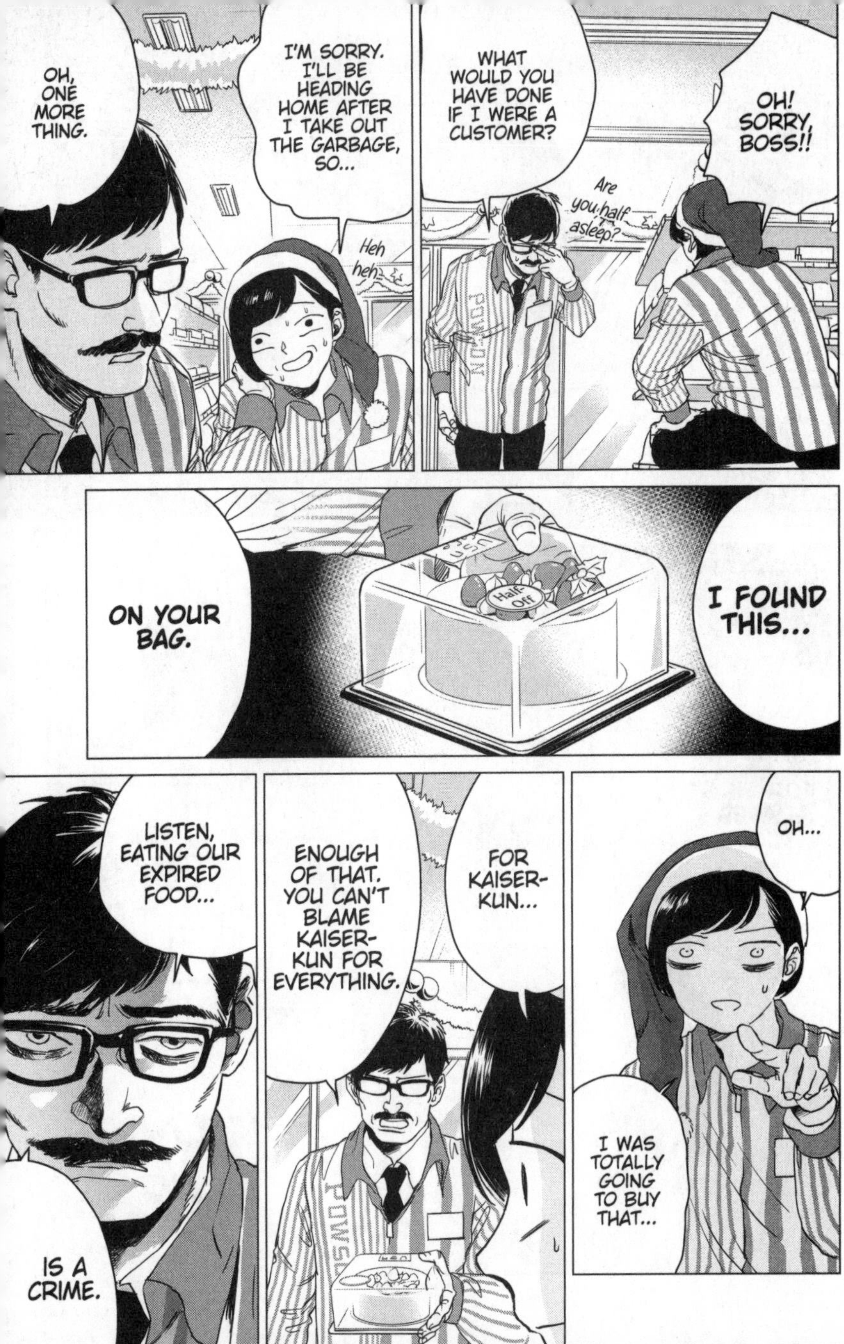
OH! SORRY, BOSS!!
WHAT WOULD YOU HAVE DONE IF I WERE A CUSTOMER?
Are you half asleep?
I'M SORRY. I'LL BE HEADING HOME AFTER I TAKE OUT THE GARBAGE, SO...
Heh heh
OH, ONE MORE THING.
I FOUND THIS...
Half-Off
ON YOUR BAG.
OH...
I WAS TOTALLY GOING TO BUY THAT...
FOR KAISER-KUN...
ENOUGH OF THAT. YOU CAN'T BLAME KAISER-KUN FOR EVERYTHING.
LISTEN, EATING OUR EXPIRED FOOD...
IS A CRIME.

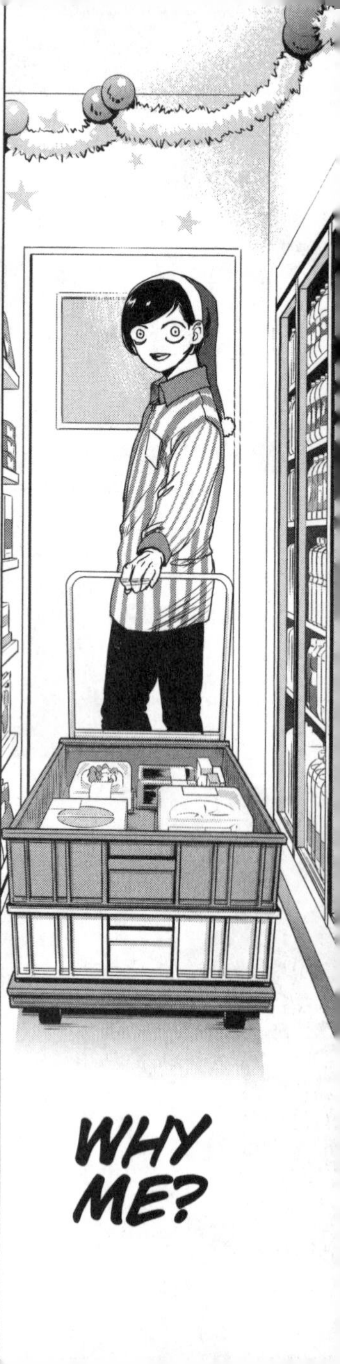
WHY ME?
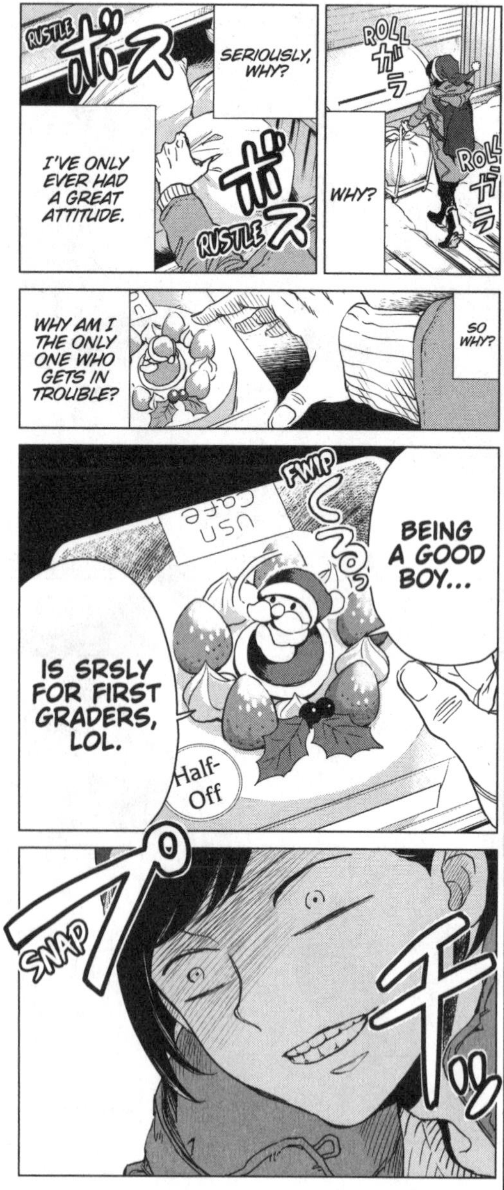
ROLL ガラ
ROLL ガラ
WHY?
SERIOUSLY, WHY?
RUSTLE ボス
I'VE ONLY EVER HAD A GREAT ATTITUDE.
RUSTLE ボス
SO WHY?
WHY AM I THE ONLY ONE WHO GETS IN TROUBLE?
FWIP くるっ
BEING A GOOD BOY...
IS SRSLY FOR FIRST GRADERS, LOL.
Half-Off
SNAP プチッ

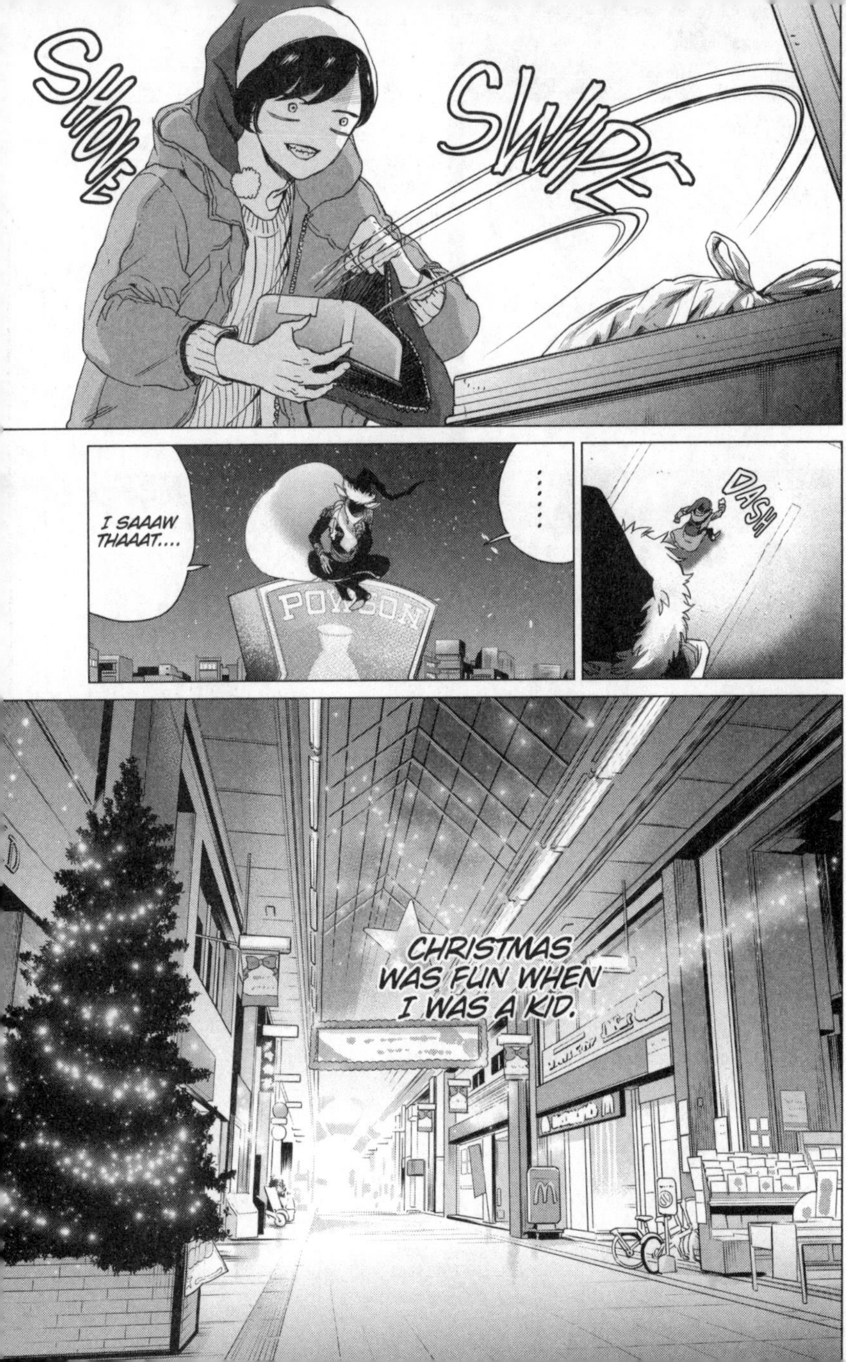
SWIPE
SHOVE
DASH
.....
I SAAAW THAAAT....
POWSON
CHRISTMAS WAS FUN WHEN I WAS A KID.

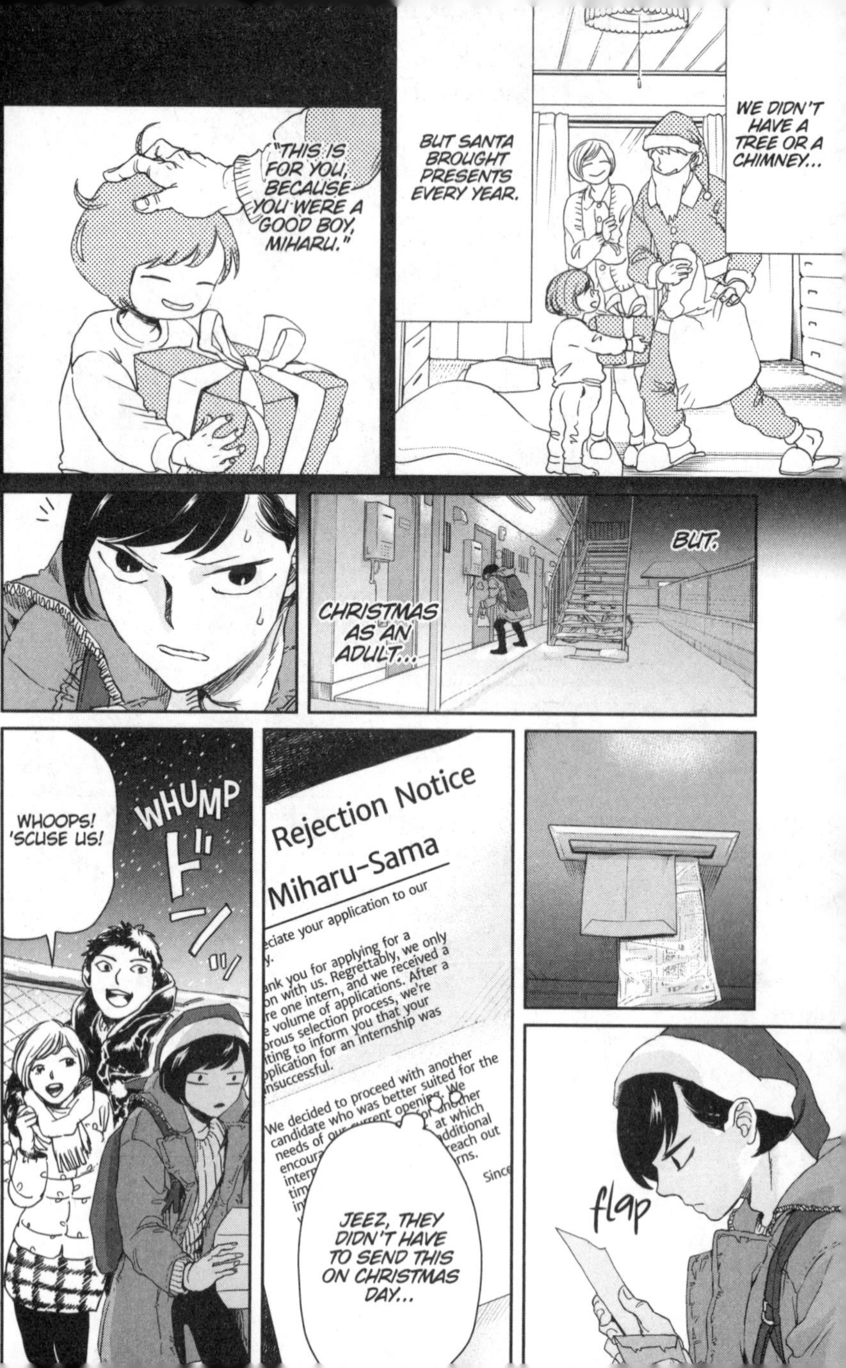
WE DIDN'T HAVE A TREE OR A CHIMNEY...
BUT SANTA BROUGHT PRESENTS EVERY YEAR.
"THIS IS FOR YOU, BECAUSE YOU WERE A GOOD BOY, MIHARU."
BUT.
CHRISTMAS AS AN ADULT...
flap
Rejection Notice
Miharu-Sama
eciate your application to our
y.
ank you for applying for a
on with us. Regrettably, we only
re one intern, and we received a
e volume of applications. After a
orous selection process, we're
iting to inform you that your
application for an internship was
unsuccessful.
We decided to proceed with another
candidate who was better suited for the
needs of our current opening. We
Since
JEEZ, THEY DIDN'T HAVE TO SEND THIS ON CHRISTMAS DAY...
WHUMP
ド
WHOOPS! 'SCUSE US!

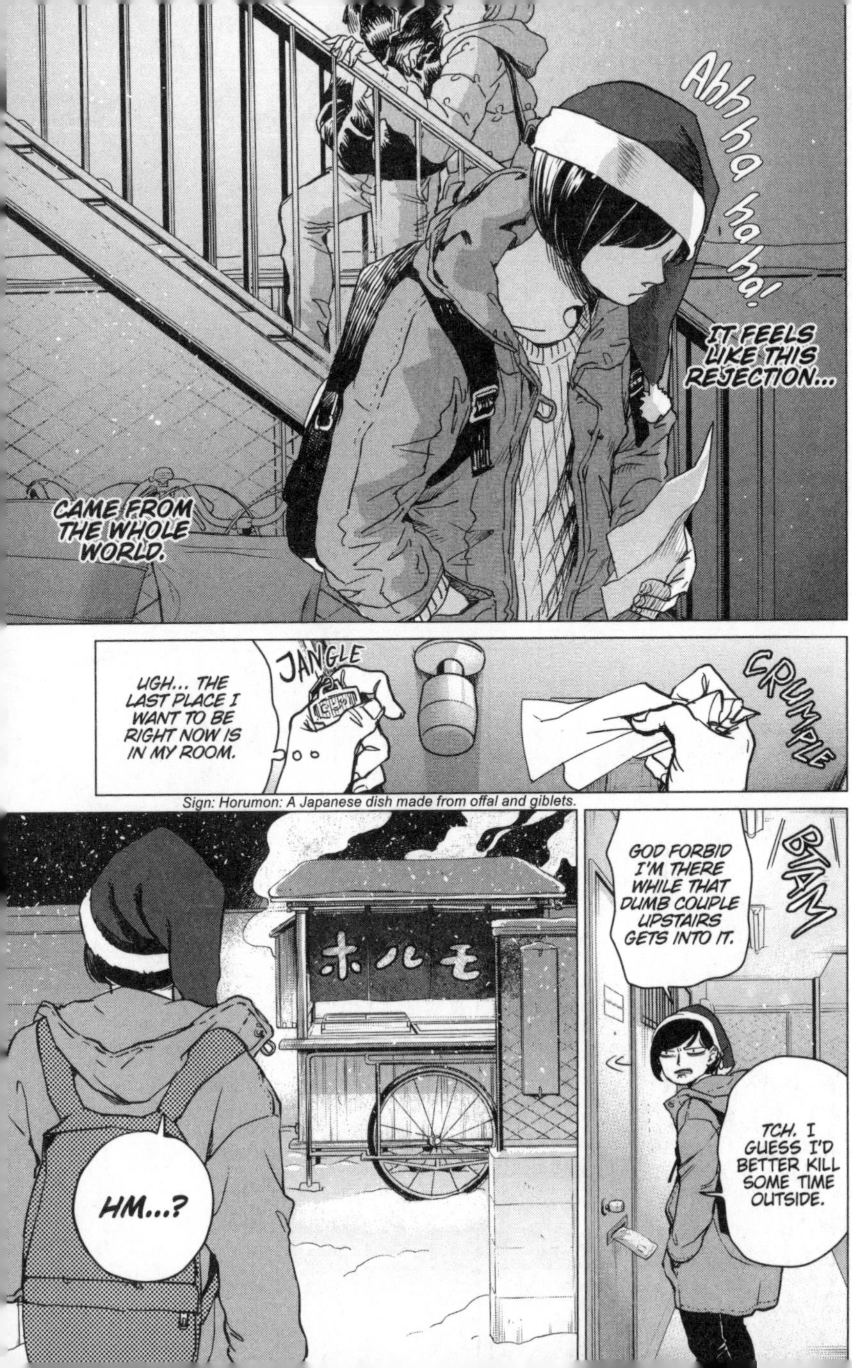
Ahhha ha ha!
IT FEELS LIKE THIS REJECTION...
CAME FROM THE WHOLE WORLD.
CRUMPLE
JANGLE
UGH... THE LAST PLACE I WANT TO BE RIGHT NOW IS IN MY ROOM.
BTAM
GOD FORBID I'M THERE WHILE THAT DUMB COUPLE UPSTAIRS GETS INTO IT.
TCH. I GUESS I'D BETTER KILL SOME TIME OUTSIDE.
ホルモ
HM...?
Sign: Horumon: A Japanese dish made from offal and giblets.

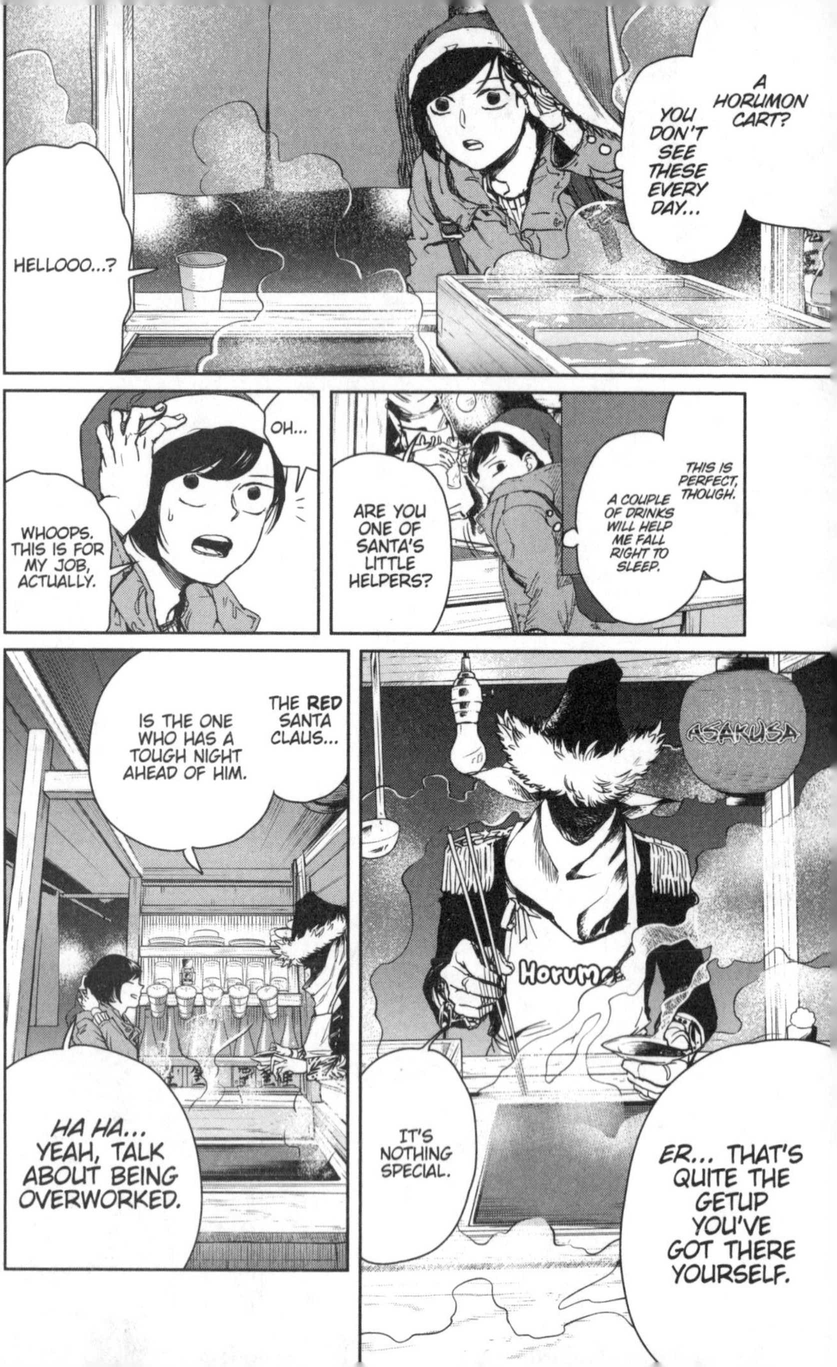
A HORUMON CART?
YOU DON'T SEE THESE EVERY DAY...
HELLOOO...?
THIS IS PERFECT, THOUGH.
A COUPLE OF DRINKS WILL HELP ME FALL RIGHT TO SLEEP.
ARE YOU ONE OF SANTA'S LITTLE HELPERS?
OH...
WHOOPS. THIS IS FOR MY JOB, ACTUALLY.
ASAKUSA
ER... THAT'S QUITE THE GETUP YOU'VE GOT THERE YOURSELF.
IT'S NOTHING SPECIAL.
THE **RED** SANTA CLAUS...
IS THE ONE WHO HAS A TOUGH NIGHT AHEAD OF HIM.
HA HA... YEAH, TALK ABOUT BEING OVERWORKED.

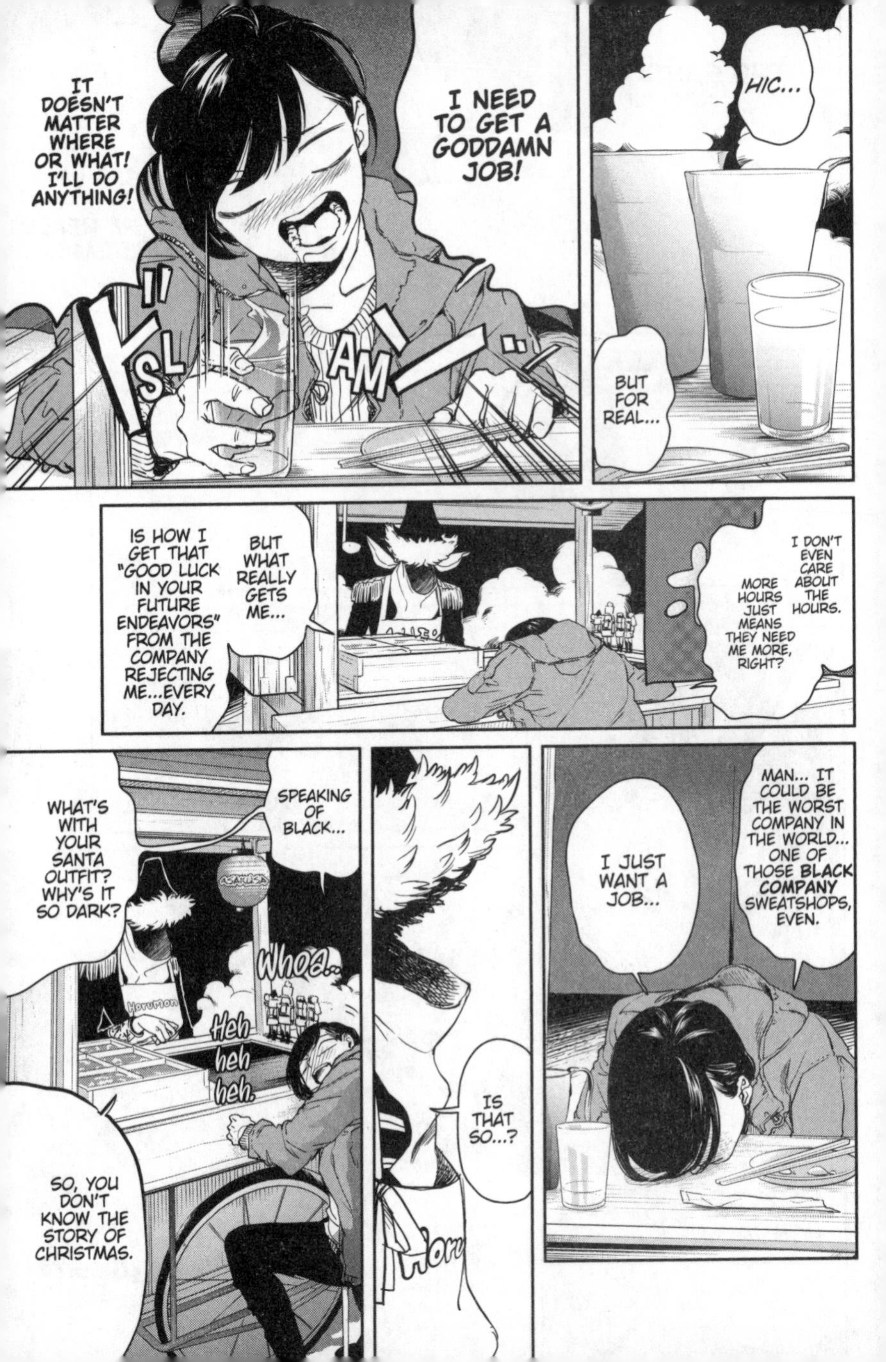

HIC...
BUT FOR REAL...
I NEED TO GET A GODDAMN JOB!
IT DOESN'T MATTER WHERE OR WHAT! I'LL DO ANYTHING!
SLAM
I DON'T EVEN CARE ABOUT THE HOURS.
MORE HOURS JUST MEANS THEY NEED ME MORE, RIGHT?
BUT WHAT REALLY GETS ME...
IS HOW I GET THAT "GOOD LUCK IN YOUR FUTURE ENDEAVORS" FROM THE COMPANY REJECTING ME...EVERY DAY.
MAN... IT COULD BE THE WORST COMPANY IN THE WORLD... ONE OF THOSE **BLACK COMPANY** SWEATSHOPS, EVEN.
I JUST WANT A JOB...
IS THAT SO...?
SPEAKING OF BLACK...
WHAT'S WITH YOUR SANTA OUTFIT? WHY'S IT SO DARK?
Whoa...
Horumon
Heh heh heh.
SO, YOU DON'T KNOW THE STORY OF CHRISTMAS.

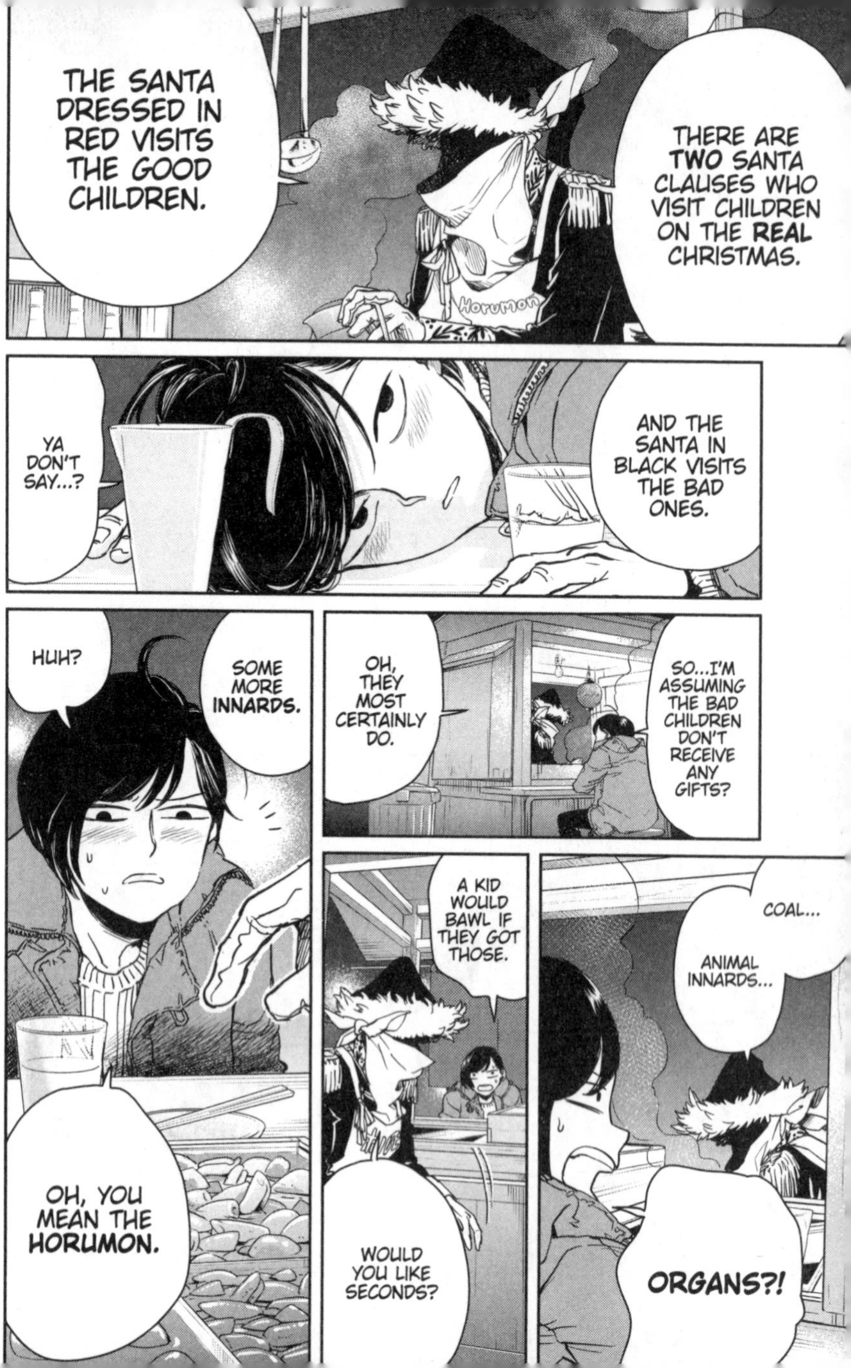
THERE ARE TWO SANTA CLAUSES WHO VISIT CHILDREN ON THE REAL CHRISTMAS.
THE SANTA DRESSED IN RED VISITS THE GOOD CHILDREN.
Horumon
AND THE SANTA IN BLACK VISITS THE BAD ONES.
YA DON'T SAY...?
SO...I'M ASSUMING THE BAD CHILDREN DON'T RECEIVE ANY GIFTS?
OH, THEY MOST CERTAINLY DO.
COAL...
ANIMAL INNARDS...
ORGANS?!
A KID WOULD BAWL IF THEY GOT THOSE.
WOULD YOU LIKE SECONDS?
SOME MORE INNARDS.
HUH?
OH, YOU MEAN THE HORUMON.

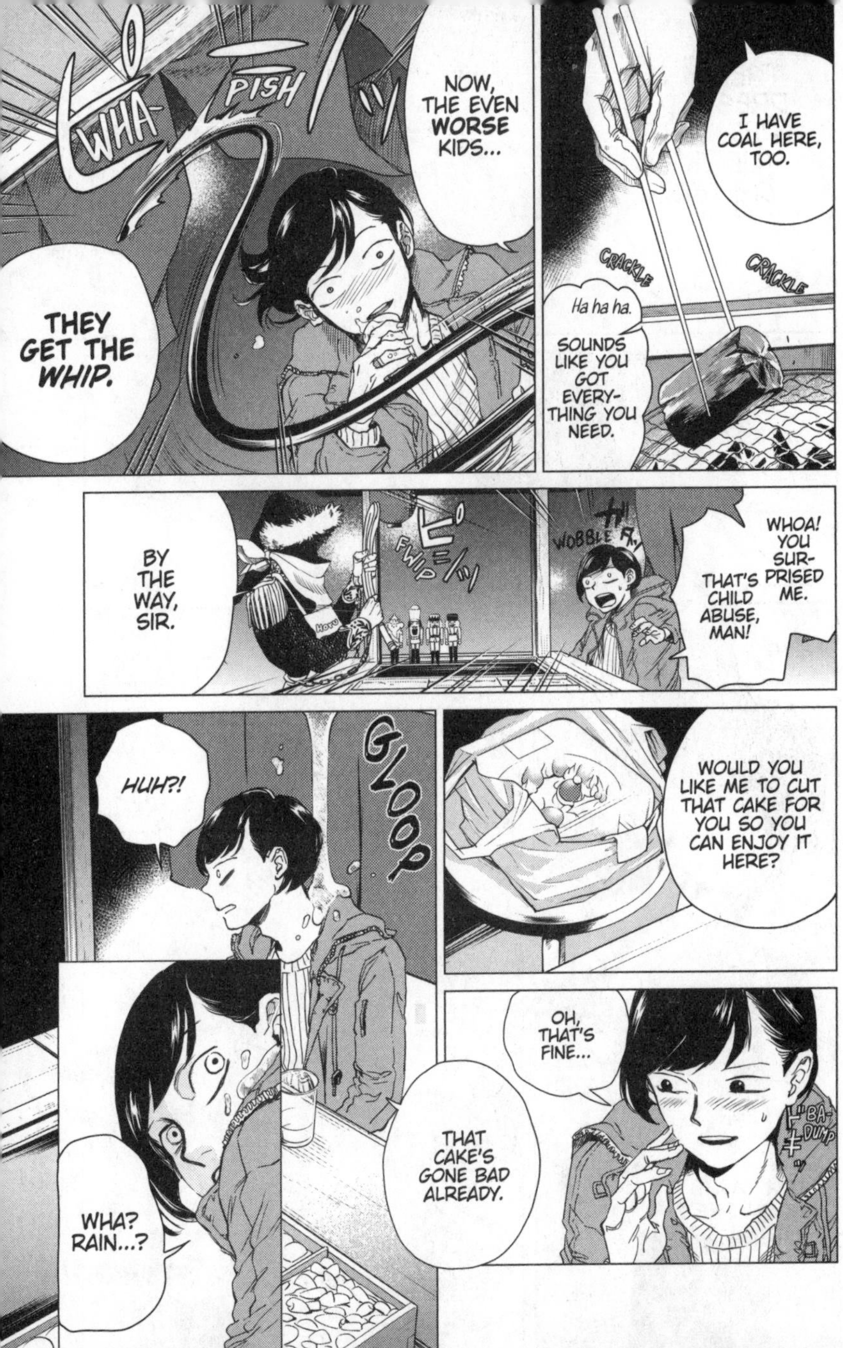
I HAVE COAL HERE, TOO.
CRACKLE
CRACKLE
Ha ha ha.
SOUNDS LIKE YOU GOT EVERY-THING YOU NEED.
NOW, THE EVEN WORSE KIDS...
WHA-PISH
THEY GET THE WHIP.
WHOA! YOU SUR-PRISED ME.
THAT'S CHILD ABUSE, MAN!
WOBBLE
FWIP
BY THE WAY, SIR.
WOULD YOU LIKE ME TO CUT THAT CAKE FOR YOU SO YOU CAN ENJOY IT HERE?
GLOOP
HUH?!
OH, THAT'S FINE...
BA-DUMP
THAT CAKE'S GONE BAD ALREADY.
WHA? RAIN...?

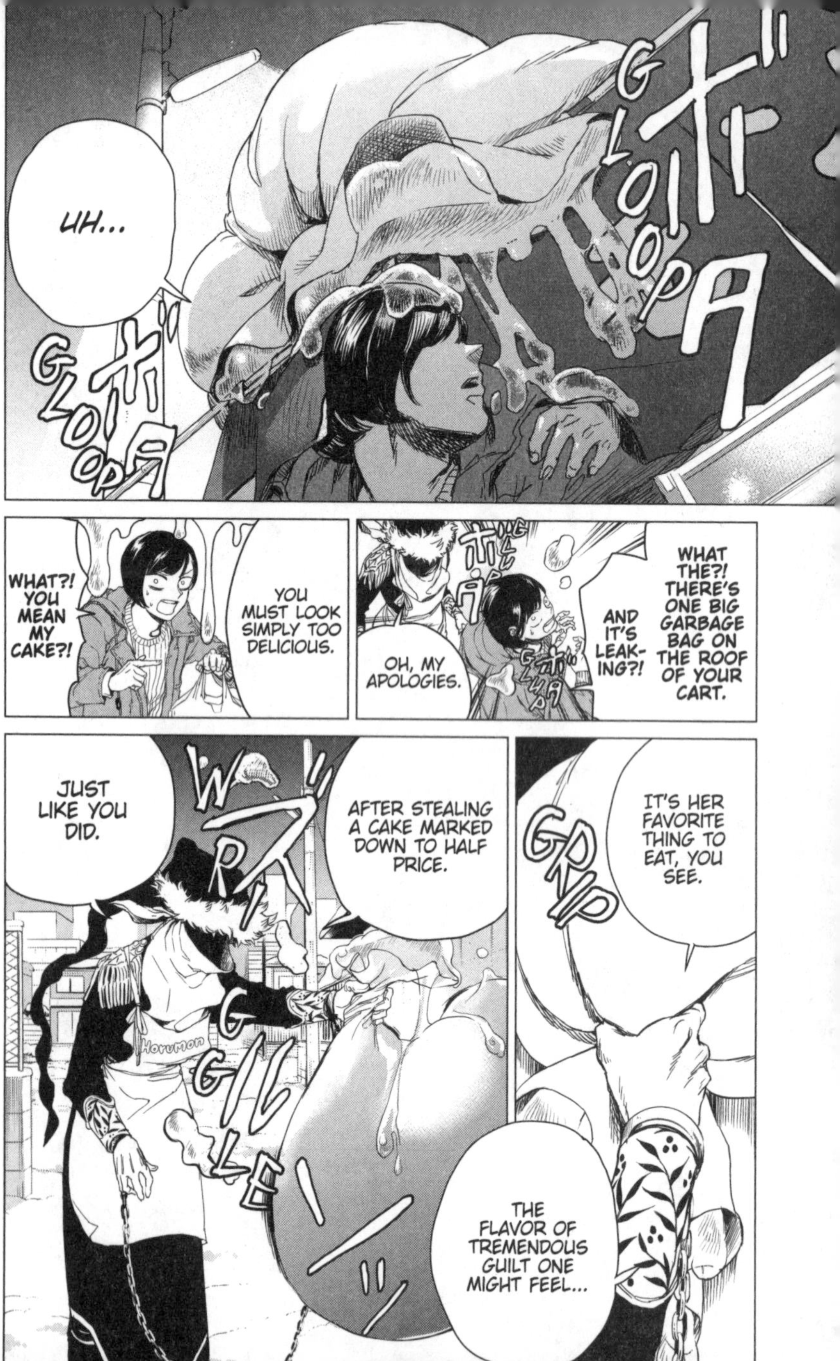
UH...
GLOOOP
GLOOP
WHAT THE?! THERE'S ONE BIG GARBAGE BAG ON THE ROOF OF YOUR CART.
AND IT'S LEAK-ING?!
OH, MY APOLOGIES.
YOU MUST LOOK SIMPLY TOO DELICIOUS.
WHAT?! YOU MEAN MY CAKE?!
GRIP
IT'S HER FAVORITE THING TO EAT, YOU SEE.
THE FLAVOR OF TREMENDOUS GUILT ONE MIGHT FEEL...
AFTER STEALING A CAKE MARKED DOWN TO HALF PRICE.
JUST LIKE YOU DID.
WRIGGLE
Horumon

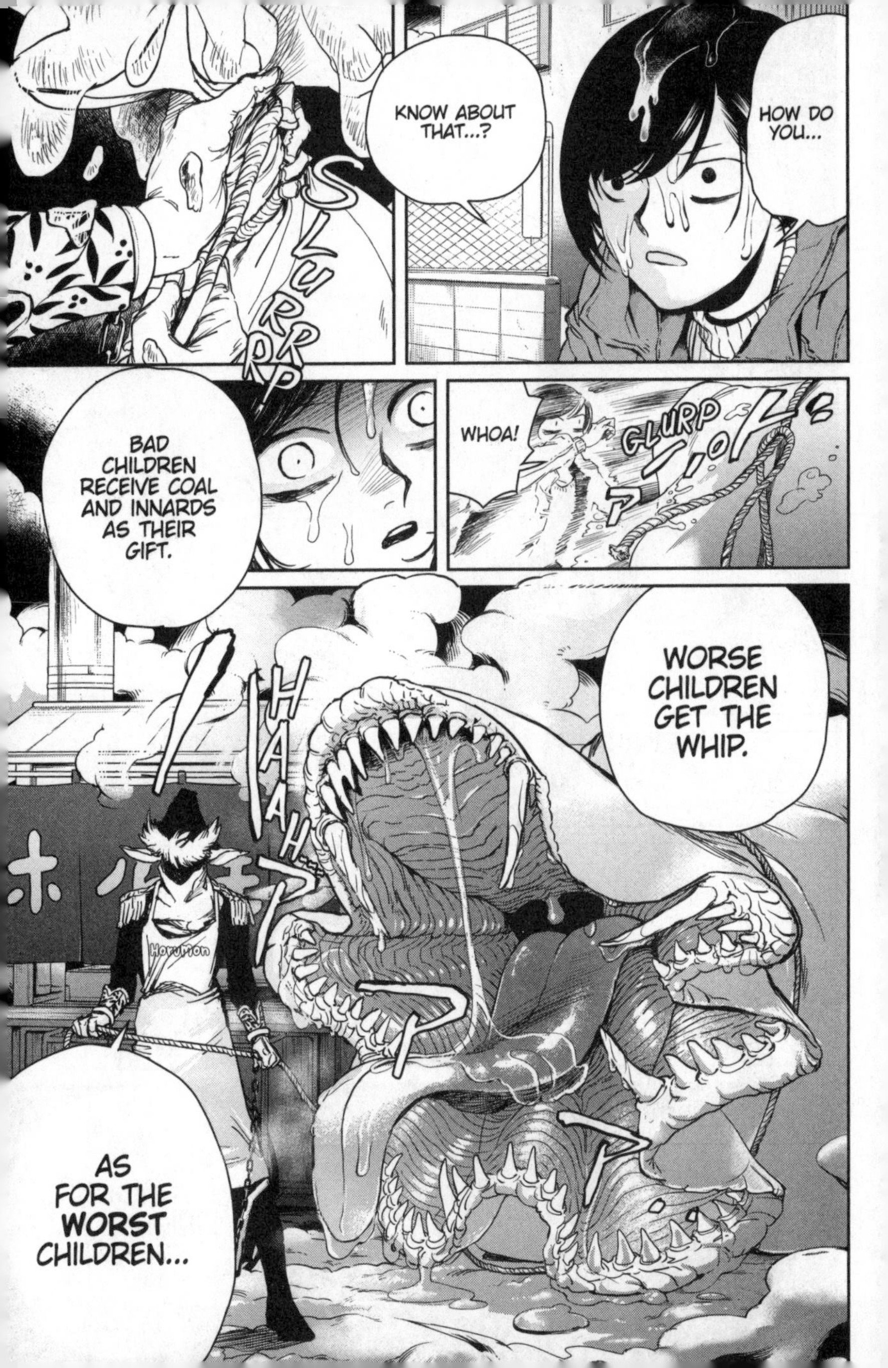
HOW DO YOU...
KNOW ABOUT THAT...?
SLURRRP
WHOA!
GLURP
BAD CHILDREN RECEIVE COAL AND INNARDS AS THEIR GIFT.
WORSE CHILDREN GET THE WHIP.
HAAAH
Horumon
AS FOR THE WORST CHILDREN...

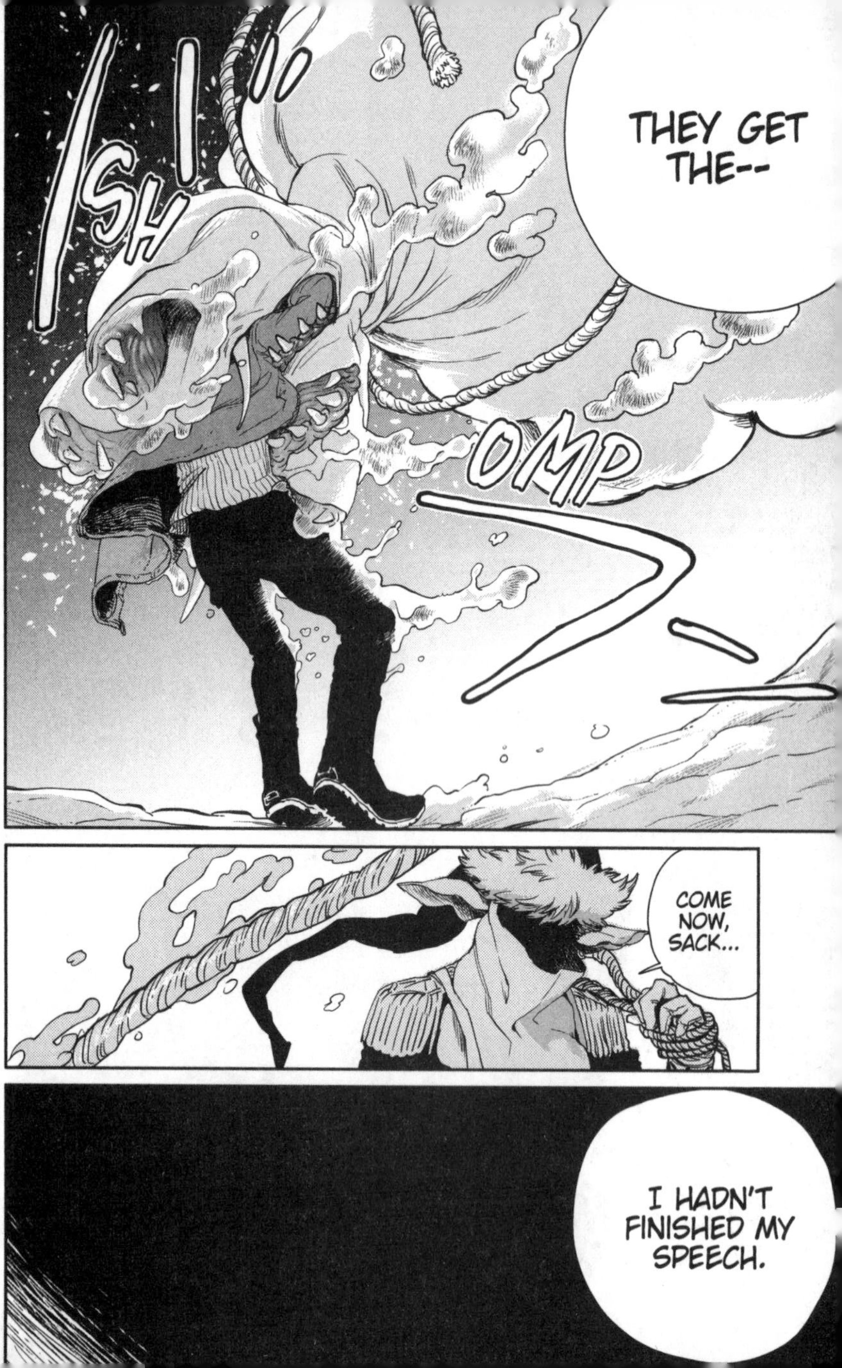
THEY GET THE--
SH
OMP
COME NOW, SACK...
I HADN'T FINISHED MY SPEECH.

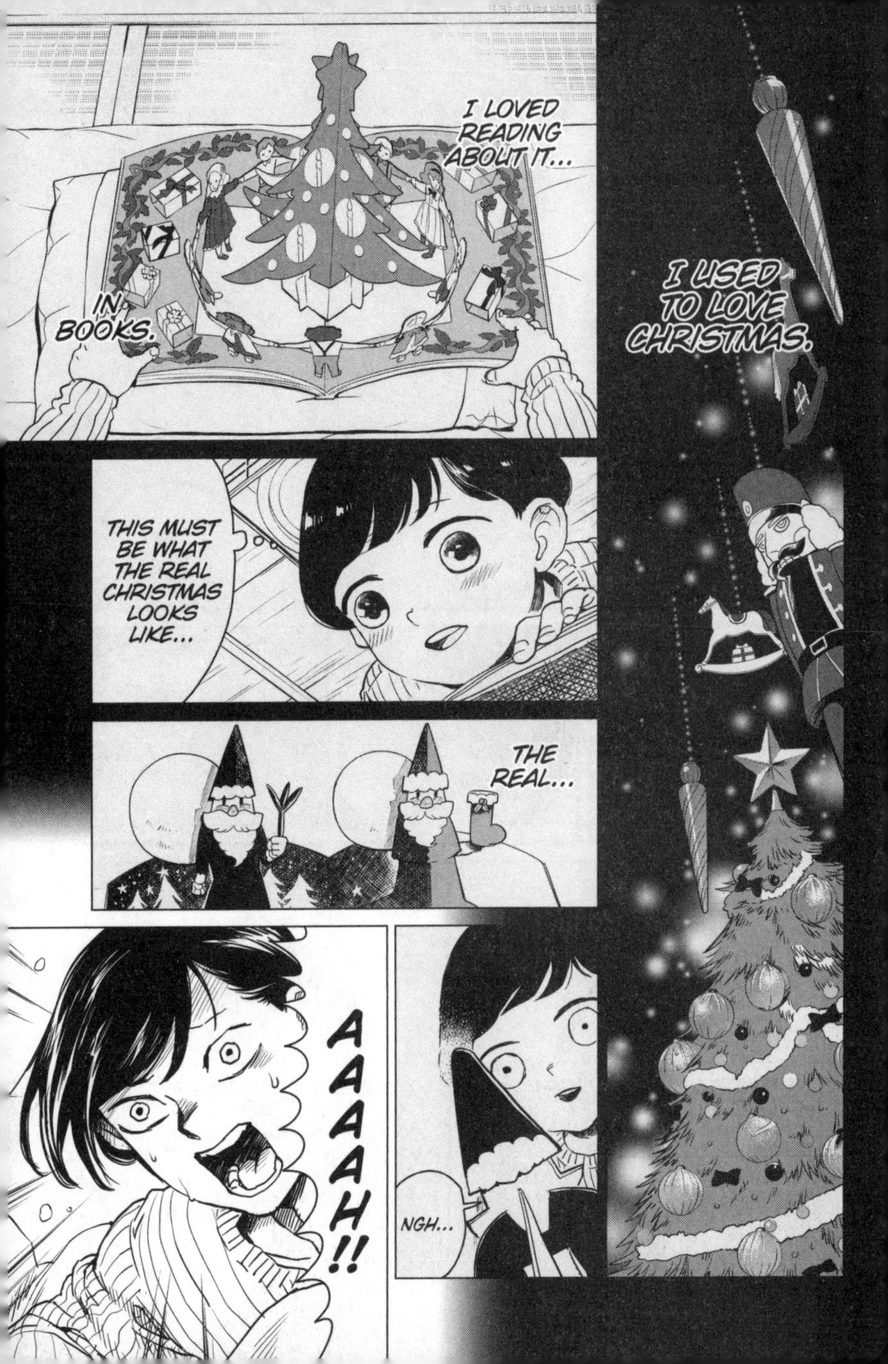
I USED TO LOVE CHRISTMAS.
I LOVED READING ABOUT IT...
IN BOOKS.
THIS MUST BE WHAT THE REAL CHRISTMAS LOOKS LIKE...
THE REAL...
NGH...
AAAAAH!!

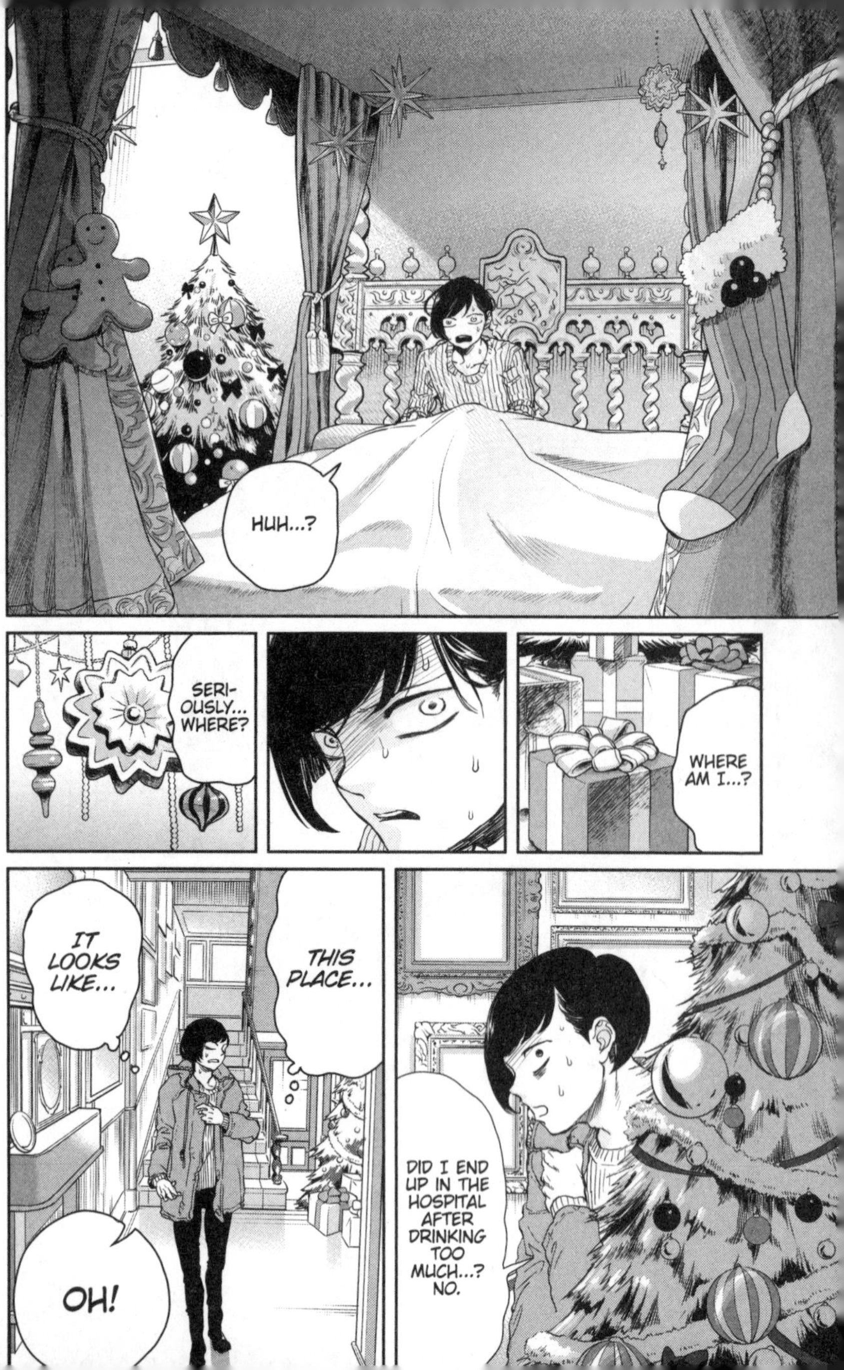
HUH...?
WHERE AM I...?
SERI-OUSLY... WHERE?
DID I END UP IN THE HOSPITAL AFTER DRINKING TOO MUCH...? NO.
THIS PLACE...
IT LOOKS LIKE...
OH!

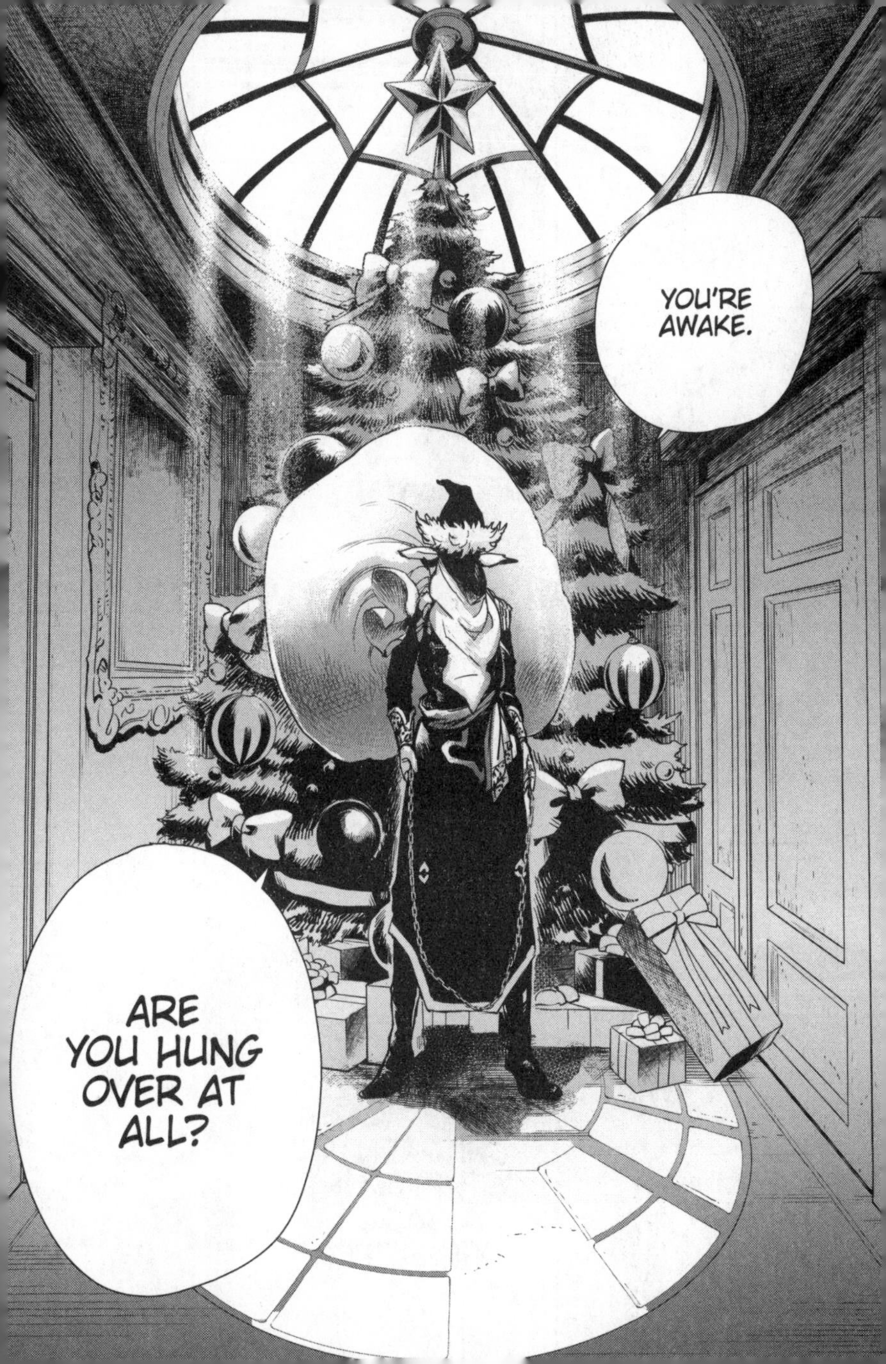
YOU'RE AWAKE.
ARE YOU HUNG OVER AT ALL?

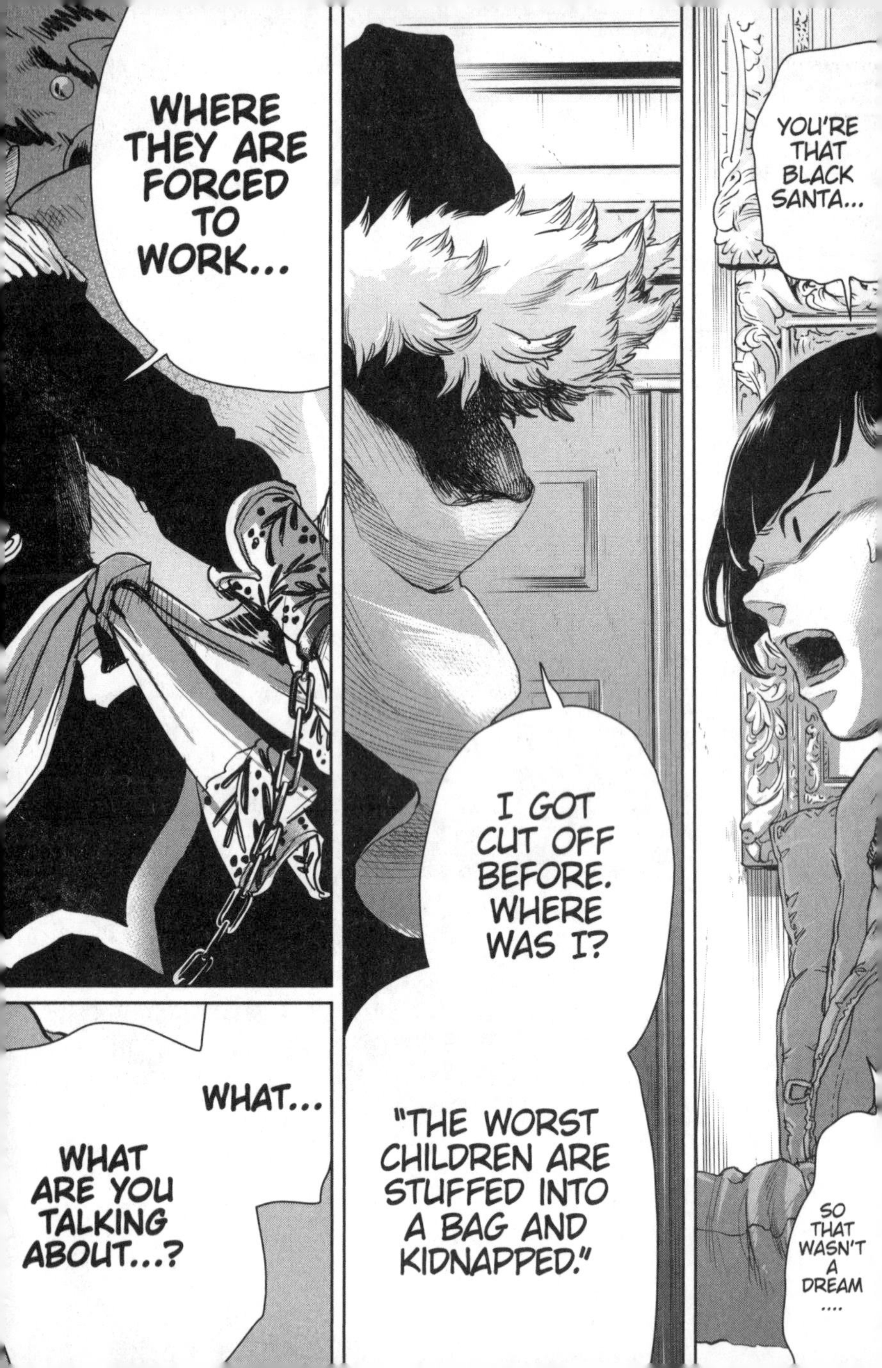
YOU'RE THAT BLACK SANTA...
SO THAT WASN'T A DREAM....
I GOT CUT OFF BEFORE. WHERE WAS I?
"THE WORST CHILDREN ARE STUFFED INTO A BAG AND KIDNAPPED."
WHERE THEY ARE FORCED TO WORK...
WHAT...
WHAT ARE YOU TALKING ABOUT...?

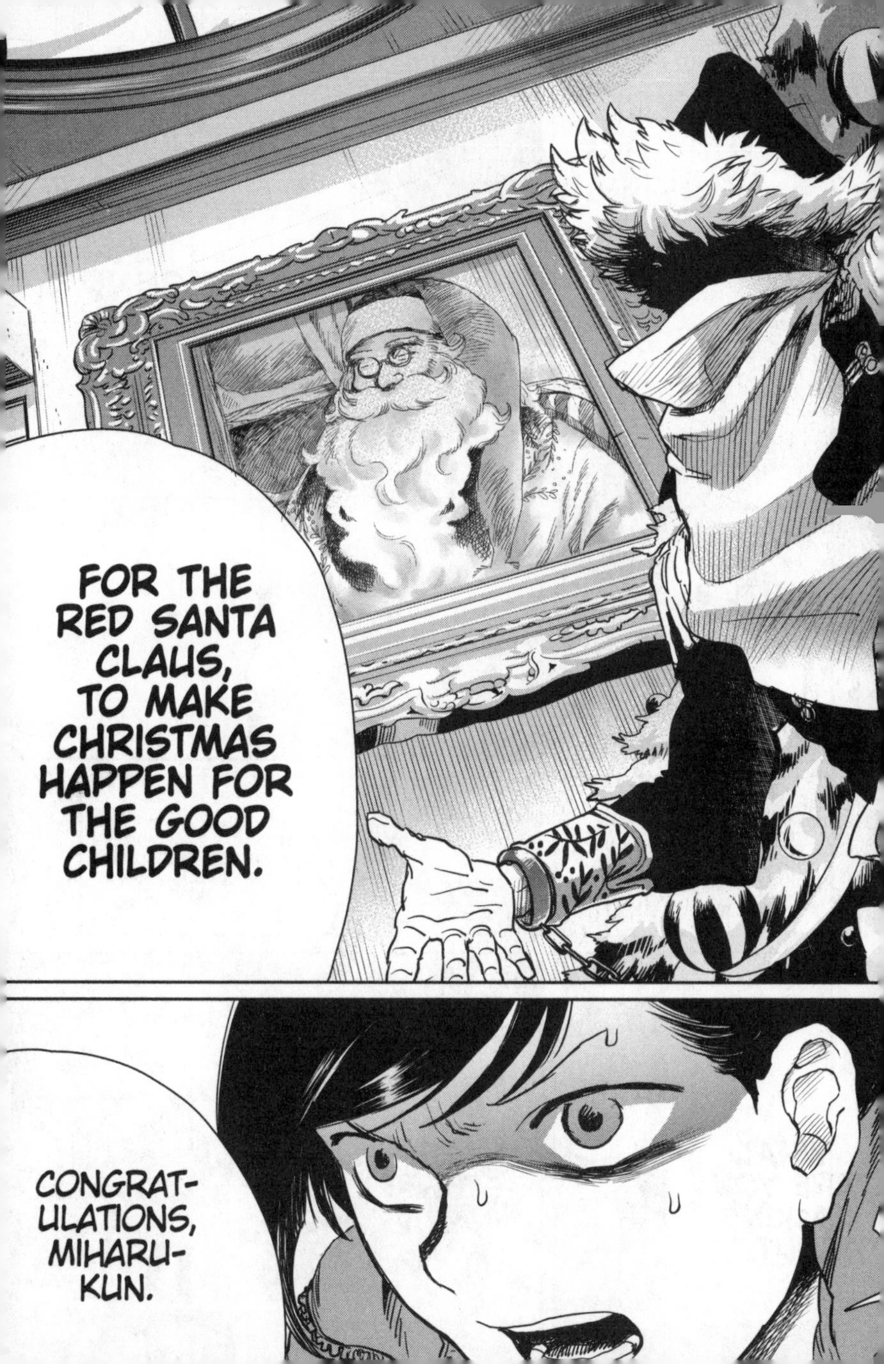
FOR THE RED SANTA CLAUS, TO MAKE CHRISTMAS HAPPEN FOR THE GOOD CHILDREN.
CONGRAT-ULATIONS, MIHARU-KUN.

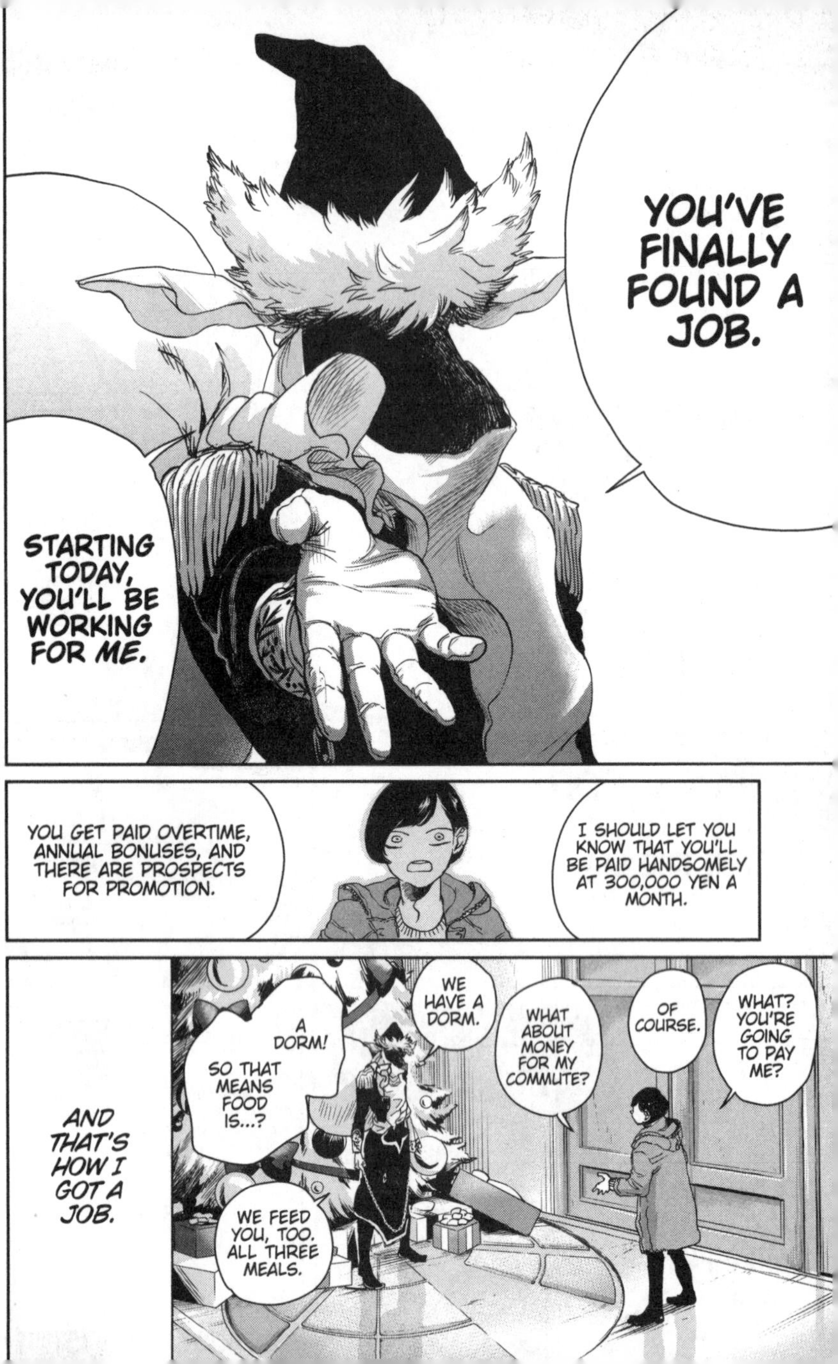
YOU'VE FINALLY FOUND A JOB.
STARTING TODAY, YOU'LL BE WORKING FOR ME.
I SHOULD LET YOU KNOW THAT YOU'LL BE PAID HANDSOMELY AT 300,000 YEN A MONTH.
YOU GET PAID OVERTIME, ANNUAL BONUSES, AND THERE ARE PROSPECTS FOR PROMOTION.
WHAT? YOU'RE GOING TO PAY ME?
OF COURSE.
WHAT ABOUT MONEY FOR MY COMMUTE?
WE HAVE A DORM.
A DORM!
SO THAT MEANS FOOD IS...?
WE FEED YOU, TOO. ALL THREE MEALS.
AND THAT'S HOW I GOT A JOB.

Chapter 2: My Nightmare Job

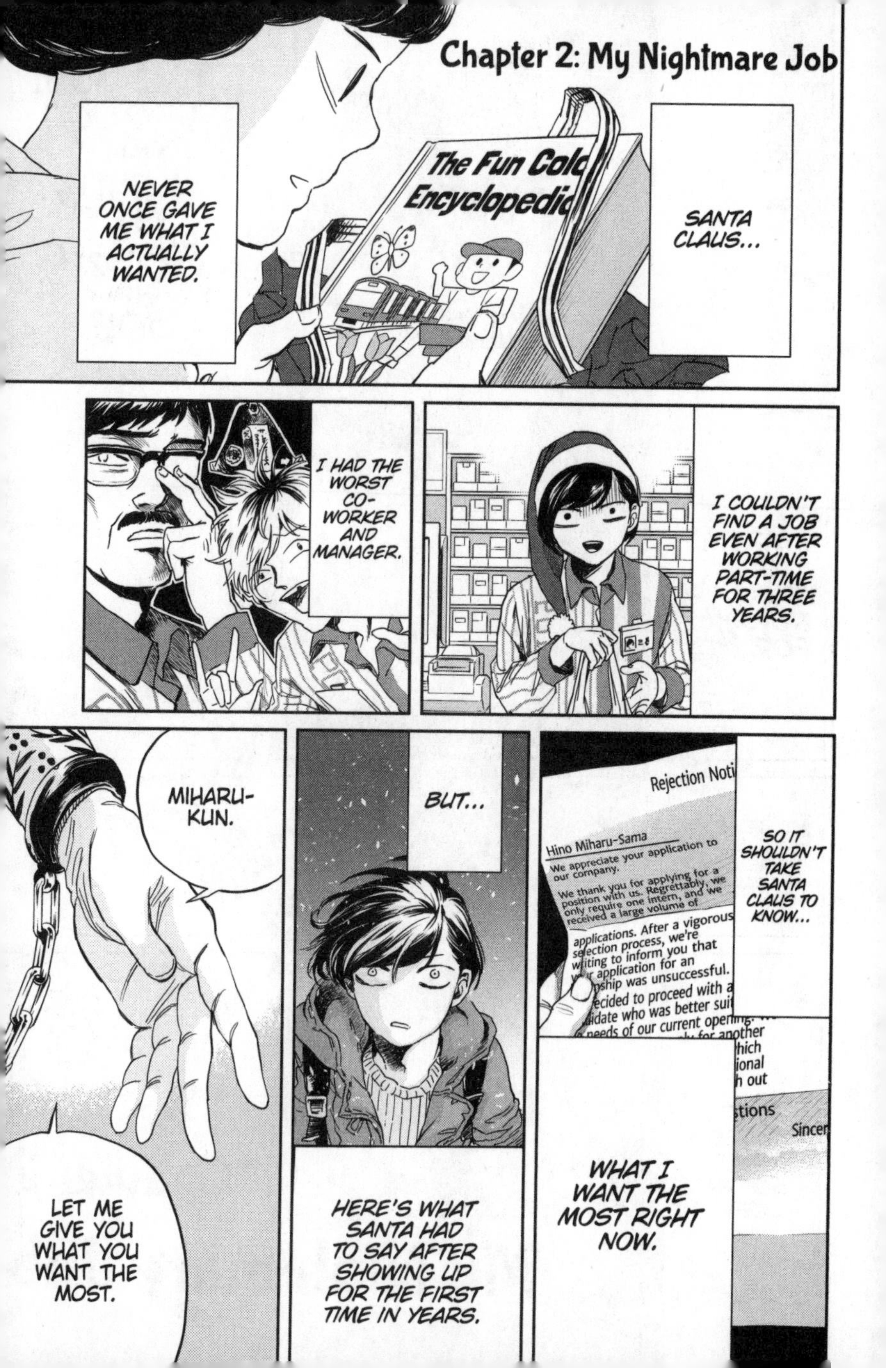
SANTA CLAUS...
NEVER ONCE GAVE ME WHAT I ACTUALLY WANTED.
I COULDN'T FIND A JOB EVEN AFTER WORKING PART-TIME FOR THREE YEARS.
I HAD THE WORST CO-WORKER AND MANAGER.
Hino Miharu-Sama
We appreciate your application to our company.
We thank you for applying for a position with us. Regrettably, we only require one intern, and we received a large volume of
applications. After a vigorous
SO IT SHOULDN'T TAKE SANTA CLAUS TO KNOW...
WHAT I WANT THE MOST RIGHT NOW.
BUT...
HERE'S WHAT SANTA HAD TO SAY AFTER SHOWING UP FOR THE FIRST TIME IN YEARS.
MIHARU-KUN.
LET ME GIVE YOU WHAT YOU WANT THE MOST.

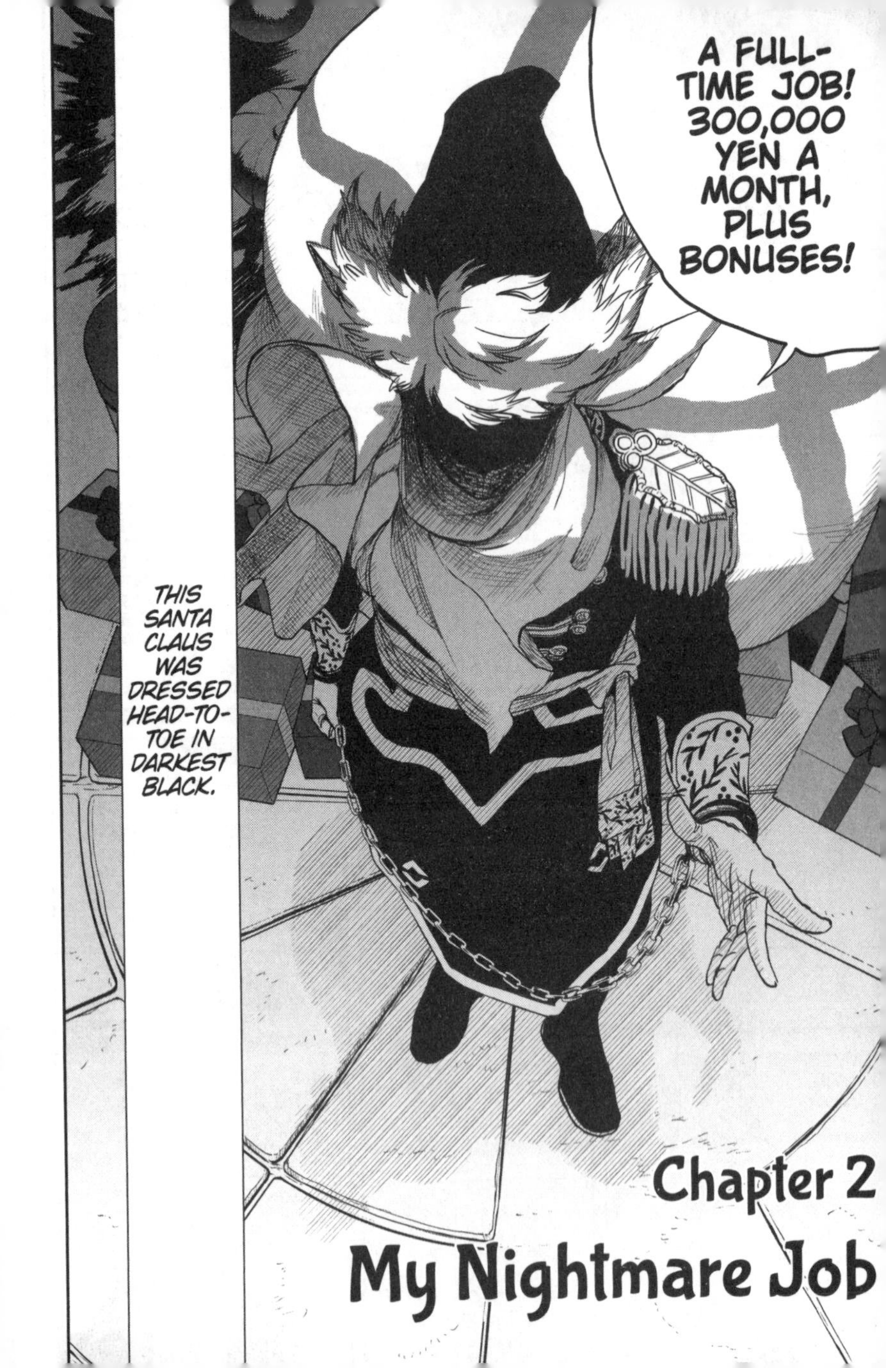
A FULL-TIME JOB! 300,000 YEN A MONTH, PLUS BONUSES!
Chapter 2
My Nightmare Job
THIS SANTA CLAUS WAS DRESSED HEAD-TO-TOE IN DARKEST BLACK.

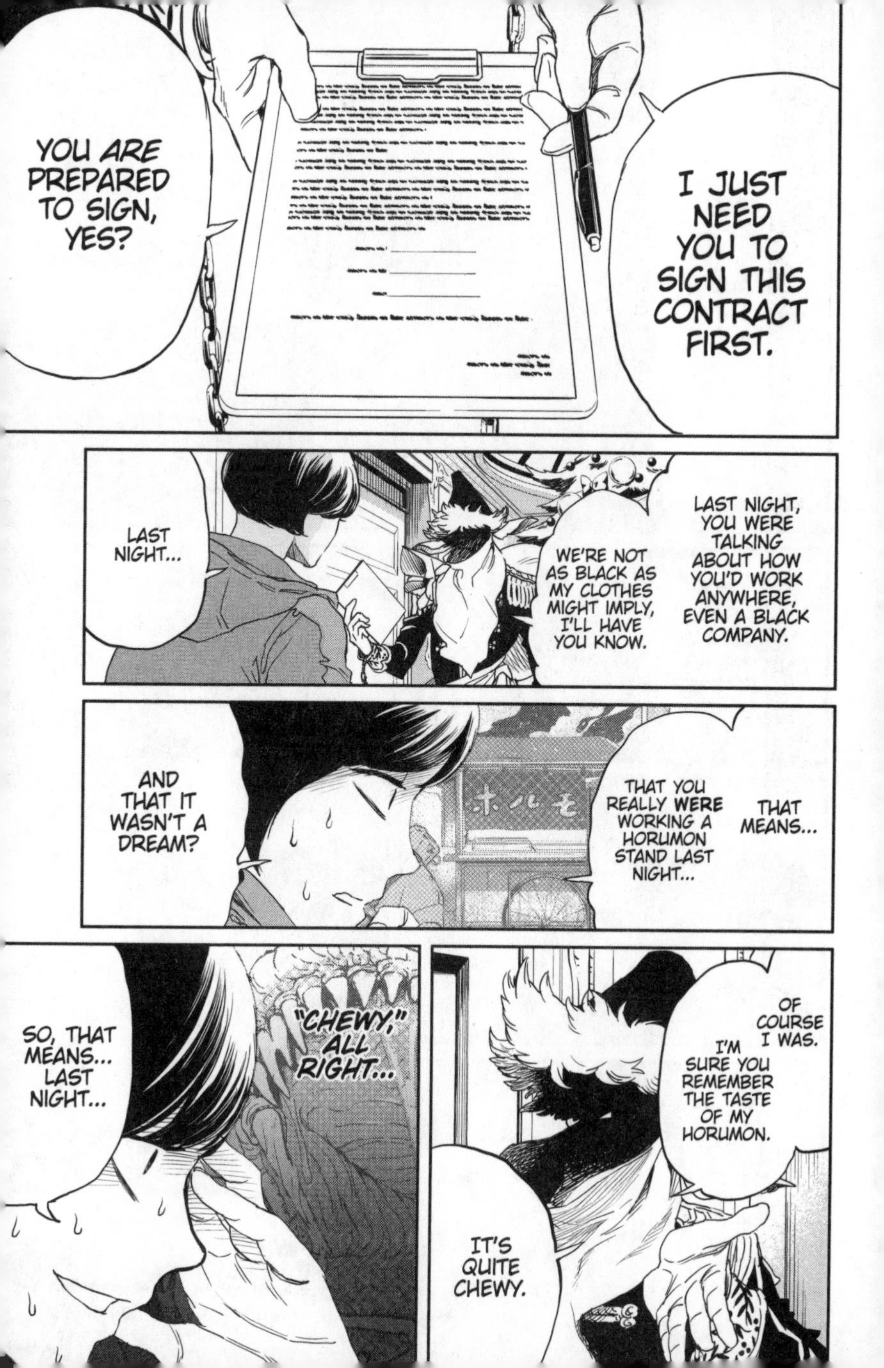
I JUST NEED YOU TO SIGN THIS CONTRACT FIRST.
YOU ARE PREPARED TO SIGN, YES?
LAST NIGHT, YOU WERE TALKING ABOUT HOW YOU'D WORK ANYWHERE, EVEN A BLACK COMPANY.
WE'RE NOT AS BLACK AS MY CLOTHES MIGHT IMPLY, I'LL HAVE YOU KNOW.
LAST NIGHT...
THAT MEANS...
THAT YOU REALLY WERE WORKING A HORUMON STAND LAST NIGHT...
AND THAT IT WASN'T A DREAM?
OF COURSE I WAS.
I'M SURE YOU REMEMBER THE TASTE OF MY HORUMON.
IT'S QUITE CHEWY.
"CHEWY," ALL RIGHT...
SO, THAT MEANS... LAST NIGHT...

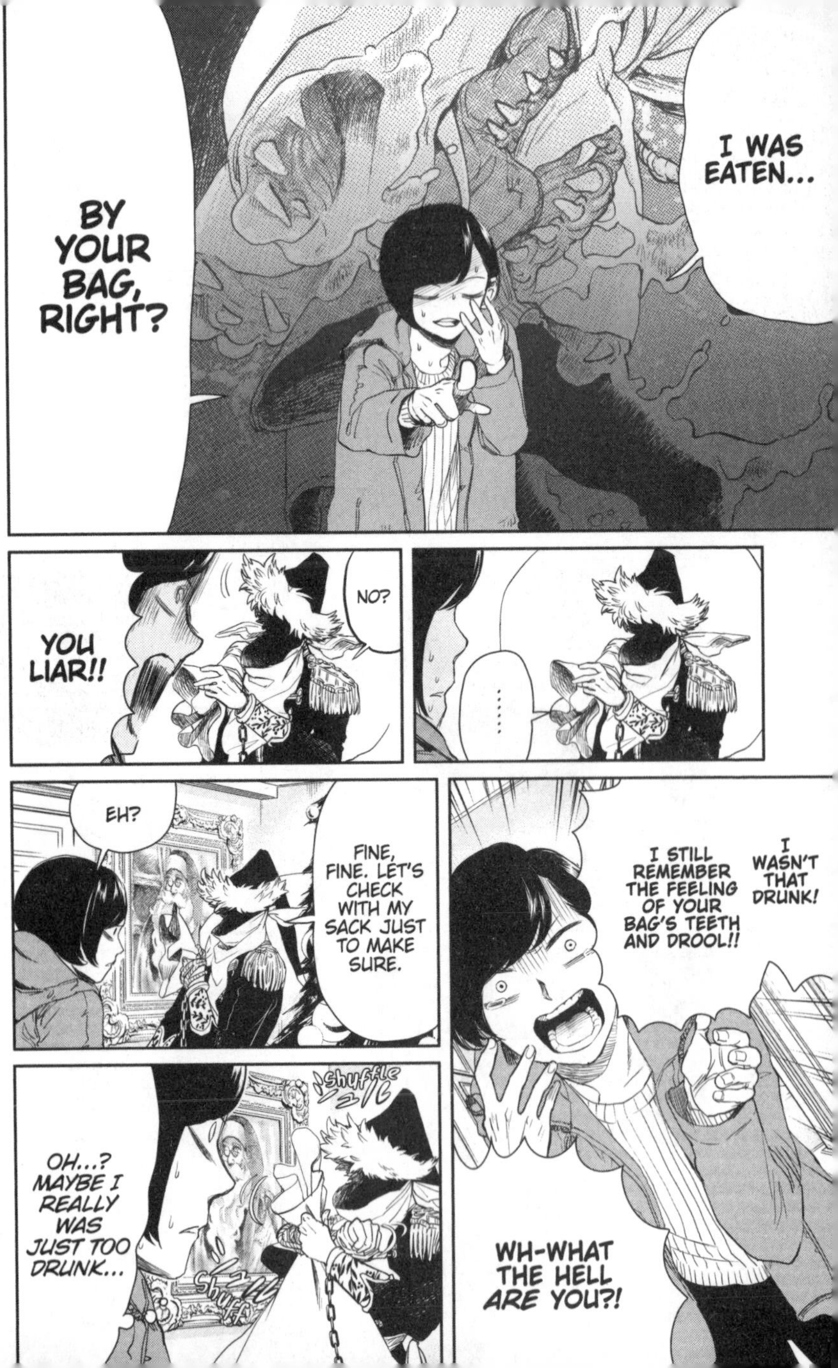

I WAS EATEN...
BY YOUR BAG, RIGHT?
......
NO?
YOU LIAR!!
I WASN'T THAT DRUNK!
I STILL REMEMBER THE FEELING OF YOUR BAG'S TEETH AND DROOL!!
WH-WHAT THE HELL ARE YOU?!
FINE, FINE. LET'S CHECK WITH MY SACK JUST TO MAKE SURE.
EH?
SHUFFLE
OH...? MAYBE I REALLY WAS JUST TOO DRUNK...
SHUFF

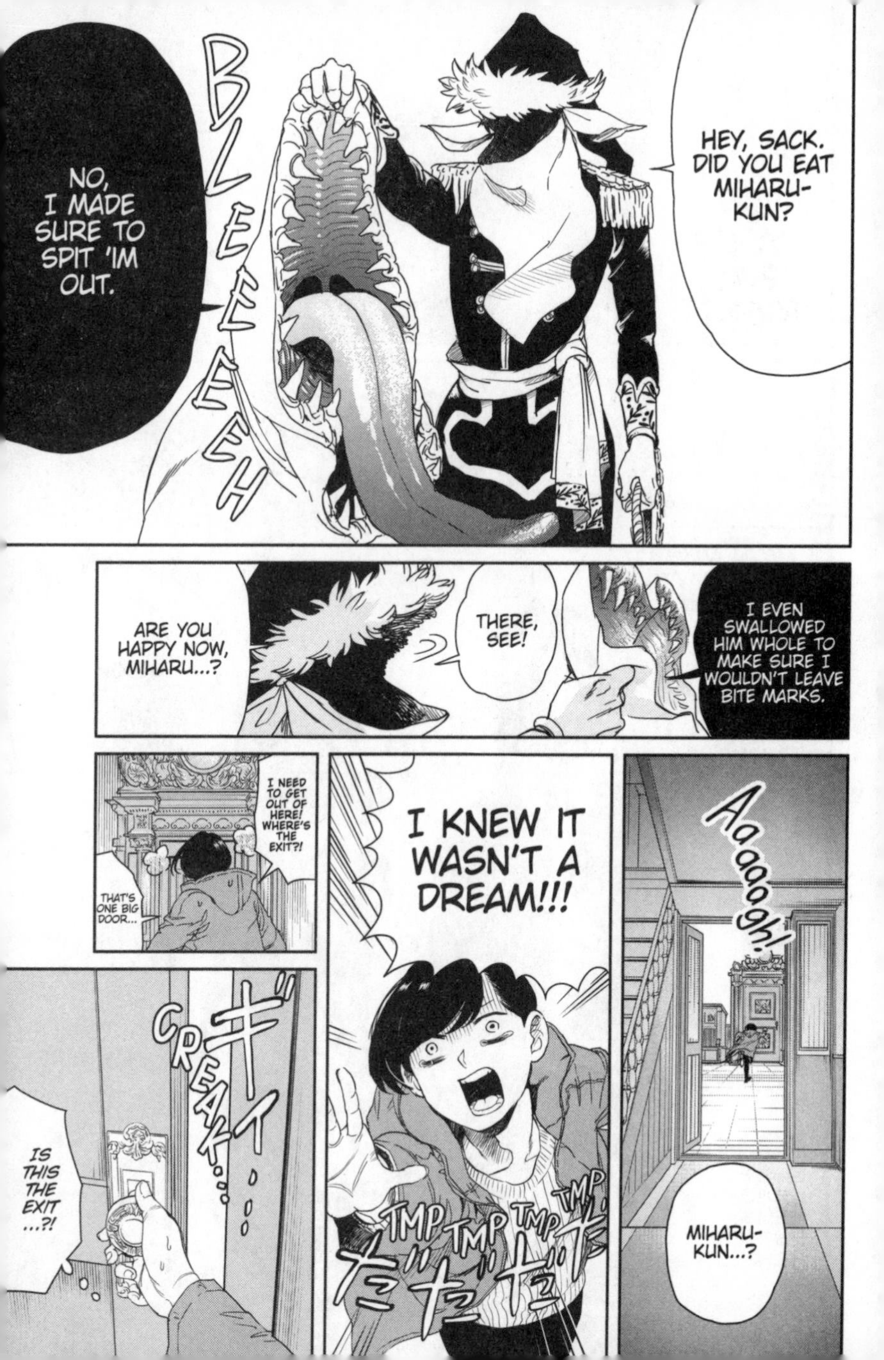

HEY, SACK. DID YOU EAT MIHARU-KUN?
BLEEEEH
NO, I MADE SURE TO SPIT 'IM OUT.
I EVEN SWALLOWED HIM WHOLE TO MAKE SURE I WOULDN'T LEAVE BITE MARKS.
THERE, SEE!
ARE YOU HAPPY NOW, MIHARU...?
Aaaaagh!
MIHARU-KUN...?
I KNEW IT WASN'T A DREAM!!!
TMP TMP TMP TMP
I NEED TO GET OUT OF HERE! WHERE'S THE EXIT?!
THAT'S ONE BIG DOOR...
CREAK...
ギイ...
IS THIS THE EXIT...?!

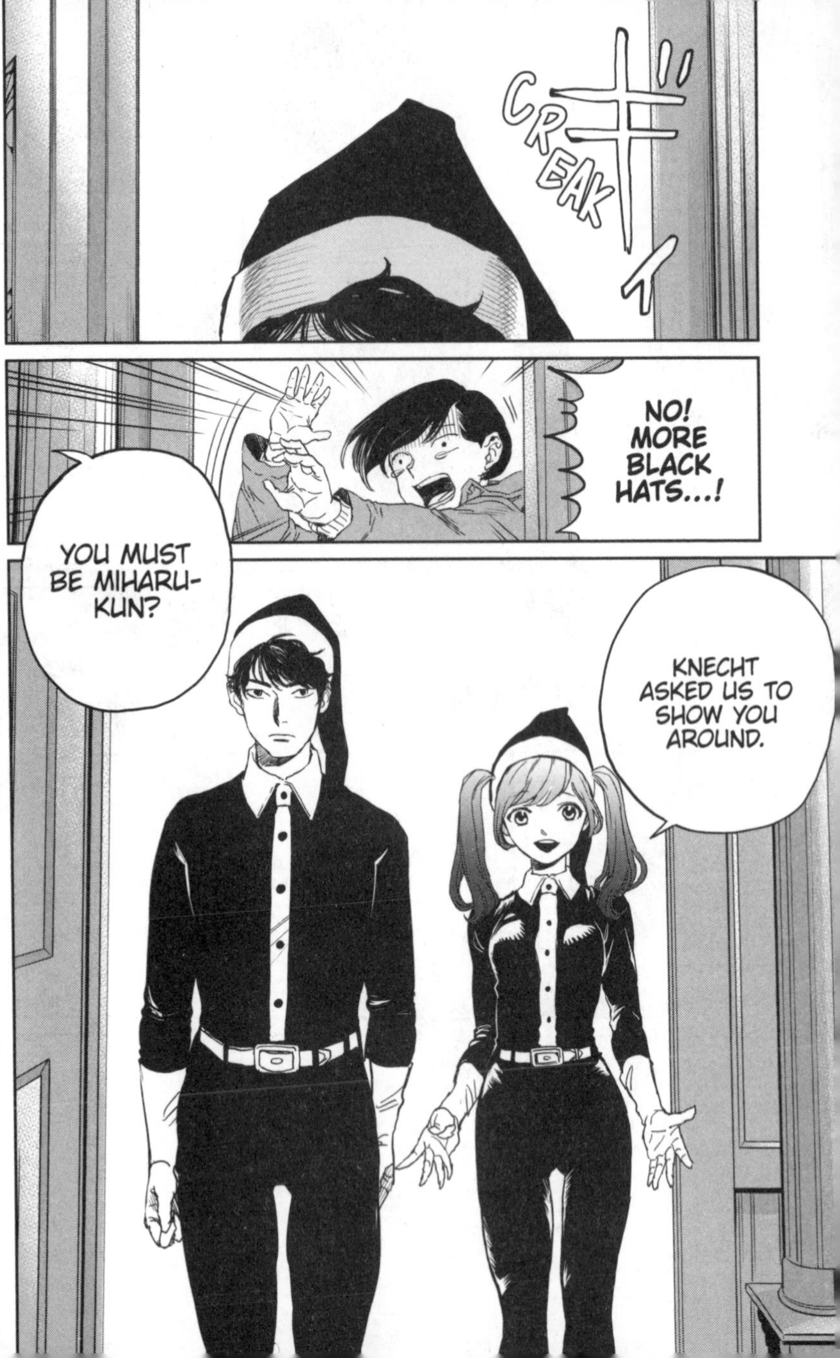
CREAK
ギィ
NO! MORE BLACK HATS...!
YOU MUST BE MIHARU-KUN?
KNECHT ASKED US TO SHOW YOU AROUND.

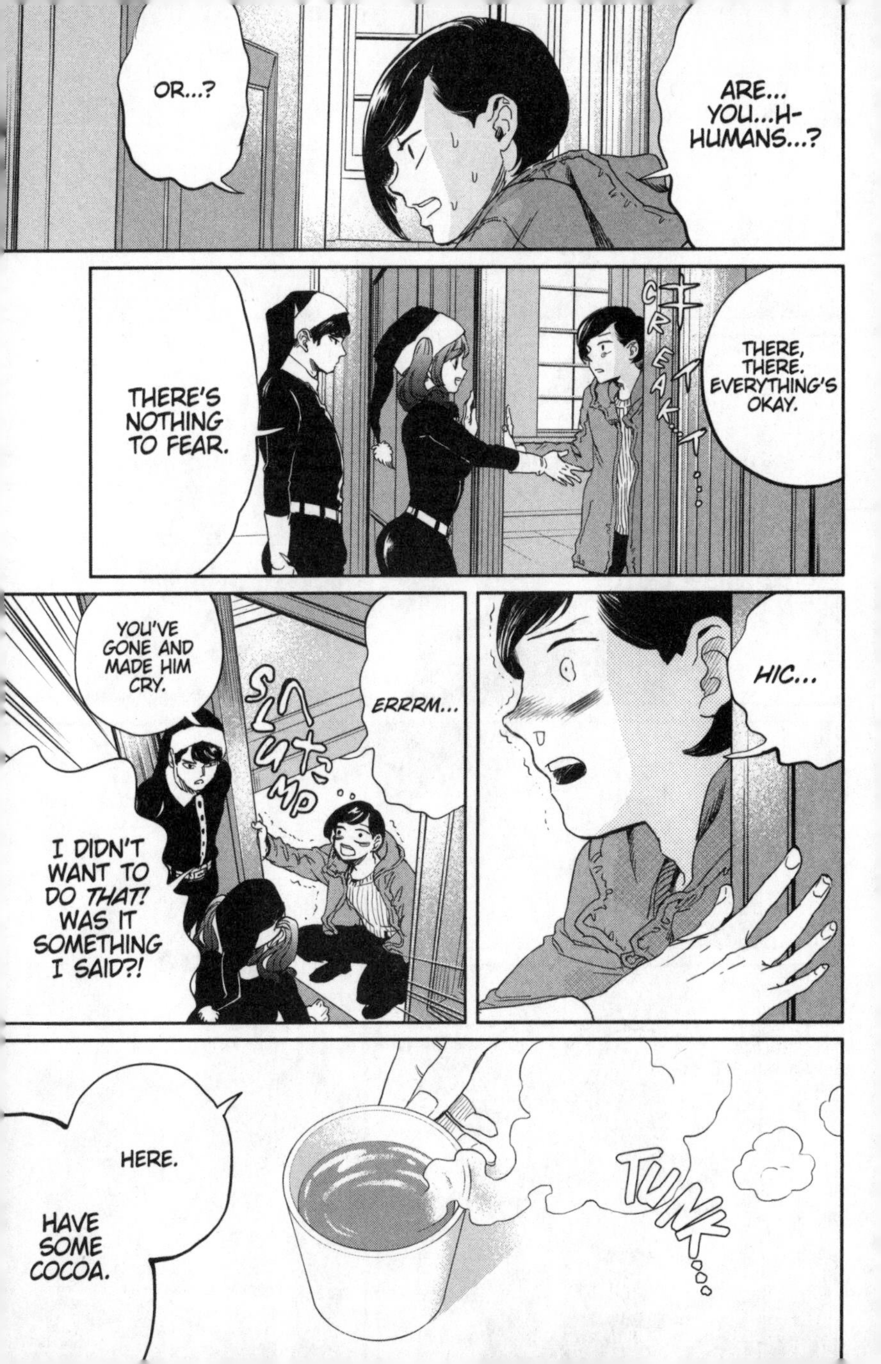
ARE... YOU...H-HUMANS...?
OR...?
THERE, THERE. EVERYTHING'S OKAY.
CREAK...
THERE'S NOTHING TO FEAR.
HIC...
ERRRM...
YOU'VE GONE AND MADE HIM CRY.
SLUMP
I DIDN'T WANT TO DO *THAT!* WAS IT SOMETHING I SAID?!
TUNK...
HERE.
HAVE SOME COCOA.

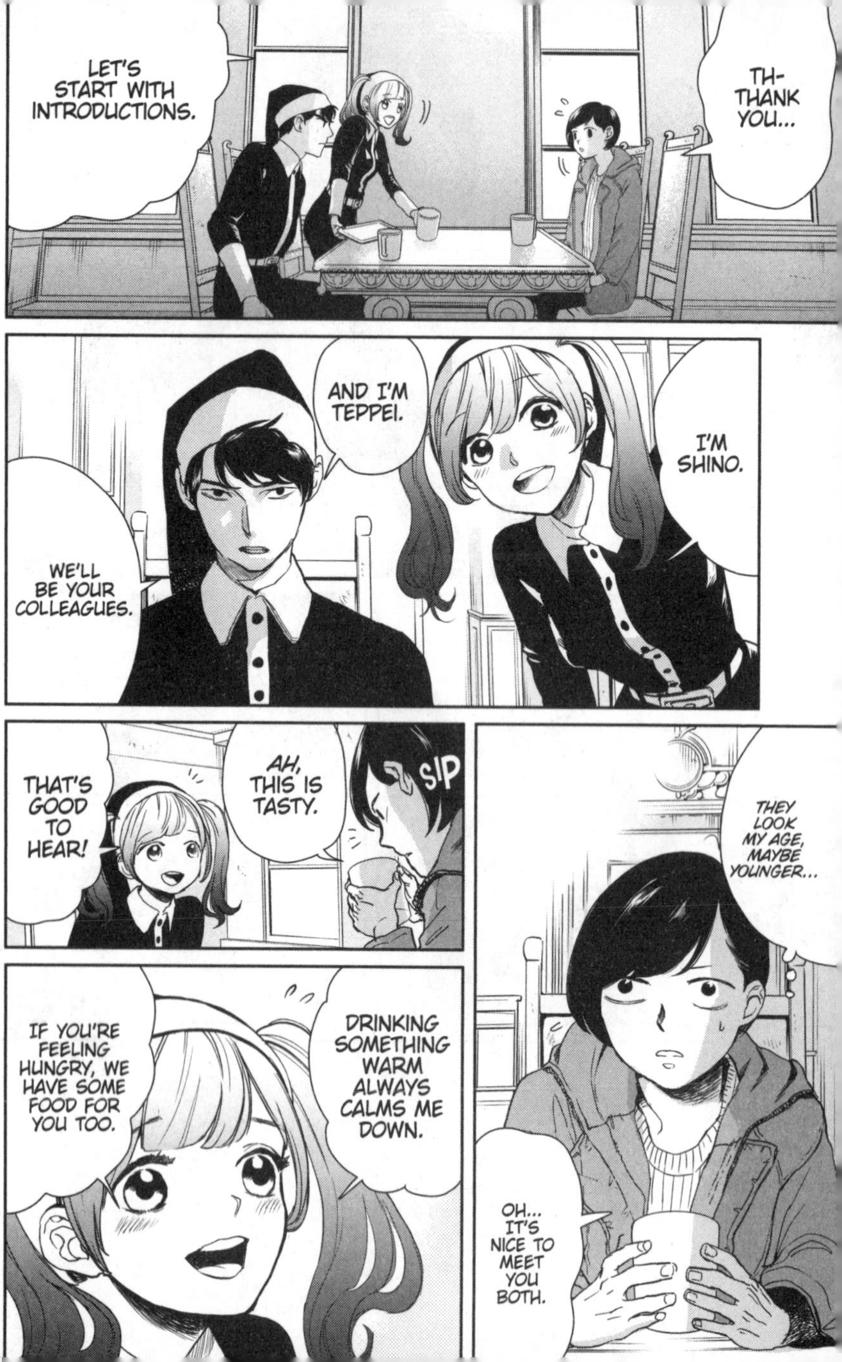
TH- THANK YOU...
LET'S START WITH INTRODUCTIONS.
I'M SHINO.
AND I'M TEPPEI.
WE'LL BE YOUR COLLEAGUES.
THEY LOOK MY AGE, MAYBE YOUNGER...
OH... IT'S NICE TO MEET YOU BOTH.
SIP
AH, THIS IS TASTY.
THAT'S GOOD TO HEAR!
DRINKING SOMETHING WARM ALWAYS CALMS ME DOWN.
IF YOU'RE FEELING HUNGRY, WE HAVE SOME FOOD FOR YOU TOO.

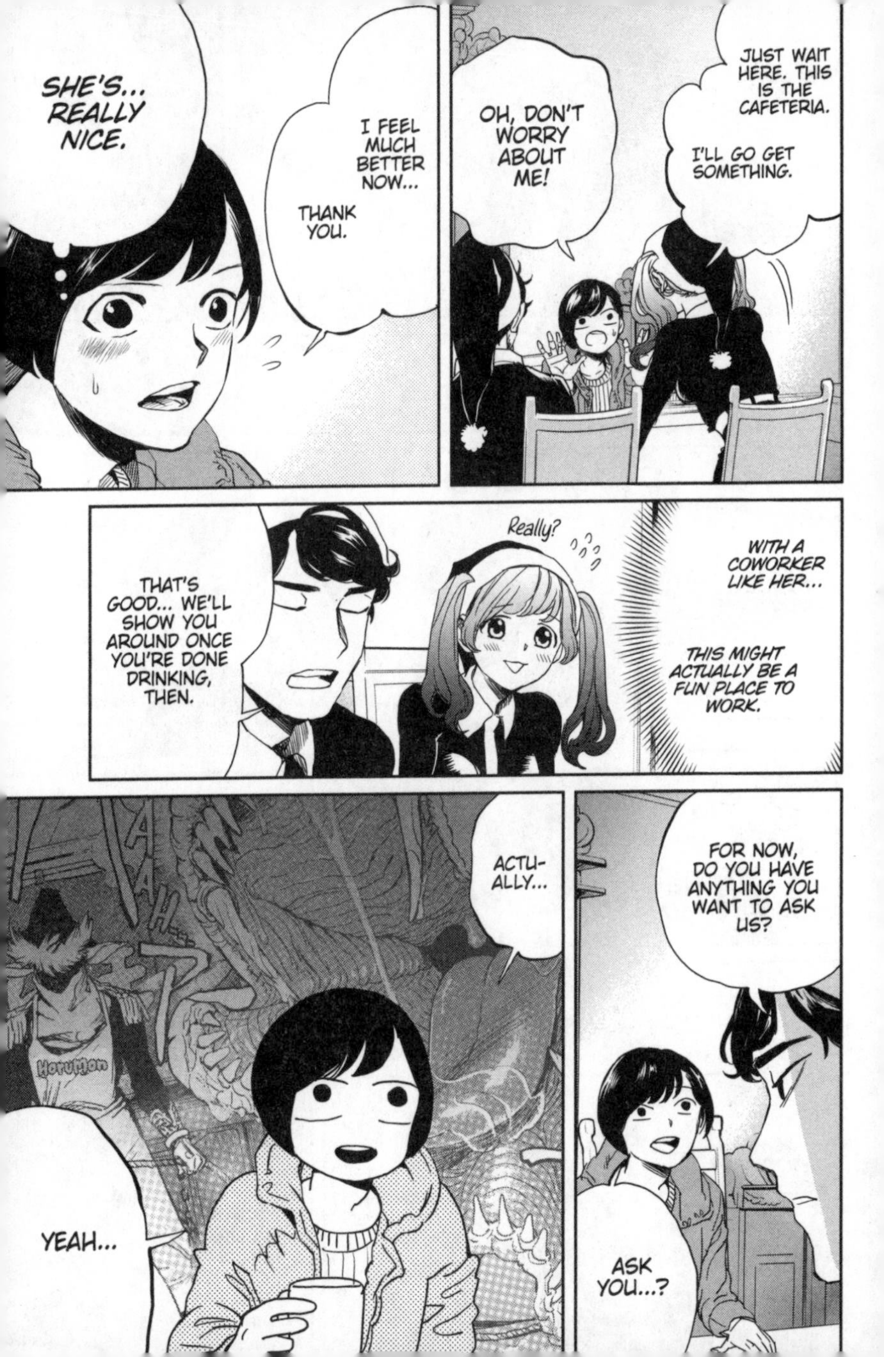
JUST WAIT HERE. THIS IS THE CAFETERIA.
I'LL GO GET SOMETHING.
OH, DON'T WORRY ABOUT ME!
I FEEL MUCH BETTER NOW...
THANK YOU.
SHE'S... REALLY NICE.
WITH A COWORKER LIKE HER...
THIS MIGHT ACTUALLY BE A FUN PLACE TO WORK.
Really?
THAT'S GOOD... WE'LL SHOW YOU AROUND ONCE YOU'RE DONE DRINKING, THEN.
FOR NOW, DO YOU HAVE ANYTHING YOU WANT TO ASK US?
ASK YOU...?
ACTU-ALLY...
Horumon
YEAH...

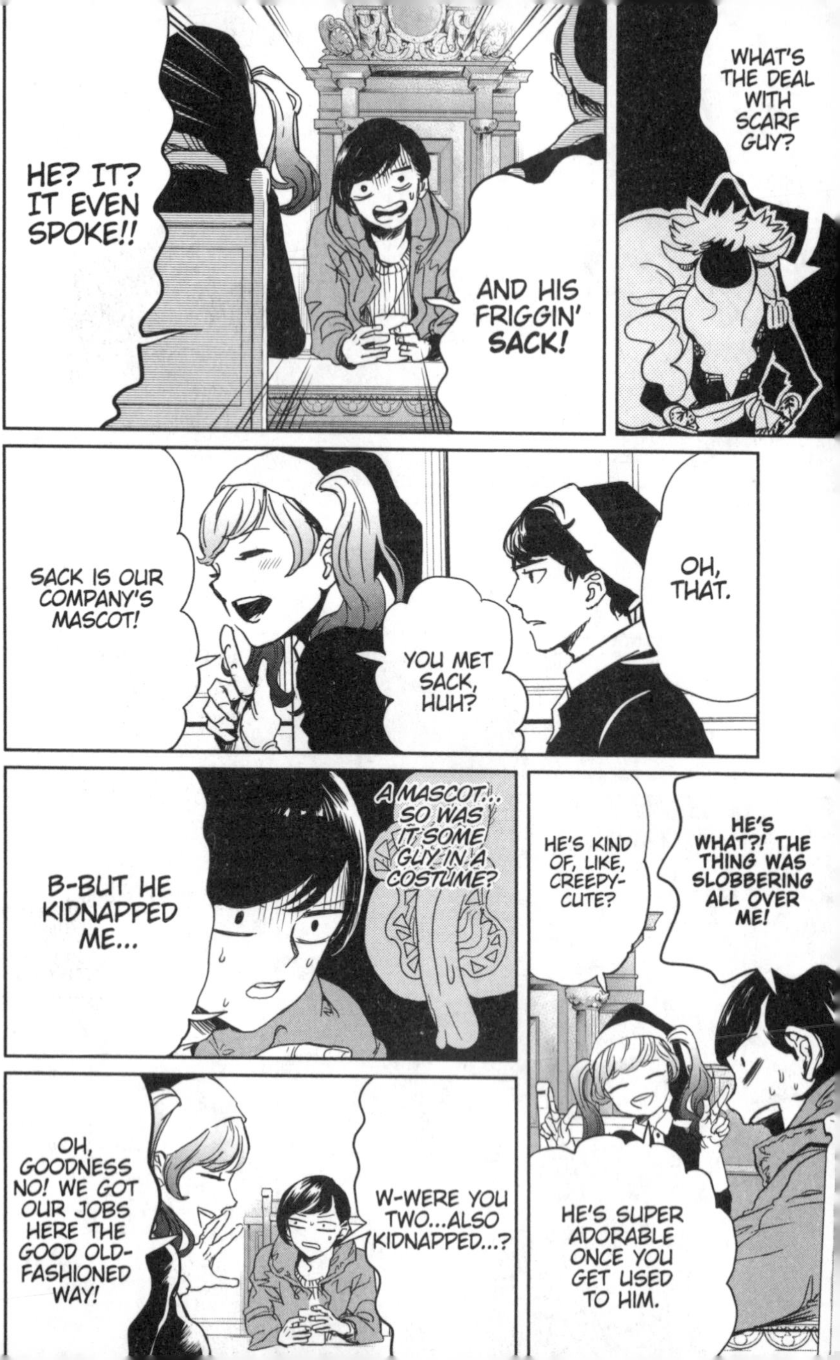
WHAT'S THE DEAL WITH SCARF GUY?
HE? IT? IT EVEN SPOKE!!
AND HIS FRIGGIN' SACK!
OH, THAT.
YOU MET SACK, HUH?
SACK IS OUR COMPANY'S MASCOT!
HE'S WHAT?! THE THING WAS SLOBBERING ALL OVER ME!
HE'S KIND OF, LIKE, CREEPY-CUTE?
HE'S SUPER ADORABLE ONCE YOU GET USED TO HIM.
A MASCOT... SO WAS IT SOME GUY IN A COSTUME?
B-BUT HE KIDNAPPED ME...
W-WERE YOU TWO...ALSO KIDNAPPED...?
OH, GOODNESS NO! WE GOT OUR JOBS HERE THE GOOD OLD-FASHIONED WAY!

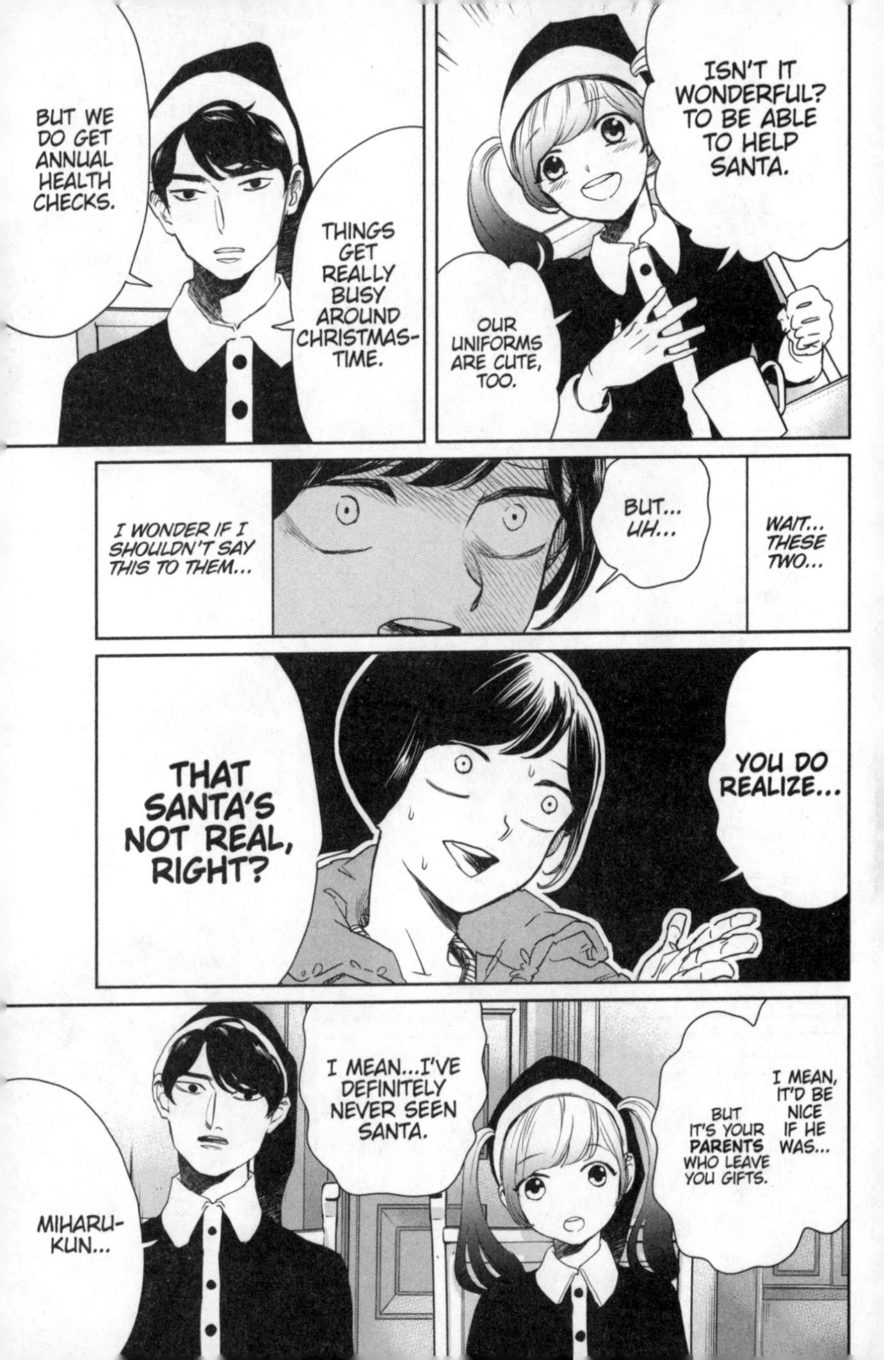
ISN'T IT WONDERFUL? TO BE ABLE TO HELP SANTA.
OUR UNIFORMS ARE CUTE, TOO.
THINGS GET REALLY BUSY AROUND CHRISTMAS-TIME.
BUT WE DO GET ANNUAL HEALTH CHECKS.
WAIT... THESE TWO...
BUT... UH...
I WONDER IF I SHOULDN'T SAY THIS TO THEM...
YOU DO REALIZE...
THAT SANTA'S NOT REAL, RIGHT?
I MEAN, IT'D BE NICE IF HE WAS...
BUT IT'S YOUR PARENTS WHO LEAVE YOU GIFTS.
I MEAN...I'VE DEFINITELY NEVER SEEN SANTA.
MIHARU-KUN...

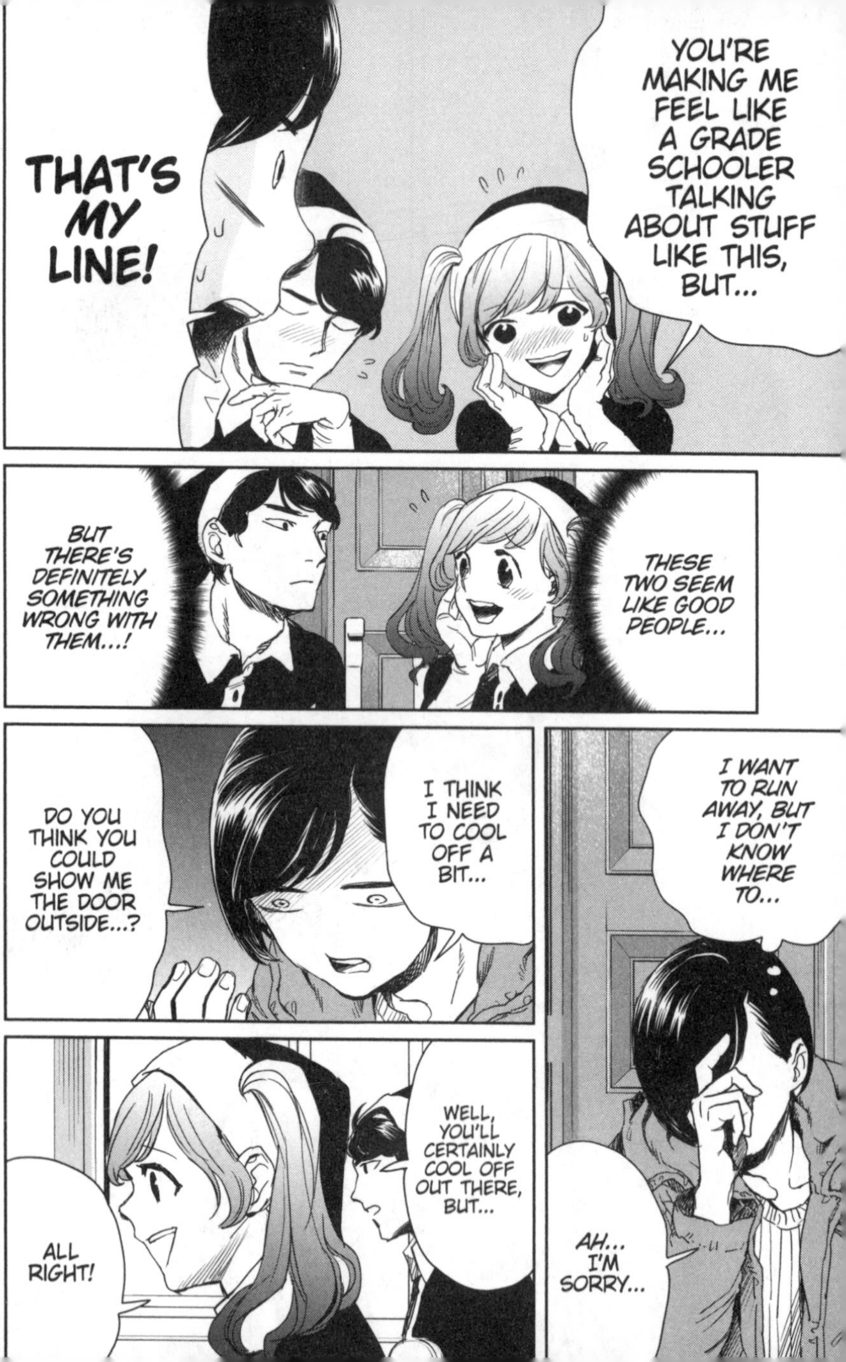
YOU'RE MAKING ME FEEL LIKE A GRADE SCHOOLER TALKING ABOUT STUFF LIKE THIS, BUT...
THAT'S *MY* LINE!
THESE TWO SEEM LIKE GOOD PEOPLE...
BUT THERE'S DEFINITELY SOMETHING WRONG WITH THEM...!
I WANT TO RUN AWAY, BUT I DON'T KNOW WHERE TO...
AH... I'M SORRY...
I THINK I NEED TO COOL OFF A BIT...
DO YOU THINK YOU COULD SHOW ME THE DOOR OUTSIDE...?
WELL, YOU'LL CERTAINLY COOL OFF OUT THERE, BUT...
ALL RIGHT!

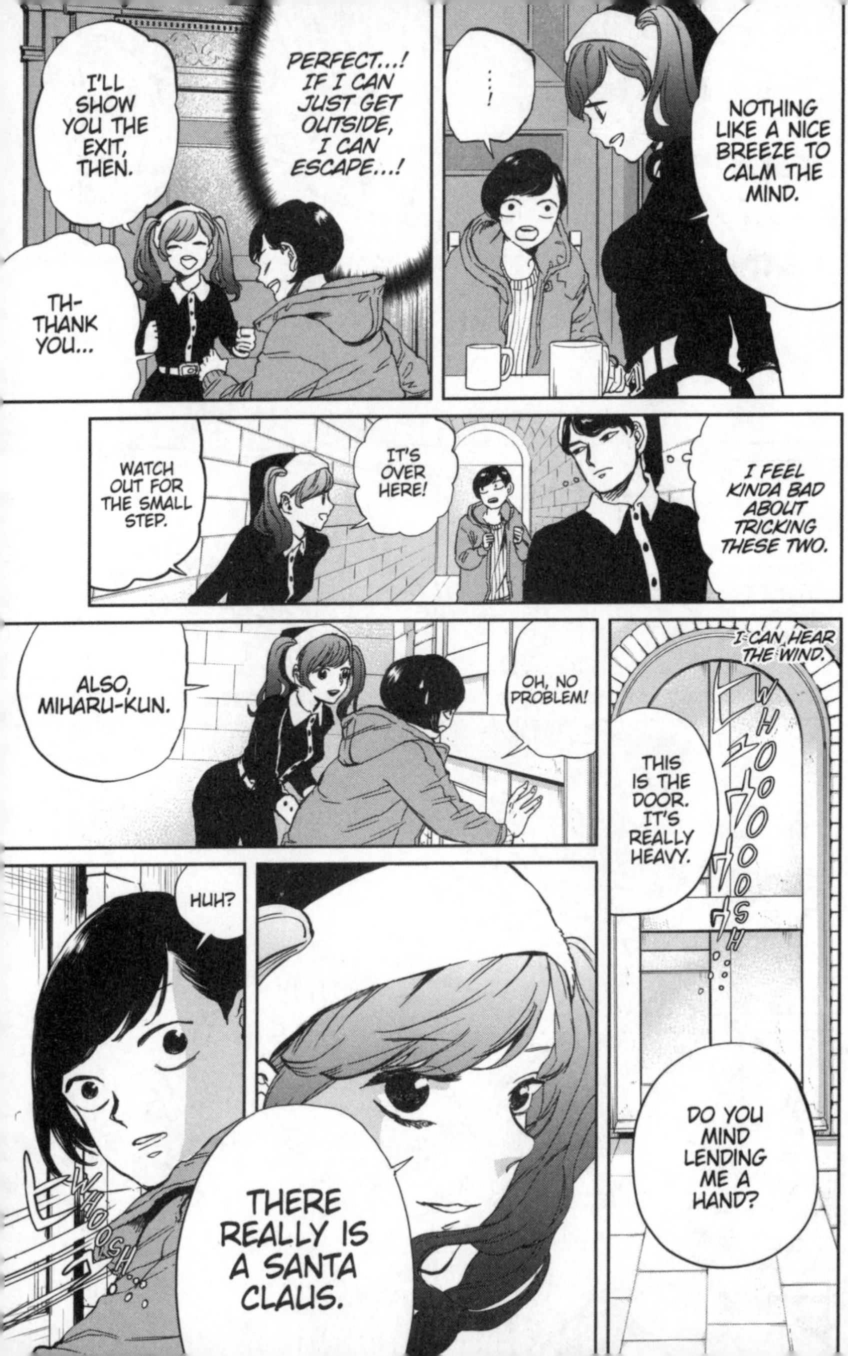

NOTHING LIKE A NICE BREEZE TO CALM THE MIND.
...!
PERFECT...! IF I CAN JUST GET OUTSIDE, I CAN ESCAPE...!
I'LL SHOW YOU THE EXIT, THEN.
TH-THANK YOU...
I FEEL KINDA BAD ABOUT TRICKING THESE TWO.
IT'S OVER HERE!
WATCH OUT FOR THE SMALL STEP.
I CAN HEAR THE WIND.
WHOOOOOOOSH
THIS IS THE DOOR. IT'S REALLY HEAVY.
DO YOU MIND LENDING ME A HAND?
OH, NO PROBLEM!
ALSO, MIHARU-KUN.
THERE REALLY IS A SANTA CLAUS.
HUH?
WHOOSH...

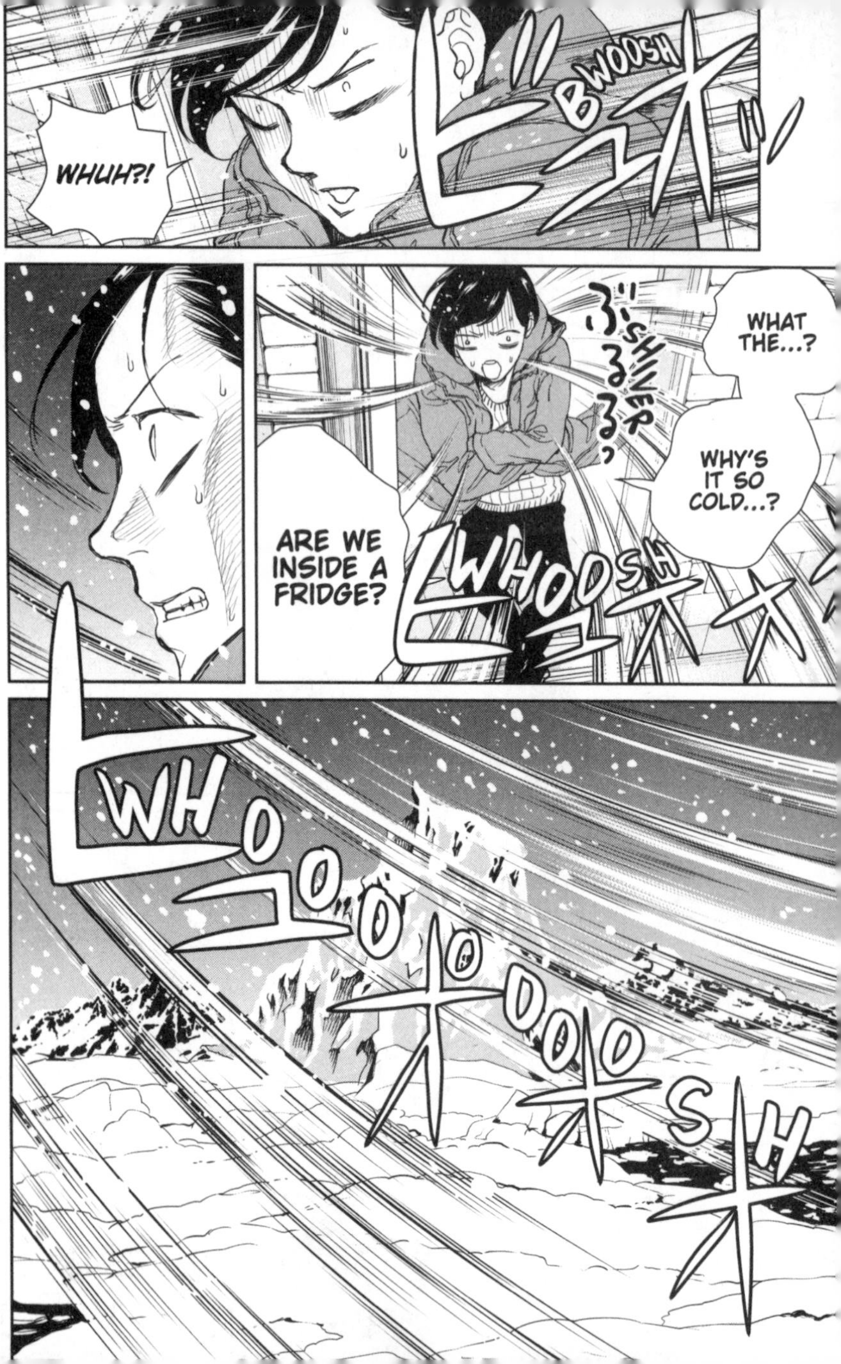
BWOOSH
WHUH?!
WHAT THE...?
WHY'S IT SO COLD...?
SHIVER
ARE WE INSIDE A FRIDGE?
WHOOSH
WHOOOOOOOSH

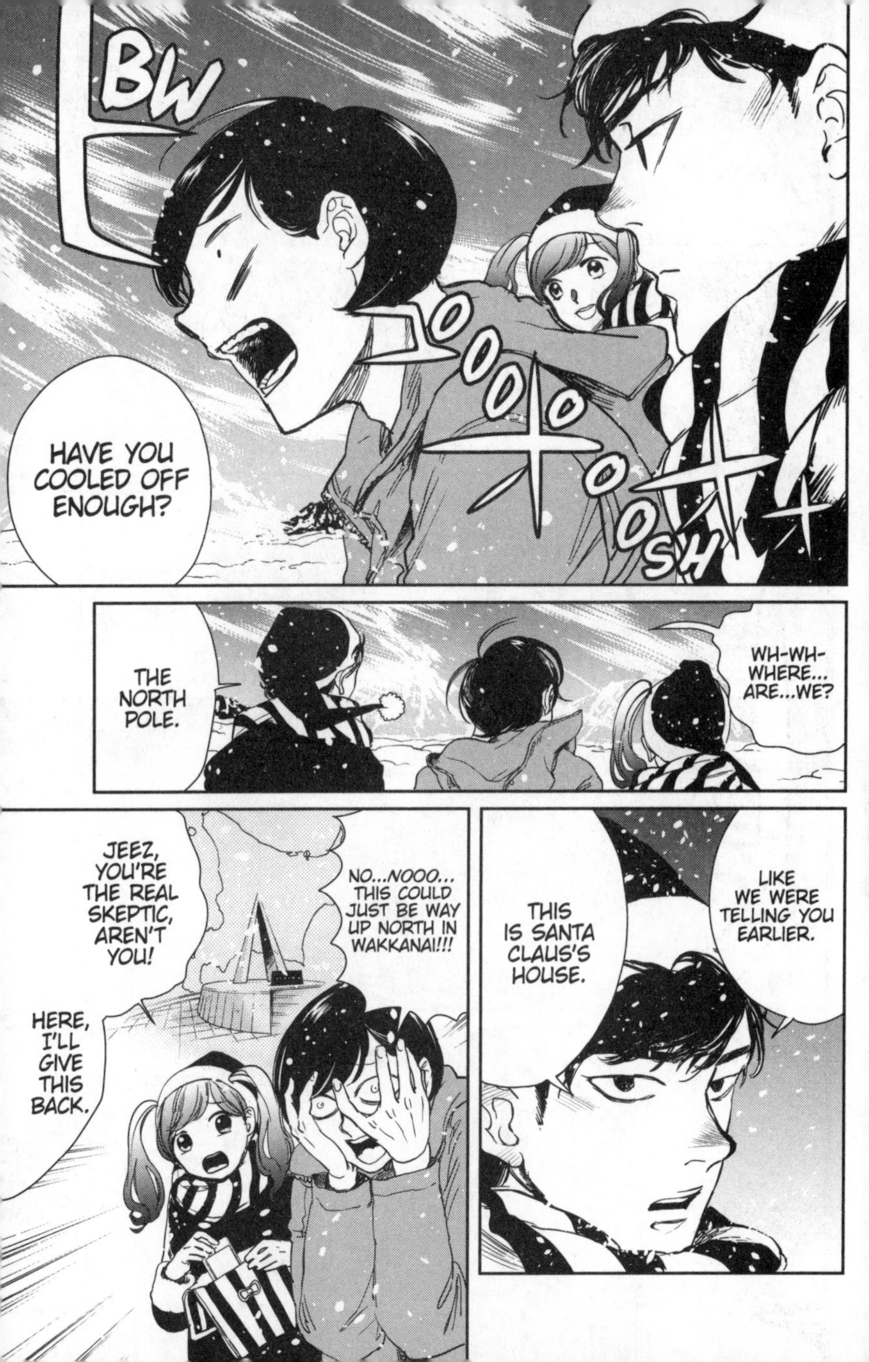
BWOOOOOOSH
HAVE YOU COOLED OFF ENOUGH?
WH-WH-WHERE... ARE...WE?
THE NORTH POLE.
LIKE WE WERE TELLING YOU EARLIER.
THIS IS SANTA CLAUS'S HOUSE.
NO...NOOO... THIS COULD JUST BE WAY UP NORTH IN WAKKANAI!!!
JEEZ, YOU'RE THE REAL SKEPTIC, AREN'T YOU!
HERE, I'LL GIVE THIS BACK.

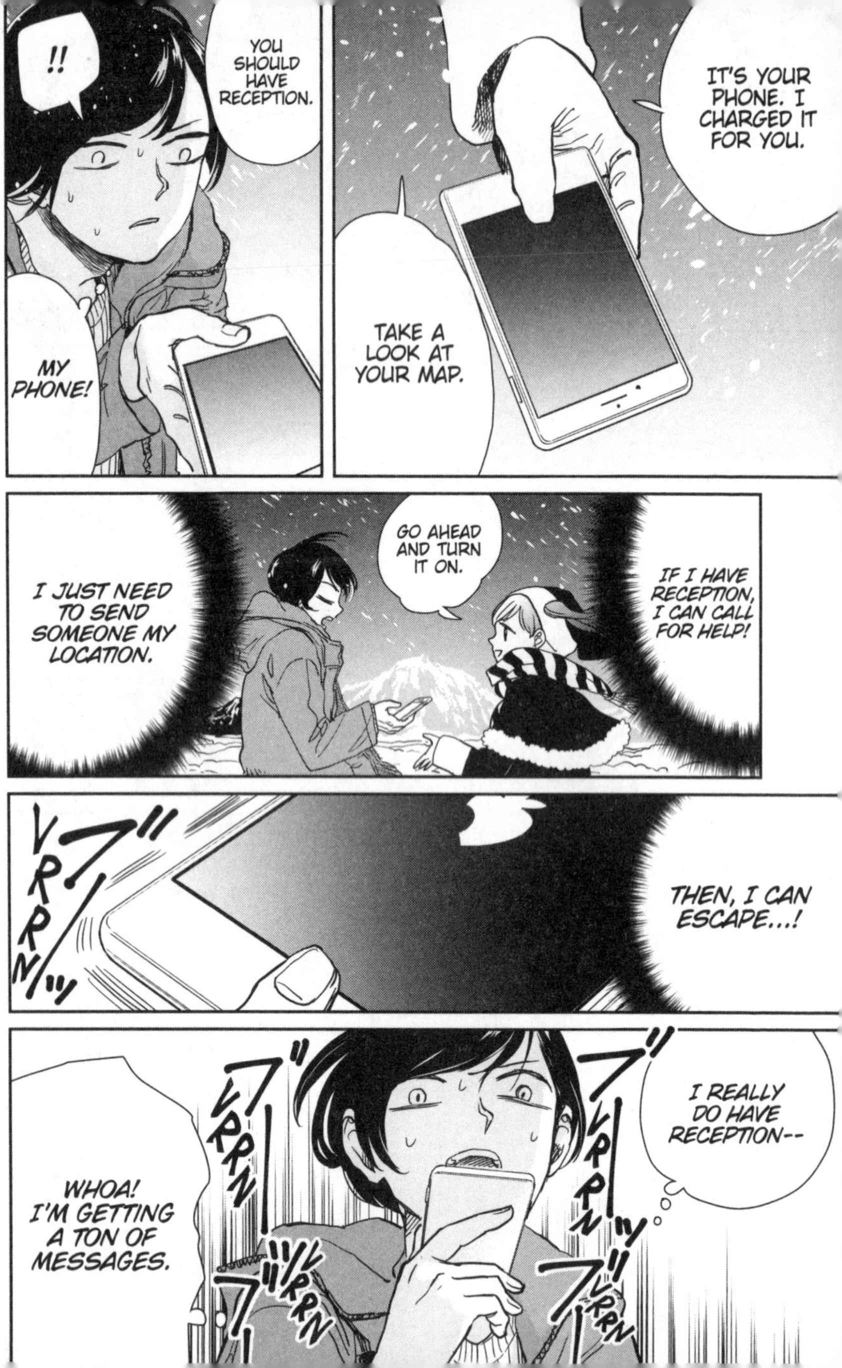
IT'S YOUR PHONE. I CHARGED IT FOR YOU.
TAKE A LOOK AT YOUR MAP.
YOU SHOULD HAVE RECEPTION.
!!
MY PHONE!
IF I HAVE RECEPTION, I CAN CALL FOR HELP!
GO AHEAD AND TURN IT ON.
I JUST NEED TO SEND SOMEONE MY LOCATION.
THEN, I CAN ESCAPE...!
VRRRN
I REALLY DO HAVE RECEPTION--
VRRRN
VRRN
VRRN
VRRN
WHOA! I'M GETTING A TON OF MESSAGES.

All | Missed Calls

Manager	16:55	To
Manager	17:00	
Manager	17:01	
		To

WHO'S BEEN TRYING TO...

I'M GOING TO REPORT THIS TO UPPER MANAGEMENT, ALONG WITH YOUR SHOPLIFTING.

DO YOU UNDERSTAND HOW BIG OF A PROBLEM THIS IS?

MIHARU-KUN. YOU NEED TO CALL ME IF YOU'RE GOING TO TAKE THE DAY OFF. YOU'RE AN ADULT, ACT LIKE ONE.

Mom
Message

UH...

Hey, it's mom. Did you get the rice I sent you for Christmas? It would be nice if you came home this year. Everyone knows you're doing your best to get a job, so you don't have to worry about it. Just come spend time with your family.

You have 11 new notifications.

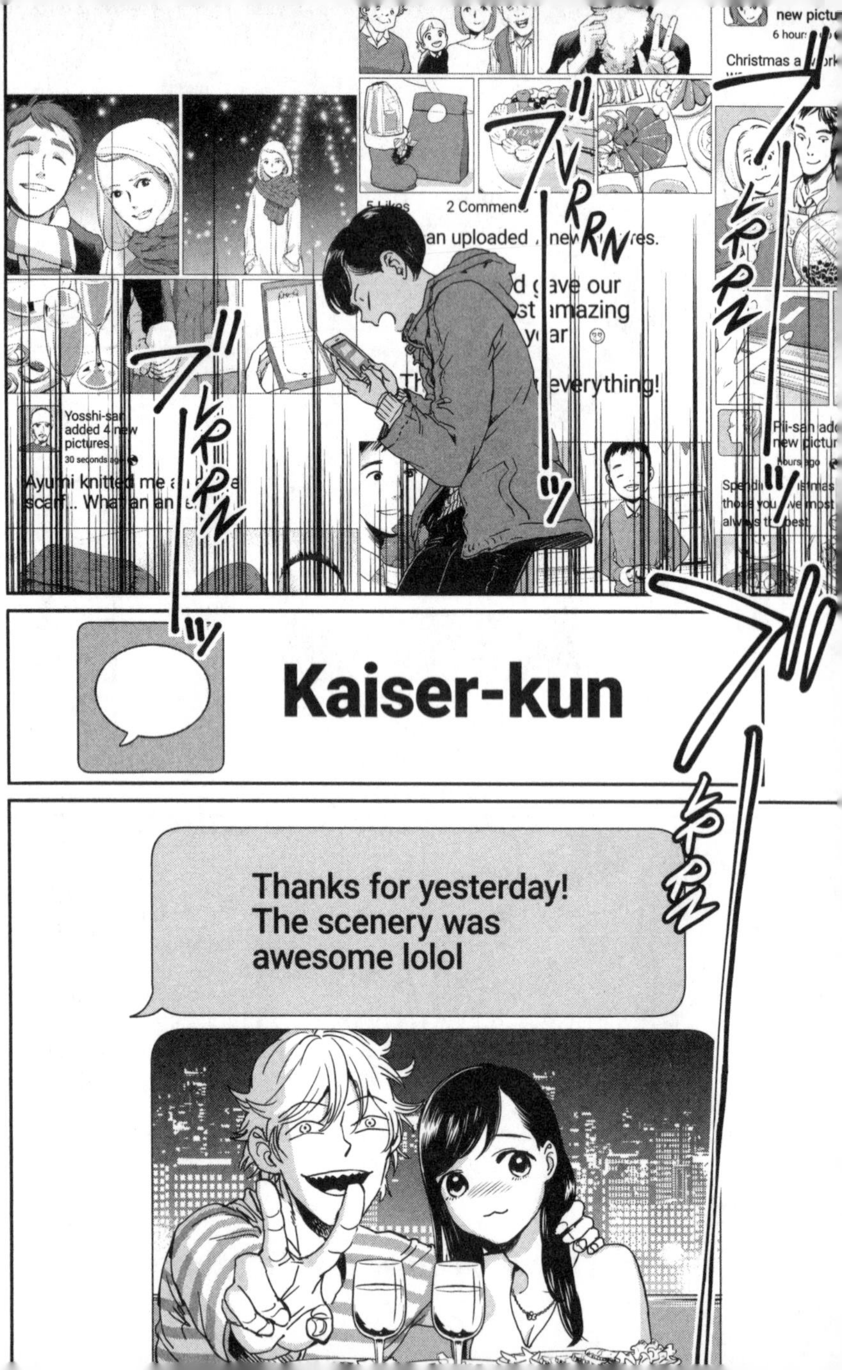
new pictu
Christmas a
5 Likes
2 Comments
an uploaded
VRRN
everything!
Yosshi-san added 4 new pictures.
30 seconds ago
Ayumi knitted me a
scarf... What an an
VRRN
Pii-san add new pictur
VRRN
VRRN
Kaiser-kun
Thanks for yesterday! The scenery was awesome lolol

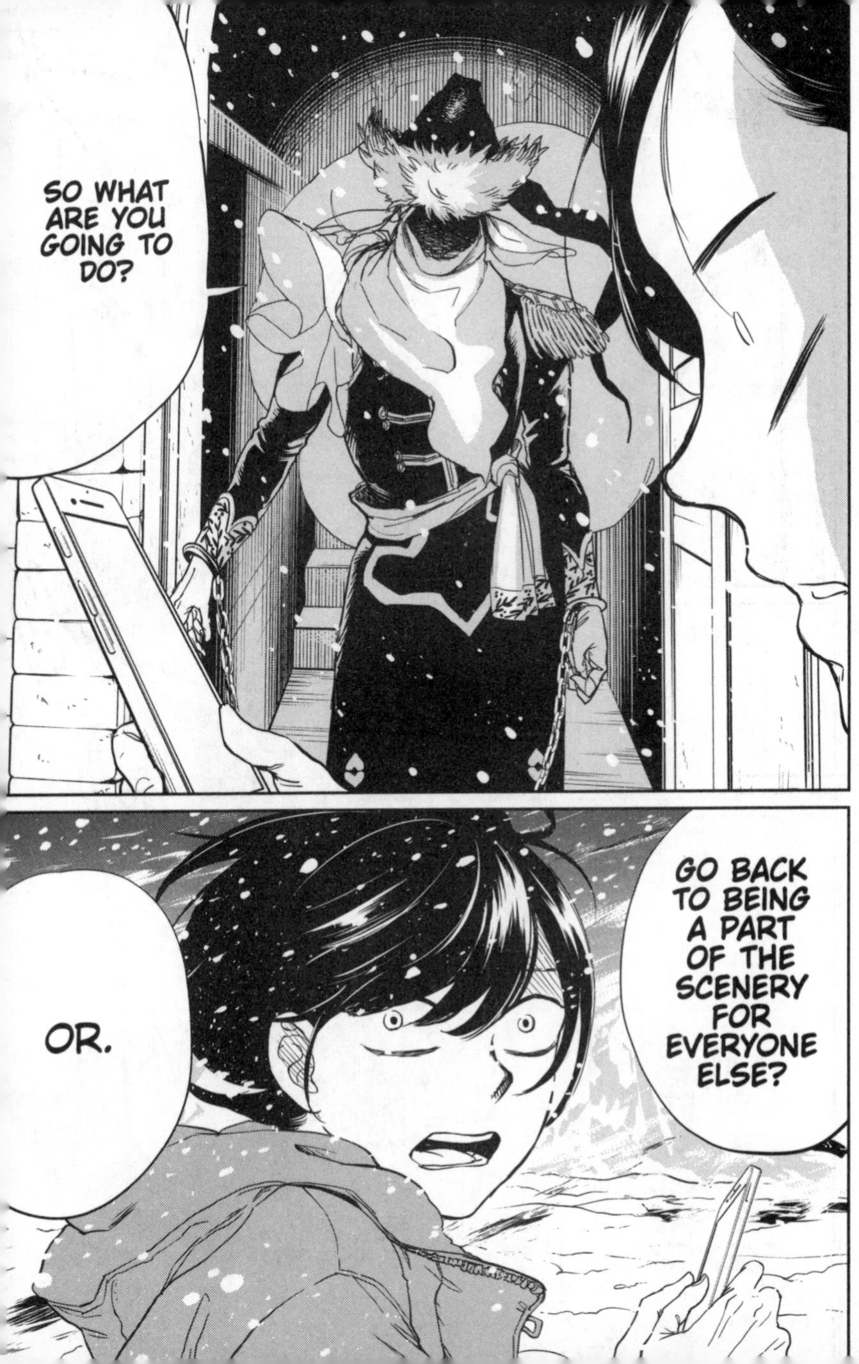
SO WHAT ARE YOU GOING TO DO?
GO BACK TO BEING A PART OF THE SCENERY FOR EVERYONE ELSE?
OR.

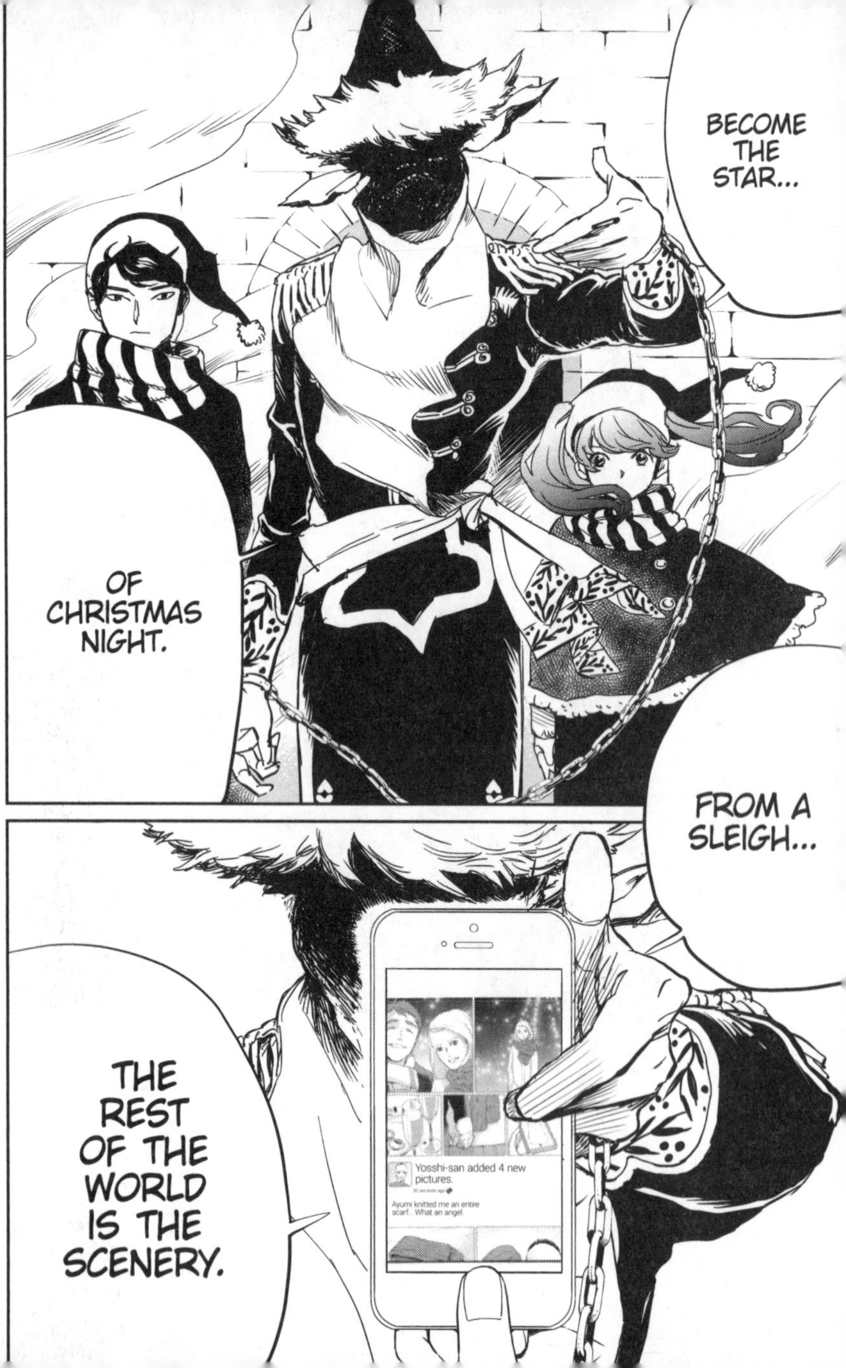
BECOME THE STAR...
OF CHRISTMAS NIGHT.
FROM A SLEIGH...
Yosshi-san added 4 new pictures.
Ayumi knitted me an entire scarf... What an angel.
THE REST OF THE WORLD IS THE SCENERY.

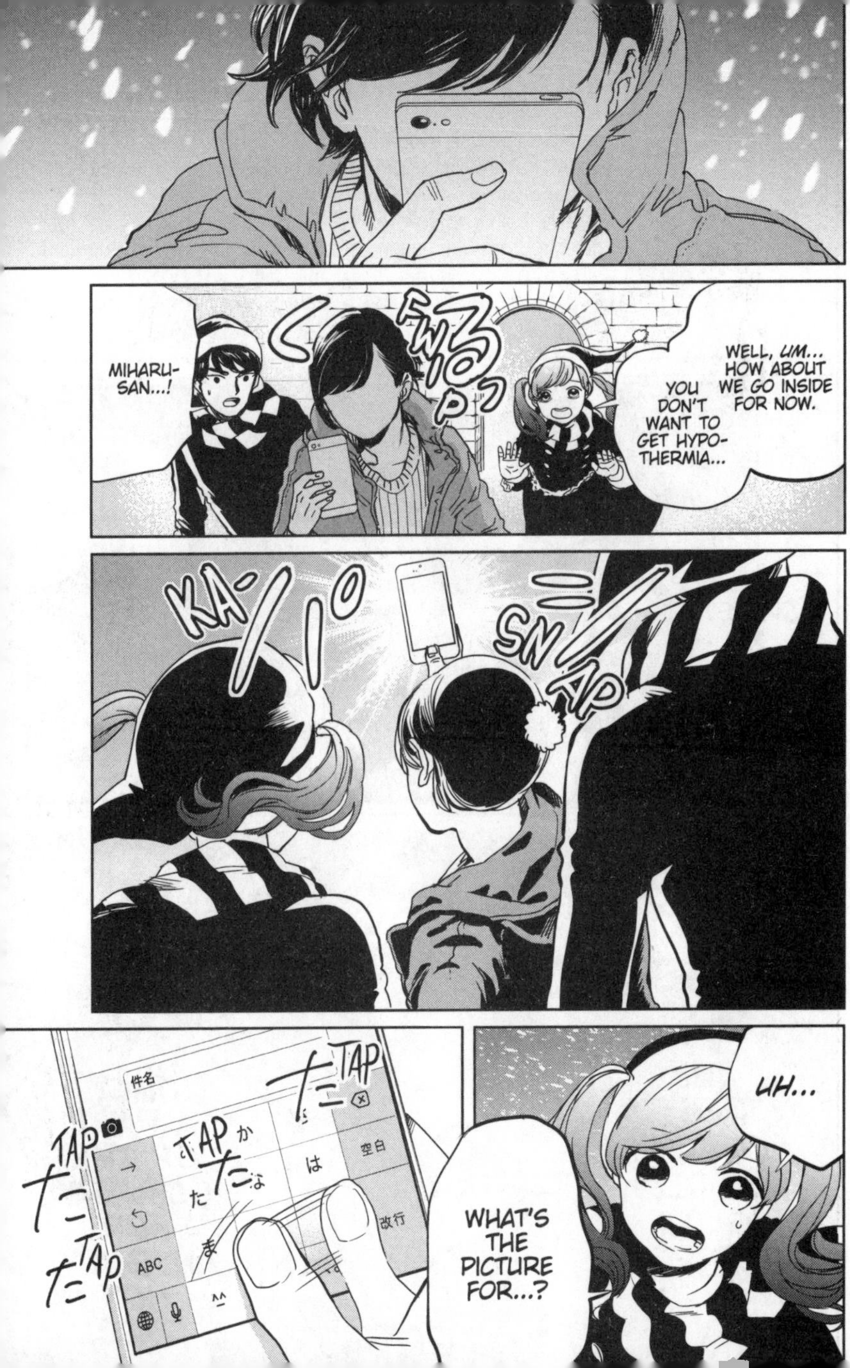
WELL, UM... HOW ABOUT WE GO INSIDE FOR NOW.
YOU DON'T WANT TO GET HYPO-THERMIA...
FWOOP
MIHARU-SAN...!
SNAP
KA-
UH...
WHAT'S THE PICTURE FOR...?
TAP
件名
空白
改行
ABC
TAP
TAP
TAP

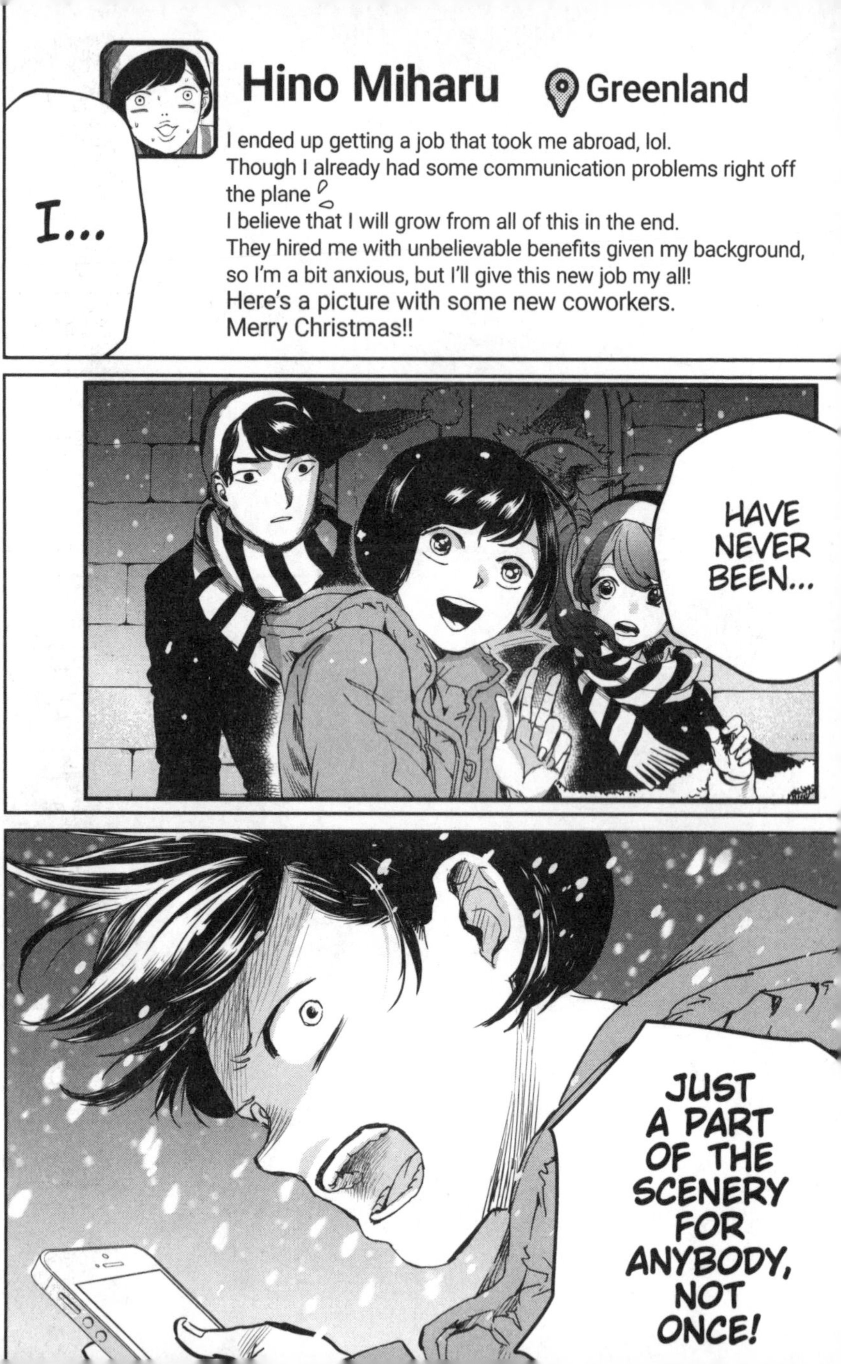
Hino Miharu
Greenland
I ended up getting a job that took me abroad, lol.
Though I already had some communication problems right off the plane
I believe that I will grow from all of this in the end.
They hired me with unbelievable benefits given my background, so I'm a bit anxious, but I'll give this new job my all!
Here's a picture with some new coworkers.
Merry Christmas!!
I...
HAVE NEVER BEEN...
JUST A PART OF THE SCENERY FOR ANYBODY, NOT ONCE!

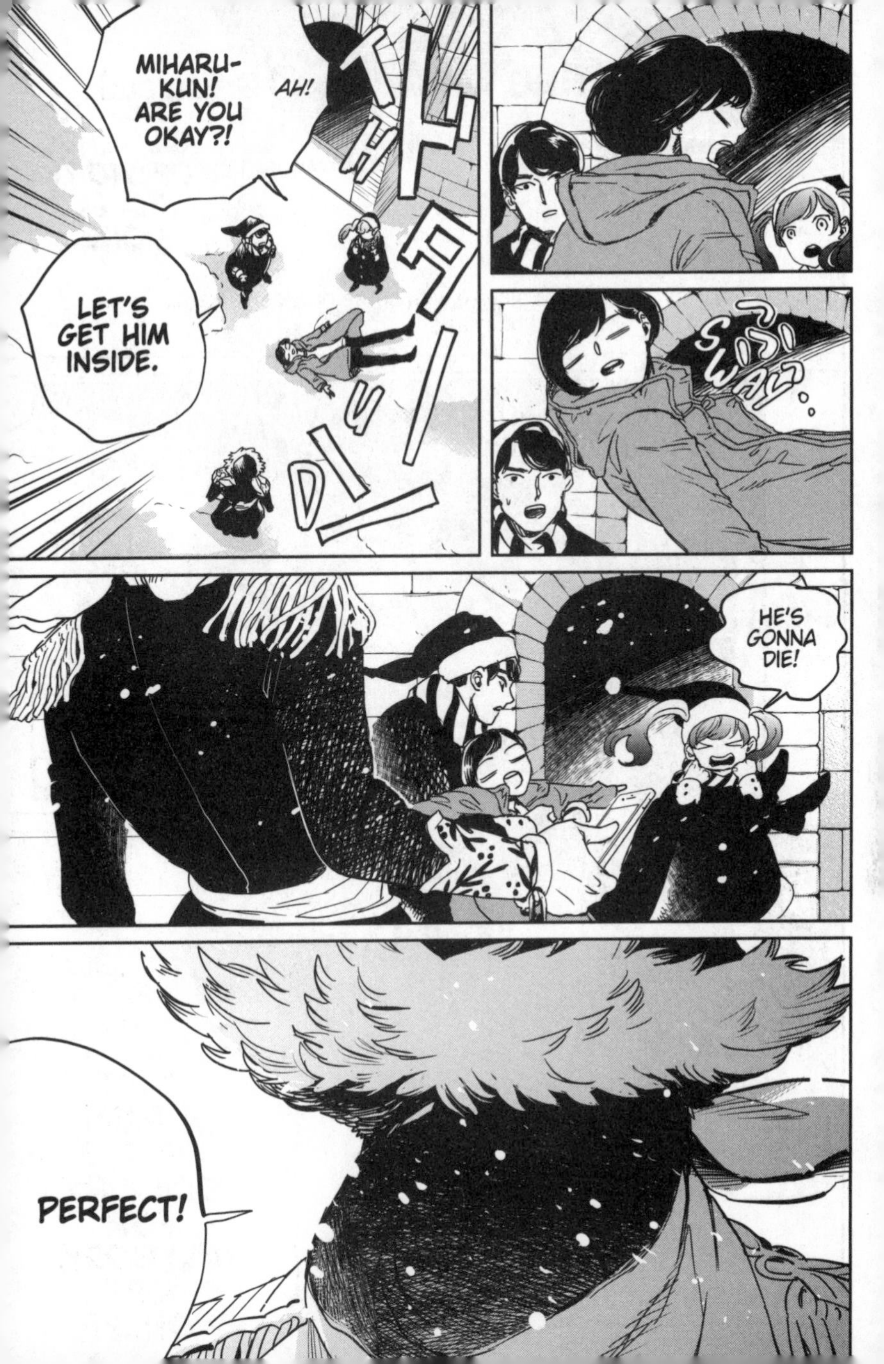
SWAY
AH!
MIHARU-KUN! ARE YOU OKAY?!
LET'S GET HIM INSIDE.
HE'S GONNA DIE!
PERFECT!

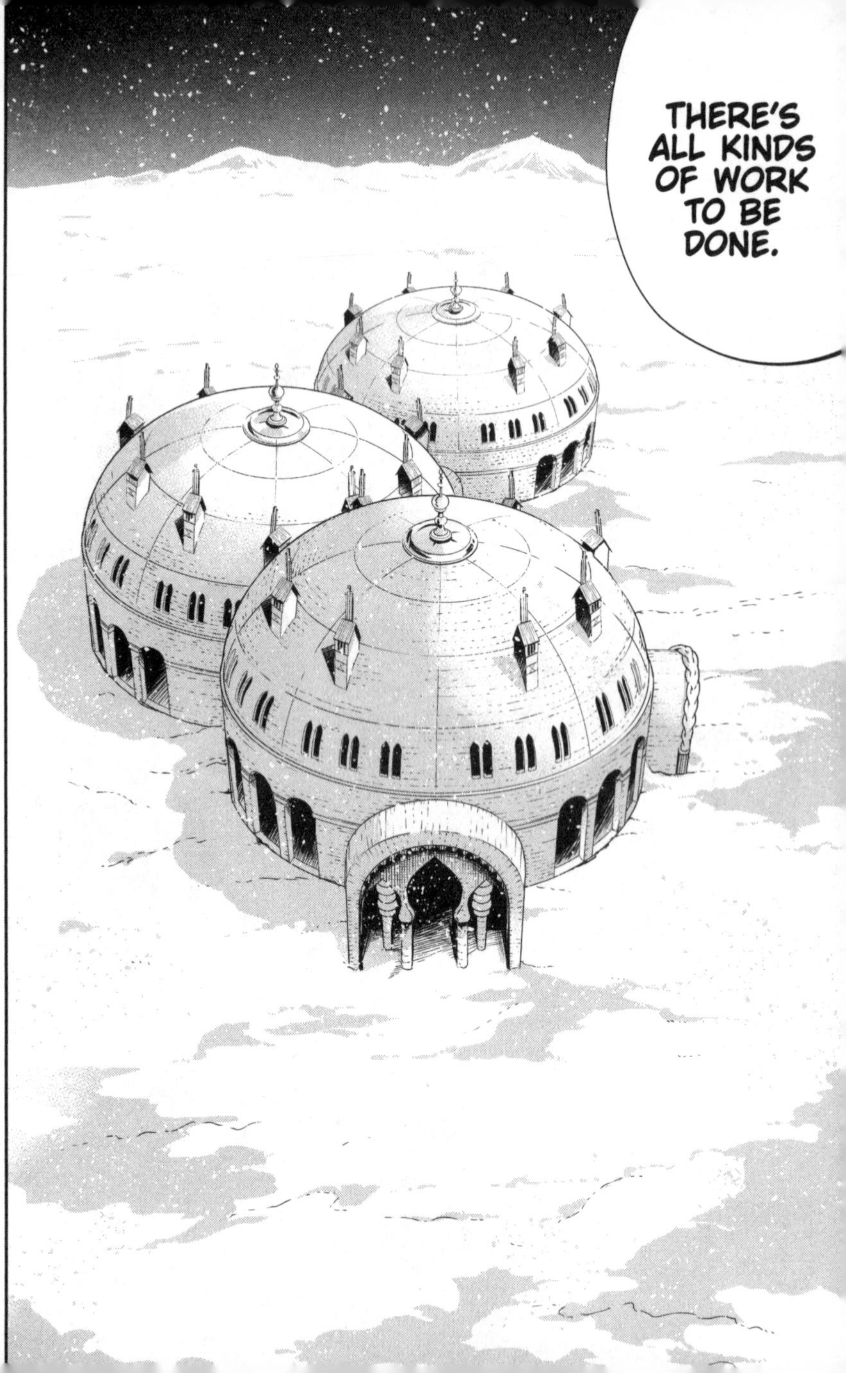
THERE'S ALL KINDS OF WORK TO BE DONE.

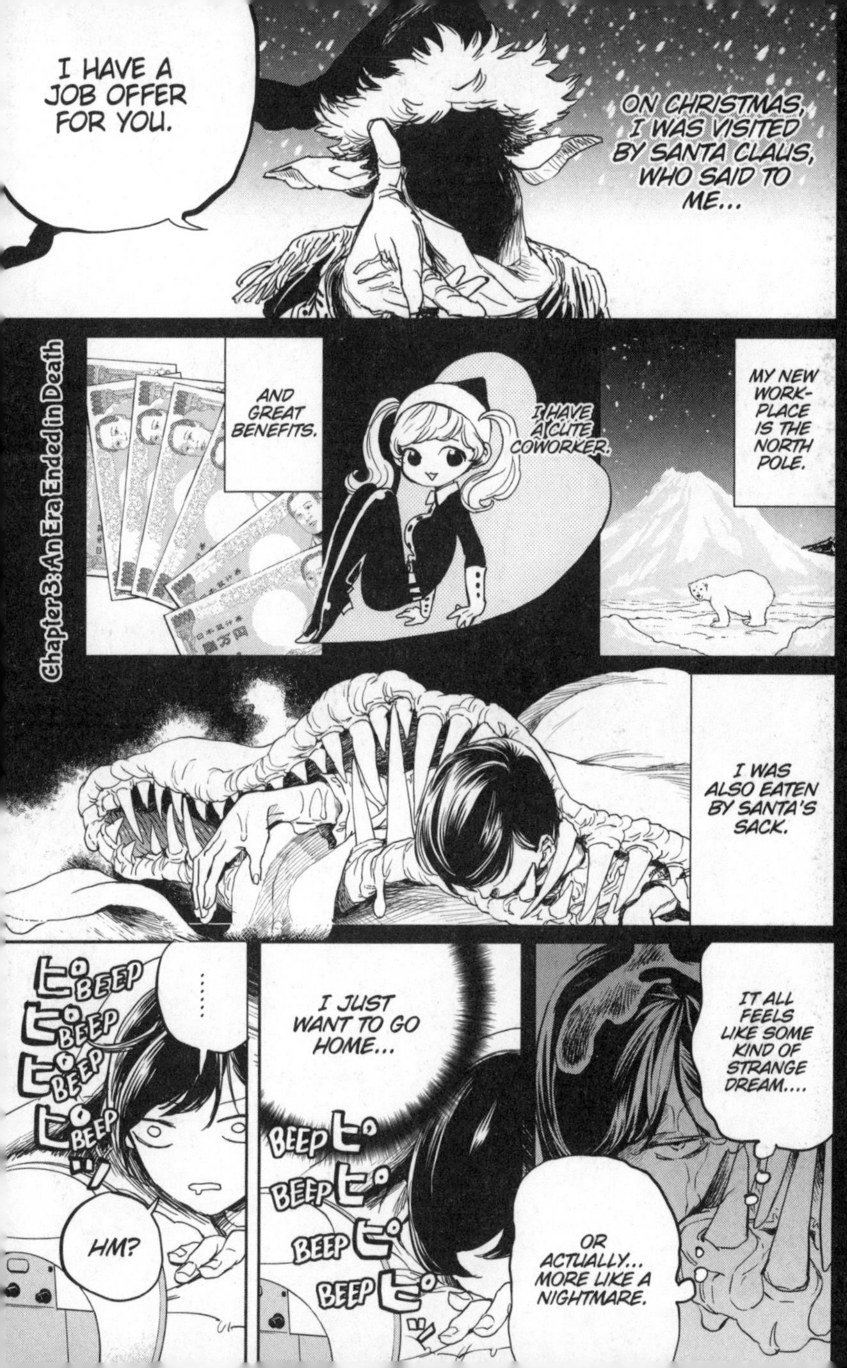
ON CHRISTMAS, I WAS VISITED BY SANTA CLAUS, WHO SAID TO ME...
I HAVE A JOB OFFER FOR YOU.
Chapter 3: An Era Ended in Death
MY NEW WORK-PLACE IS THE NORTH POLE.
I HAVE A CUTE COWORKER.
AND GREAT BENEFITS.
I WAS ALSO EATEN BY SANTA'S SACK.
IT ALL FEELS LIKE SOME KIND OF STRANGE DREAM....
OR ACTUALLY... MORE LIKE A NIGHTMARE.
I JUST WANT TO GO HOME...
BEEP ピ
BEEP ピ
BEEP ピ
BEEP ピッ
......
ピ BEEP
ピ BEEP
ピ BEEP
ピ BEEP
ッ
HM?

Chapter 3
An Era Ended in Death

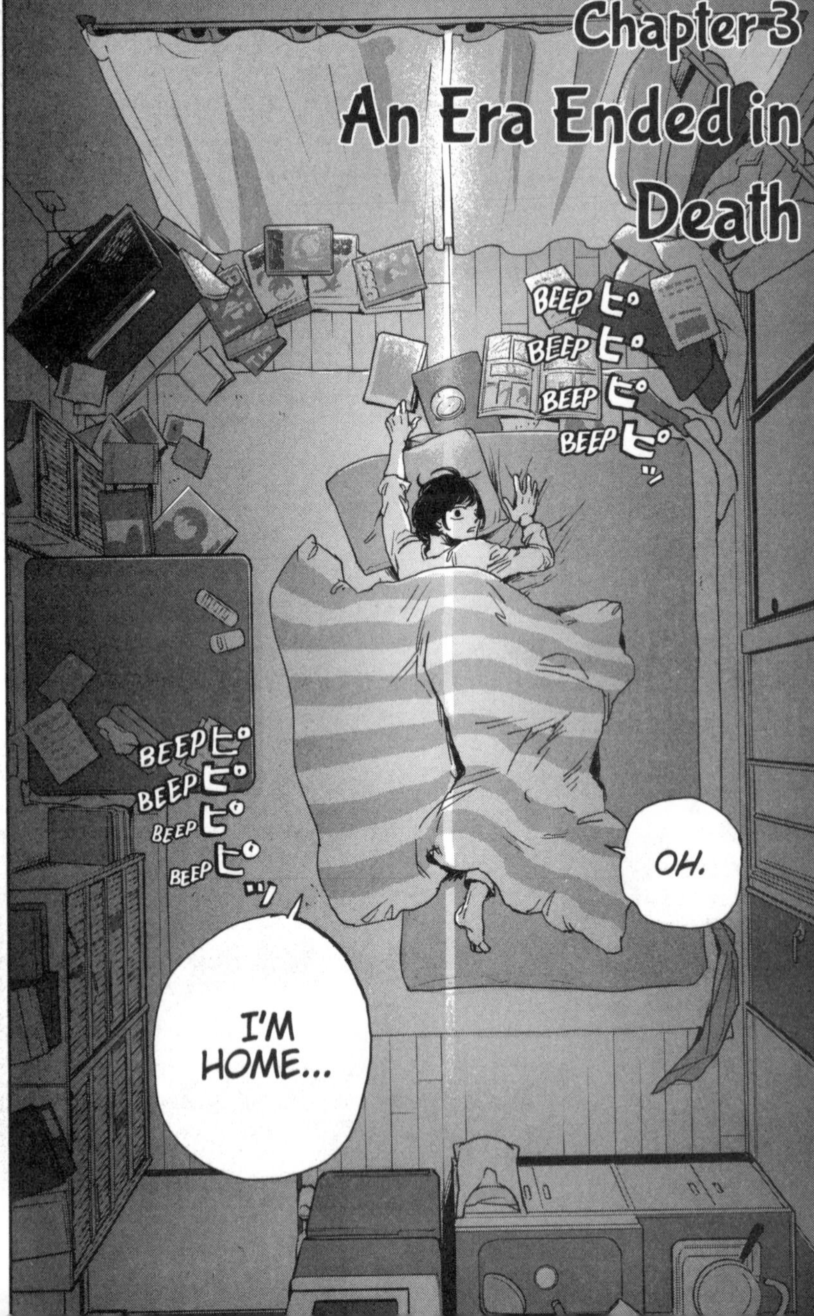
BEEP ピ BEEP ピ BEEP ピ BEEP ピッ
BEEP ピ BEEP ピ BEEP ピ BEEP ピッ
OH.
I'M HOME...

JEEZ...

SO IT REALLY WAS A DREAM.

BEEP BEEP BEEP

CHAK

CRAP... I DO! I DON'T WANT TO GO...

12

SUN	MON	TUE	WED	THU	FRI	SAT
				1	2	3
4	5	6	7	8	9	10
11	12	13	14	15	16	17
18	19	20	21	22	23	24
25	26	27	28	29	30	31

DO I HAVE WORK TODAY...?

THAT MAKES SENSE, THOUGH...

scratch scratch

OUCH!!

THUD

I GUESS I'M GLAD CHRISTMAS IS OVER, THOUGH.

I'D BETTER CHECK WHAT SHE SENT, JUST TO MAKE SURE I DON'T NEED TO REFRIGERATE ANYTHING.

RIP

Mom

KOSHIHIKARI Northern Rice

THE HECK IS...

OH, IT'S FROM MOM.

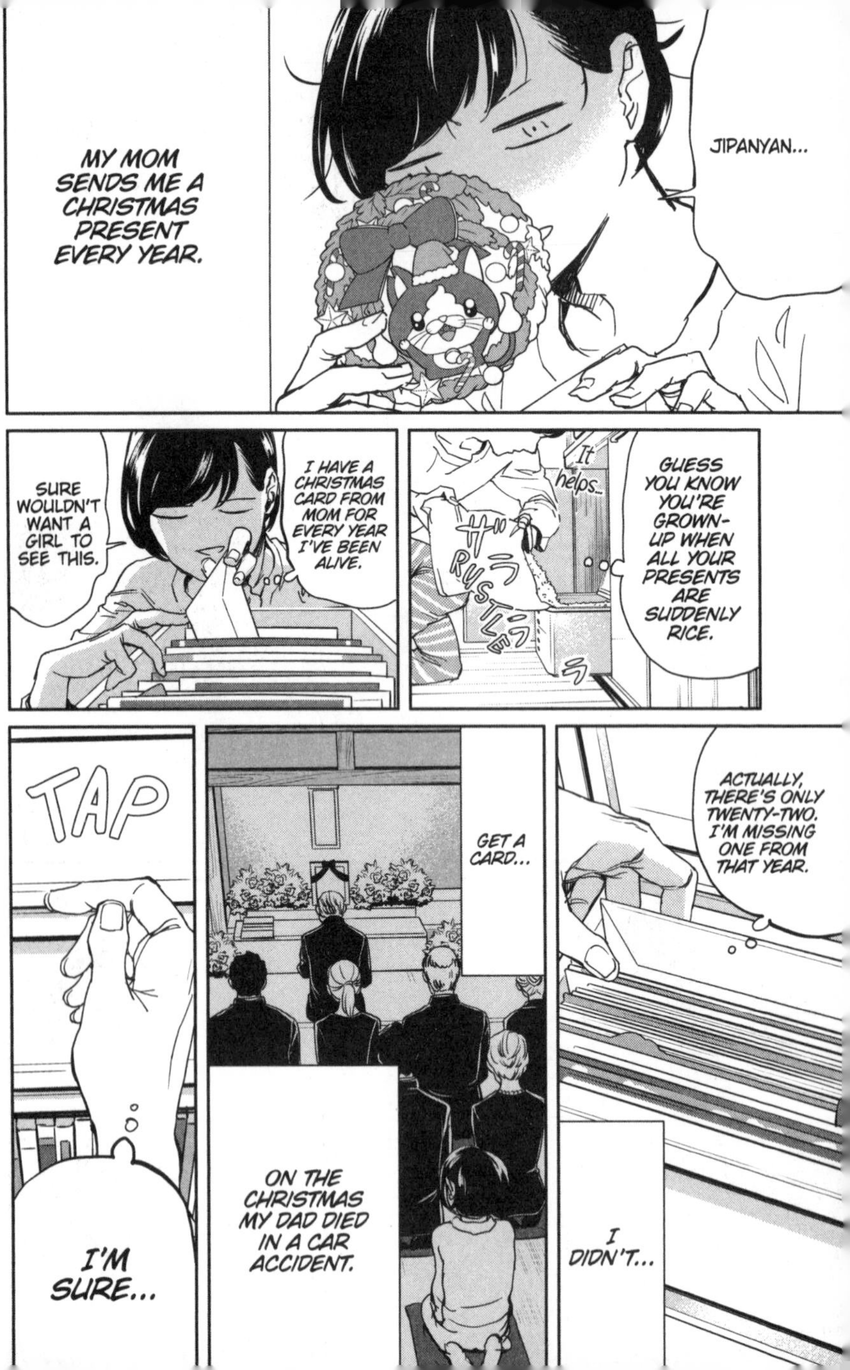
JIPANYAN...
MY MOM SENDS ME A CHRISTMAS PRESENT EVERY YEAR.
GUESS YOU KNOW YOU'RE GROWN-UP WHEN ALL YOUR PRESENTS ARE SUDDENLY RICE.
It helps..
RUSTLE
I HAVE A CHRISTMAS CARD FROM MOM FOR EVERY YEAR I'VE BEEN ALIVE.
SURE WOULDN'T WANT A GIRL TO SEE THIS.
ACTUALLY, THERE'S ONLY TWENTY-TWO. I'M MISSING ONE FROM THAT YEAR.
I DIDN'T...
GET A CARD...
ON THE CHRISTMAS MY DAD DIED IN A CAR ACCIDENT.
TAP
I'M SURE...

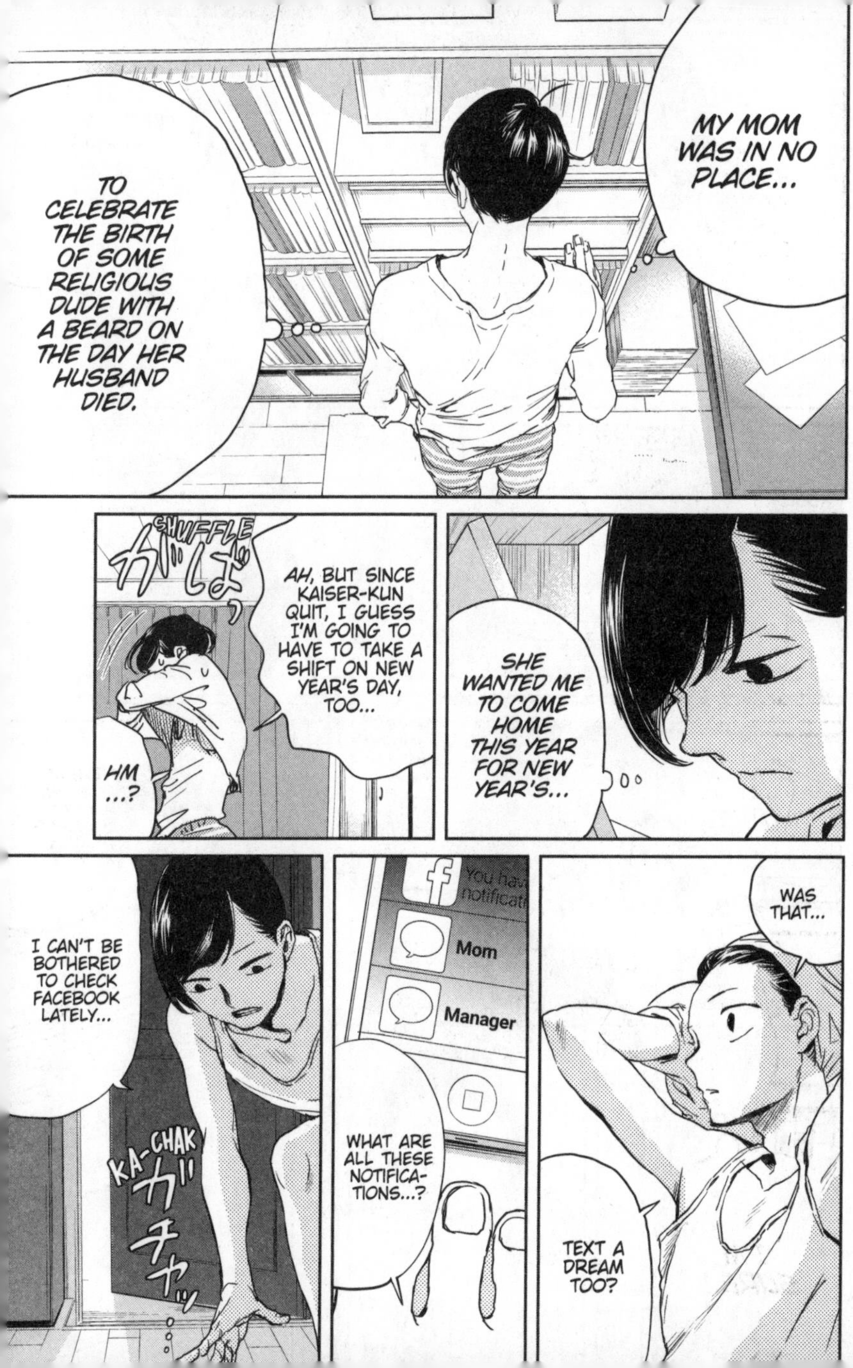
MY MOM WAS IN NO PLACE...
TO CELEBRATE THE BIRTH OF SOME RELIGIOUS DUDE WITH A BEARD ON THE DAY HER HUSBAND DIED.
SHE WANTED ME TO COME HOME THIS YEAR FOR NEW YEAR'S...
SHUFFLE
AH, BUT SINCE KAISER-KUN QUIT, I GUESS I'M GOING TO HAVE TO TAKE A SHIFT ON NEW YEAR'S DAY, TOO...
HM ...?
WAS THAT...
TEXT A DREAM TOO?
Mom
Manager
WHAT ARE ALL THESE NOTIFICA-TIONS...?
I CAN'T BE BOTHERED TO CHECK FACEBOOK LATELY...
KA-CHAK

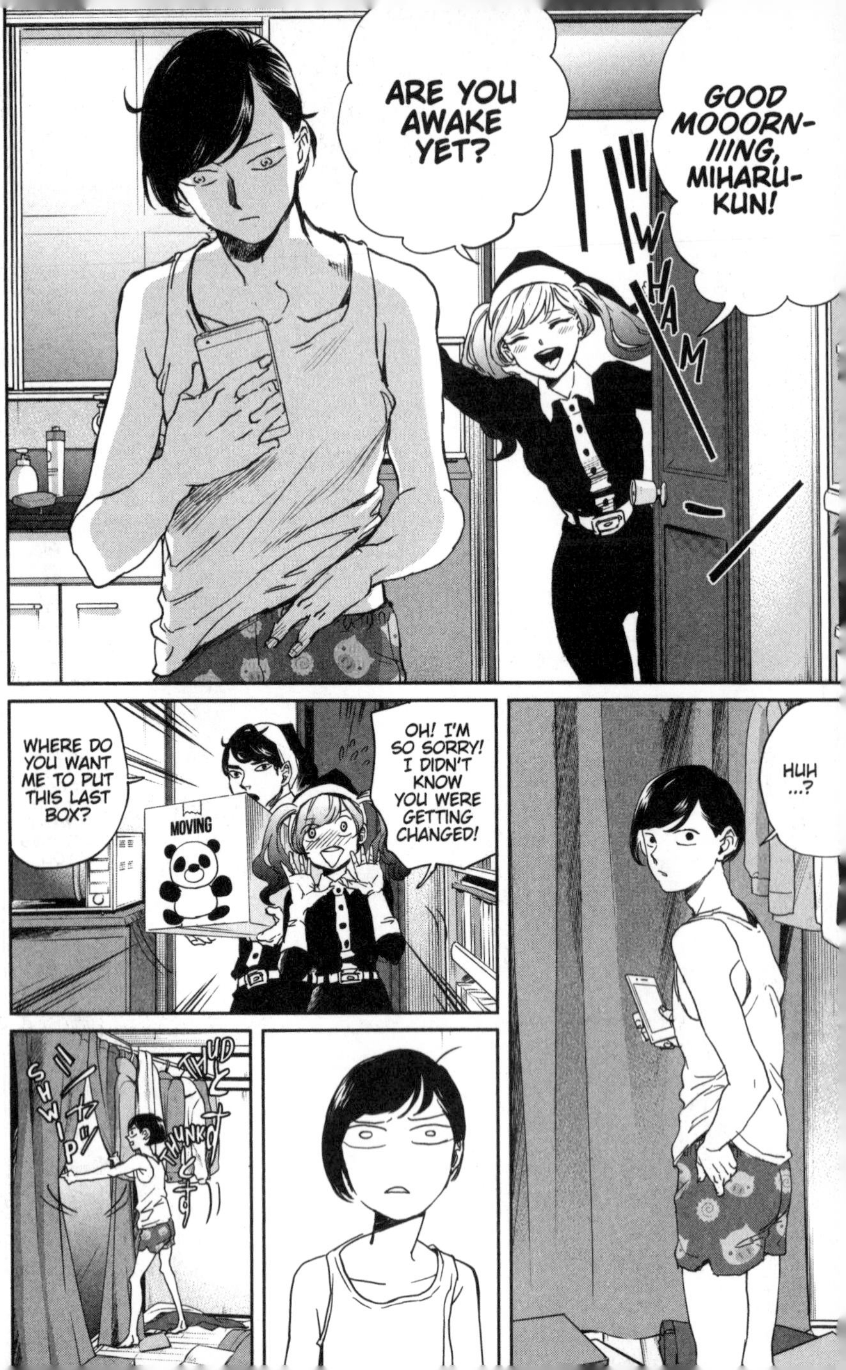
GOOD MOOORN-IIING, MIHARU-KUN!
WHAM
ARE YOU AWAKE YET?
HUH ...?
OH! I'M SO SORRY! I DIDN'T KNOW YOU WERE GETTING CHANGED!
WHERE DO YOU WANT ME TO PUT THIS LAST BOX?
MOVING
THUD
THUNK
SHWIP

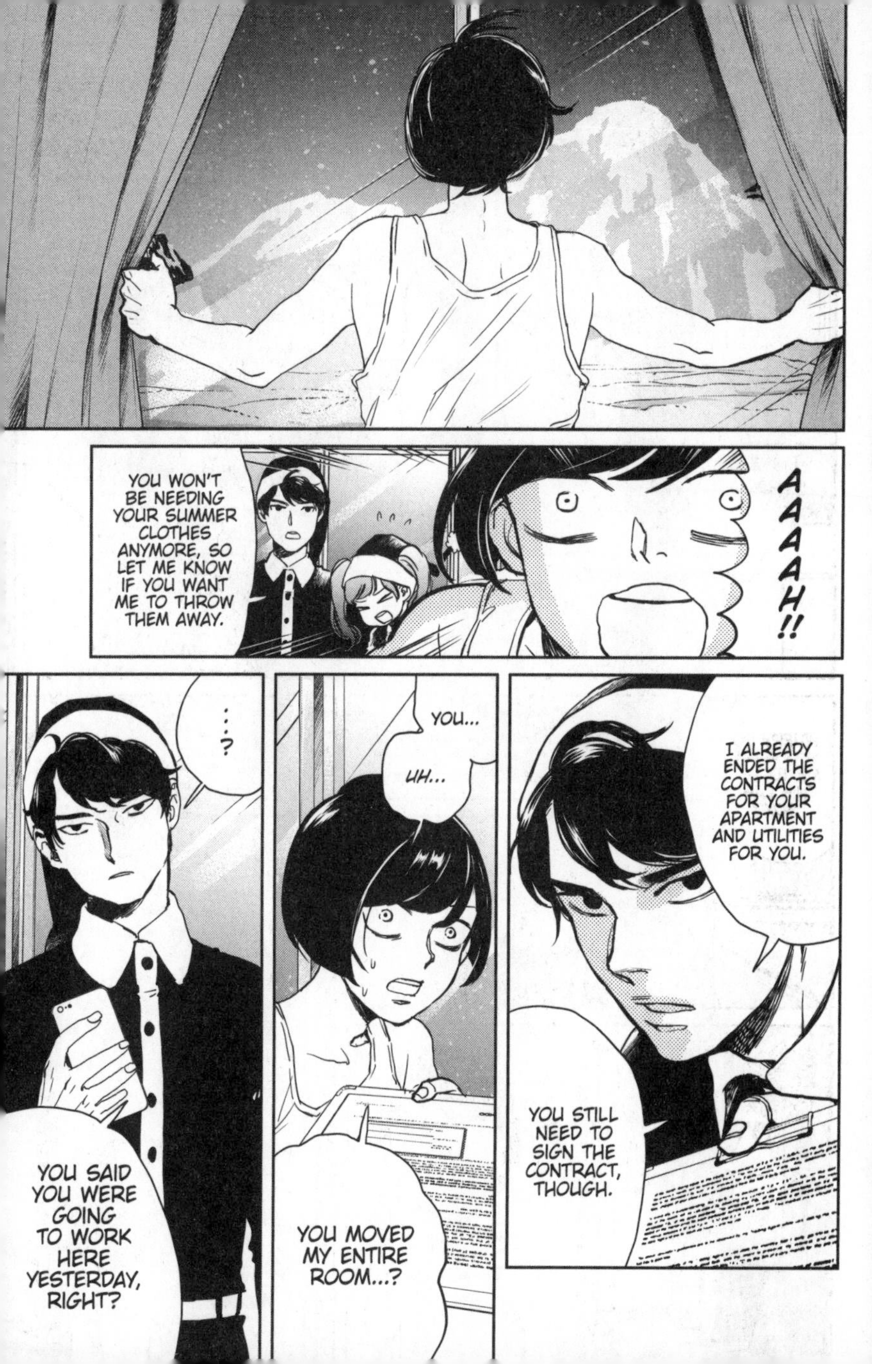
AAAAAH!!
YOU WON'T BE NEEDING YOUR SUMMER CLOTHES ANYMORE, SO LET ME KNOW IF YOU WANT ME TO THROW THEM AWAY.
I ALREADY ENDED THE CONTRACTS FOR YOUR APARTMENT AND UTILITIES FOR YOU.
YOU STILL NEED TO SIGN THE CONTRACT, THOUGH.
YOU...
UH...
YOU MOVED MY ENTIRE ROOM...?
...?
YOU SAID YOU WERE GOING TO WORK HERE YESTERDAY, RIGHT?

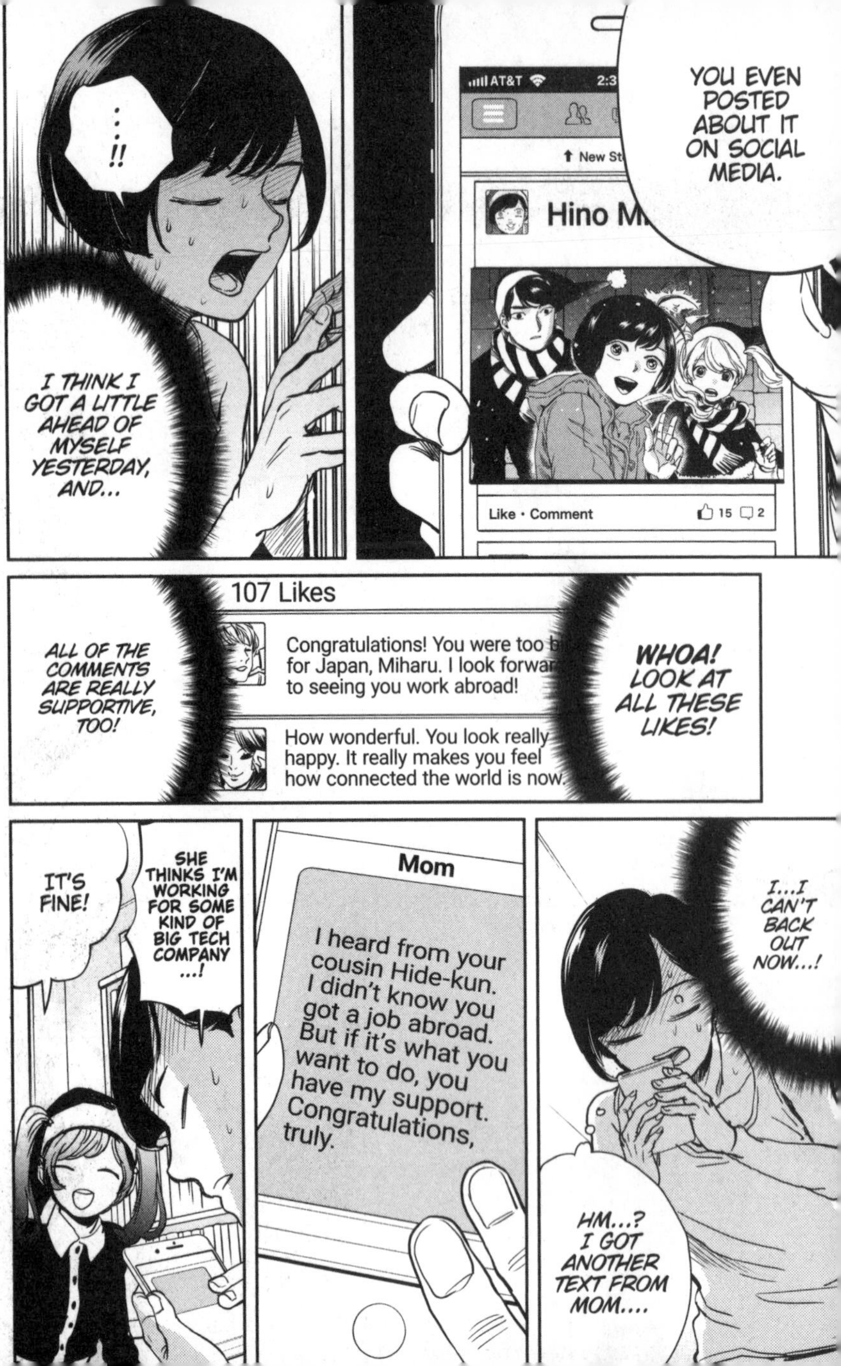
AT&T
YOU EVEN POSTED ABOUT IT ON SOCIAL MEDIA.
Like · Comment
15
2
...!!
I THINK I GOT A LITTLE AHEAD OF MYSELF YESTERDAY, AND...
WHOA! LOOK AT ALL THESE LIKES!
107 Likes
Congratulations! You were too b for Japan, Miharu. I look forwar to seeing you work abroad!
How wonderful. You look really happy. It really makes you feel how connected the world is now.
ALL OF THE COMMENTS ARE REALLY SUPPORTIVE, TOO!
I...I CAN'T BACK OUT NOW...!
HM...? I GOT ANOTHER TEXT FROM MOM....
Mom
I heard from your cousin Hide-kun. I didn't know you got a job abroad. But if it's what you want to do, you have my support. Congratulations, truly.
SHE THINKS I'M WORKING FOR SOME KIND OF BIG TECH COMPANY ...!
IT'S FINE!

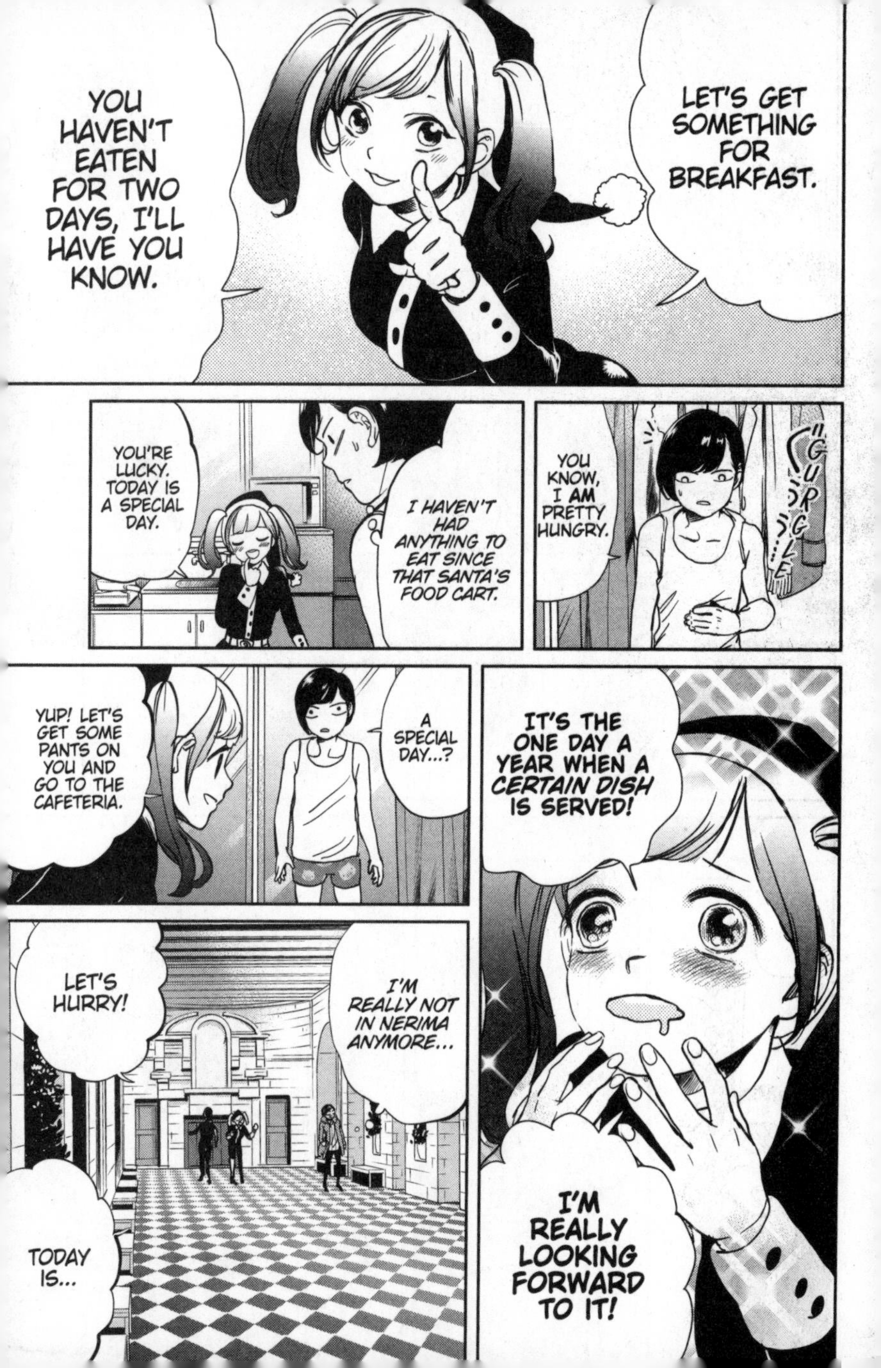
LET'S GET SOMETHING FOR BREAKFAST.
YOU HAVEN'T EATEN FOR TWO DAYS, I'LL HAVE YOU KNOW.
GURGLE...
YOU KNOW, I AM PRETTY HUNGRY.
I HAVEN'T HAD ANYTHING TO EAT SINCE THAT SANTA'S FOOD CART.
YOU'RE LUCKY. TODAY IS A SPECIAL DAY.
A SPECIAL DAY...?
YUP! LET'S GET SOME PANTS ON YOU AND GO TO THE CAFETERIA.
IT'S THE ONE DAY A YEAR WHEN A CERTAIN DISH IS SERVED!
I'M REALLY LOOKING FORWARD TO IT!
I'M REALLY NOT IN NERIMA ANYMORE...
LET'S HURRY!
TODAY IS...

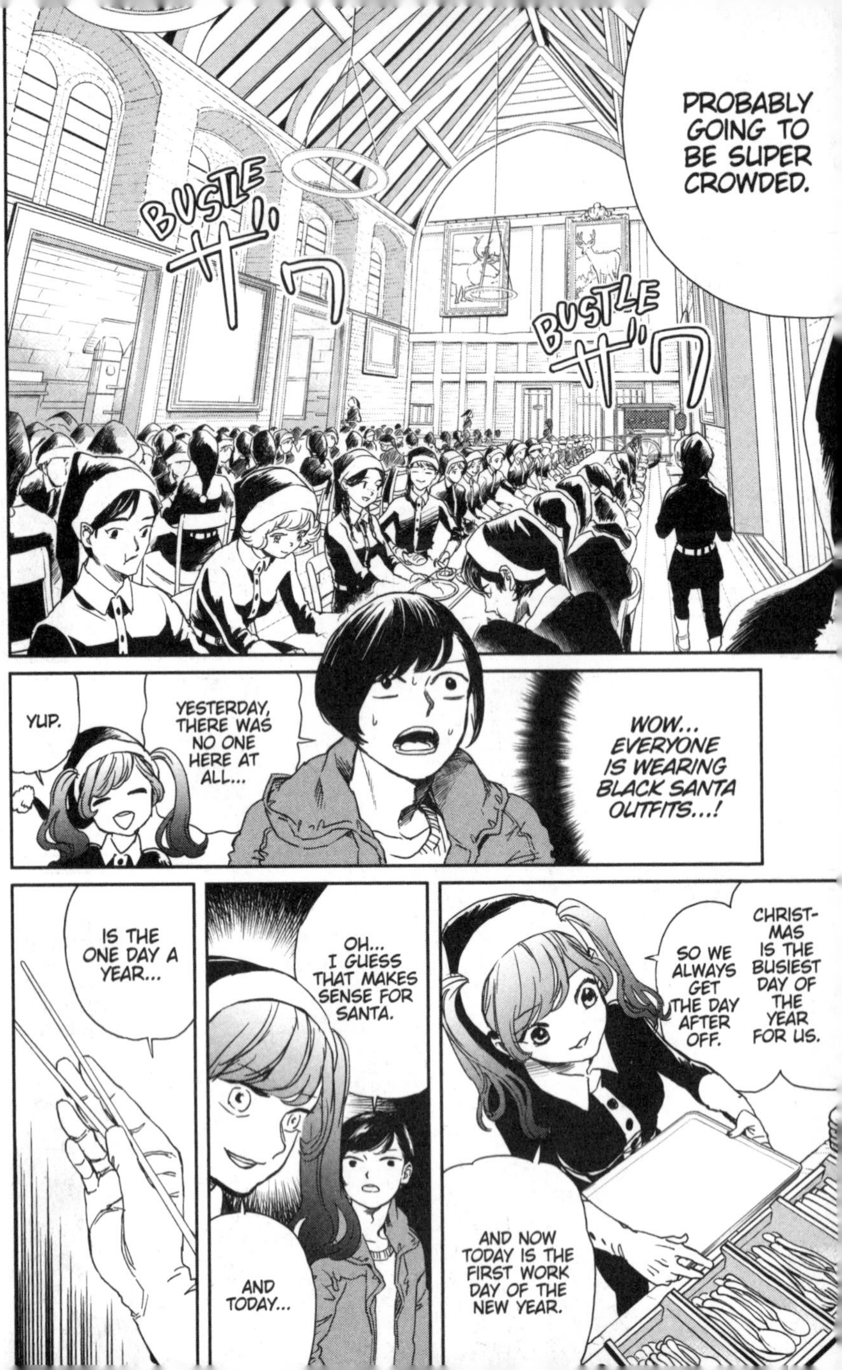
PROBABLY GOING TO BE SUPER CROWDED.
BUSTLE
BUSTLE
WOW... EVERYONE IS WEARING BLACK SANTA OUTFITS...!
YESTERDAY, THERE WAS NO ONE HERE AT ALL...
YUP.
CHRISTMAS IS THE BUSIEST DAY OF THE YEAR FOR US.
SO WE ALWAYS GET THE DAY AFTER OFF.
AND NOW TODAY IS THE FIRST WORK DAY OF THE NEW YEAR.
OH... I GUESS THAT MAKES SENSE FOR SANTA.
AND TODAY...
IS THE ONE DAY A YEAR...

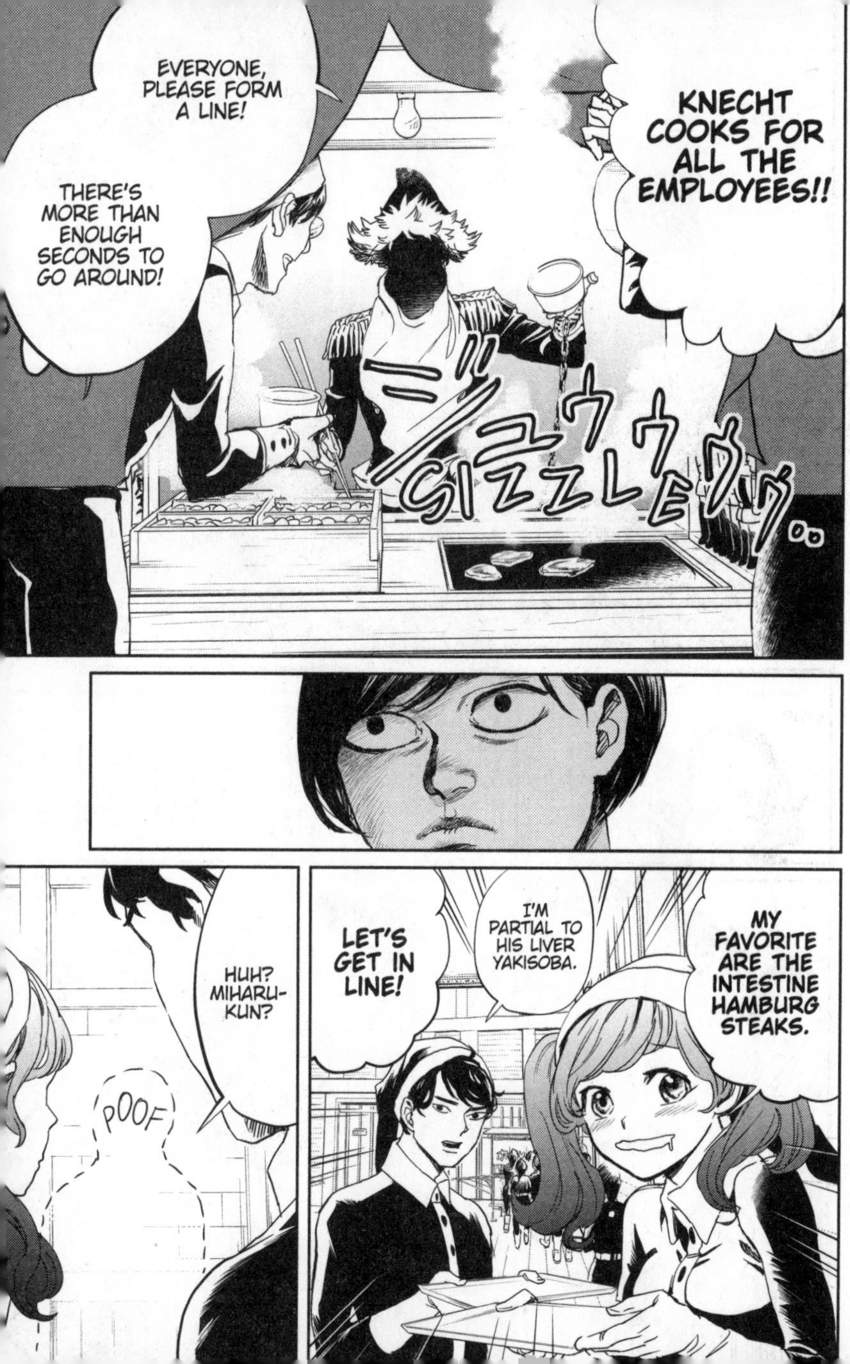
KNECHT COOKS FOR ALL THE EMPLOYEES!!
EVERYONE, PLEASE FORM A LINE!
THERE'S MORE THAN ENOUGH SECONDS TO GO AROUND!
ジュウウウウ
SIZZLE
MY FAVORITE ARE THE INTESTINE HAMBURG STEAKS.
I'M PARTIAL TO HIS LIVER YAKISOBA.
LET'S GET IN LINE!
HUH? MIHARU-KUN?
POOF

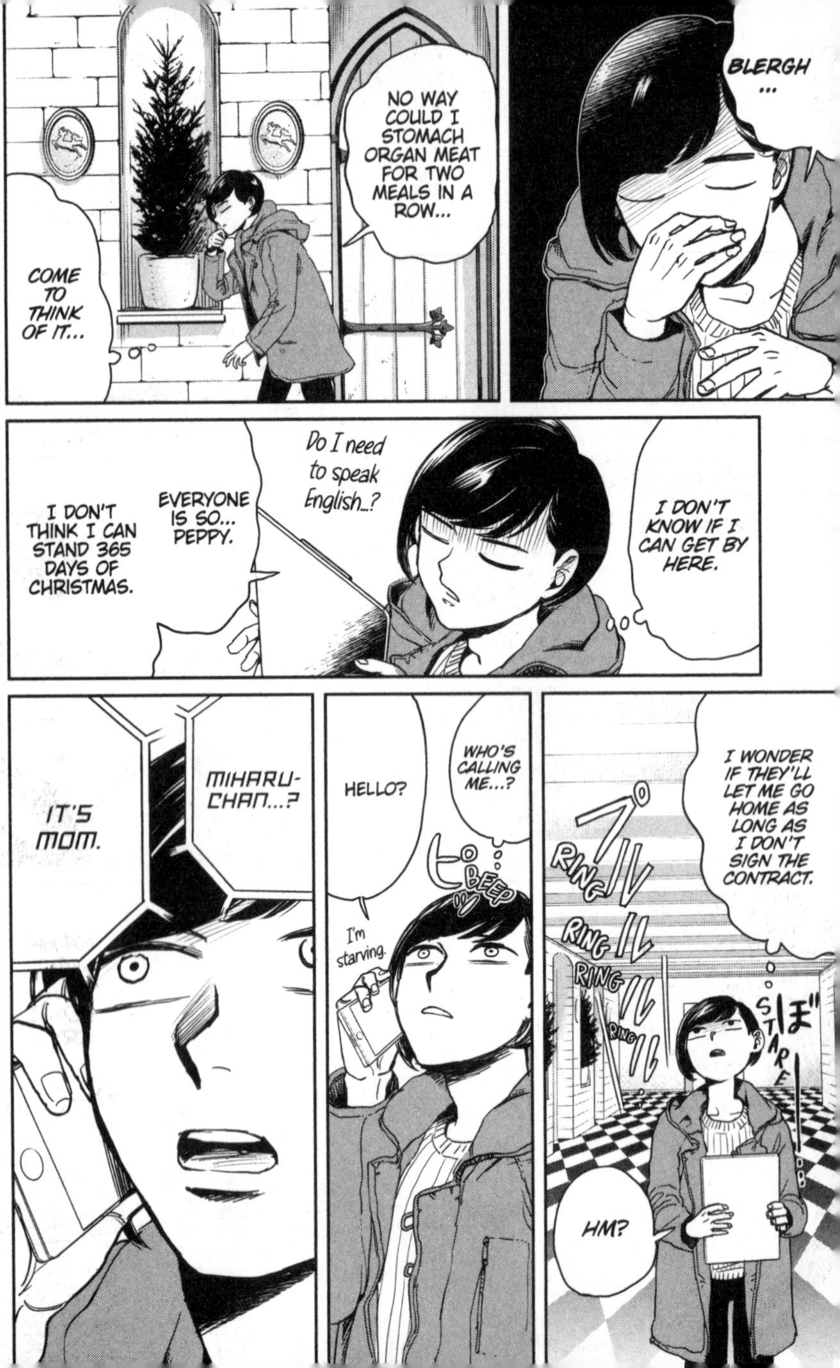
BLERGH ...
NO WAY COULD I STOMACH ORGAN MEAT FOR TWO MEALS IN A ROW...
COME TO THINK OF IT...
I DON'T KNOW IF I CAN GET BY HERE.
Do I need to speak English...?
EVERYONE IS SO... PEPPY.
I DON'T THINK I CAN STAND 365 DAYS OF CHRISTMAS.
I WONDER IF THEY'LL LET ME GO HOME AS LONG AS I DON'T SIGN THE CONTRACT.
RING
RING
RING
RING
STARE
HM?
WHO'S CALLING ME...?
BEEP
HELLO?
I'm starving.
MIHARU-CHAN...?
IT'S MOM.

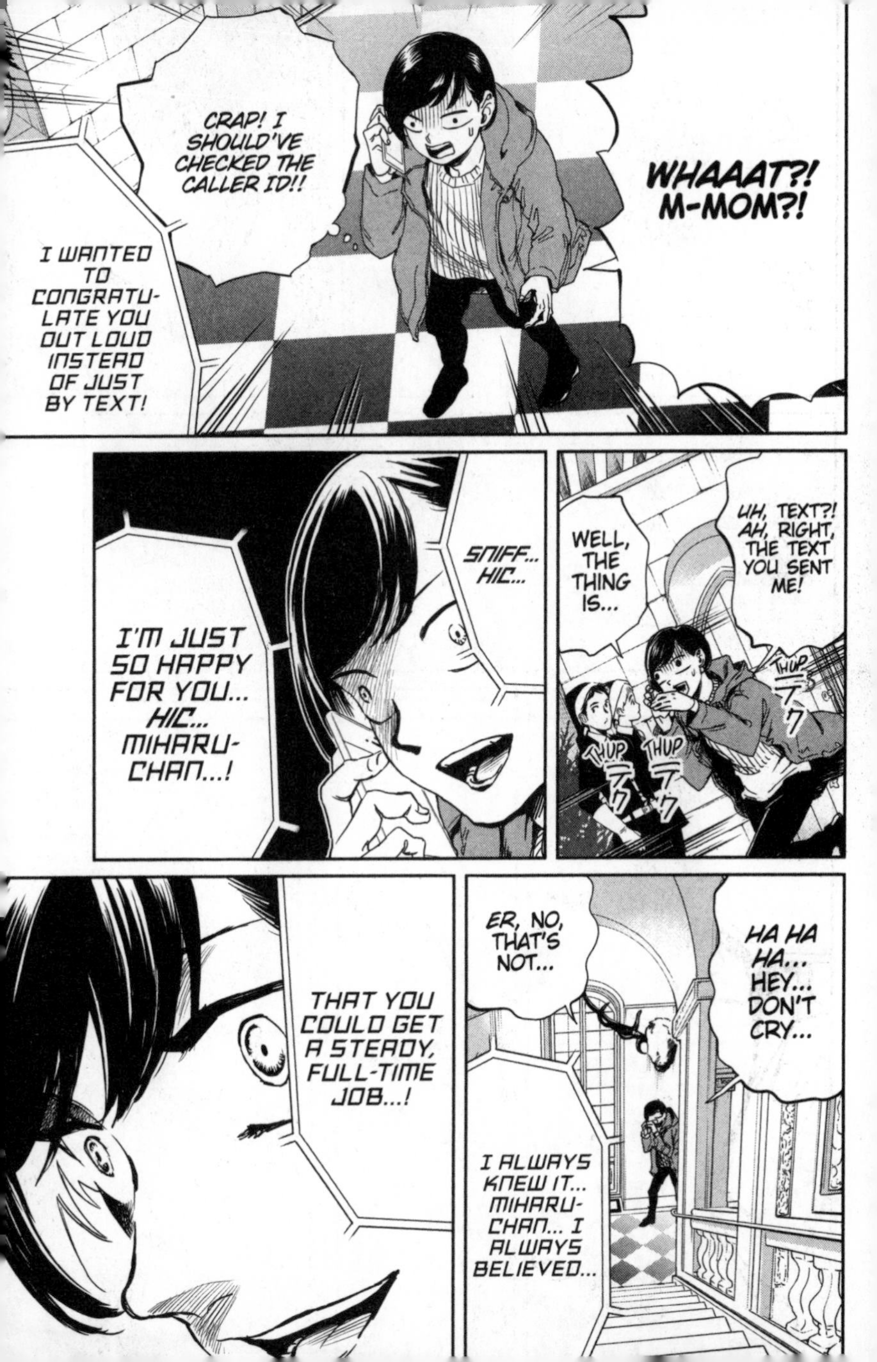
WHAAAT?! M-MOM?!
CRAP! I SHOULD'VE CHECKED THE CALLER ID!!
I WANTED TO CONGRATULATE YOU OUT LOUD INSTEAD OF JUST BY TEXT!
UH, TEXT?! AH, RIGHT, THE TEXT YOU SENT ME!
THUP
WELL, THE THING IS...
THUP
THUP
SNIFF... HIC...
I'M JUST SO HAPPY FOR YOU... HIC... MIHARU-CHAN...!
HA HA HA... HEY... DON'T CRY...
ER, NO, THAT'S NOT...
I ALWAYS KNEW IT... MIHARU-CHAN... I ALWAYS BELIEVED...
THAT YOU COULD GET A STEADY, FULL-TIME JOB...!

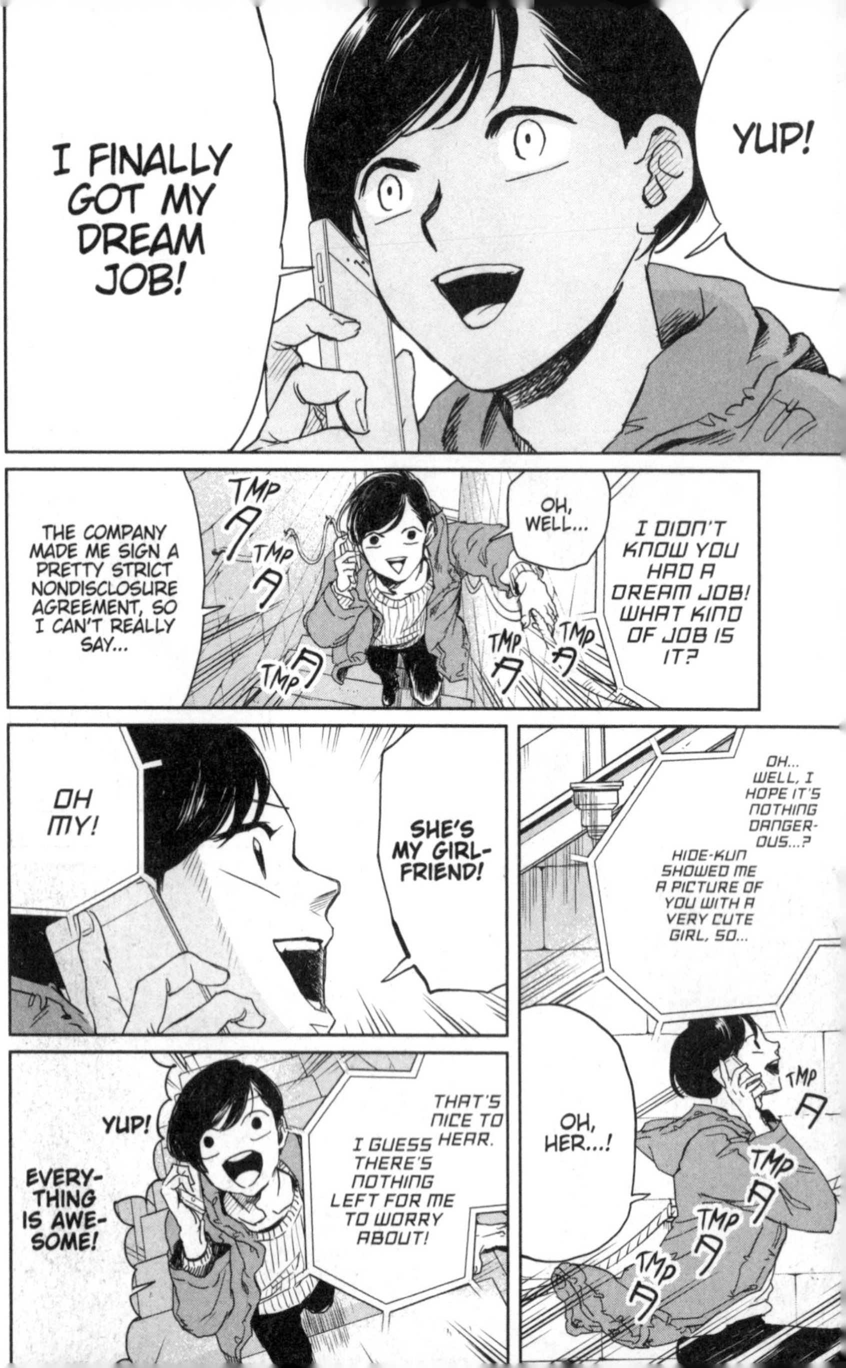
YUP!
I FINALLY GOT MY DREAM JOB!
I DIDN'T KNOW YOU HAD A DREAM JOB! WHAT KIND OF JOB IS IT?
TMP
TMP
OH, WELL...
TMP
TMP
TMP
THE COMPANY MADE ME SIGN A PRETTY STRICT NONDISCLOSURE AGREEMENT, SO I CAN'T REALLY SAY...
OH... WELL, I HOPE IT'S NOTHING DANGEROUS...?
HIDE-KUN SHOWED ME A PICTURE OF YOU WITH A VERY CUTE GIRL, SO...
TMP
OH, HER...!
TMP
TMP
TMP
SHE'S MY GIRLFRIEND!
OH MY!
THAT'S NICE TO HEAR.
I GUESS THERE'S NOTHING LEFT FOR ME TO WORRY ABOUT!
YUP!
EVERYTHING IS AWESOME!

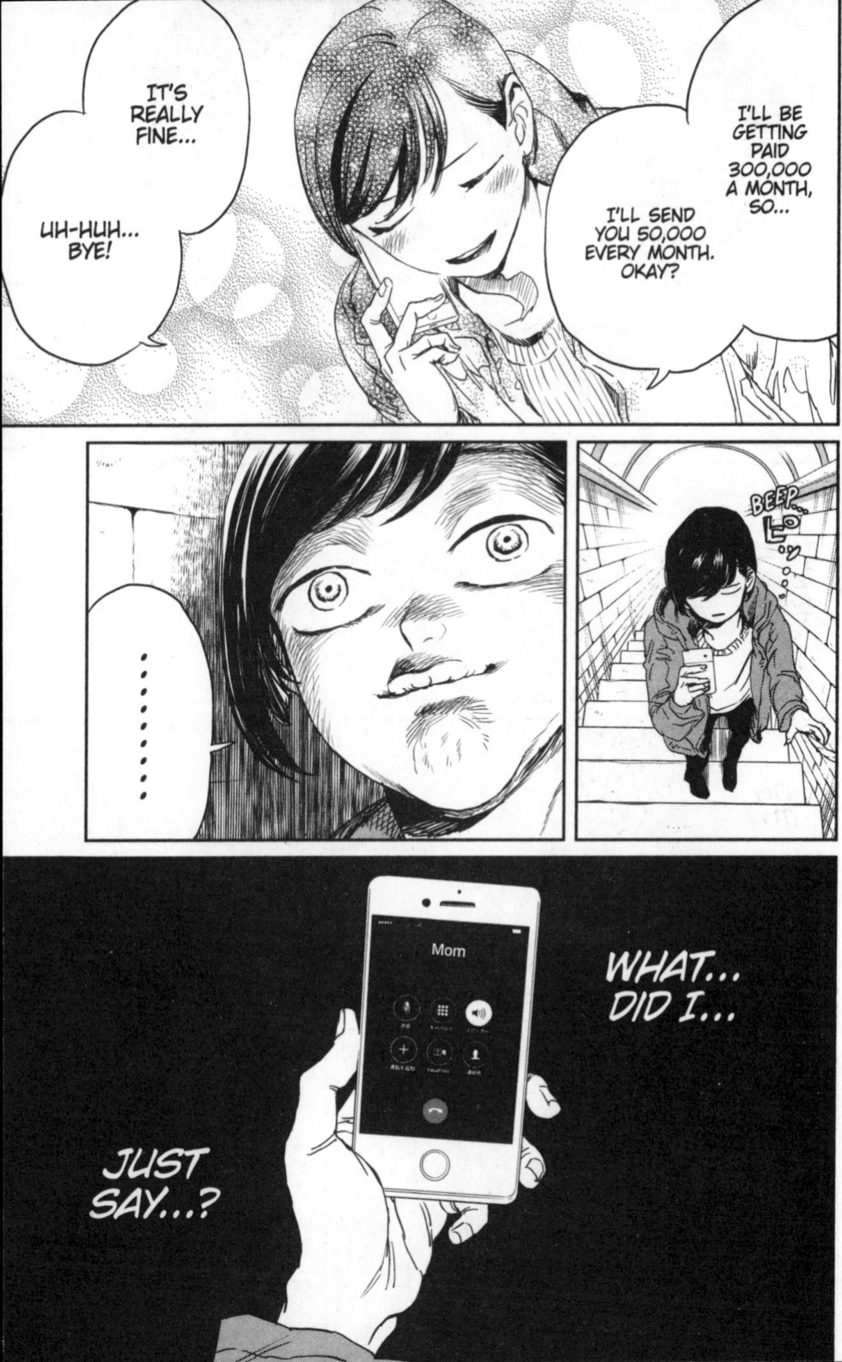
I'LL BE GETTING PAID 300,000 A MONTH, SO...
I'LL SEND YOU 50,000 EVERY MONTH. OKAY?
IT'S REALLY FINE...
UH-HUH... BYE!
BEEP...
....
Mom
WHAT... DID I...
JUST SAY...?

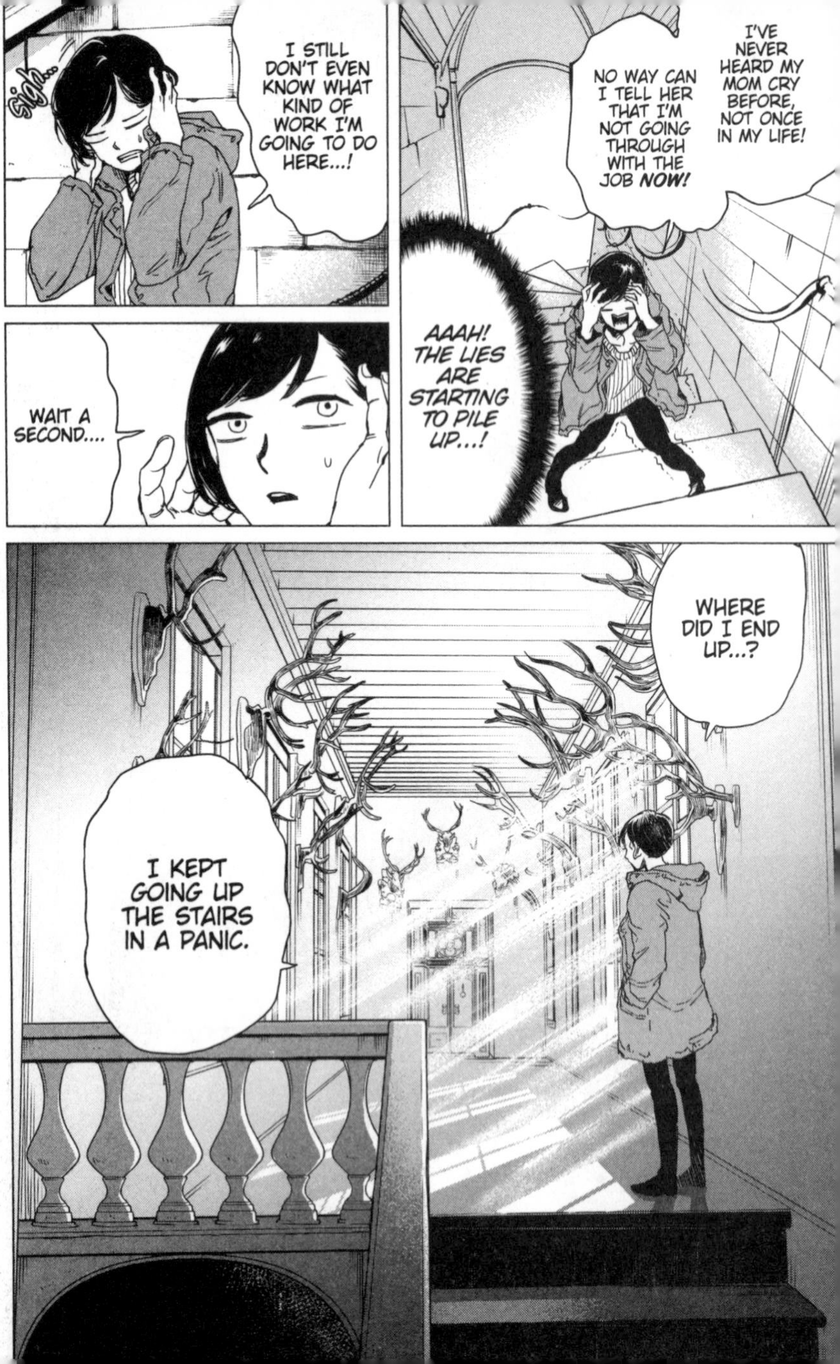
I'VE NEVER HEARD MY MOM CRY BEFORE, NOT ONCE IN MY LIFE!
NO WAY CAN I TELL HER THAT I'M NOT GOING THROUGH WITH THE JOB ***NOW!***
AAAH! THE LIES ARE STARTING TO PILE UP...!
sigh...
I STILL DON'T EVEN KNOW WHAT KIND OF WORK I'M GOING TO DO HERE...!
WAIT A SECOND....
WHERE DID I END UP...?
I KEPT GOING UP THE STAIRS IN A PANIC.

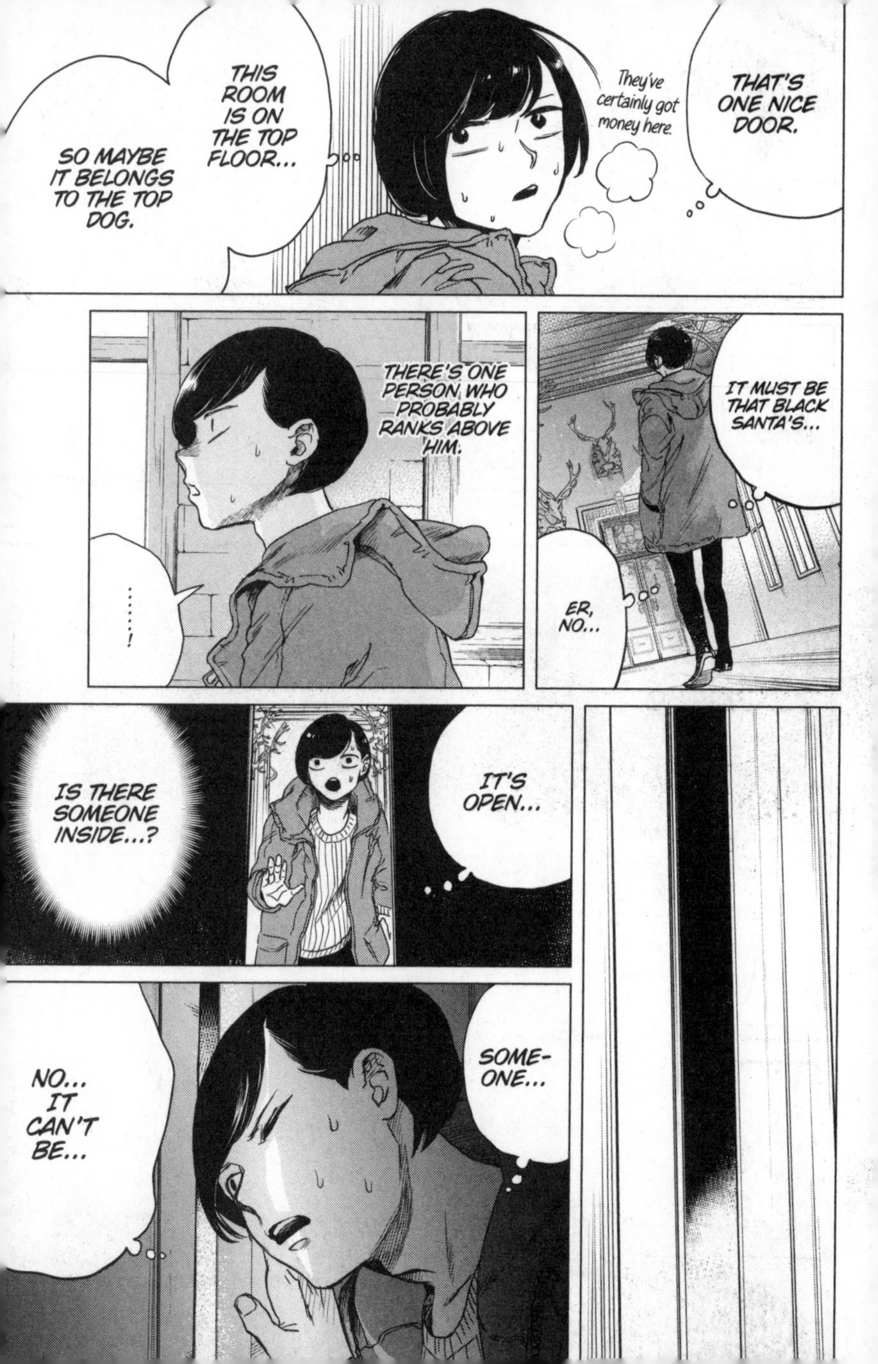
THAT'S ONE NICE DOOR.
They've certainly got money here.
THIS ROOM IS ON THE TOP FLOOR...
SO MAYBE IT BELONGS TO THE TOP DOG.
IT MUST BE THAT BLACK SANTA'S...
ER, NO...
THERE'S ONE PERSON WHO PROBABLY RANKS ABOVE HIM.
......!
IT'S OPEN...
IS THERE SOMEONE INSIDE...?
SOME-ONE...
NO... IT CAN'T BE...

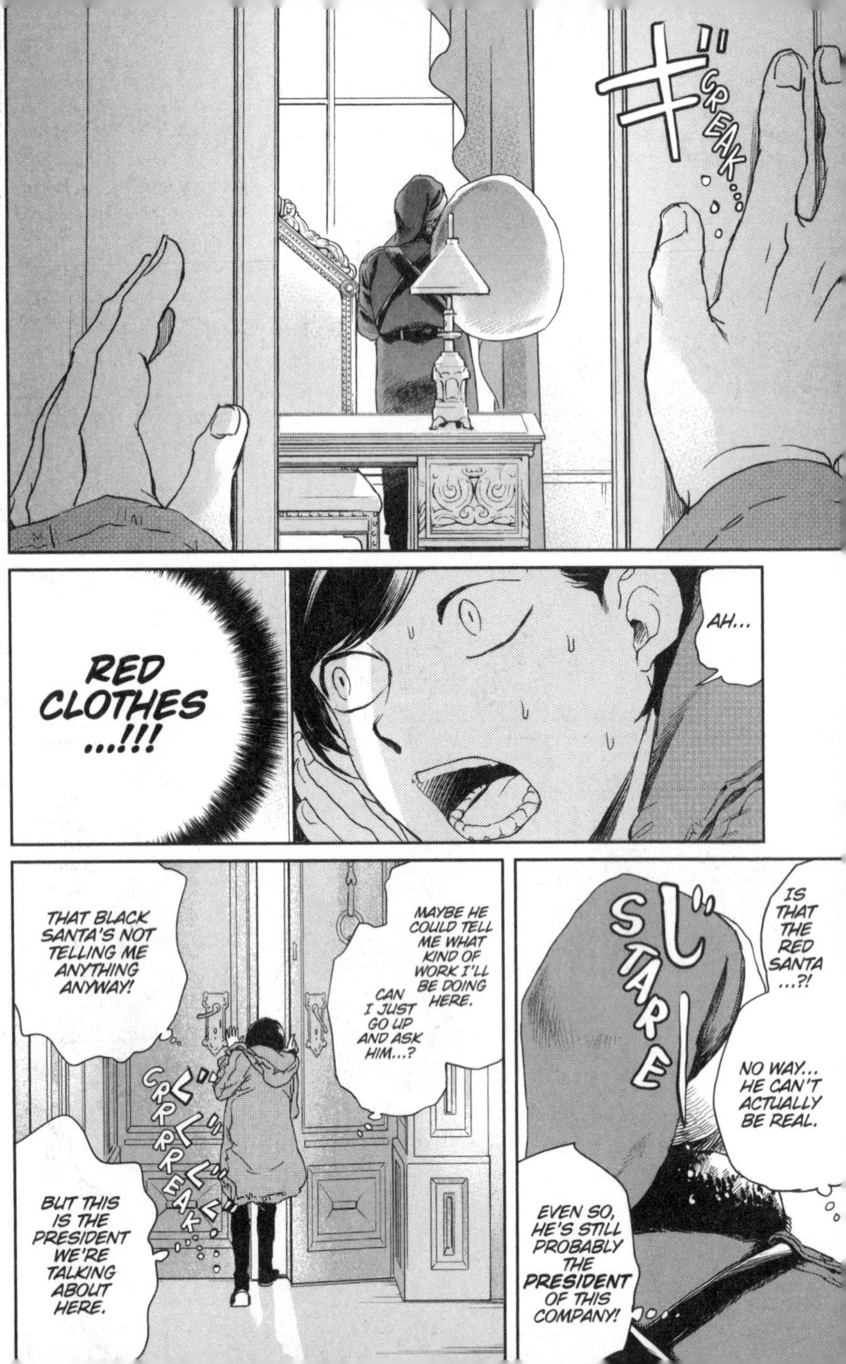
CREAK...
AH...
RED CLOTHES ...!!!
IS THAT THE RED SANTA ...?!
STARE
NO WAY... HE CAN'T ACTUALLY BE REAL.
EVEN SO, HE'S STILL PROBABLY THE PRESIDENT OF THIS COMPANY!
MAYBE HE COULD TELL ME WHAT KIND OF WORK I'LL BE DOING HERE.
CAN I JUST GO UP AND ASK HIM...?
THAT BLACK SANTA'S NOT TELLING ME ANYTHING ANYWAY!
CRRREAK...
BUT THIS IS THE PRESIDENT WE'RE TALKING ABOUT HERE.

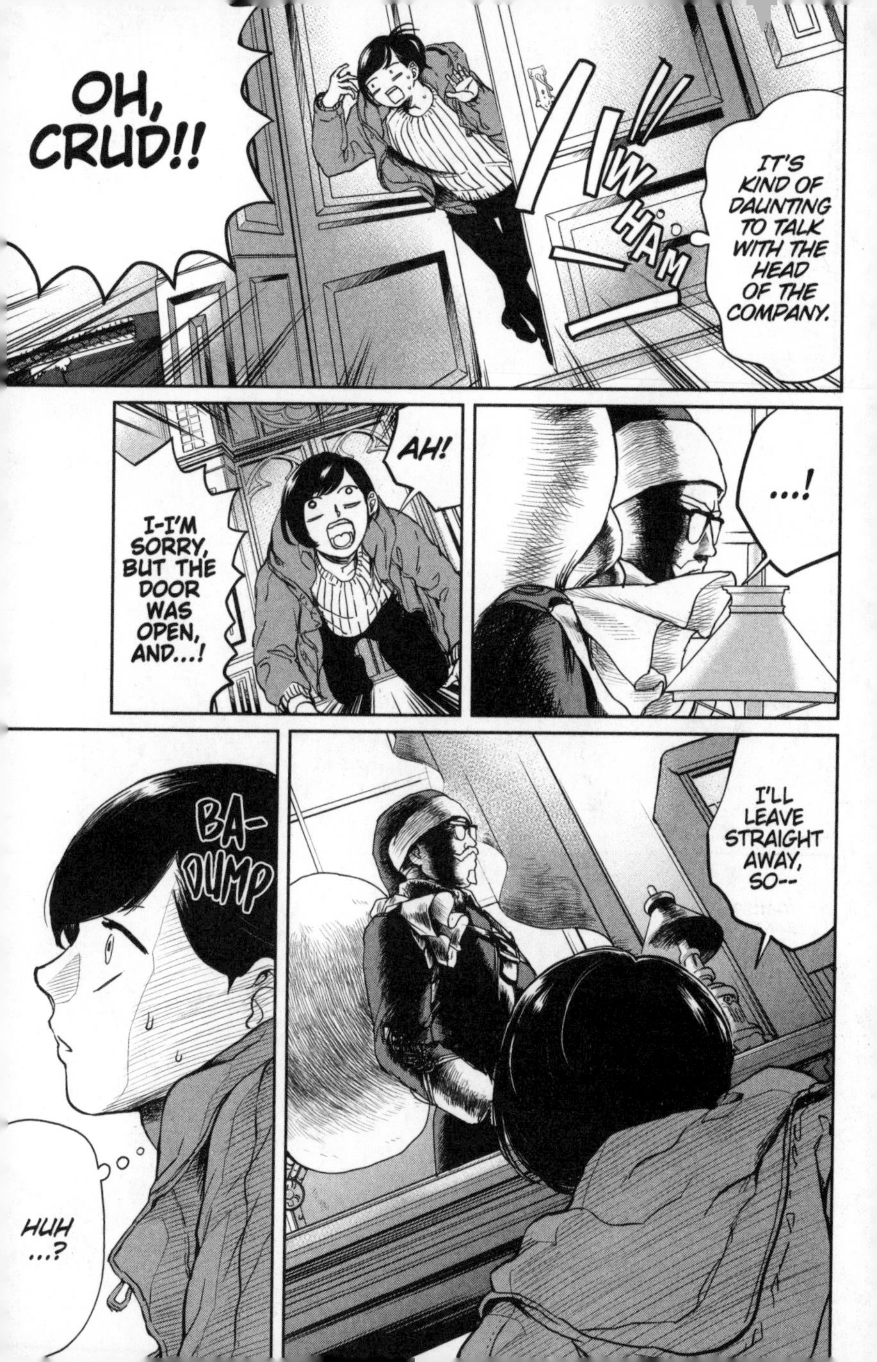
IT'S KIND OF DAUNTING TO TALK WITH THE HEAD OF THE COMPANY.
WHAM
OH, CRUD!!
...!
AH!
I-I'M SORRY, BUT THE DOOR WAS OPEN, AND...!
I'LL LEAVE STRAIGHT AWAY, SO--
BA-DUMP
HUH ...?

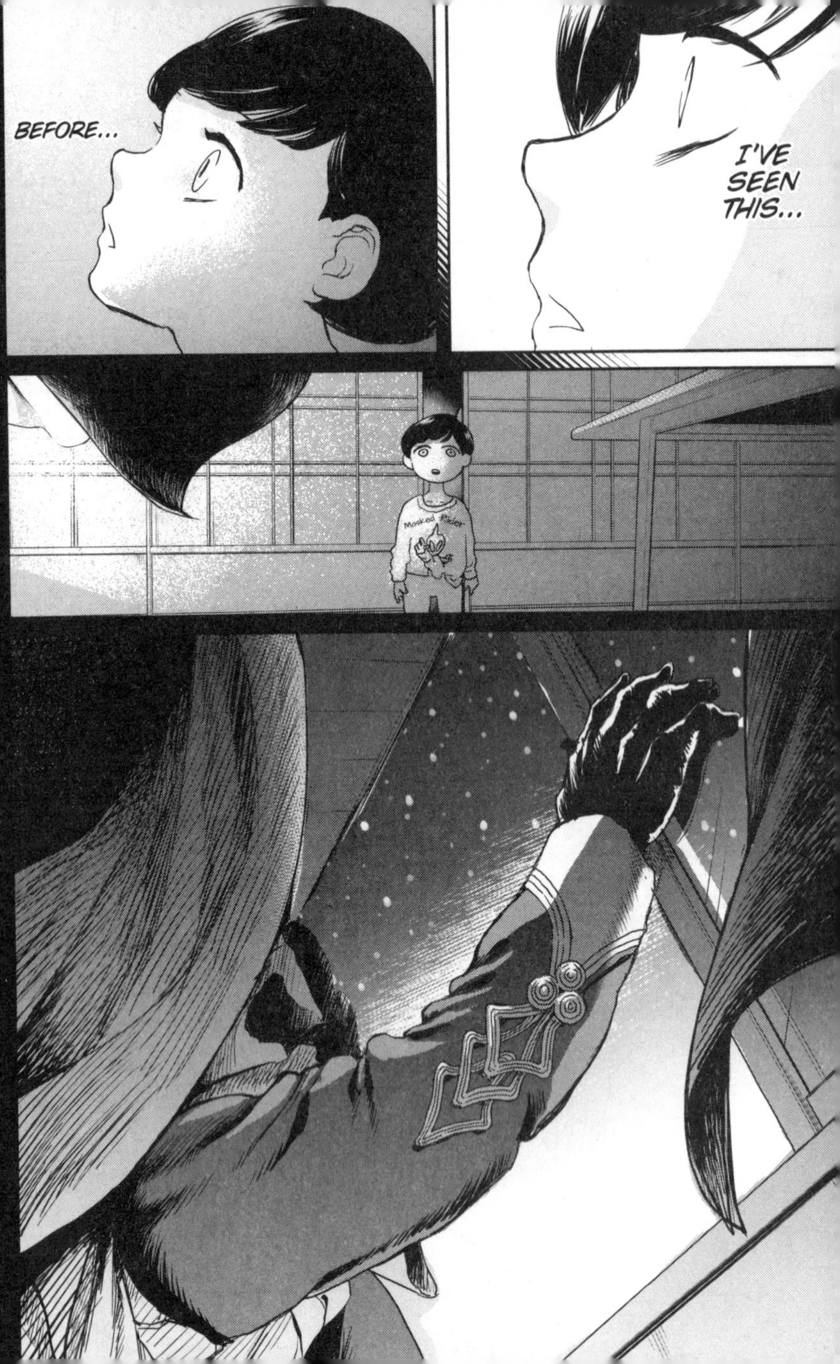
I'VE SEEN THIS...
BEFORE...
Masked Rider

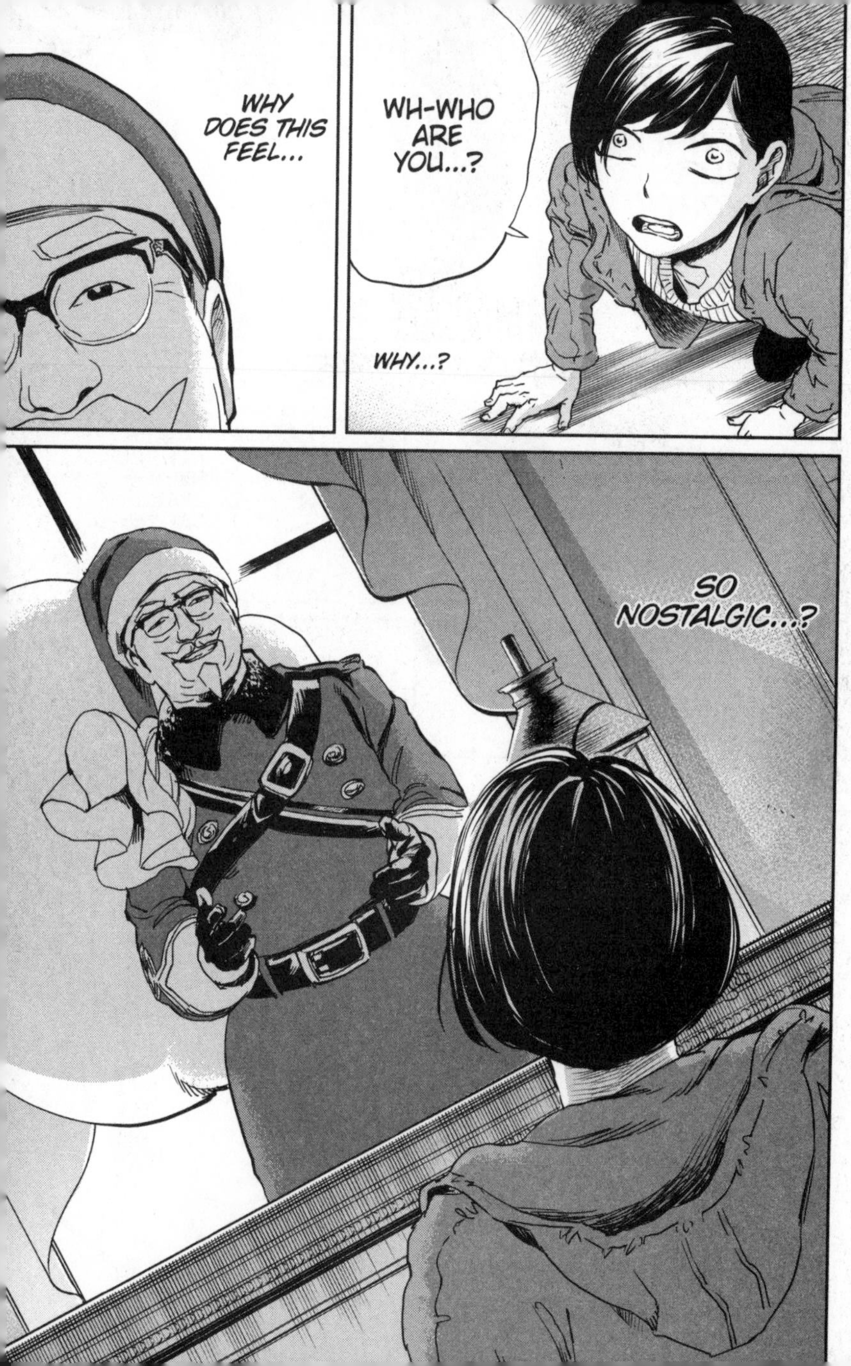
WH-WHO ARE YOU...?
WHY...?
WHY DOES THIS FEEL...
SO NOSTALGIC...?

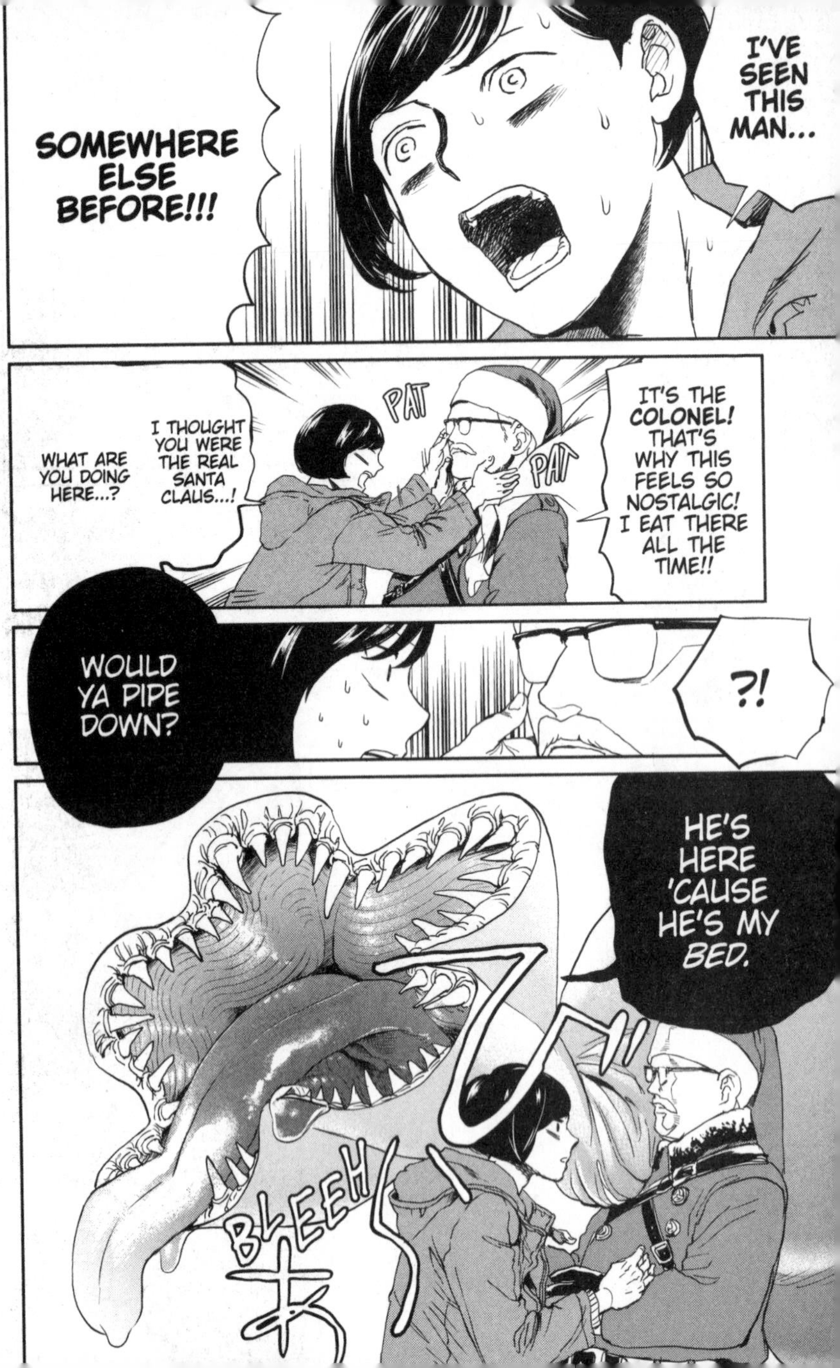
I'VE SEEN THIS MAN...
SOMEWHERE ELSE BEFORE!!!
IT'S THE COLONEL! THAT'S WHY THIS FEELS SO NOSTALGIC! I EAT THERE ALL THE TIME!!
PAT
PAT
I THOUGHT YOU WERE THE REAL SANTA CLAUS...!
WHAT ARE YOU DOING HERE...?
?!
WOULD YA PIPE DOWN?
HE'S HERE 'CAUSE HE'S MY BED.
BLEEH

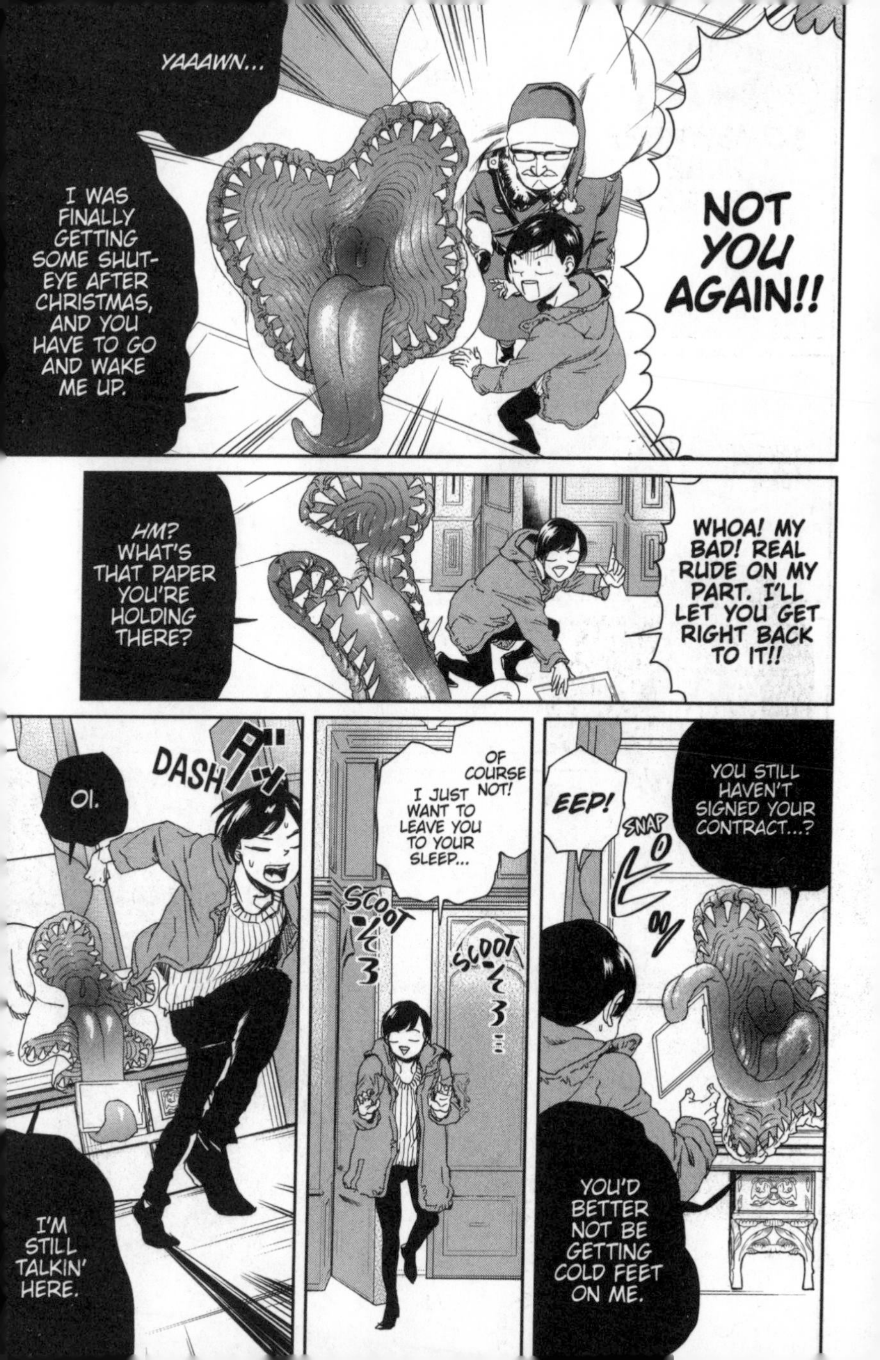
NOT YOU AGAIN!!
YAAAWN...
I WAS FINALLY GETTING SOME SHUT-EYE AFTER CHRISTMAS, AND YOU HAVE TO GO AND WAKE ME UP.
WHOA! MY BAD! REAL RUDE ON MY PART. I'LL LET YOU GET RIGHT BACK TO IT!!
HM? WHAT'S THAT PAPER YOU'RE HOLDING THERE?
YOU STILL HAVEN'T SIGNED YOUR CONTRACT...?
SNAP
EEP!
YOU'D BETTER NOT BE GETTING COLD FEET ON ME.
OF COURSE NOT!
I JUST WANT TO LEAVE YOU TO YOUR SLEEP...
SCOOT
SCOOT
DASH
OI.
I'M STILL TALKIN' HERE.

TCH.

IS THIS REALLY THE GUY?

KNECHT.

CHIK

I'MMA GIVE 'IM A LITTLE TEST...

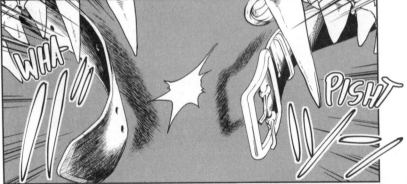

WHA—

PISHT

OKAY, I'M ALMOST OUT...

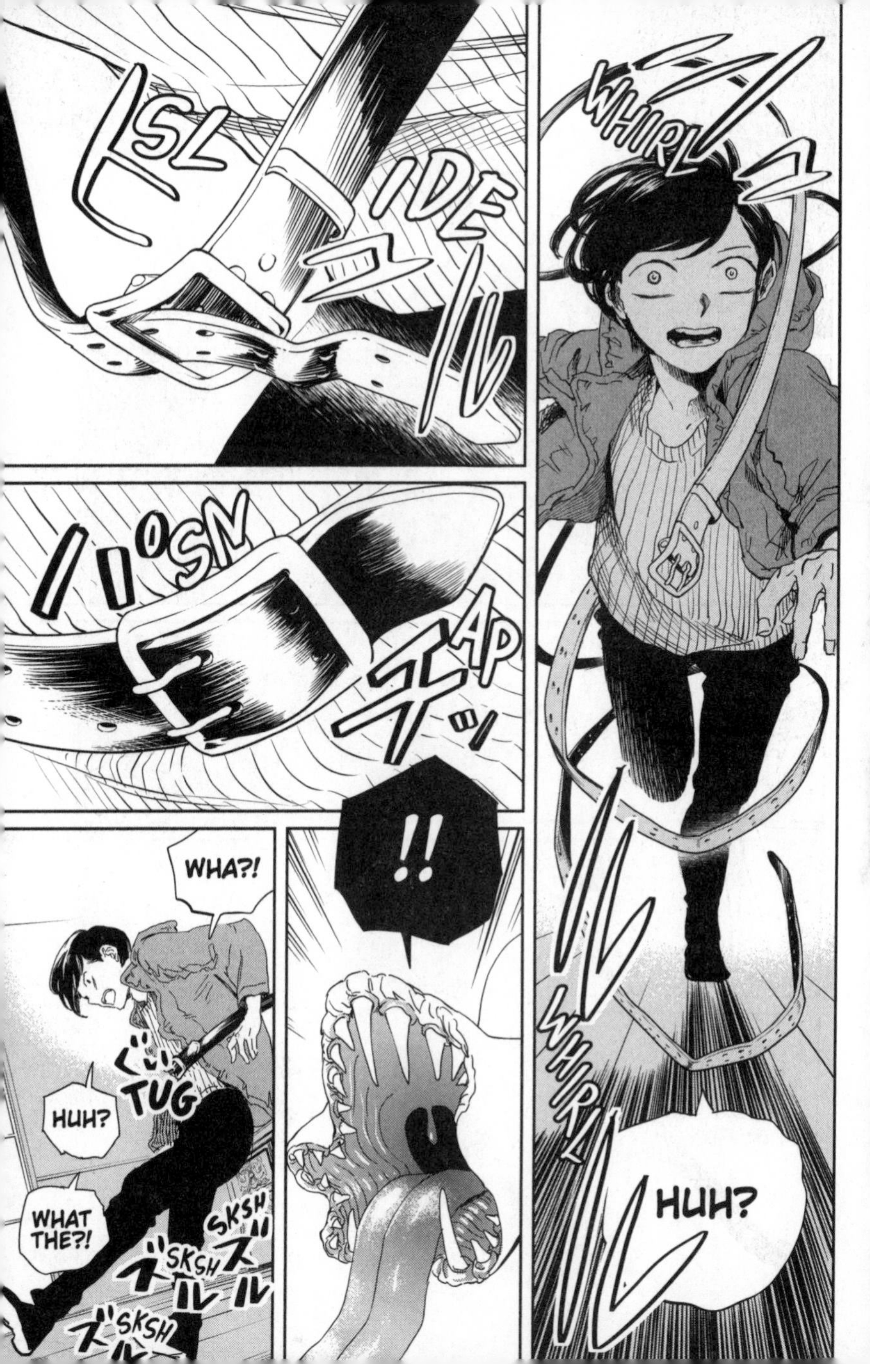
WHIRL
WHIRL
HUH?
SL
IDE
!!
WHA?!
TUG
HUH?
WHAT THE?!
SKSH
SKSH
SKSH

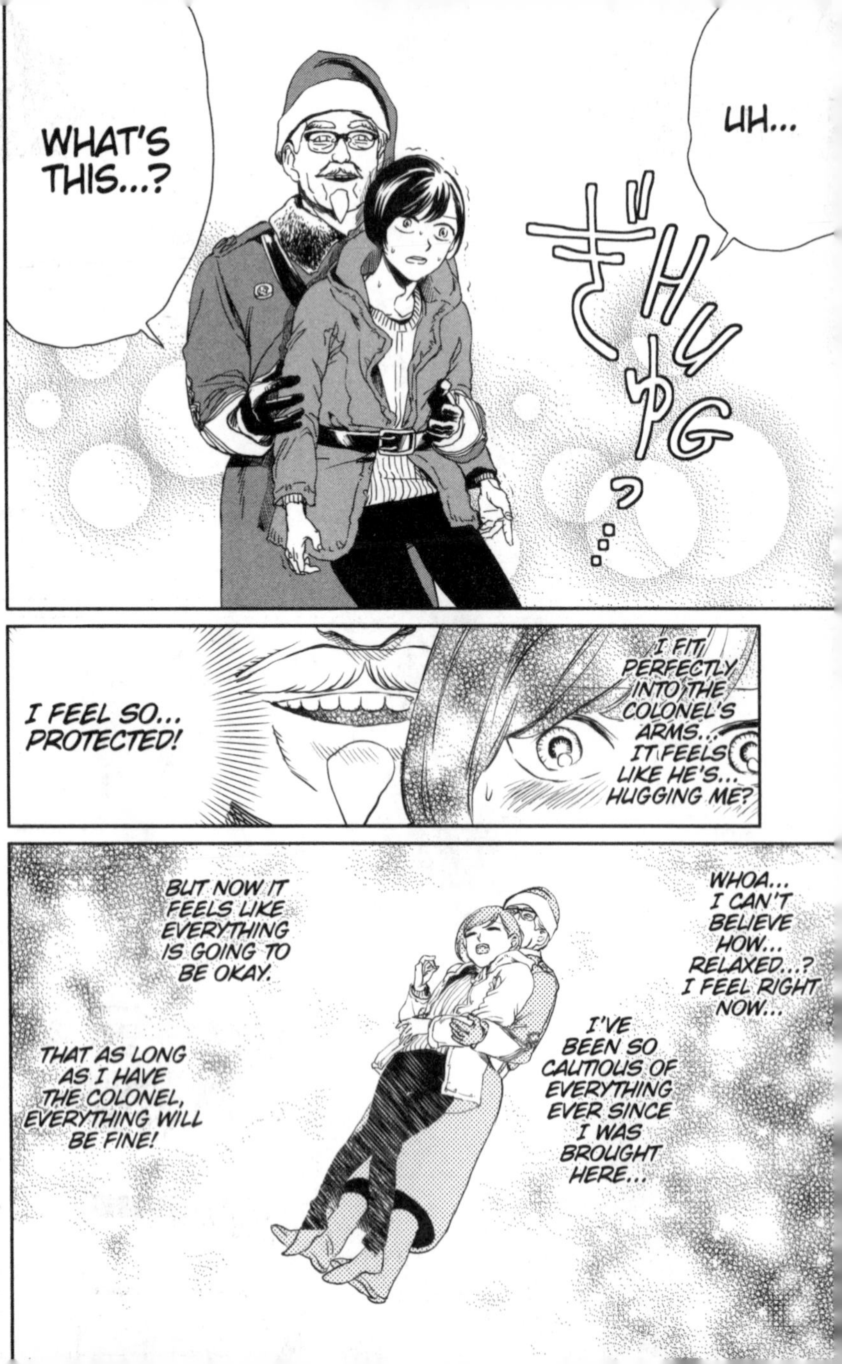
UH...
ぎゅっ
HUG
WHAT'S THIS...?
I FIT PERFECTLY INTO THE COLONEL'S ARMS... IT FEELS LIKE HE'S... HUGGING ME?
I FEEL SO... PROTECTED!
WHOA... I CAN'T BELIEVE HOW... RELAXED...? I FEEL RIGHT NOW...
I'VE BEEN SO CAUTIOUS OF EVERYTHING EVER SINCE I WAS BROUGHT HERE...
BUT NOW IT FEELS LIKE EVERYTHING IS GOING TO BE OKAY.
THAT AS LONG AS I HAVE THE COLONEL, EVERYTHING WILL BE FINE!

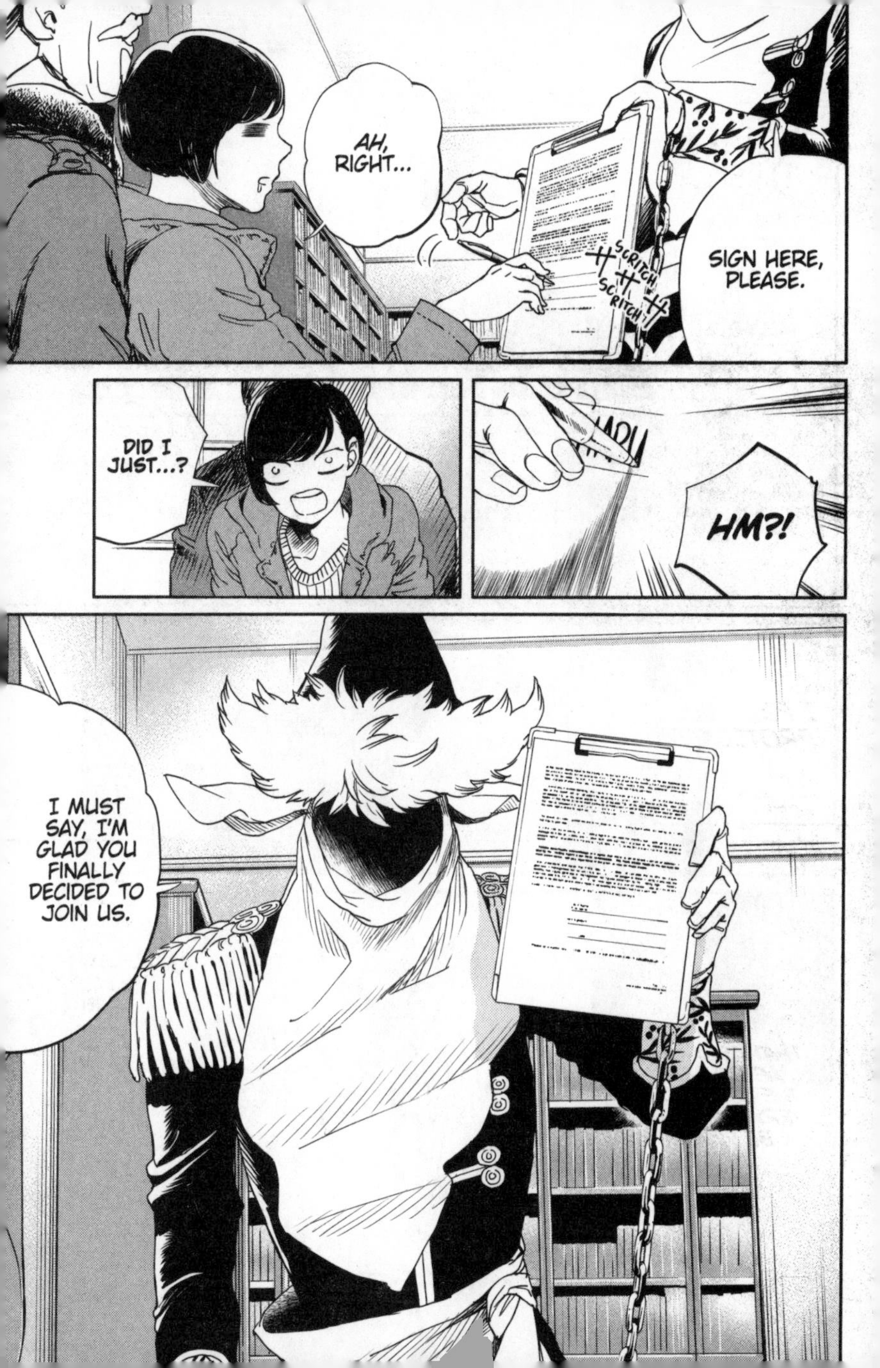
SIGN HERE, PLEASE.
SCRITCH SCRITCH
AH, RIGHT...
HM?!
DID I JUST...?
I MUST SAY, I'M GLAD YOU FINALLY DECIDED TO JOIN US.

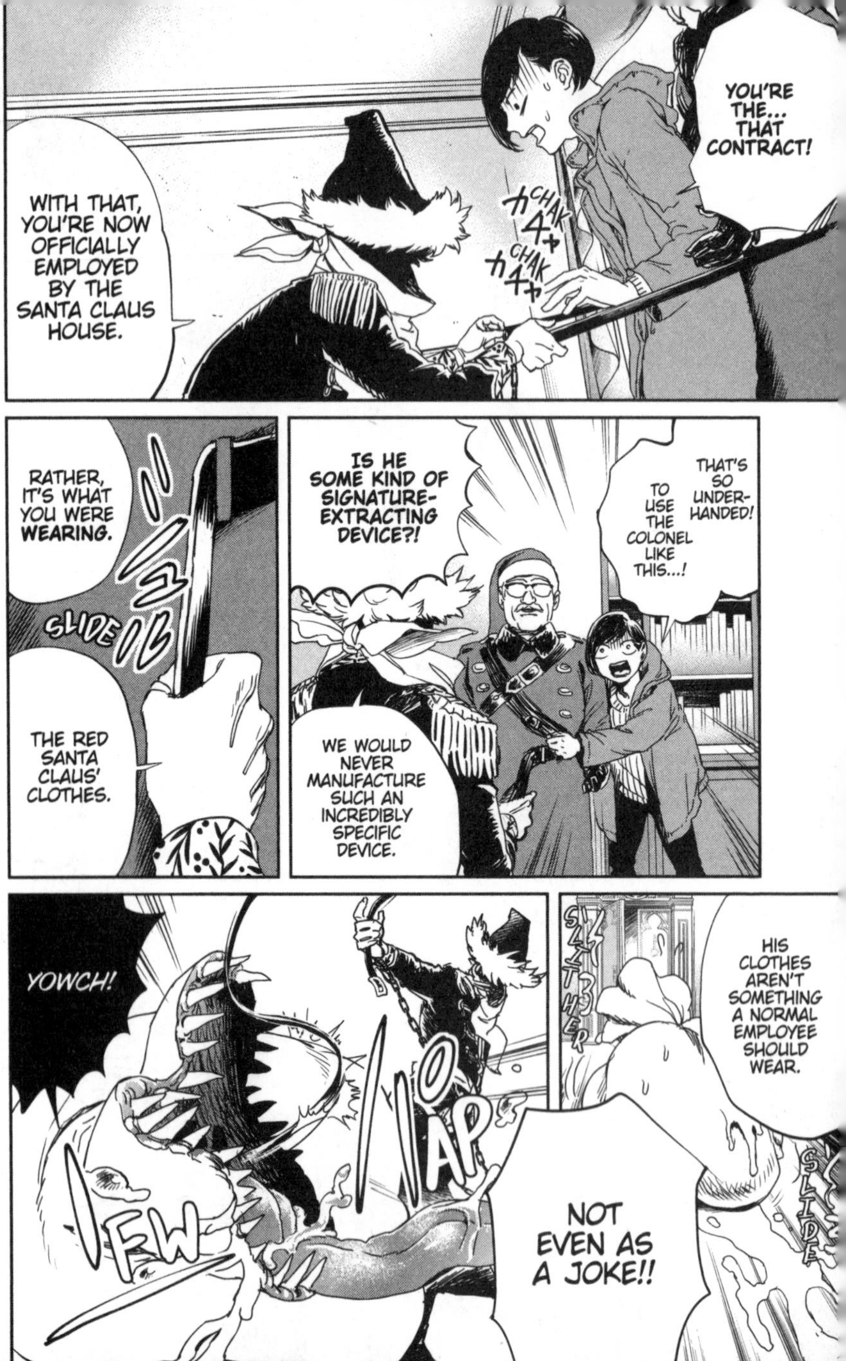
YOU'RE THE... THAT CONTRACT!
CHAK CHAK
WITH THAT, YOU'RE NOW OFFICIALLY EMPLOYED BY THE SANTA CLAUS HOUSE.
THAT'S SO UNDER-HANDED!
TO USE THE COLONEL LIKE THIS...!
IS HE SOME KIND OF SIGNATURE-EXTRACTING DEVICE?!
WE WOULD NEVER MANUFACTURE SUCH AN INCREDIBLY SPECIFIC DEVICE.
RATHER, IT'S WHAT YOU WERE WEARING.
SLIDE
THE RED SANTA CLAUS' CLOTHES.
HIS CLOTHES AREN'T SOMETHING A NORMAL EMPLOYEE SHOULD WEAR.
SLITHER
SLIDE
NOT EVEN AS A JOKE!!
YOWCH!
FWAP

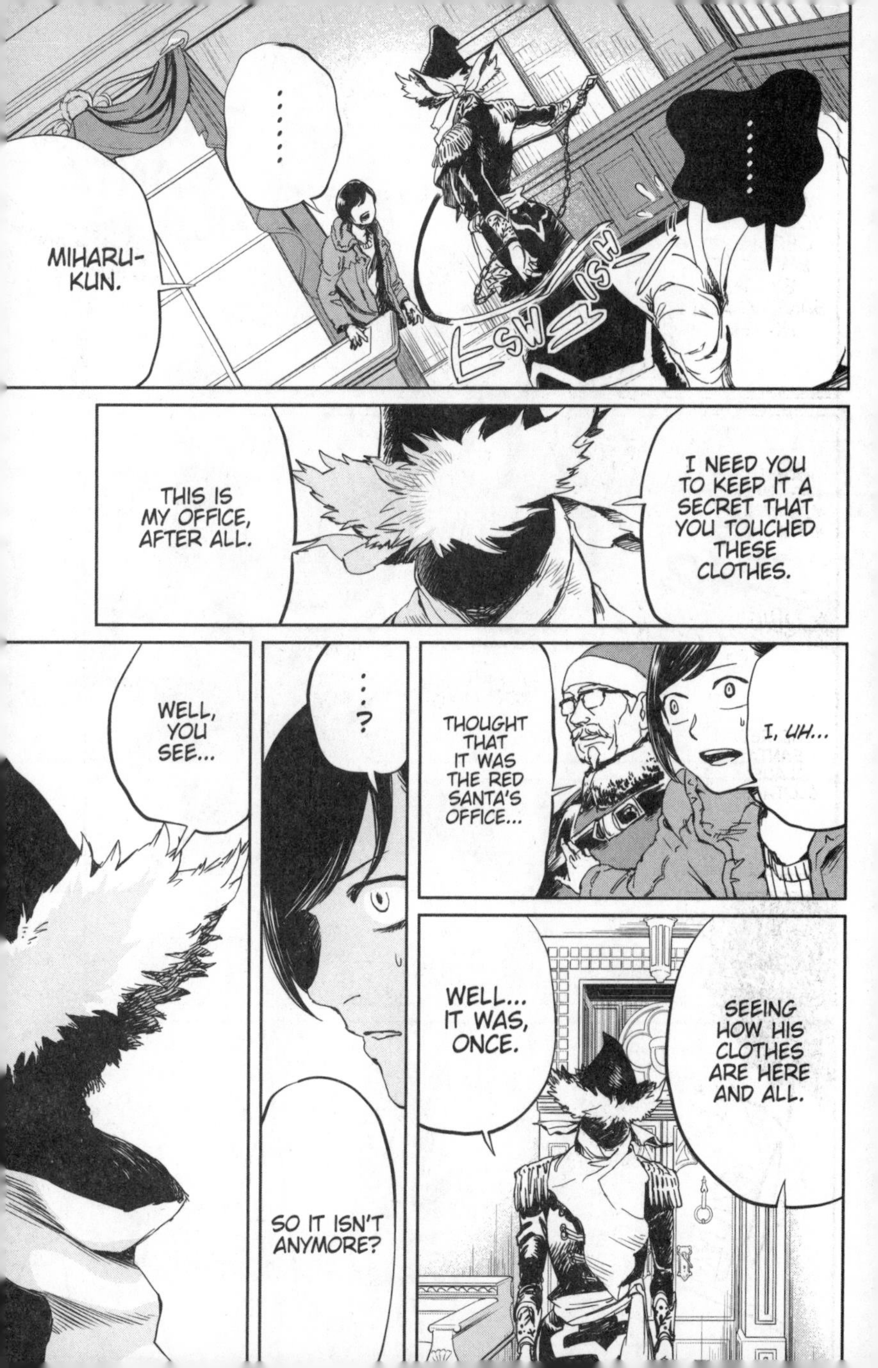
......
SWISH—
......
MIHARU-KUN.
I NEED YOU TO KEEP IT A SECRET THAT YOU TOUCHED THESE CLOTHES.
THIS IS MY OFFICE, AFTER ALL.
I, UH...
THOUGHT THAT IT WAS THE RED SANTA'S OFFICE...
SEEING HOW HIS CLOTHES ARE HERE AND ALL.
WELL... IT WAS, ONCE.
...?
SO IT ISN'T ANYMORE?
WELL, YOU SEE...

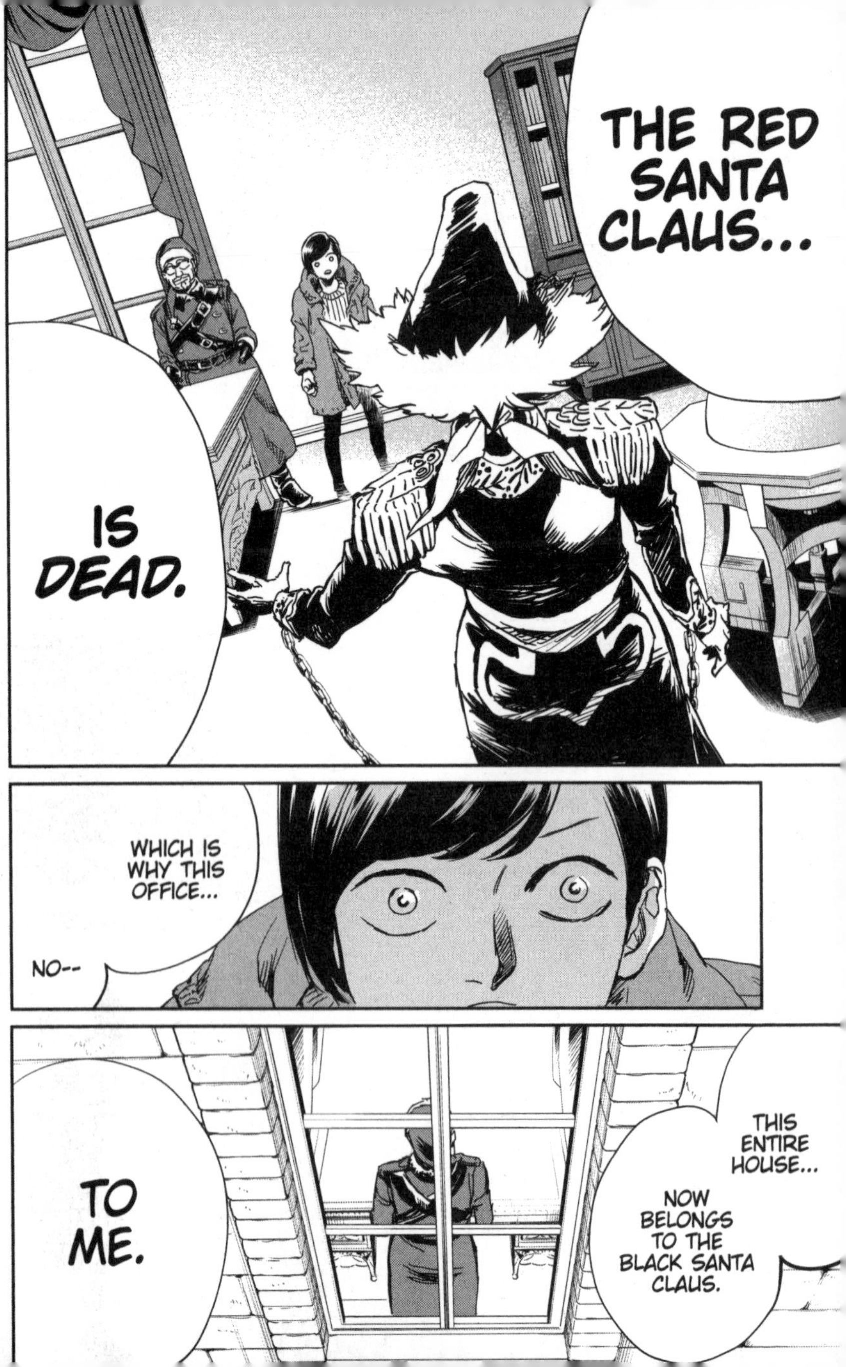
THE RED SANTA CLAUS...
IS DEAD.
WHICH IS WHY THIS OFFICE...
NO--
THIS ENTIRE HOUSE...
NOW BELONGS TO THE BLACK SANTA CLAUS.
TO ME.

Chapter 4: The Shady Magic that Makes Christmas Happen

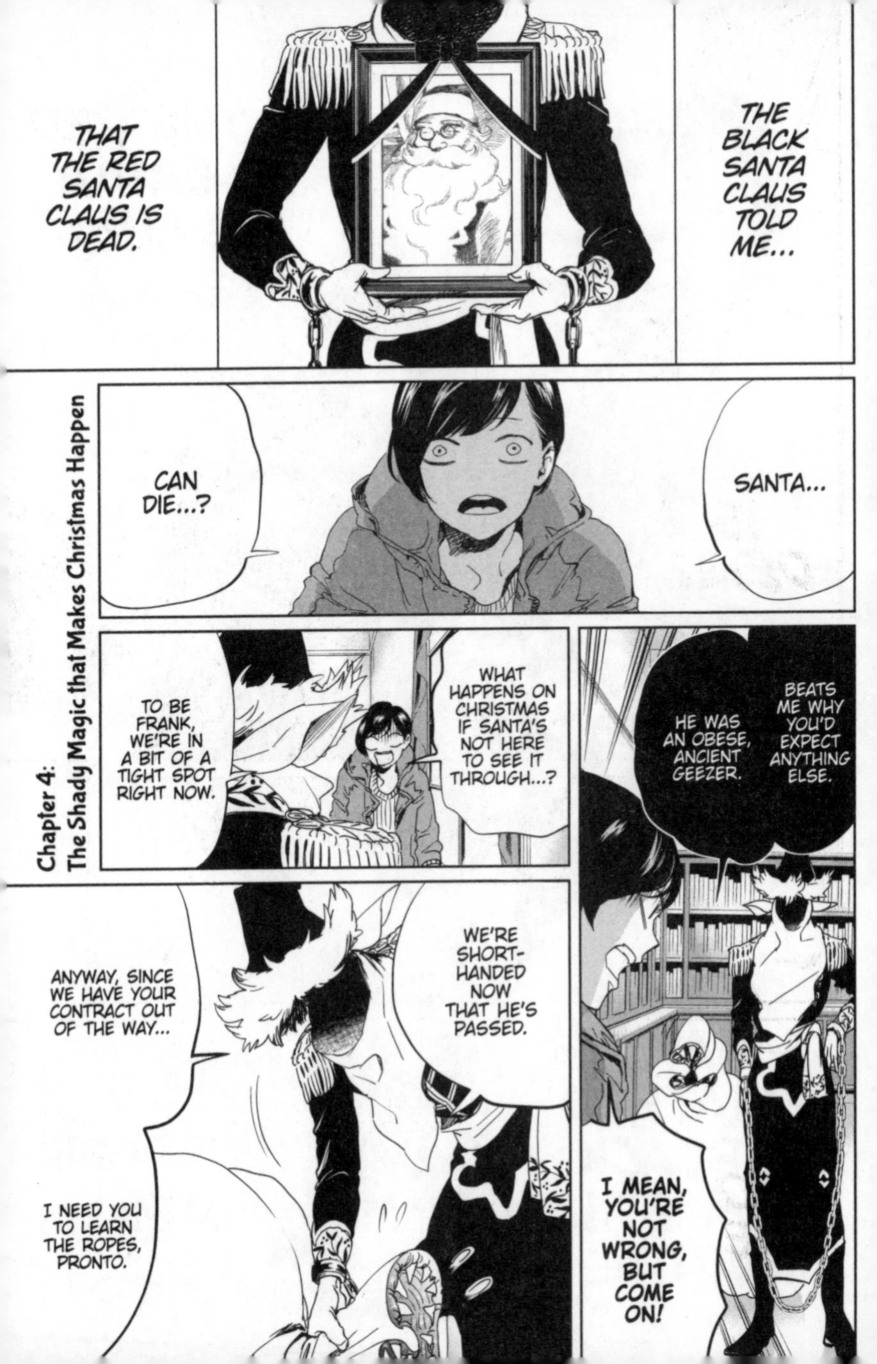
THE BLACK SANTA CLAUS TOLD ME...
THAT THE RED SANTA CLAUS IS DEAD.
SANTA...
CAN DIE...?
BEATS ME WHY YOU'D EXPECT ANYTHING ELSE.
HE WAS AN OBESE, ANCIENT GEEZER.
I MEAN, YOU'RE NOT WRONG, BUT COME ON!
WHAT HAPPENS ON CHRISTMAS IF SANTA'S NOT HERE TO SEE IT THROUGH...?
TO BE FRANK, WE'RE IN A BIT OF A TIGHT SPOT RIGHT NOW.
WE'RE SHORT-HANDED NOW THAT HE'S PASSED.
ANYWAY, SINCE WE HAVE YOUR CONTRACT OUT OF THE WAY...
I NEED YOU TO LEARN THE ROPES, PRONTO.

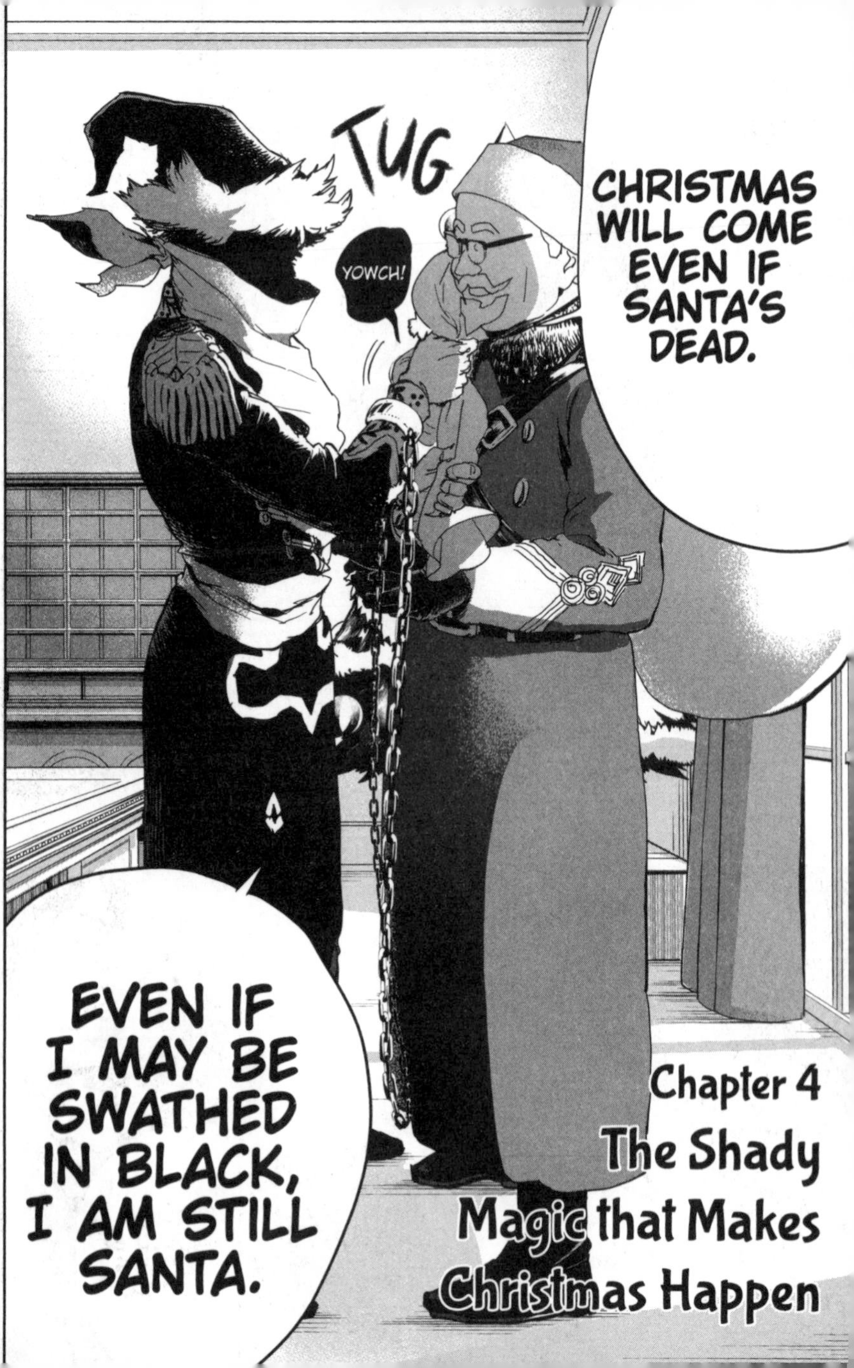
CHRISTMAS WILL COME EVEN IF SANTA'S DEAD.
TUG
YOWCH!
Chapter 4
The Shady Magic that Makes Christmas Happen
EVEN IF I MAY BE SWATHED IN BLACK, I AM STILL SANTA.

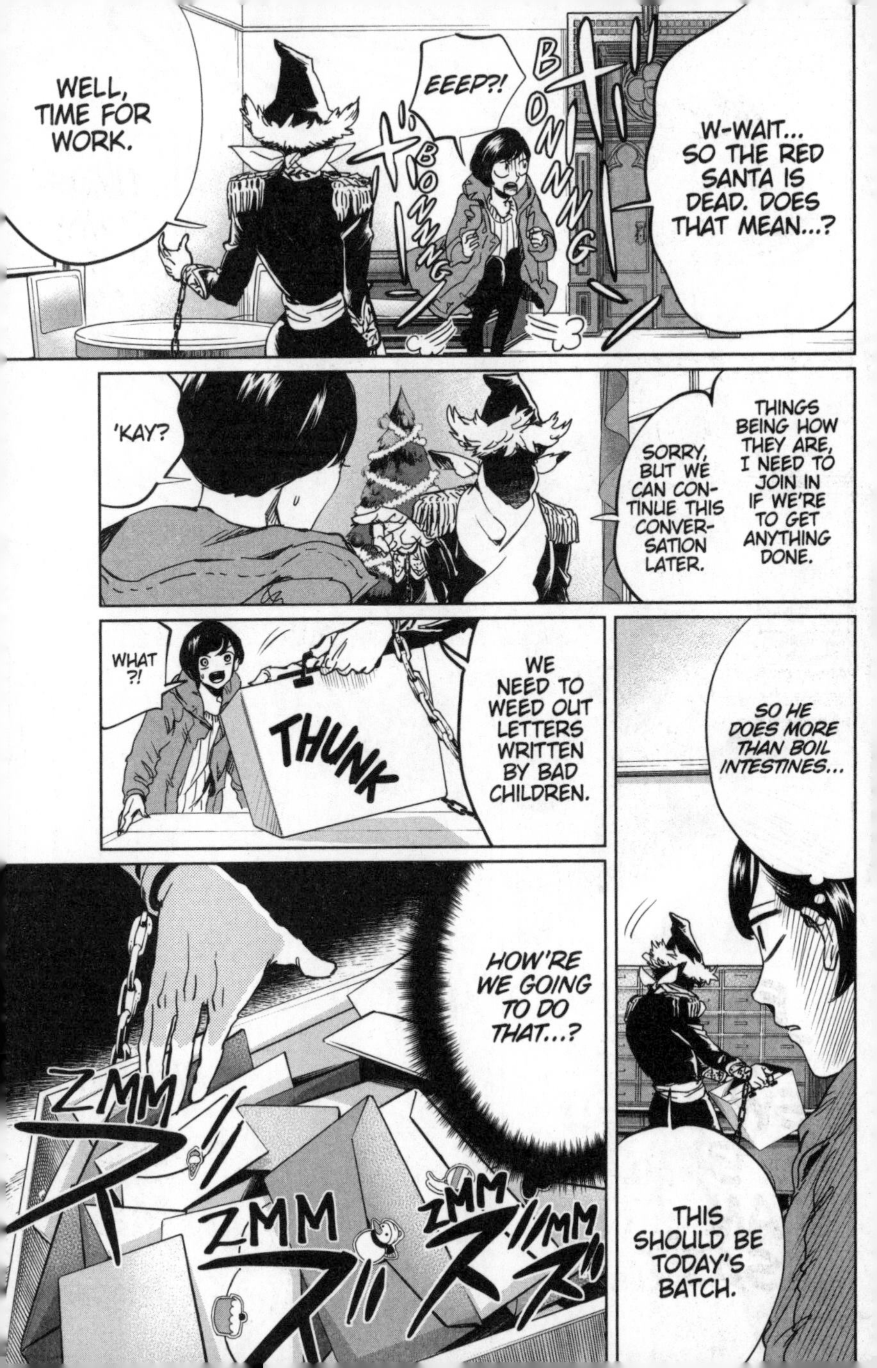
W-WAIT... SO THE RED SANTA IS DEAD. DOES THAT MEAN...?
BONNNNG
EEEP?!
BONNNG
WELL, TIME FOR WORK.
THINGS BEING HOW THEY ARE, I NEED TO JOIN IN IF WE'RE TO GET ANYTHING DONE.
SORRY, BUT WE CAN CONTINUE THIS CONVERSATION LATER.
'KAY?
SO HE DOES MORE THAN BOIL INTESTINES...
THIS SHOULD BE TODAY'S BATCH.
WE NEED TO WEED OUT LETTERS WRITTEN BY BAD CHILDREN.
THUNK
WHAT?!
HOW'RE WE GOING TO DO THAT...?
ZMM
ZMM
ZMM
MM

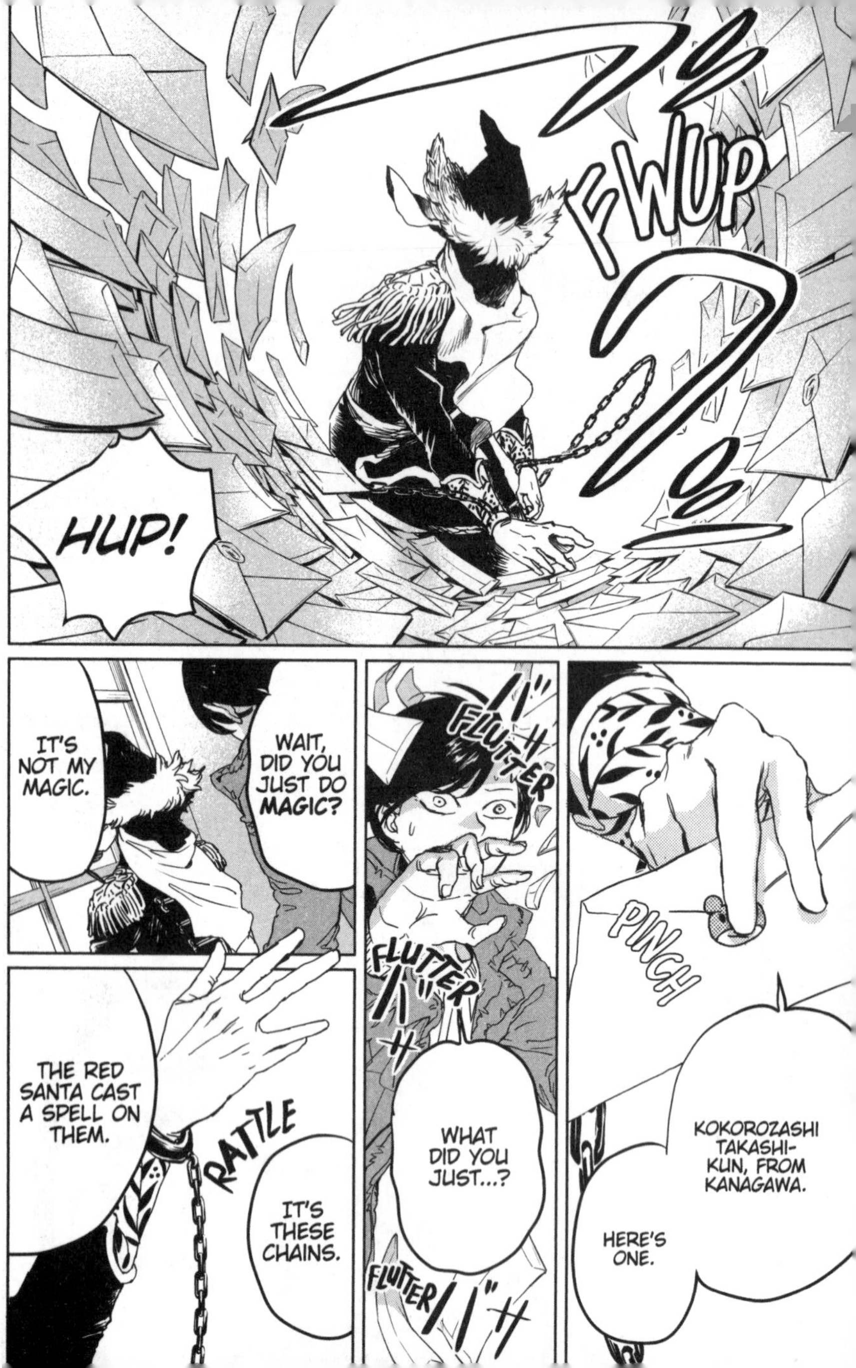
FWUP
HUP!
PINCH
KOKOROZASHI TAKASHI-KUN, FROM KANAGAWA.
HERE'S ONE.
FLUTTER
FLUTTER
WHAT DID YOU JUST...?
FLUTTER
WAIT, DID YOU JUST DO MAGIC?
IT'S NOT MY MAGIC.
RATTLE
IT'S THESE CHAINS.
THE RED SANTA CAST A SPELL ON THEM.

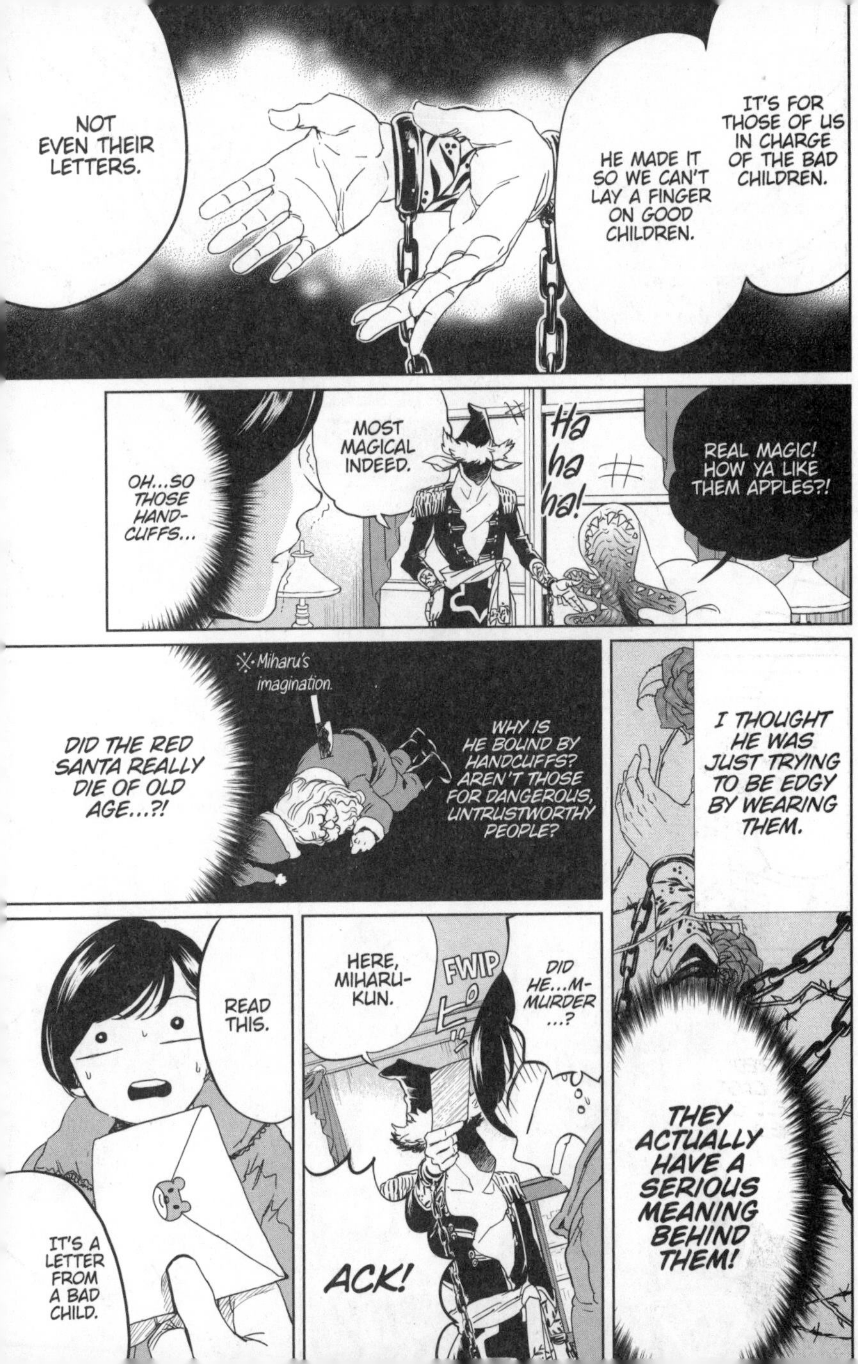
IT'S FOR THOSE OF US IN CHARGE OF THE BAD CHILDREN.
HE MADE IT SO WE CAN'T LAY A FINGER ON GOOD CHILDREN.
NOT EVEN THEIR LETTERS.
REAL MAGIC! HOW YA LIKE THEM APPLES?!
Ha ha ha!
MOST MAGICAL INDEED.
OH...SO THOSE HAND-CUFFS...
I THOUGHT HE WAS JUST TRYING TO BE EDGY BY WEARING THEM.
THEY ACTUALLY HAVE A SERIOUS MEANING BEHIND THEM!
WHY IS HE BOUND BY HANDCUFFS? AREN'T THOSE FOR DANGEROUS, UNTRUSTWORTHY PEOPLE?
※ Miharu's imagination.
DID THE RED SANTA REALLY DIE OF OLD AGE...?!
DID HE...M-MURDER...?
FWIP
HERE, MIHARU-KUN.
ACK!
READ THIS.
IT'S A LETTER FROM A BAD CHILD.

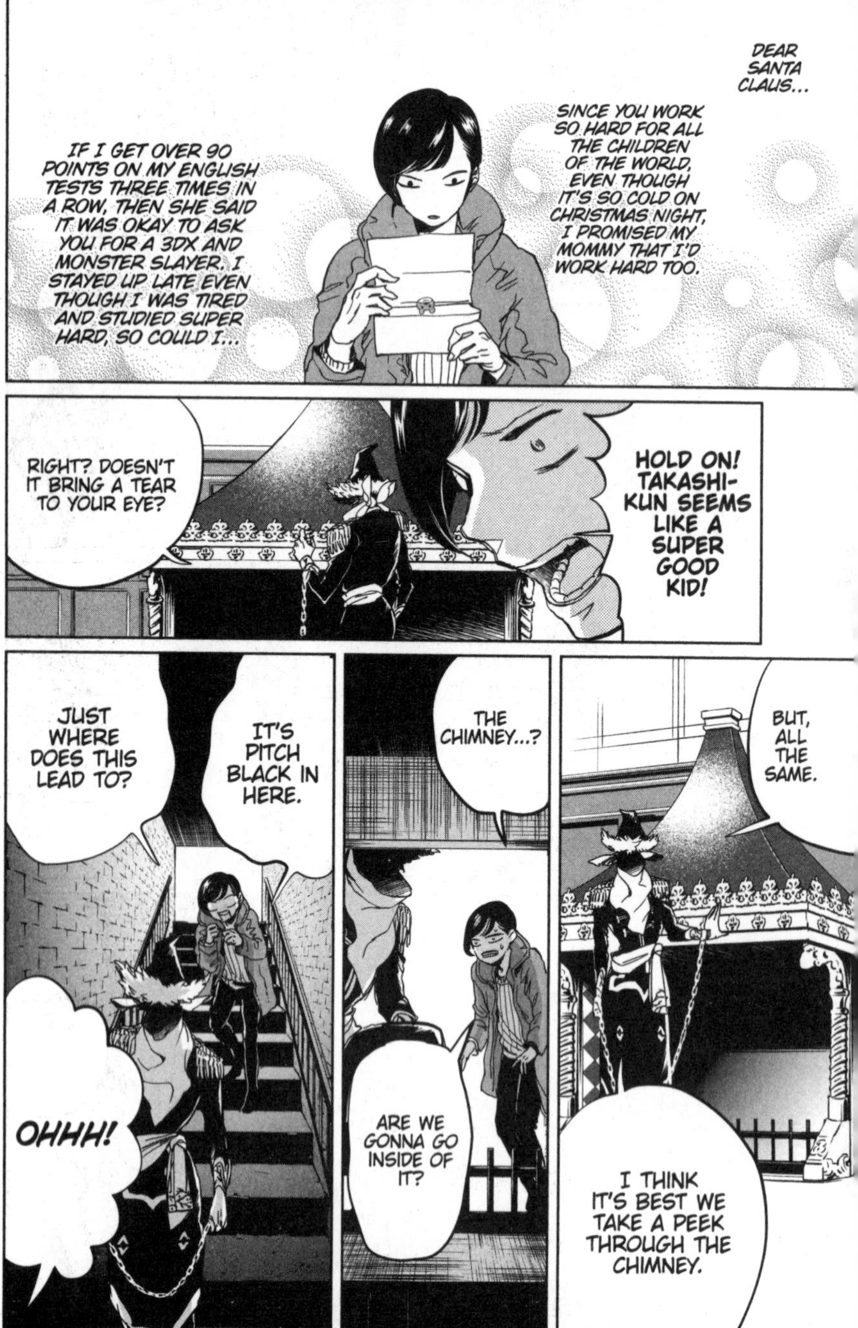

DEAR SANTA CLAUS...
SINCE YOU WORK SO HARD FOR ALL THE CHILDREN OF THE WORLD, EVEN THOUGH IT'S SO COLD ON CHRISTMAS NIGHT, I PROMISED MY MOMMY THAT I'D WORK HARD TOO.
IF I GET OVER 90 POINTS ON MY ENGLISH TESTS THREE TIMES IN A ROW, THEN SHE SAID IT WAS OKAY TO ASK YOU FOR A 3DX AND MONSTER SLAYER. I STAYED UP LATE EVEN THOUGH I WAS TIRED AND STUDIED SUPER HARD, SO COULD I...
HOLD ON! TAKASHI-KUN SEEMS LIKE A SUPER GOOD KID!
RIGHT? DOESN'T IT BRING A TEAR TO YOUR EYE?
BUT, ALL THE SAME.
I THINK IT'S BEST WE TAKE A PEEK THROUGH THE CHIMNEY.
THE CHIMNEY...?
ARE WE GONNA GO INSIDE OF IT?
IT'S PITCH BLACK IN HERE.
JUST WHERE DOES THIS LEAD TO?
OHHH!

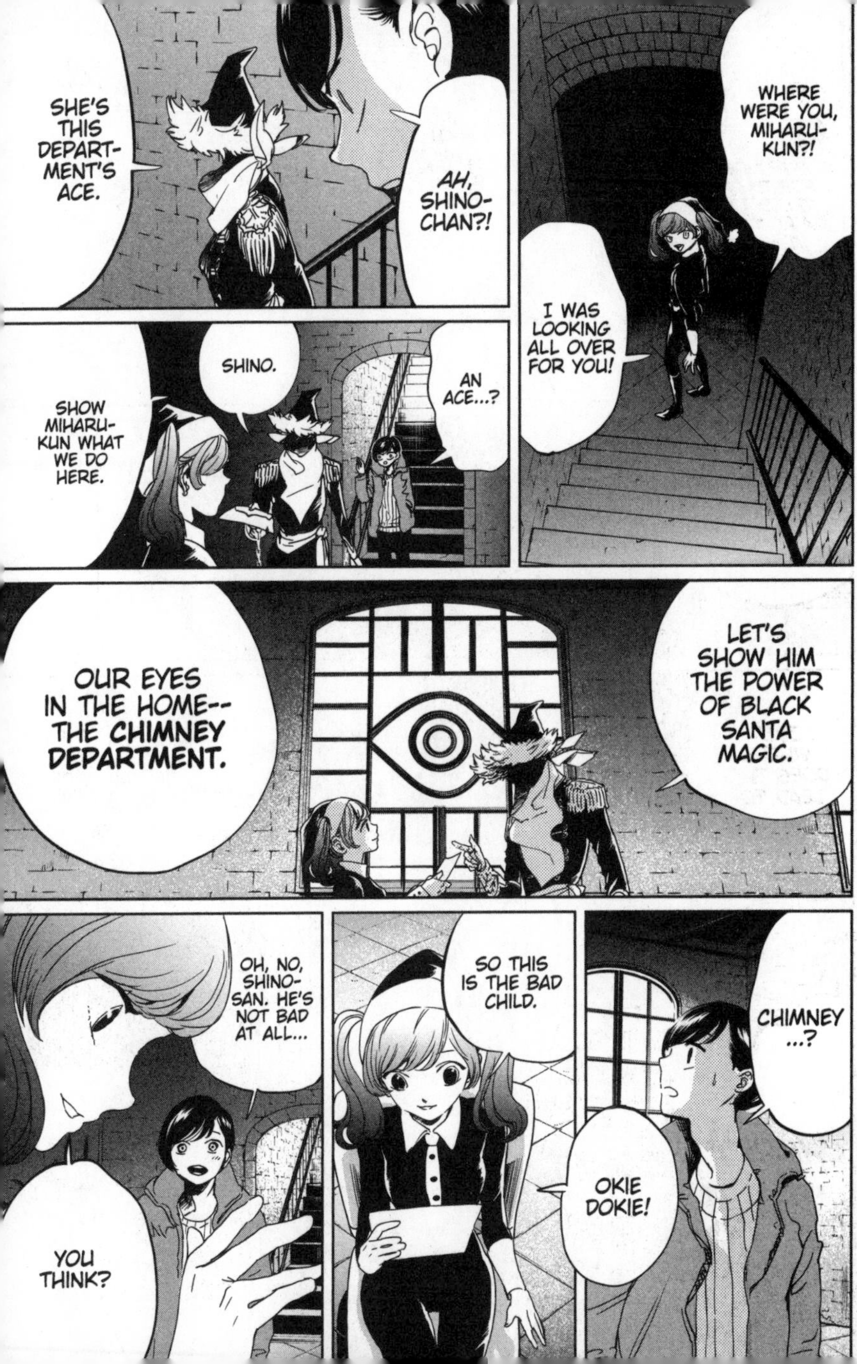
WHERE WERE YOU, MIHARU-KUN?!
I WAS LOOKING ALL OVER FOR YOU!
AH, SHINO-CHAN?!
SHE'S THIS DEPART-MENT'S ACE.
AN ACE...?
SHINO.
SHOW MIHARU-KUN WHAT WE DO HERE.
LET'S SHOW HIM THE POWER OF BLACK SANTA MAGIC.
OUR EYES IN THE HOME-- THE **CHIMNEY DEPARTMENT.**
CHIMNEY ...?
OKIE DOKIE!
SO THIS IS THE BAD CHILD.
OH, NO, SHINO-SAN. HE'S NOT BAD AT ALL...
YOU THINK?

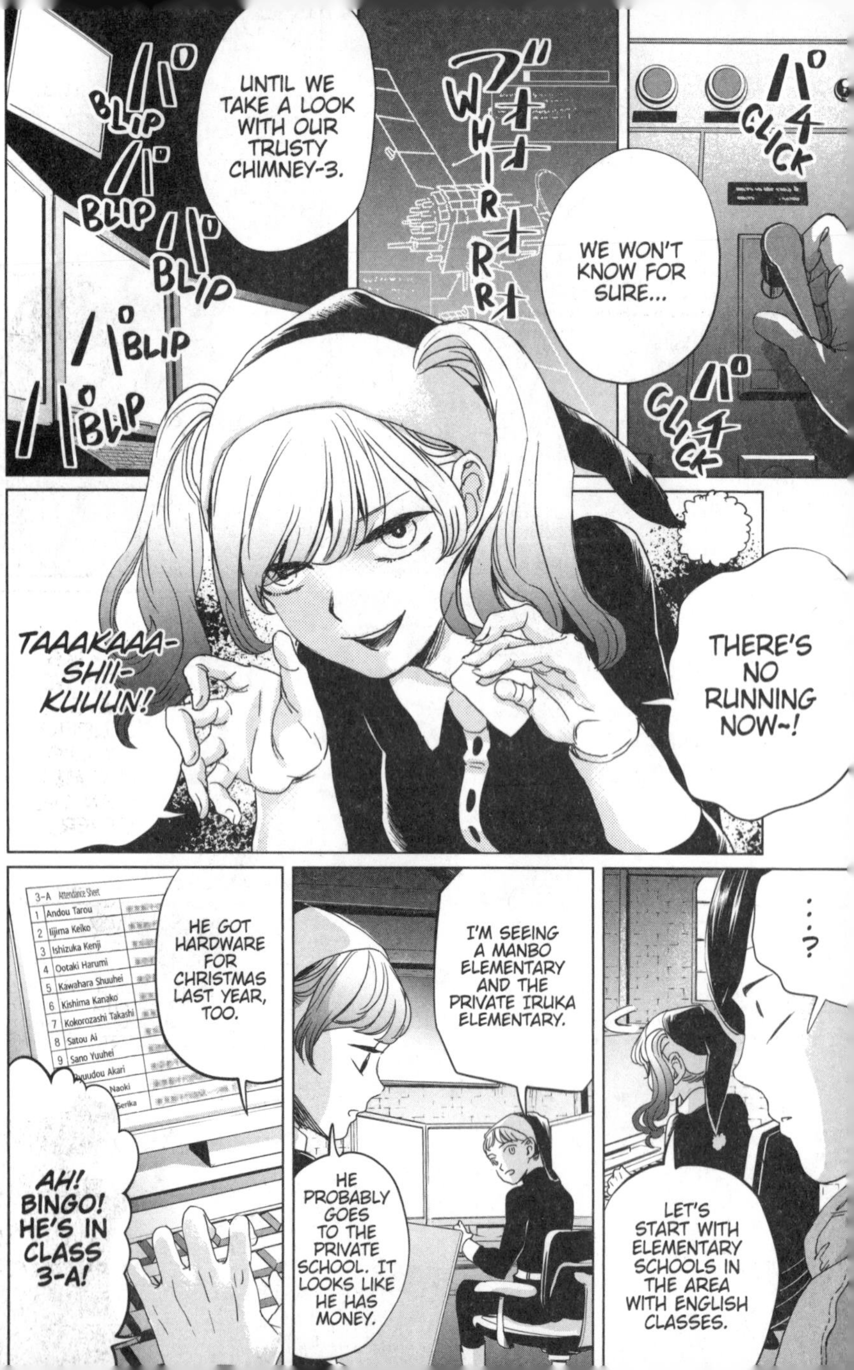
パ
CLICK
WE WON'T KNOW FOR SURE...
パ
CLICK
ブォォォ
WHIRRR
UNTIL WE TAKE A LOOK WITH OUR TRUSTY CHIMNEY-3.
パ BLIP
パ BLIP
パ BLIP
パ BLIP
パ BLIP
THERE'S NO RUNNING NOW~!
TAAAKAAA-SHII-KUUUN!
...?
LET'S START WITH ELEMENTARY SCHOOLS IN THE AREA WITH ENGLISH CLASSES.
I'M SEEING A MANBO ELEMENTARY AND THE PRIVATE IRUKA ELEMENTARY.
HE PROBABLY GOES TO THE PRIVATE SCHOOL. IT LOOKS LIKE HE HAS MONEY.
HE GOT HARDWARE FOR CHRISTMAS LAST YEAR, TOO.
3-A Attendance Sheet
1 Andou Tarou
2 Iijima Keiko
3 Ishizuka Kenji
4 Ootaki Harumi
5 Kawahara Shuuhei
6 Kishima Kanako
7 Kokorozashi Takashi
8 Satou Ai
9 Sano Yuuhei
AH! BINGO! HE'S IN CLASS 3-A!

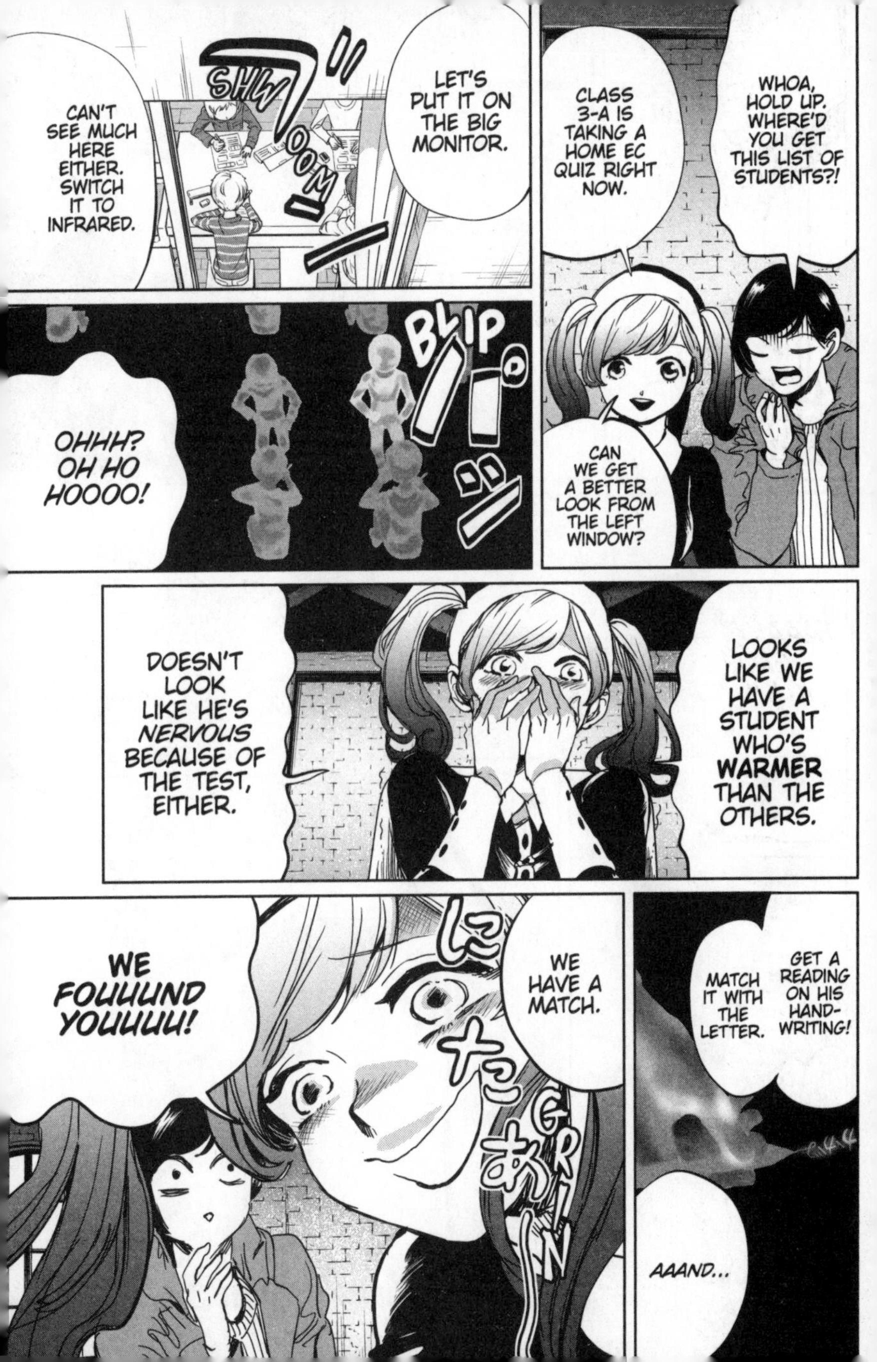
WHOA, HOLD UP. WHERE'D YOU GET THIS LIST OF STUDENTS?!
CLASS 3-A IS TAKING A HOME EC QUIZ RIGHT NOW.
CAN WE GET A BETTER LOOK FROM THE LEFT WINDOW?
LET'S PUT IT ON THE BIG MONITOR.
SHWOOM
CAN'T SEE MUCH HERE EITHER. SWITCH IT TO INFRARED.
BLIP
OHHH? OH HO HOOOO!
LOOKS LIKE WE HAVE A STUDENT WHO'S WARMER THAN THE OTHERS.
DOESN'T LOOK LIKE HE'S NERVOUS BECAUSE OF THE TEST, EITHER.
GET A READING ON HIS HAND-WRITING!
MATCH IT WITH THE LETTER.
AAAND...
WE HAVE A MATCH.
GRIN
WE FOUUUND YOUUUU!

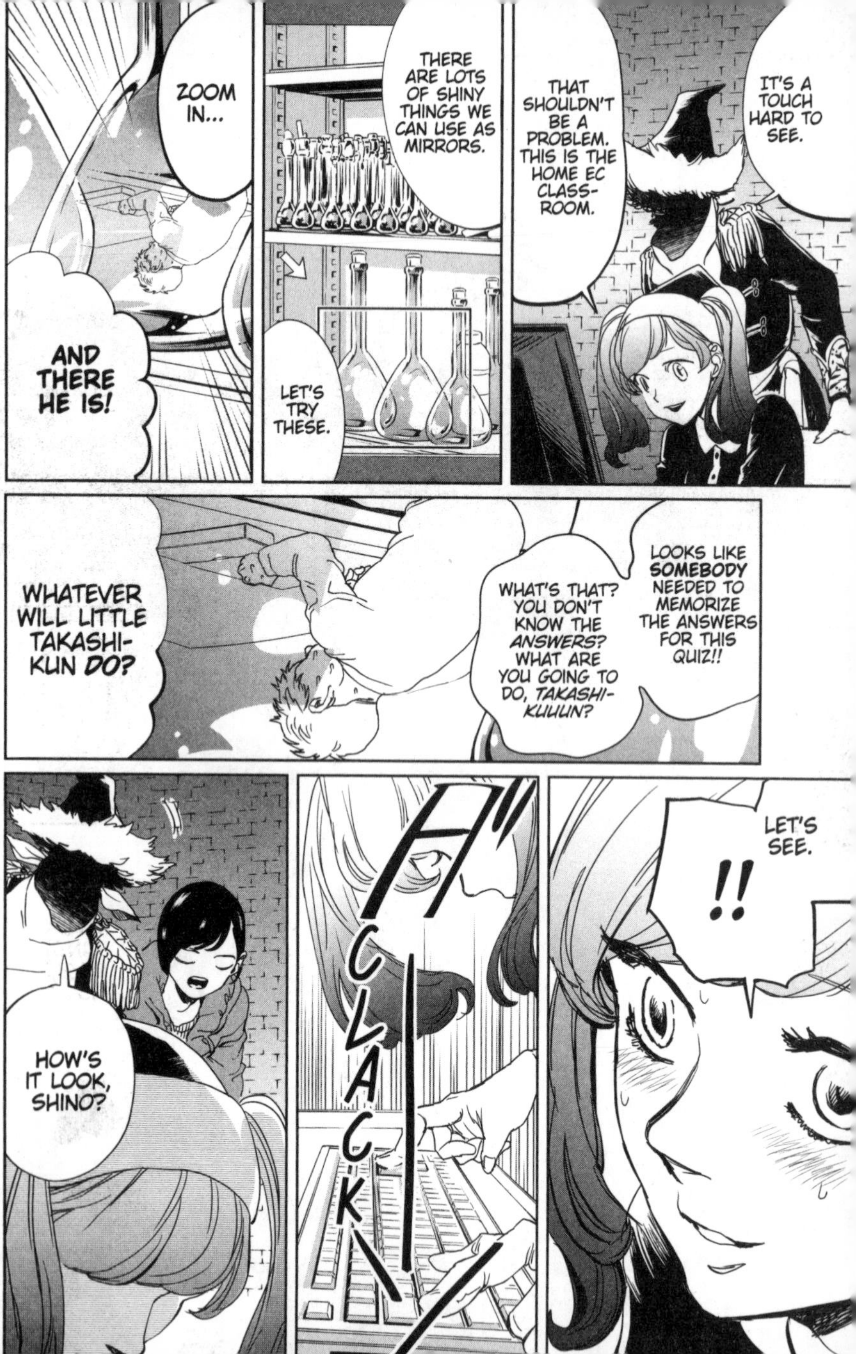
IT'S A TOUCH HARD TO SEE.
THAT SHOULDN'T BE A PROBLEM. THIS IS THE HOME EC CLASSROOM.
THERE ARE LOTS OF SHINY THINGS WE CAN USE AS MIRRORS.
LET'S TRY THESE.
ZOOM IN...
AND THERE HE IS!
LOOKS LIKE SOMEBODY NEEDED TO MEMORIZE THE ANSWERS FOR THIS QUIZ!!
WHAT'S THAT? YOU DON'T KNOW THE ANSWERS? WHAT ARE YOU GOING TO DO, TAKASHI-KUUUN?
WHATEVER WILL LITTLE TAKASHI-KUN DO?
LET'S SEE.
!!
CLACK
HOW'S IT LOOK, SHINO?

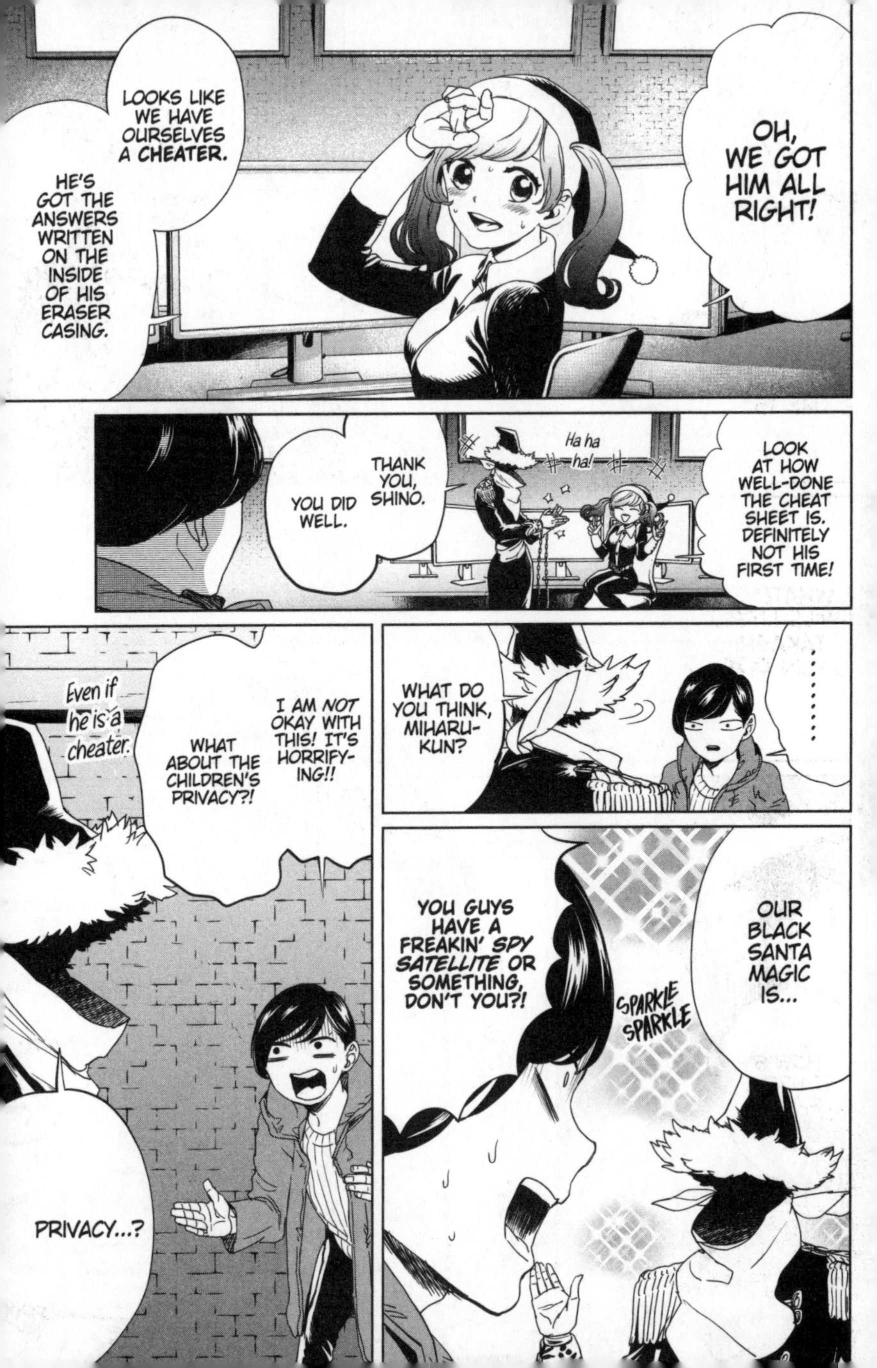
OH, WE GOT HIM ALL RIGHT!
LOOKS LIKE WE HAVE OURSELVES A CHEATER.
HE'S GOT THE ANSWERS WRITTEN ON THE INSIDE OF HIS ERASER CASING.
LOOK AT HOW WELL-DONE THE CHEAT SHEET IS. DEFINITELY NOT HIS FIRST TIME!
Ha ha ha!
THANK YOU, SHINO.
YOU DID WELL.
......
WHAT DO YOU THINK, MIHARU-KUN?
OUR BLACK SANTA MAGIC IS...
SPARKLE SPARKLE
YOU GUYS HAVE A FREAKIN' SPY SATELLITE OR SOMETHING, DON'T YOU?!
I AM NOT OKAY WITH THIS! IT'S HORRIFYING!!
WHAT ABOUT THE CHILDREN'S PRIVACY?!
Even if he is a cheater.
PRIVACY...?

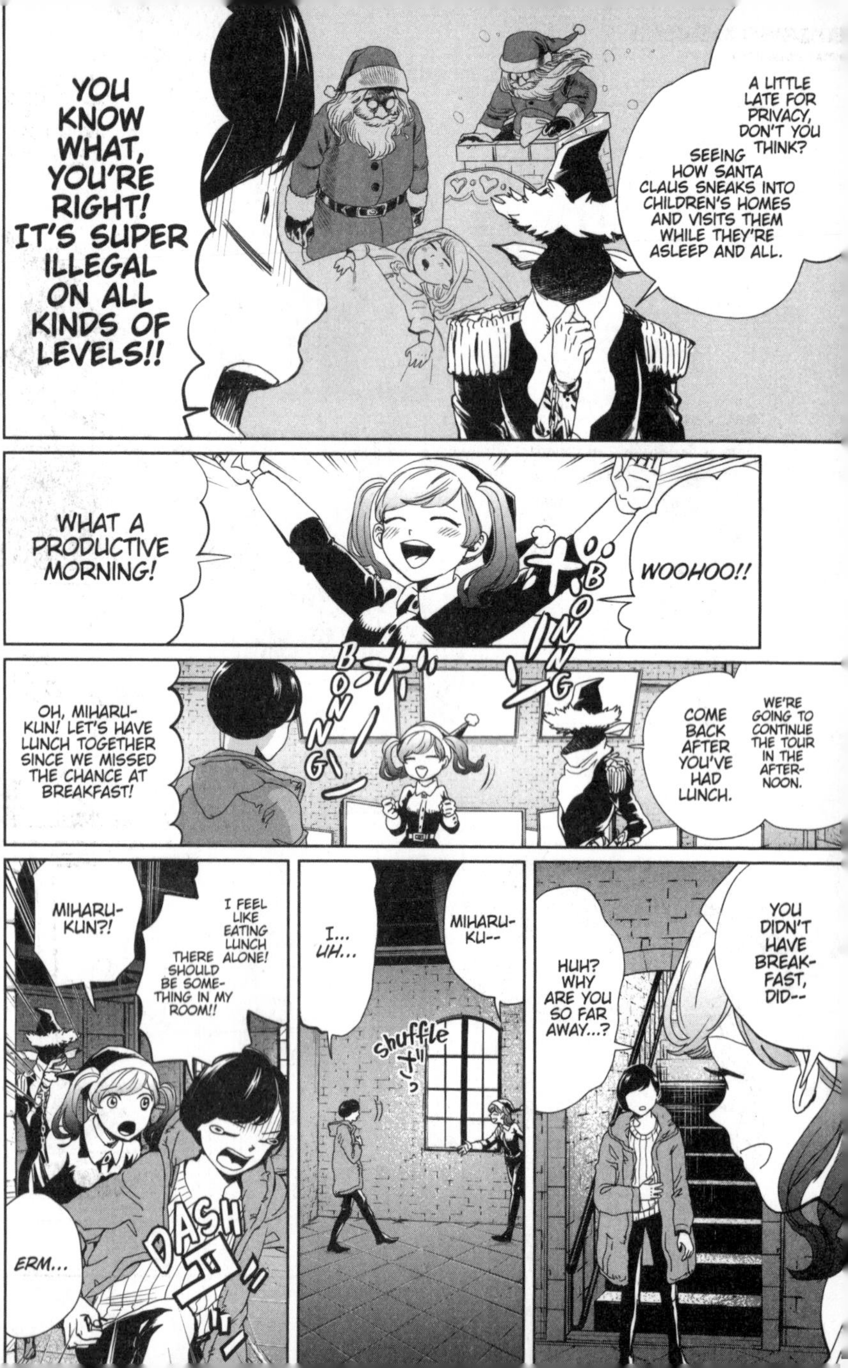
A LITTLE LATE FOR PRIVACY, DON'T YOU THINK?
SEEING HOW SANTA CLAUS SNEAKS INTO CHILDREN'S HOMES AND VISITS THEM WHILE THEY'RE ASLEEP AND ALL.
YOU KNOW WHAT, YOU'RE RIGHT! IT'S SUPER ILLEGAL ON ALL KINDS OF LEVELS!!
WOOHOO!!
BOING
WHAT A PRODUCTIVE MORNING!
WE'RE GOING TO CONTINUE THE TOUR IN THE AFTER-NOON.
COME BACK AFTER YOU'VE HAD LUNCH.
BOING
BOING
OH, MIHARU-KUN! LET'S HAVE LUNCH TOGETHER SINCE WE MISSED THE CHANCE AT BREAKFAST!
YOU DIDN'T HAVE BREAK-FAST, DID--
HUH? WHY ARE YOU SO FAR AWAY...?
MIHARU-KU--
shuffle
I... UH...
I FEEL LIKE EATING LUNCH ALONE!
THERE SHOULD BE SOME-THING IN MY ROOM!!
MIHARU-KUN?!
DASH
ERM...

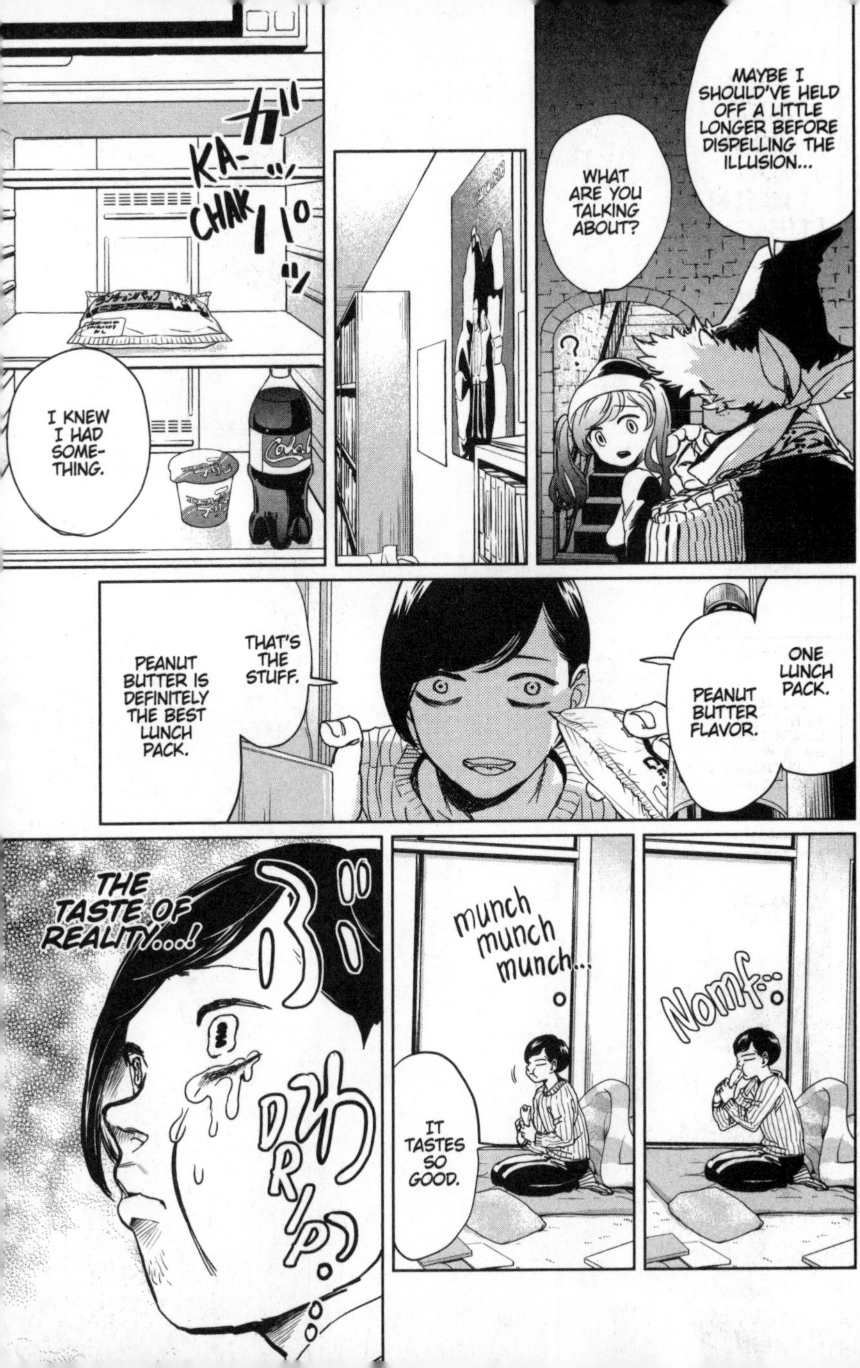
MAYBE I SHOULD'VE HELD OFF A LITTLE LONGER BEFORE DISPELLING THE ILLUSION...
WHAT ARE YOU TALKING ABOUT?
KA-CHAK
I KNEW I HAD SOME-THING.
ONE LUNCH PACK.
PEANUT BUTTER FLAVOR.
THAT'S THE STUFF.
PEANUT BUTTER IS DEFINITELY THE BEST LUNCH PACK.
Nomf...
munch munch munch...
IT TASTES SO GOOD.
THE TASTE OF REALITY...!
DRIP

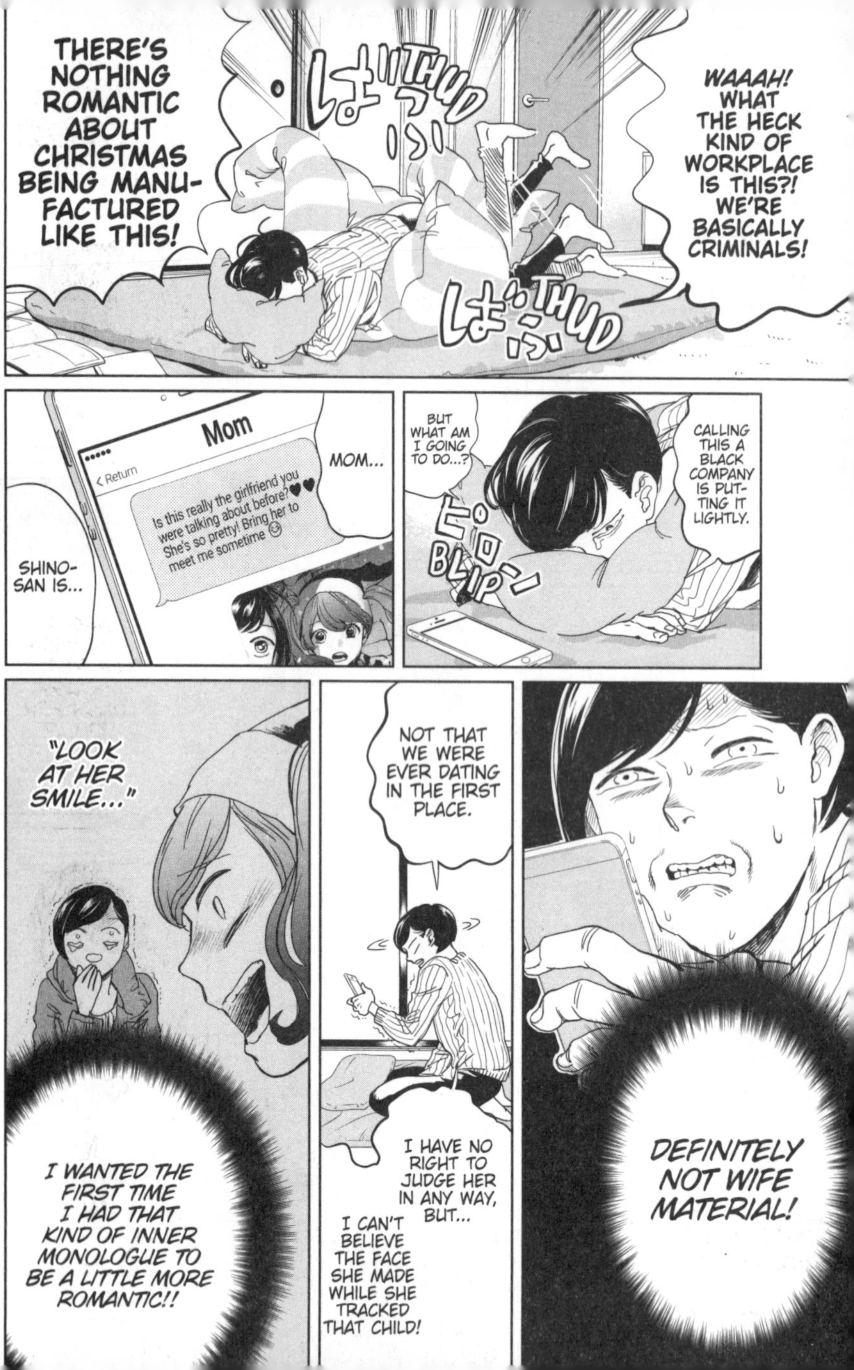
WAAAH! WHAT THE HECK KIND OF WORKPLACE IS THIS?! WE'RE BASICALLY CRIMINALS!
THUD
THERE'S NOTHING ROMANTIC ABOUT CHRISTMAS BEING MANU-FACTURED LIKE THIS!
THUD
CALLING THIS A BLACK COMPANY IS PUT-TING IT LIGHTLY.
BUT WHAT AM I GOING TO DO...?
BLIP
Mom
< Return
Is this really the girlfriend you were talking about before?♥♥ She's so pretty! Bring her to meet me sometime
MOM...
SHINO-SAN IS...
DEFINITELY NOT WIFE MATERIAL!
NOT THAT WE WERE EVER DATING IN THE FIRST PLACE.
I HAVE NO RIGHT TO JUDGE HER IN ANY WAY, BUT...
I CAN'T BELIEVE THE FACE SHE MADE WHILE SHE TRACKED THAT CHILD!
"LOOK AT HER SMILE..."
I WANTED THE FIRST TIME I HAD THAT KIND OF INNER MONOLOGUE TO BE A LITTLE MORE ROMANTIC!!

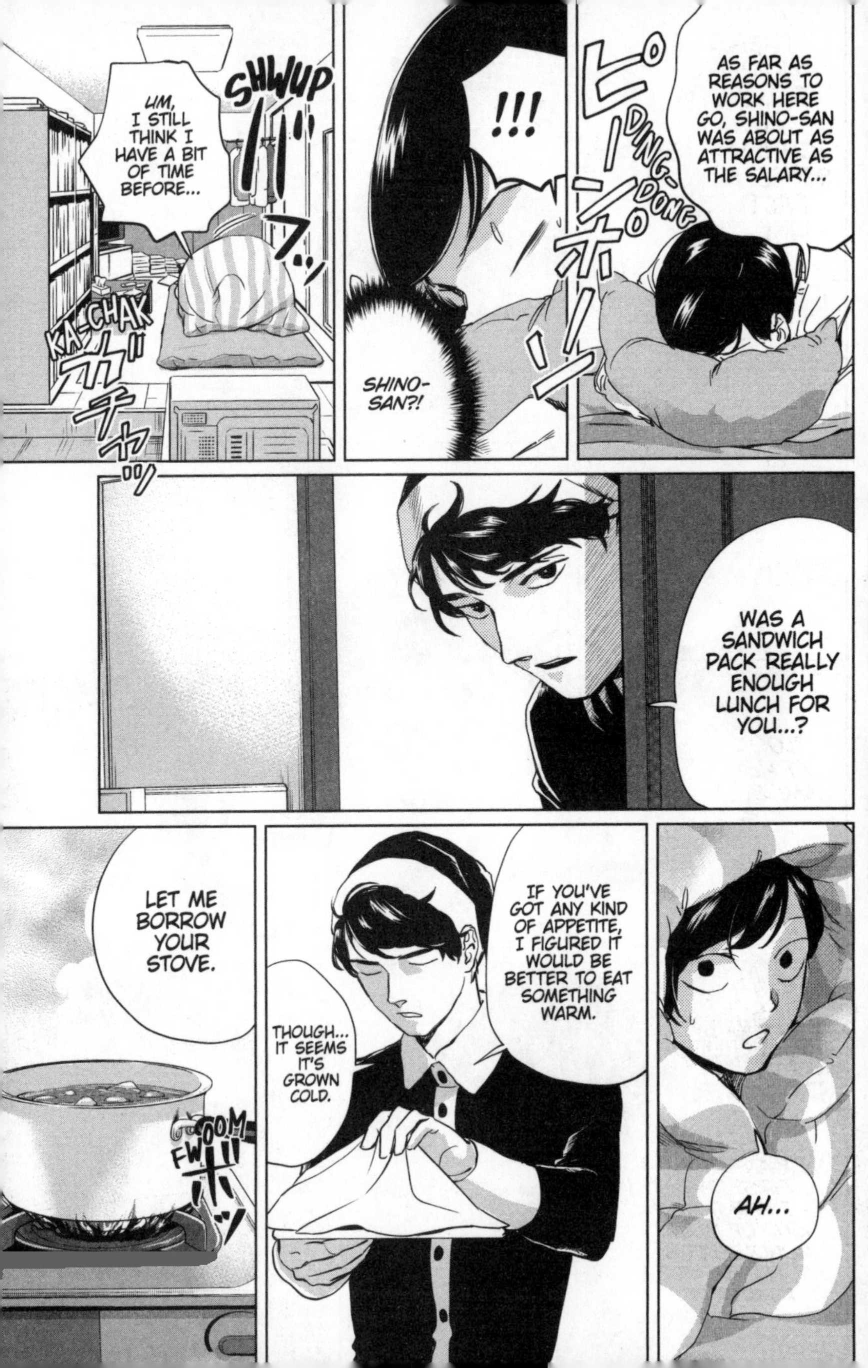
AS FAR AS REASONS TO WORK HERE GO, SHINO-SAN WAS ABOUT AS ATTRACTIVE AS THE SALARY...
DING-DONG
!!!
SHINO-SAN?!
SHWUP
UM, I STILL THINK I HAVE A BIT OF TIME BEFORE...
KA-CHAK
WAS A SANDWICH PACK REALLY ENOUGH LUNCH FOR YOU...?
AH...
IF YOU'VE GOT ANY KIND OF APPETITE, I FIGURED IT WOULD BE BETTER TO EAT SOMETHING WARM.
THOUGH... IT SEEMS IT'S GROWN COLD.
LET ME BORROW YOUR STOVE.
FWOOM

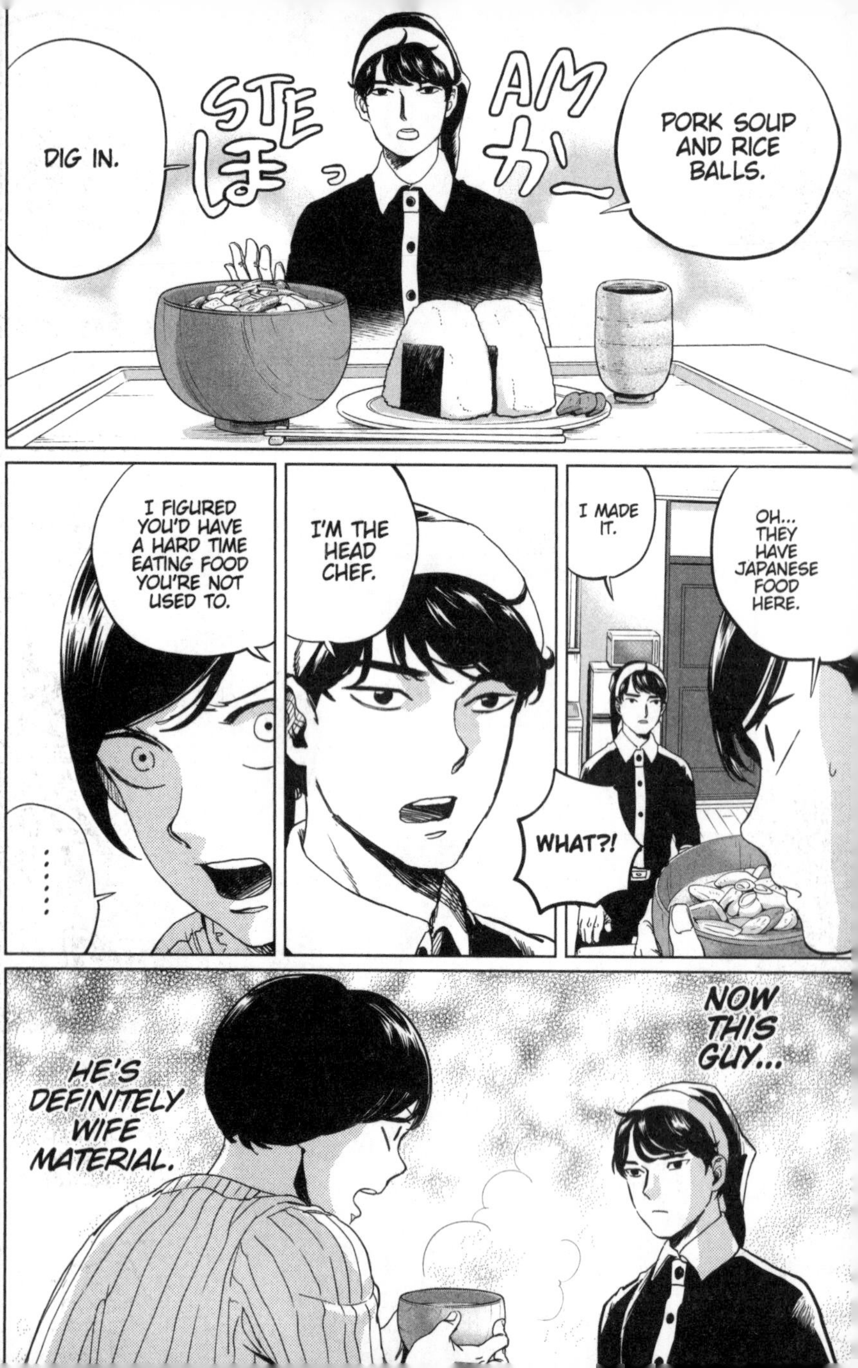
PORK SOUP AND RICE BALLS.
STEAM
ほっかー
DIG IN.
OH... THEY HAVE JAPANESE FOOD HERE.
I MADE IT.
WHAT?!
I'M THE HEAD CHEF.
I FIGURED YOU'D HAVE A HARD TIME EATING FOOD YOU'RE NOT USED TO.
......
NOW THIS GUY...
HE'S DEFINITELY WIFE MATERIAL.

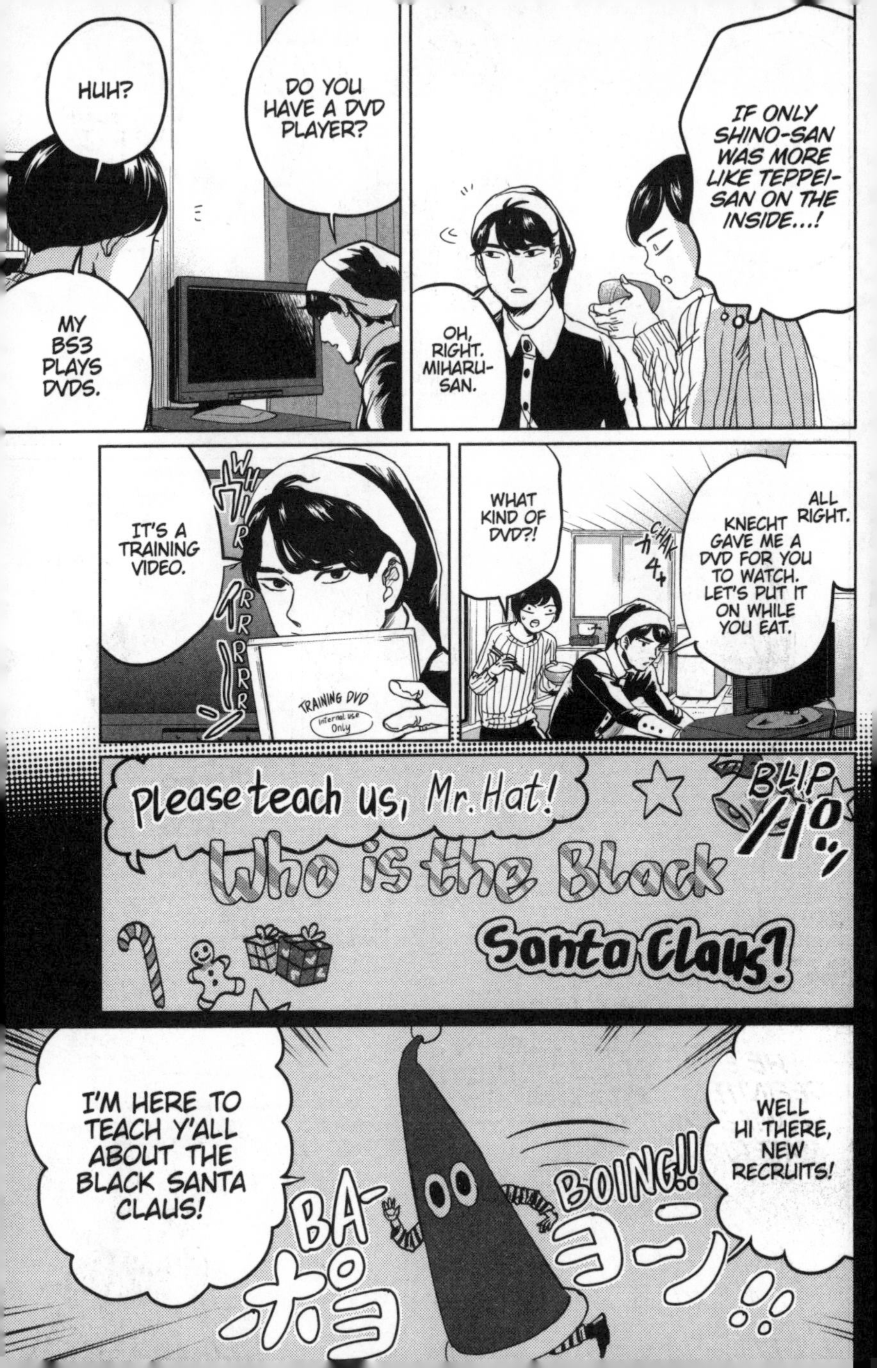
IF ONLY SHINO-SAN WAS MORE LIKE TEPPEI-SAN ON THE INSIDE...!
OH, RIGHT. MIHARU-SAN.
DO YOU HAVE A DVD PLAYER?
HUH?
MY BS3 PLAYS DVDS.
ALL RIGHT.
KNECHT GAVE ME A DVD FOR YOU TO WATCH. LET'S PUT IT ON WHILE YOU EAT.
CHAK
WHAT KIND OF DVD?!
WHIRRRRR
IT'S A TRAINING VIDEO.
TRAINING DVD
Internal use Only
BLIP
Please teach us, Mr. Hat!
Who is the Black Santa Claus?
WELL HI THERE, NEW RECRUITS!
BOING!!
I'M HERE TO TEACH Y'ALL ABOUT THE BLACK SANTA CLAUS!
BA-

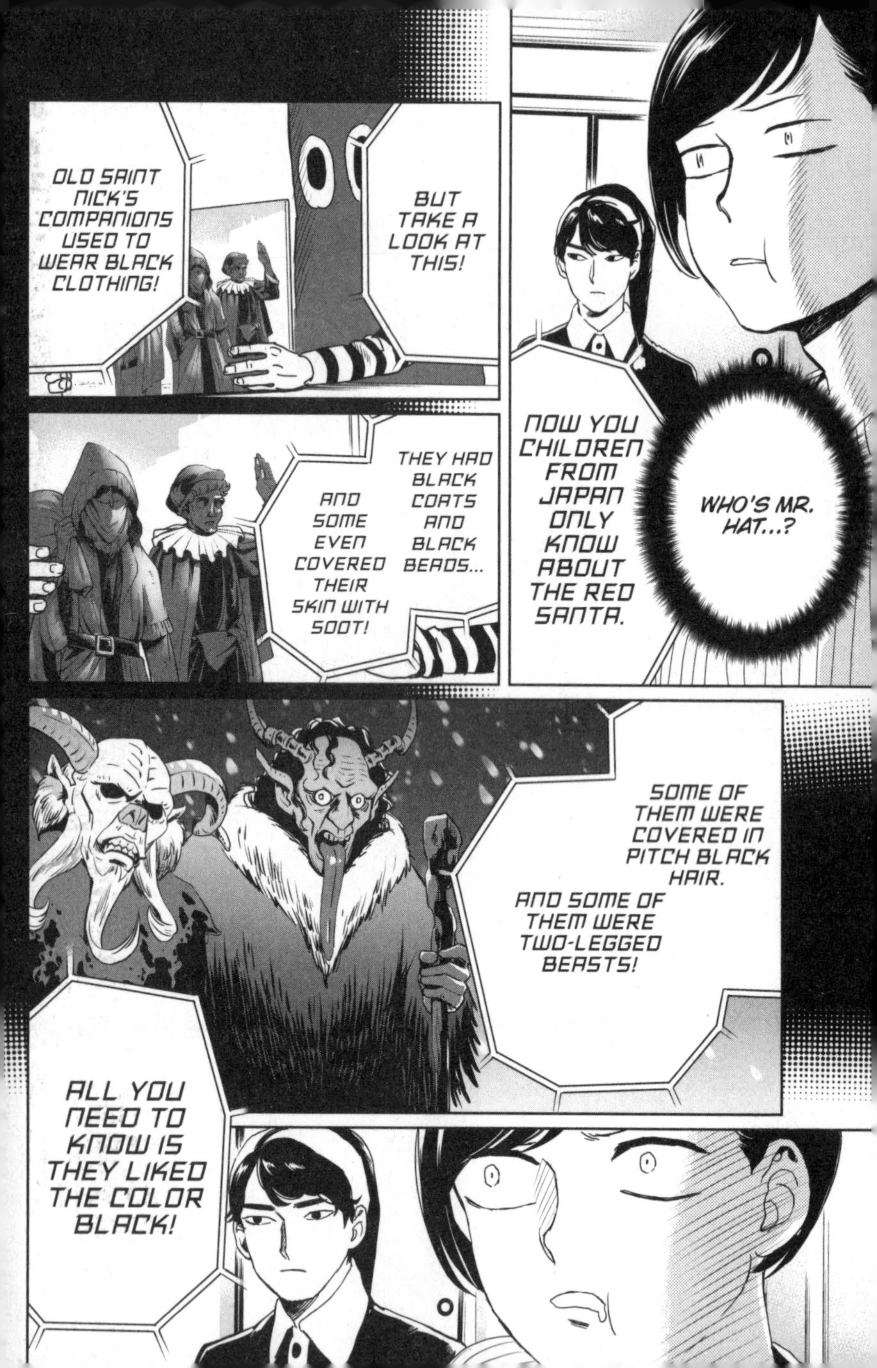
NOW YOU CHILDREN FROM JAPAN ONLY KNOW ABOUT THE RED SANTA.
WHO'S MR. HAT...?
OLD SAINT NICK'S COMPANIONS USED TO WEAR BLACK CLOTHING!
BUT TAKE A LOOK AT THIS!
THEY HAD BLACK COATS AND BLACK BEADS...
AND SOME EVEN COVERED THEIR SKIN WITH SOOT!
SOME OF THEM WERE COVERED IN PITCH BLACK HAIR.
AND SOME OF THEM WERE TWO-LEGGED BEASTS!
ALL YOU NEED TO KNOW IS THEY LIKED THE COLOR BLACK!

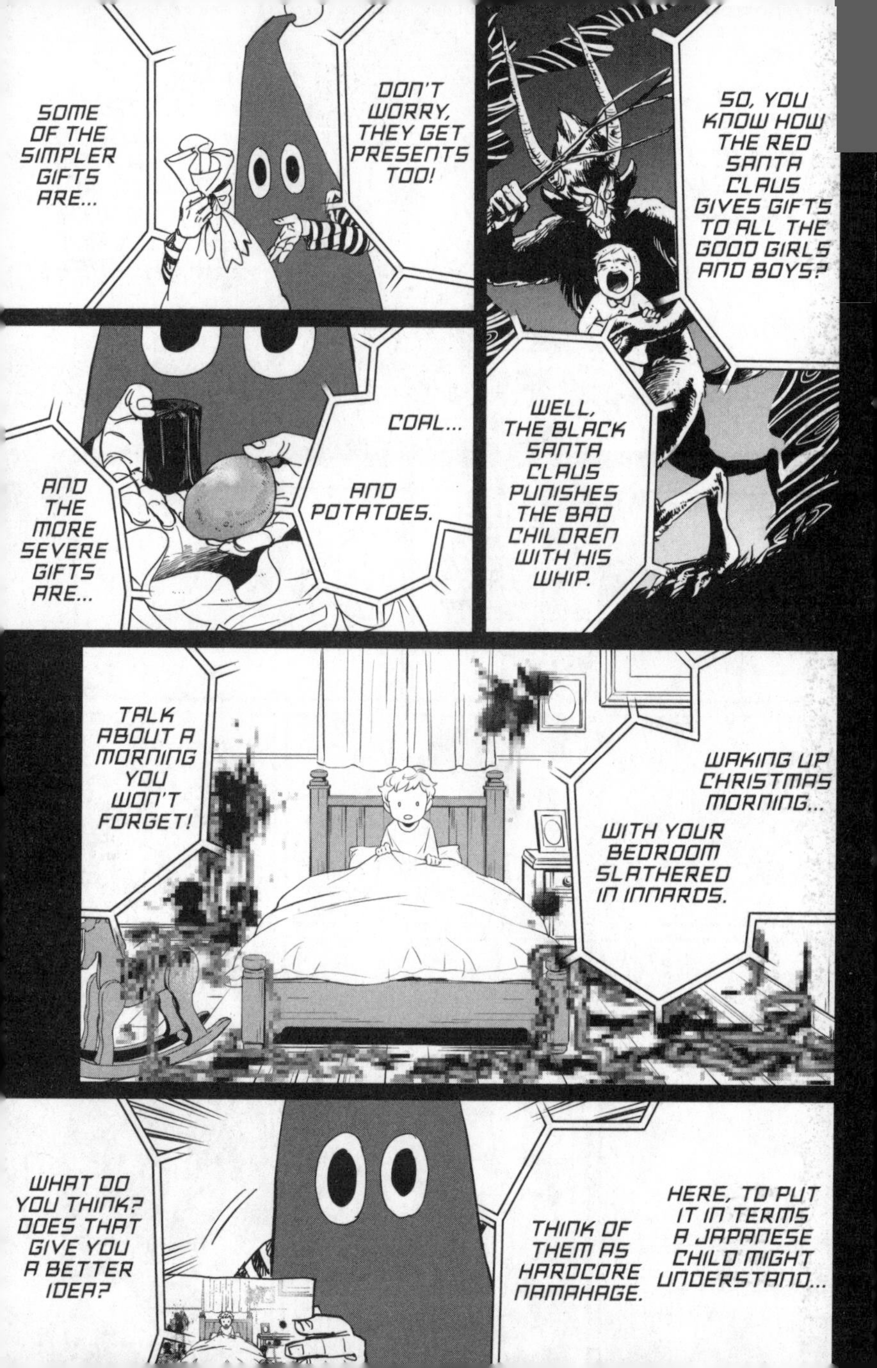
SO, YOU KNOW HOW THE RED SANTA CLAUS GIVES GIFTS TO ALL THE GOOD GIRLS AND BOYS?
WELL, THE BLACK SANTA CLAUS PUNISHES THE BAD CHILDREN WITH HIS WHIP.
DON'T WORRY, THEY GET PRESENTS TOO!
SOME OF THE SIMPLER GIFTS ARE...
AND THE MORE SEVERE GIFTS ARE...
COAL...
AND POTATOES.
WAKING UP CHRISTMAS MORNING...
WITH YOUR BEDROOM SLATHERED IN INNARDS.
TALK ABOUT A MORNING YOU WON'T FORGET!
HERE, TO PUT IT IN TERMS A JAPANESE CHILD MIGHT UNDERSTAND...
THINK OF THEM AS HARDCORE NAMAHAGE.
WHAT DO YOU THINK? DOES THAT GIVE YOU A BETTER IDEA?

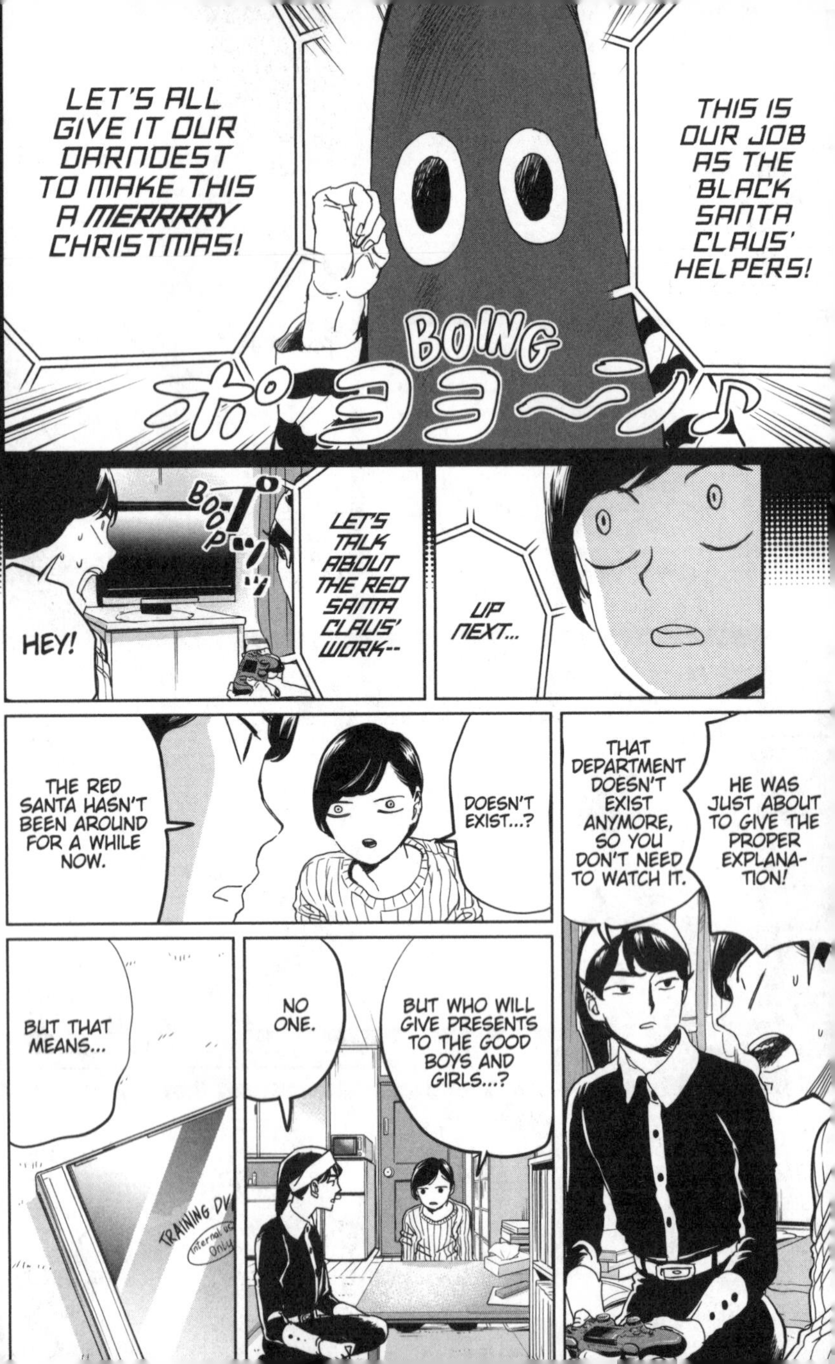
THIS IS OUR JOB AS THE BLACK SANTA CLAUS' HELPERS!
LET'S ALL GIVE IT OUR DARNDEST TO MAKE THIS A MERRRRY CHRISTMAS!
BOING
ポヨヨ〜ン♪
UP NEXT...
LET'S TALK ABOUT THE RED SANTA CLAUS' WORK--
BOOP
ブツッ
HEY!
HE WAS JUST ABOUT TO GIVE THE PROPER EXPLANATION!
THAT DEPARTMENT DOESN'T EXIST ANYMORE, SO YOU DON'T NEED TO WATCH IT.
DOESN'T EXIST...?
THE RED SANTA HASN'T BEEN AROUND FOR A WHILE NOW.
BUT WHO WILL GIVE PRESENTS TO THE GOOD BOYS AND GIRLS...?
NO ONE.
BUT THAT MEANS...
TRAINING DV
Internal us
Only

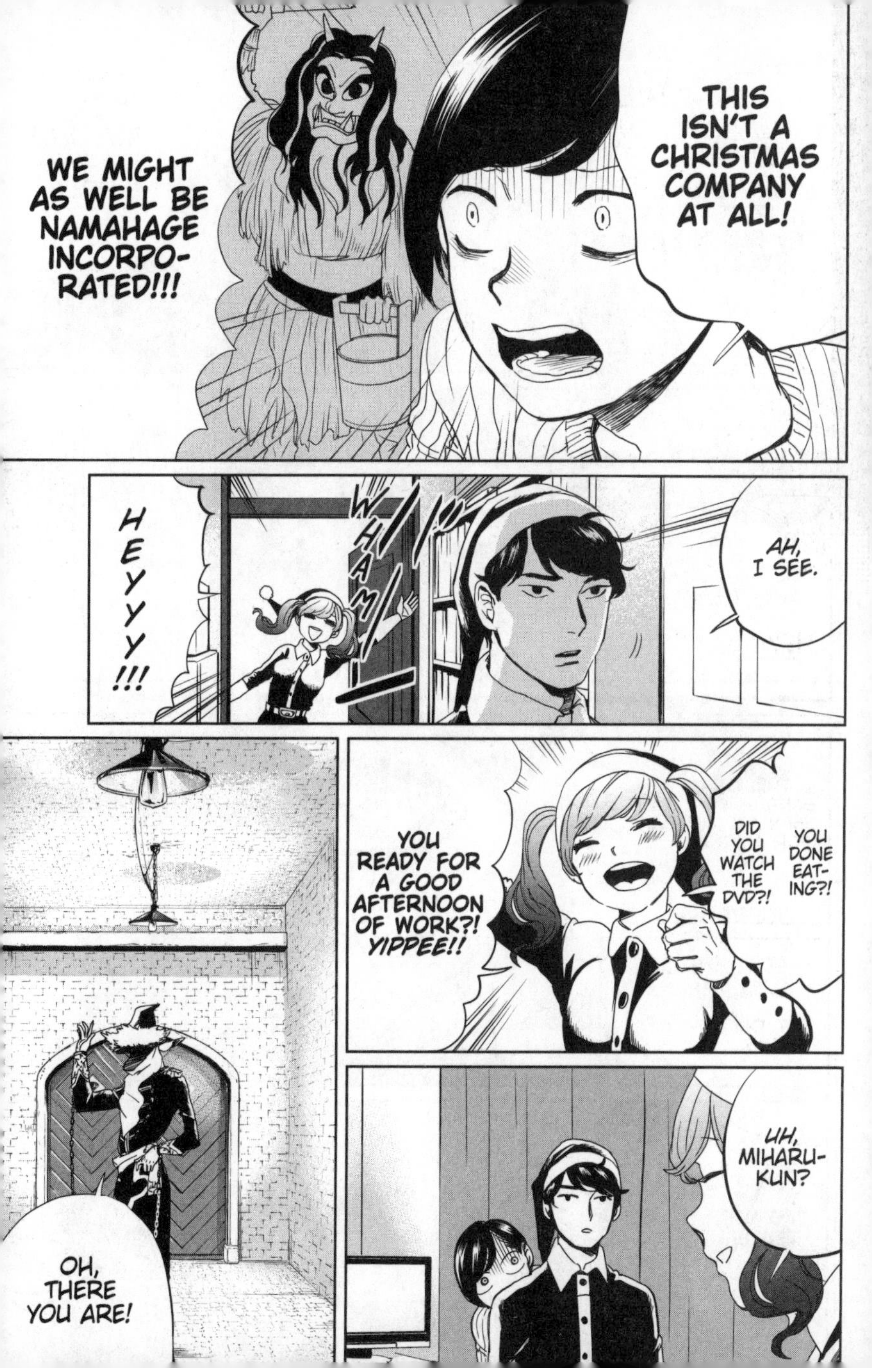
THIS ISN'T A CHRISTMAS COMPANY AT ALL!
WE MIGHT AS WELL BE NAMAHAGE INCORPO-RATED!!!
AH, I SEE.
WHAM
HEYYYY!!!
YOU DONE EAT-ING?!
DID YOU WATCH THE DVD?!
YOU READY FOR A GOOD AFTERNOON OF WORK?! YIPPEE!!
UH, MIHARU-KUN?
OH, THERE YOU ARE!

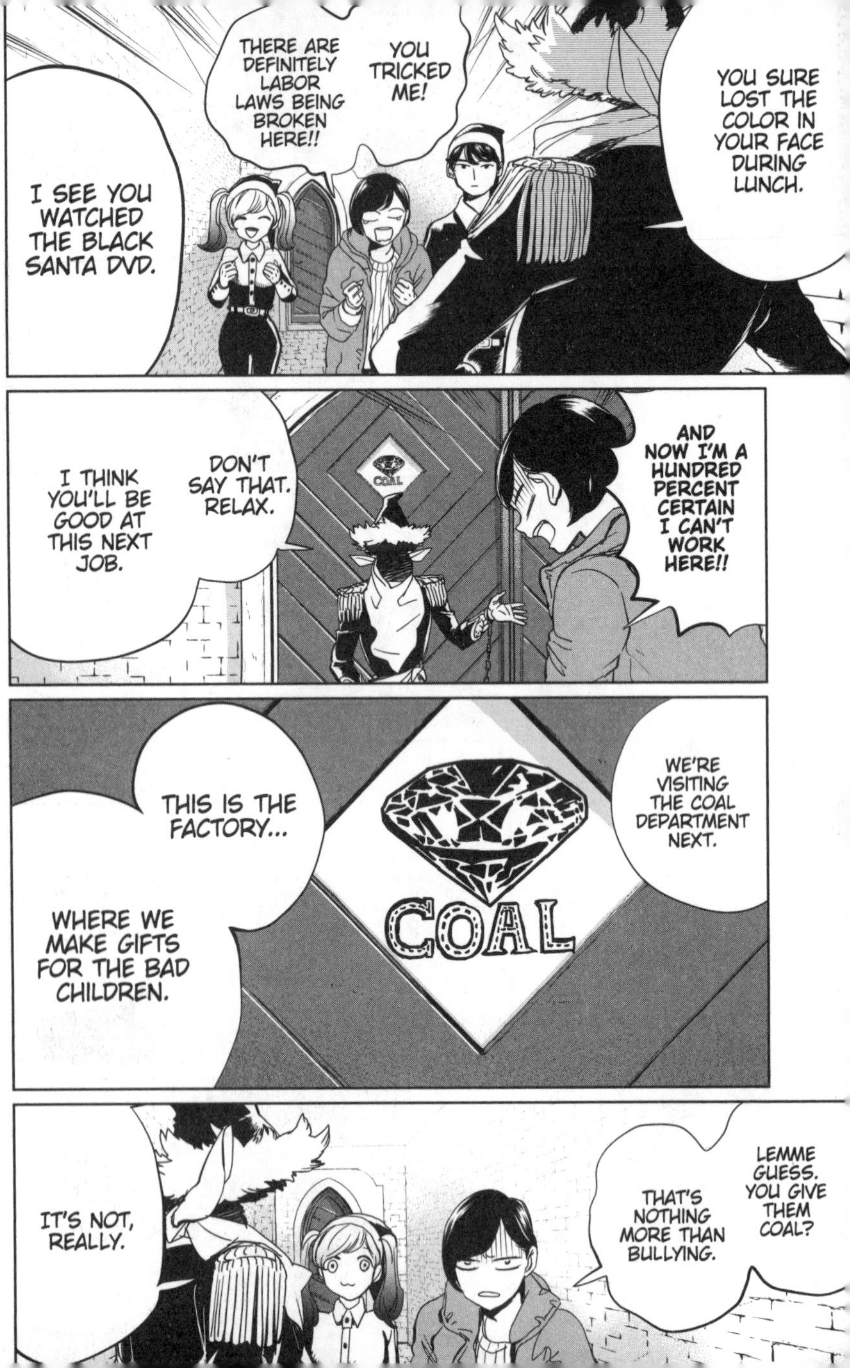
YOU SURE LOST THE COLOR IN YOUR FACE DURING LUNCH.
YOU TRICKED ME!
THERE ARE DEFINITELY LABOR LAWS BEING BROKEN HERE!!
I SEE YOU WATCHED THE BLACK SANTA DVD.
AND NOW I'M A HUNDRED PERCENT CERTAIN I CAN'T WORK HERE!!
COAL
DON'T SAY THAT. RELAX.
I THINK YOU'LL BE GOOD AT THIS NEXT JOB.
WE'RE VISITING THE COAL DEPARTMENT NEXT.
COAL
THIS IS THE FACTORY...
WHERE WE MAKE GIFTS FOR THE BAD CHILDREN.
LEMME GUESS. YOU GIVE THEM COAL?
THAT'S NOTHING MORE THAN BULLYING.
IT'S NOT, REALLY.

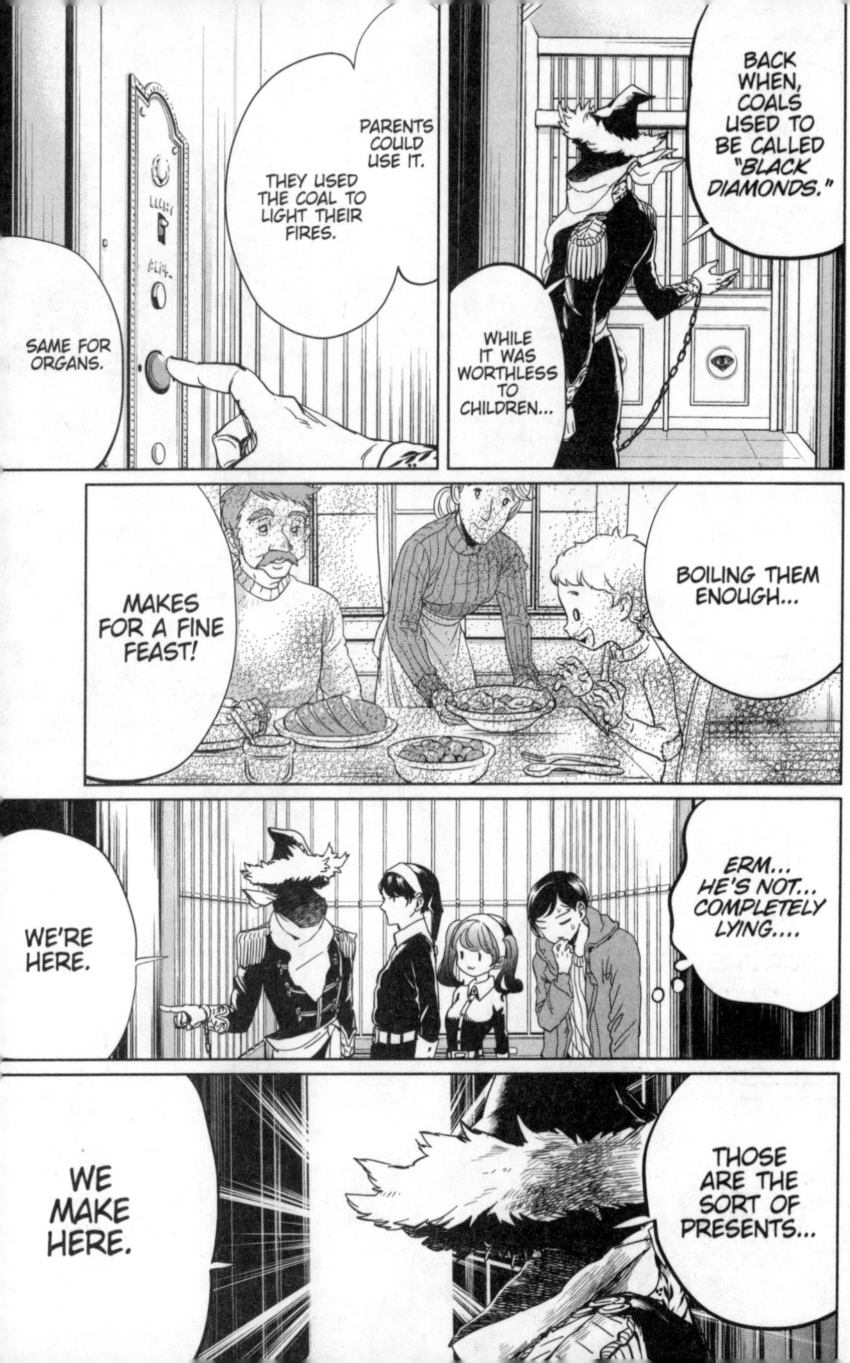
BACK WHEN, COALS USED TO BE CALLED "BLACK DIAMONDS."
WHILE IT WAS WORTHLESS TO CHILDREN...
PARENTS COULD USE IT.
THEY USED THE COAL TO LIGHT THEIR FIRES.
SAME FOR ORGANS.
BOILING THEM ENOUGH...
MAKES FOR A FINE FEAST!
ERM... HE'S NOT... COMPLETELY LYING....
WE'RE HERE.
THOSE ARE THE SORT OF PRESENTS...
WE MAKE HERE.

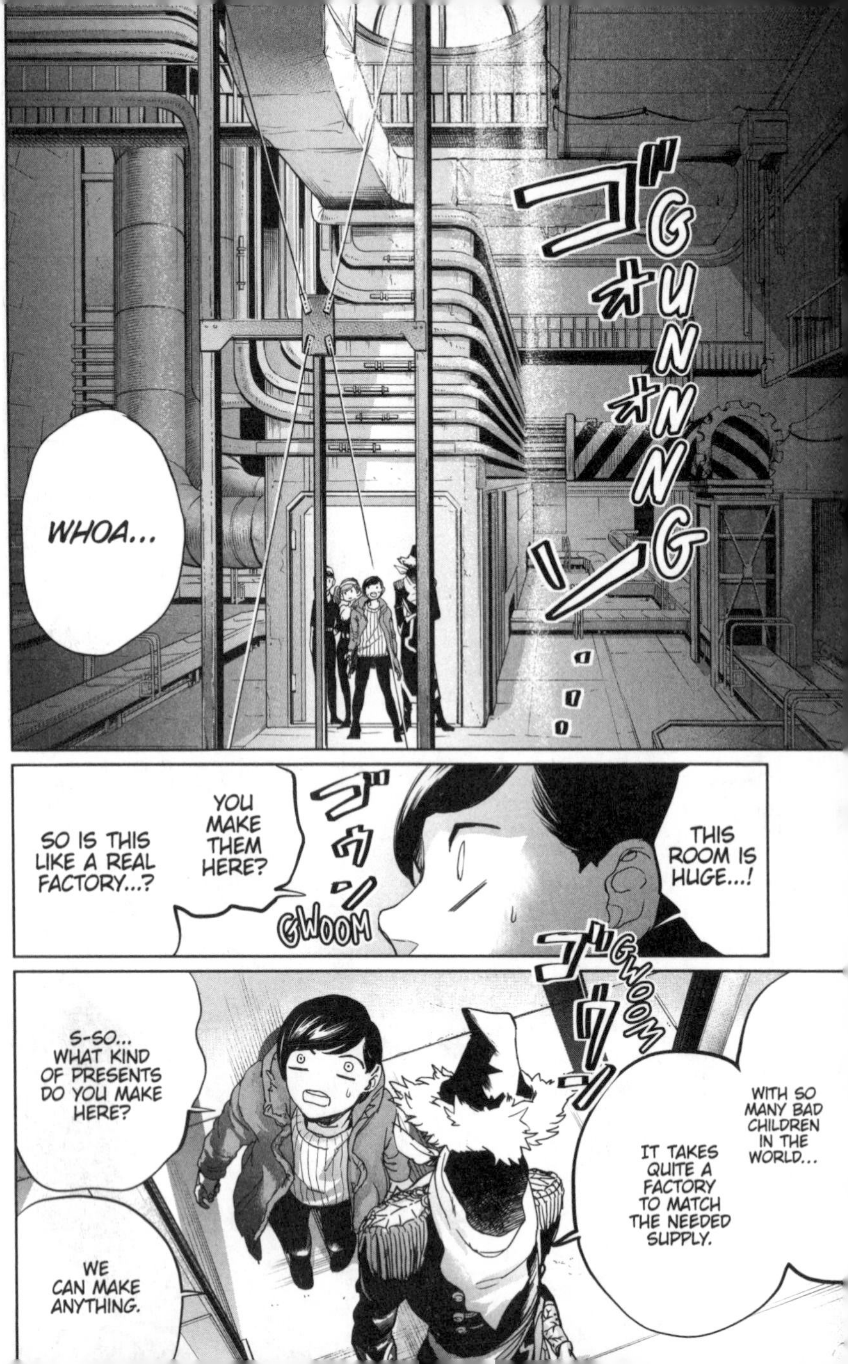
GUNNNG
WHOA...
THIS ROOM IS HUGE...!
YOU MAKE THEM HERE?
GWOOM
SO IS THIS LIKE A REAL FACTORY...?
GWOOM
WITH SO MANY BAD CHILDREN IN THE WORLD...
IT TAKES QUITE A FACTORY TO MATCH THE NEEDED SUPPLY.
S-SO... WHAT KIND OF PRESENTS DO YOU MAKE HERE?
WE CAN MAKE ANYTHING.

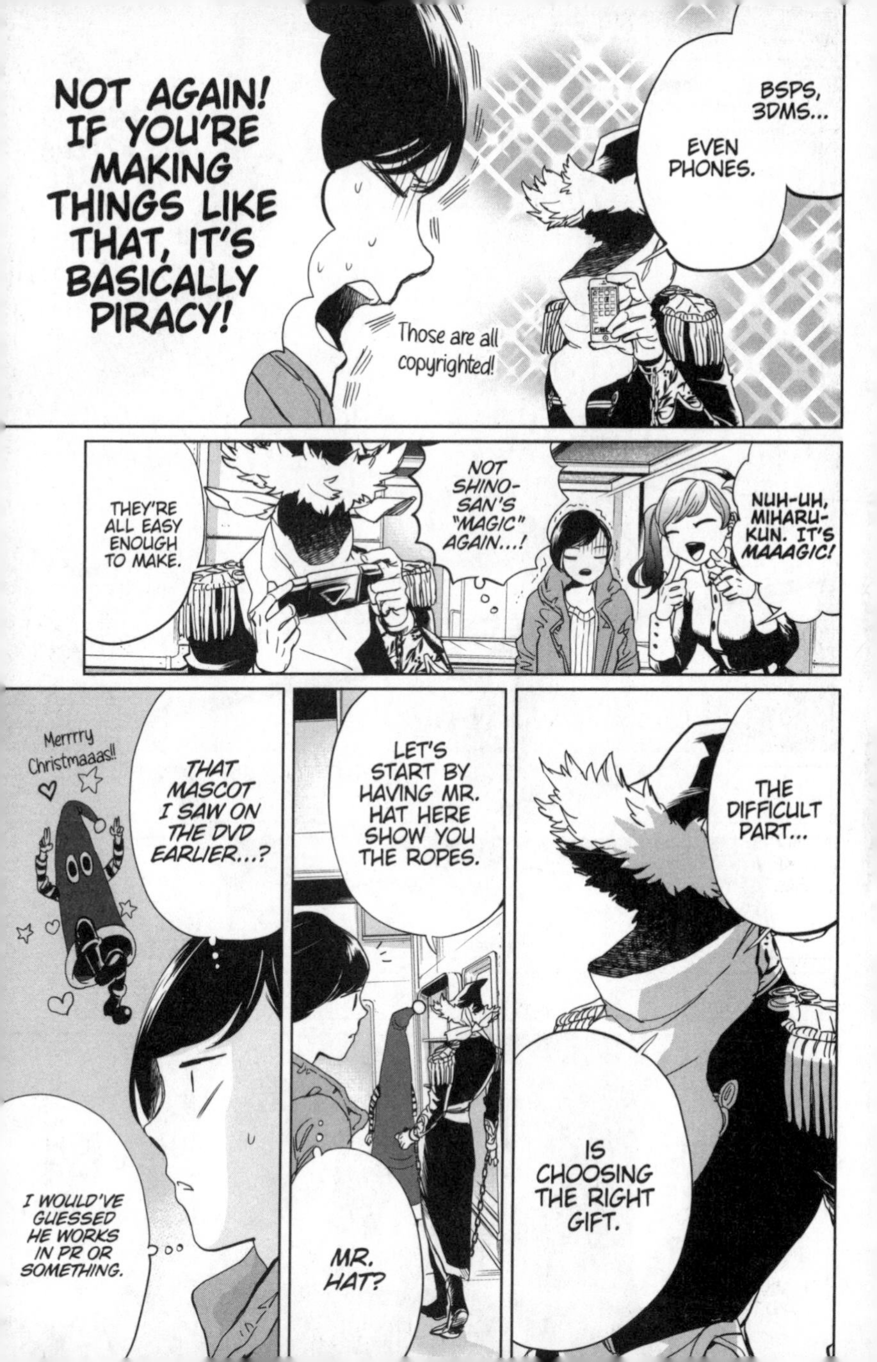
BSPS, 3DMS...
EVEN PHONES.
NOT AGAIN! IF YOU'RE MAKING THINGS LIKE THAT, IT'S BASICALLY PIRACY!
Those are all copyrighted!
NUH-UH, MIHARU-KUN. IT'S MAAAGIC!
NOT SHINO-SAN'S "MAGIC" AGAIN...!
THEY'RE ALL EASY ENOUGH TO MAKE.
THE DIFFICULT PART...
IS CHOOSING THE RIGHT GIFT.
LET'S START BY HAVING MR. HAT HERE SHOW YOU THE ROPES.
MR. HAT?
THAT MASCOT I SAW ON THE DVD EARLIER...?
Merrrry Christmaaas!!
I WOULD'VE GUESSED HE WORKS IN PR OR SOMETHING.

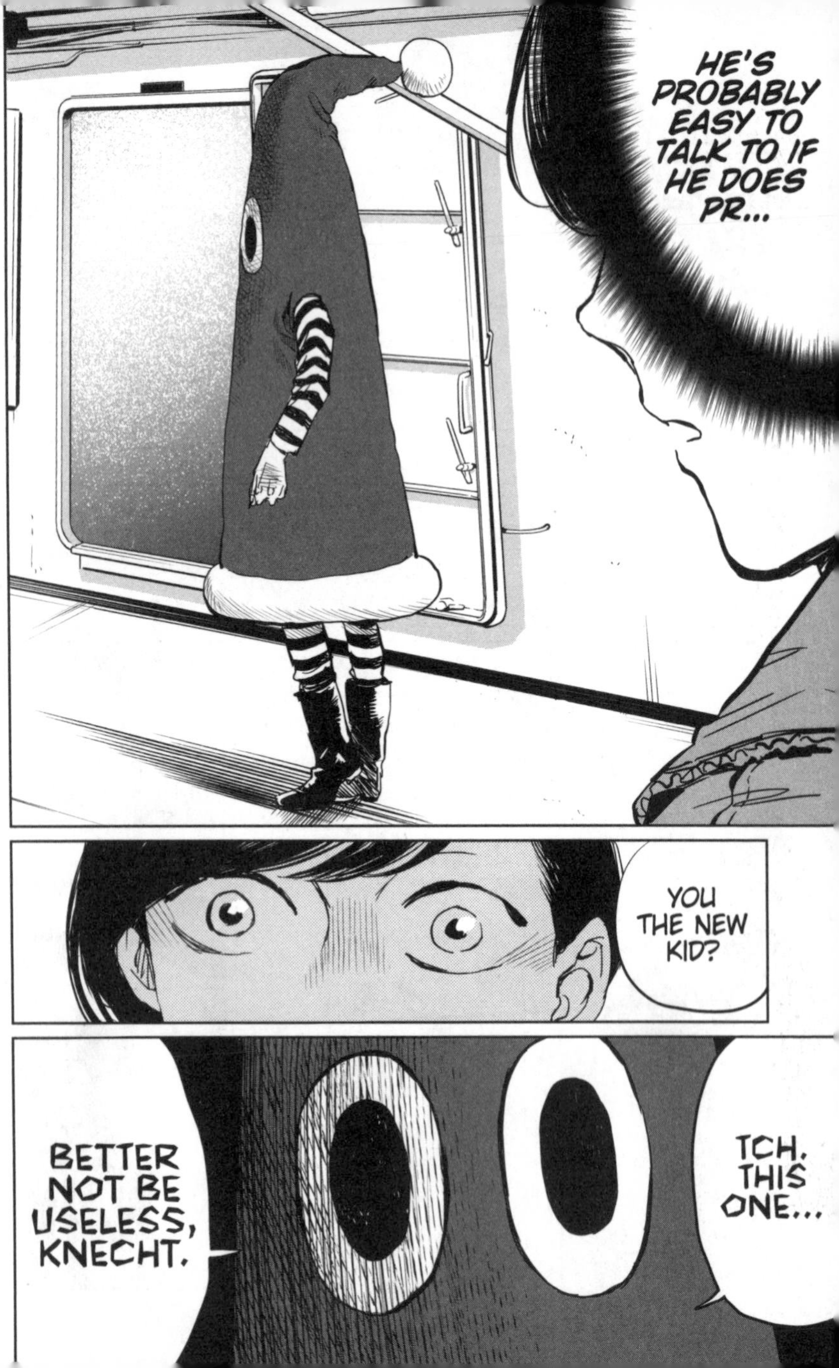
HE'S PROBABLY EASY TO TALK TO IF HE DOES PR...
YOU THE NEW KID?
TCH. THIS ONE...
BETTER NOT BE USELESS, KNECHT.

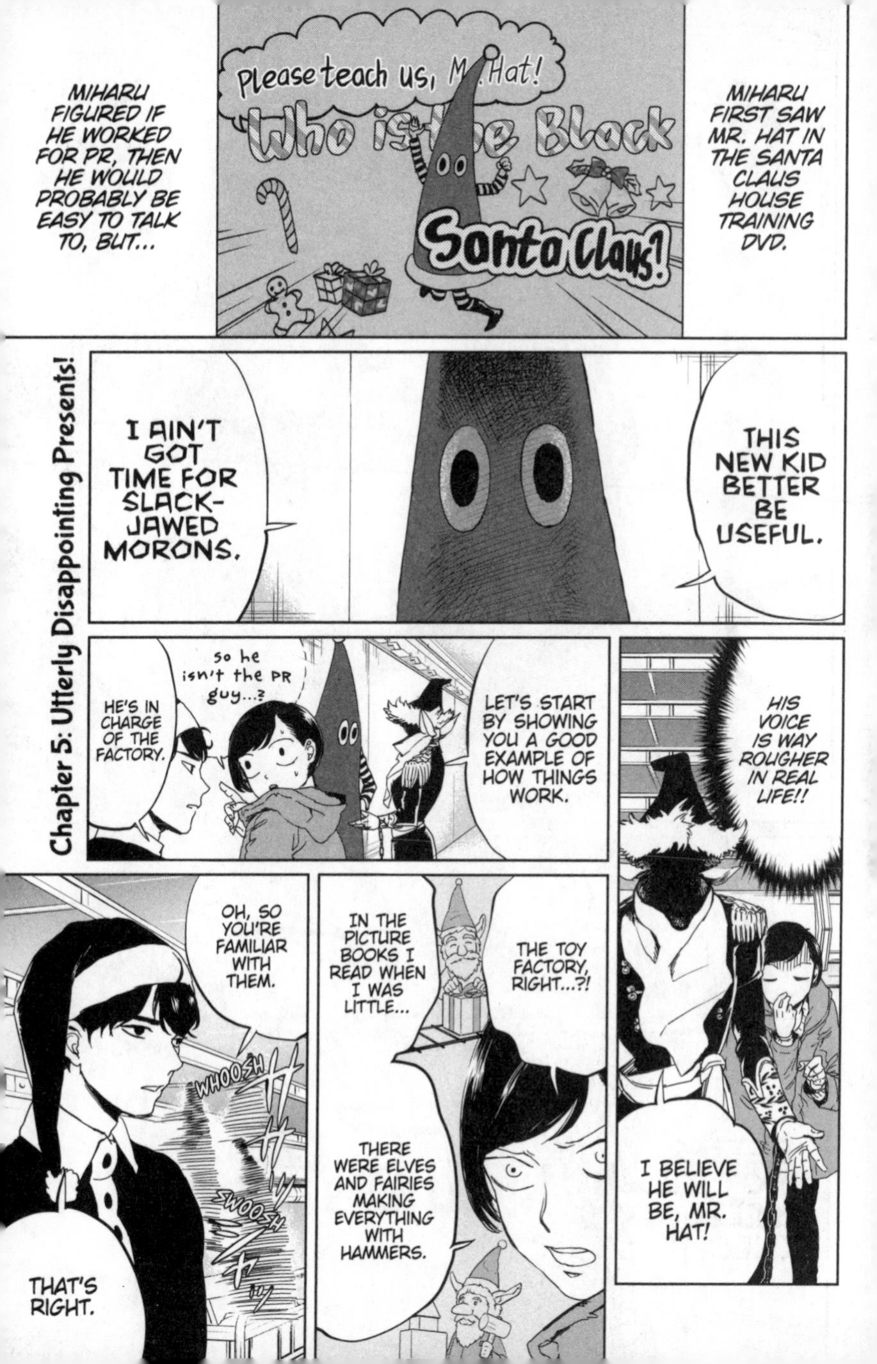
MIHARU FIRST SAW MR. HAT IN THE SANTA CLAUS HOUSE TRAINING DVD.
Please teach us, Mr. Hat!
Who is the Black Santa Claus!
MIHARU FIGURED IF HE WORKED FOR PR, THEN HE WOULD PROBABLY BE EASY TO TALK TO, BUT...
Chapter 5: Utterly Disappointing Presents!
THIS NEW KID BETTER BE USEFUL.
I AIN'T GOT TIME FOR SLACK-JAWED MORONS.
HIS VOICE IS WAY ROUGHER IN REAL LIFE!!
I BELIEVE HE WILL BE, MR. HAT!
LET'S START BY SHOWING YOU A GOOD EXAMPLE OF HOW THINGS WORK.
so he isn't the PR guy...?
HE'S IN CHARGE OF THE FACTORY.
THE TOY FACTORY, RIGHT...?!
IN THE PICTURE BOOKS I READ WHEN I WAS LITTLE...
THERE WERE ELVES AND FAIRIES MAKING EVERYTHING WITH HAMMERS.
OH, SO YOU'RE FAMILIAR WITH THEM.
WHOOSH
SWOOSH
THAT'S RIGHT.

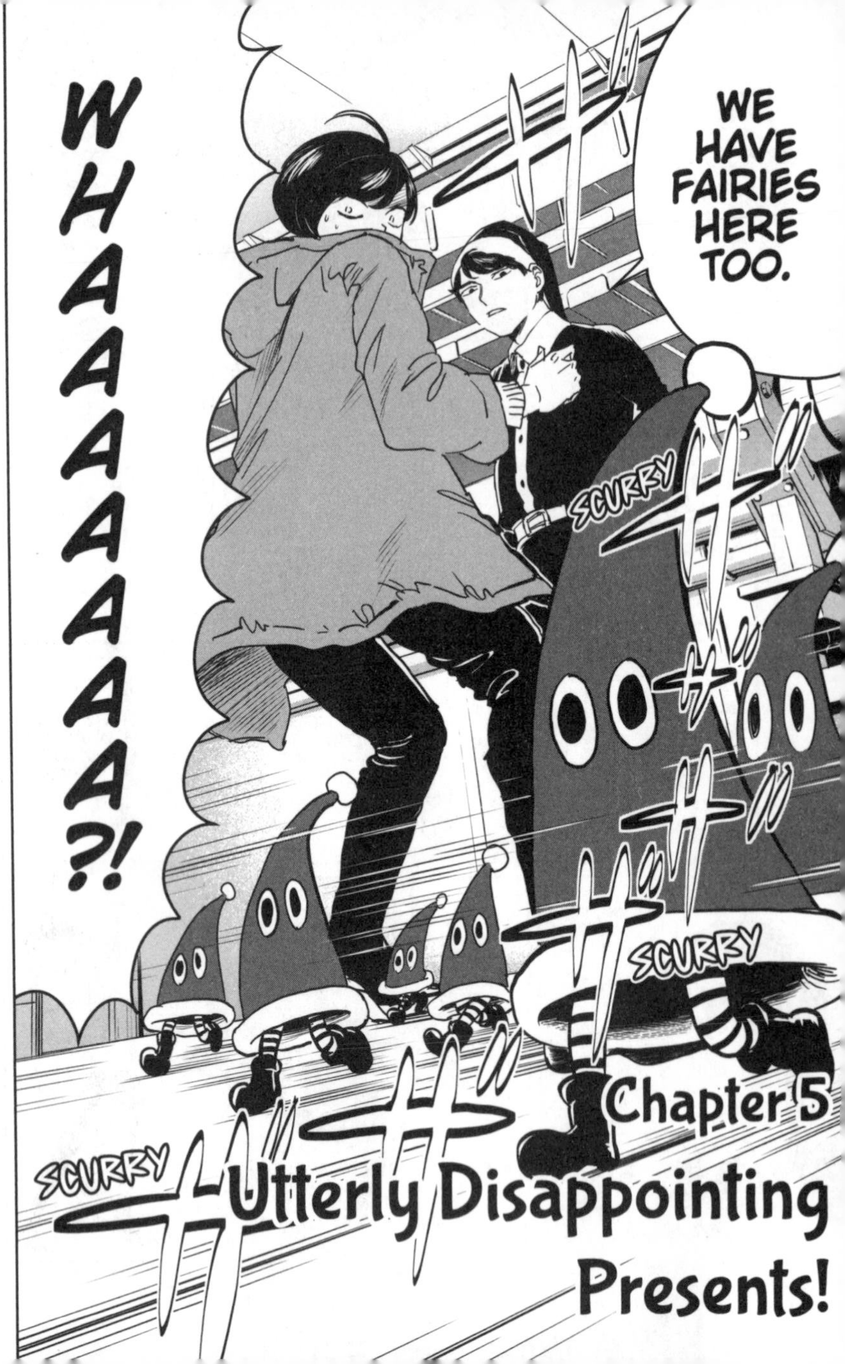
WE HAVE FAIRIES HERE TOO.
WHAAAAAAAAA?!
SCURRY
SCURRY
SCURRY
Chapter 5
Utterly Disappointing Presents!

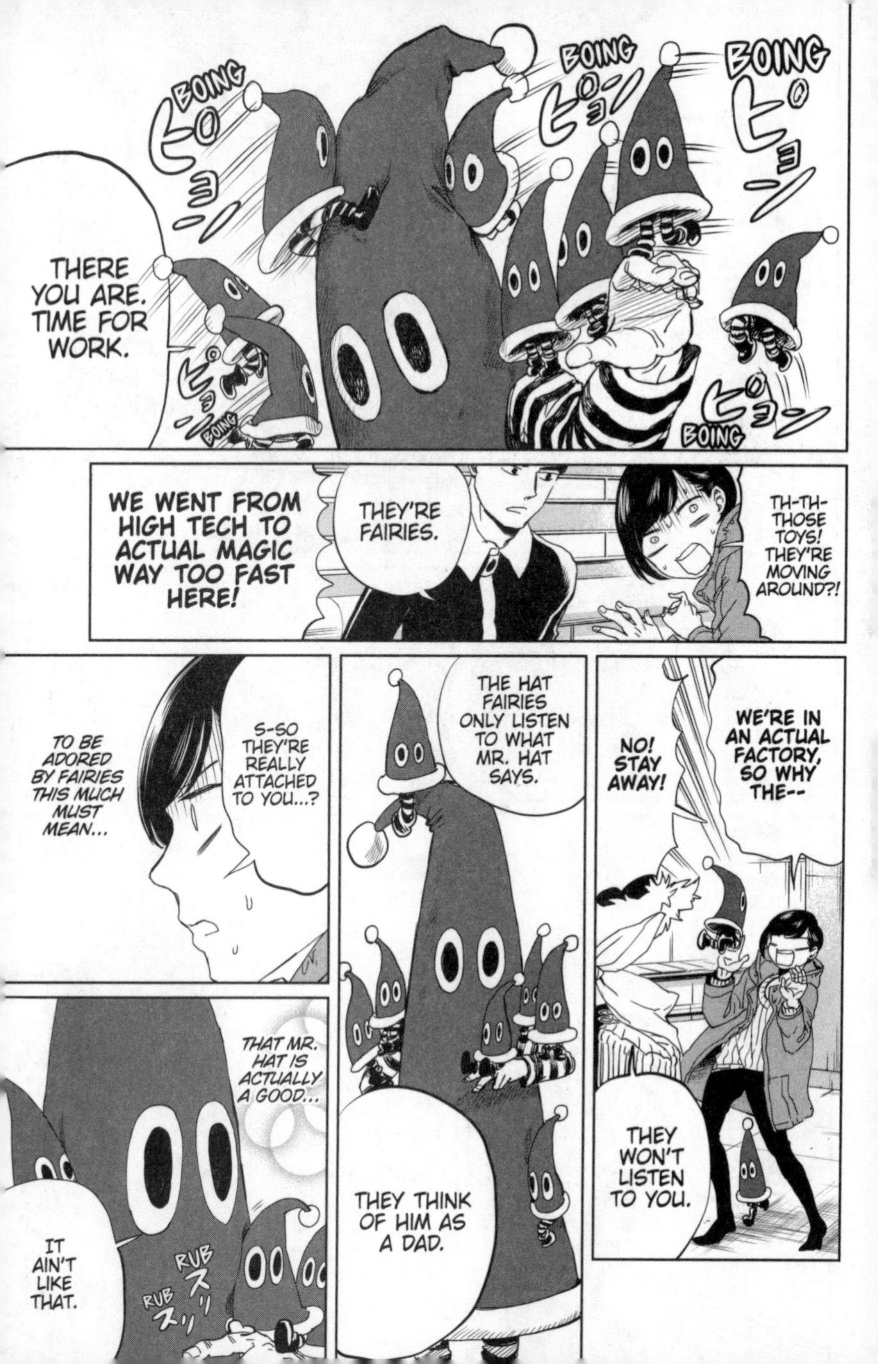

BOING
BOING
BOING
THERE YOU ARE. TIME FOR WORK.
BOING
BOING
TH-TH-THOSE TOYS! THEY'RE MOVING AROUND?!
THEY'RE FAIRIES.
WE WENT FROM HIGH TECH TO ACTUAL MAGIC WAY TOO FAST HERE!
WE'RE IN AN ACTUAL FACTORY, SO WHY THE--
NO! STAY AWAY!
THEY WON'T LISTEN TO YOU.
THE HAT FAIRIES ONLY LISTEN TO WHAT MR. HAT SAYS.
THEY THINK OF HIM AS A DAD.
S-SO THEY'RE REALLY ATTACHED TO YOU...?
TO BE ADORED BY FAIRIES THIS MUCH MUST MEAN...
THAT MR. HAT IS ACTUALLY A GOOD...
RUB
RUB
IT AIN'T LIKE THAT.

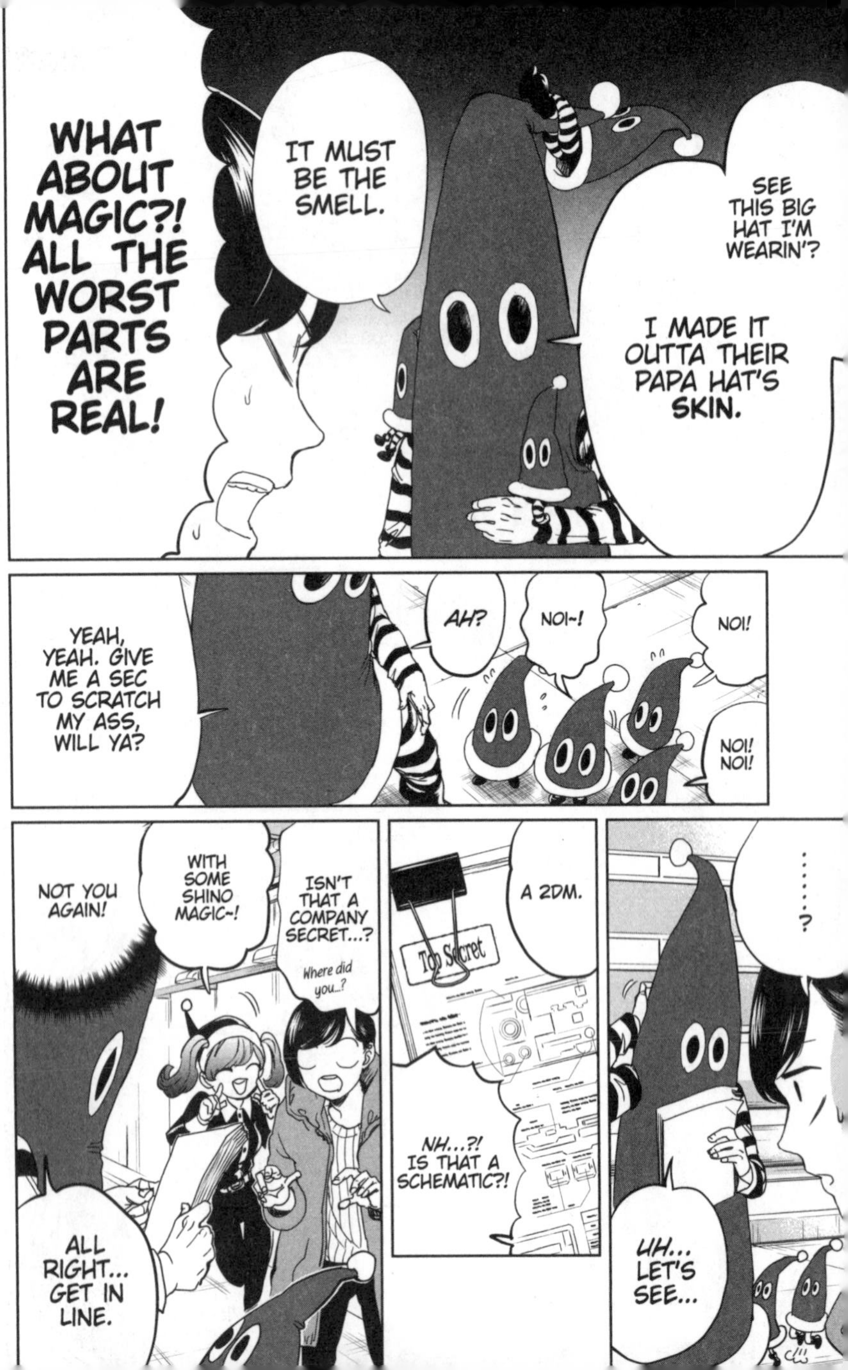
SEE THIS BIG HAT I'M WEARIN'?
I MADE IT OUTTA THEIR PAPA HAT'S SKIN.
IT MUST BE THE SMELL.
WHAT ABOUT MAGIC?! ALL THE WORST PARTS ARE REAL!
NOI!
NOI! NOI!
NOI~!
AH?
YEAH, YEAH. GIVE ME A SEC TO SCRATCH MY ASS, WILL YA?
......?
UH... LET'S SEE...
A 2DM.
Top Secret
NH...?! IS THAT A SCHEMATIC?!
ISN'T THAT A COMPANY SECRET...?
Where did you..?
WITH SOME SHINO MAGIC~!
NOT YOU AGAIN!
ALL RIGHT... GET IN LINE.

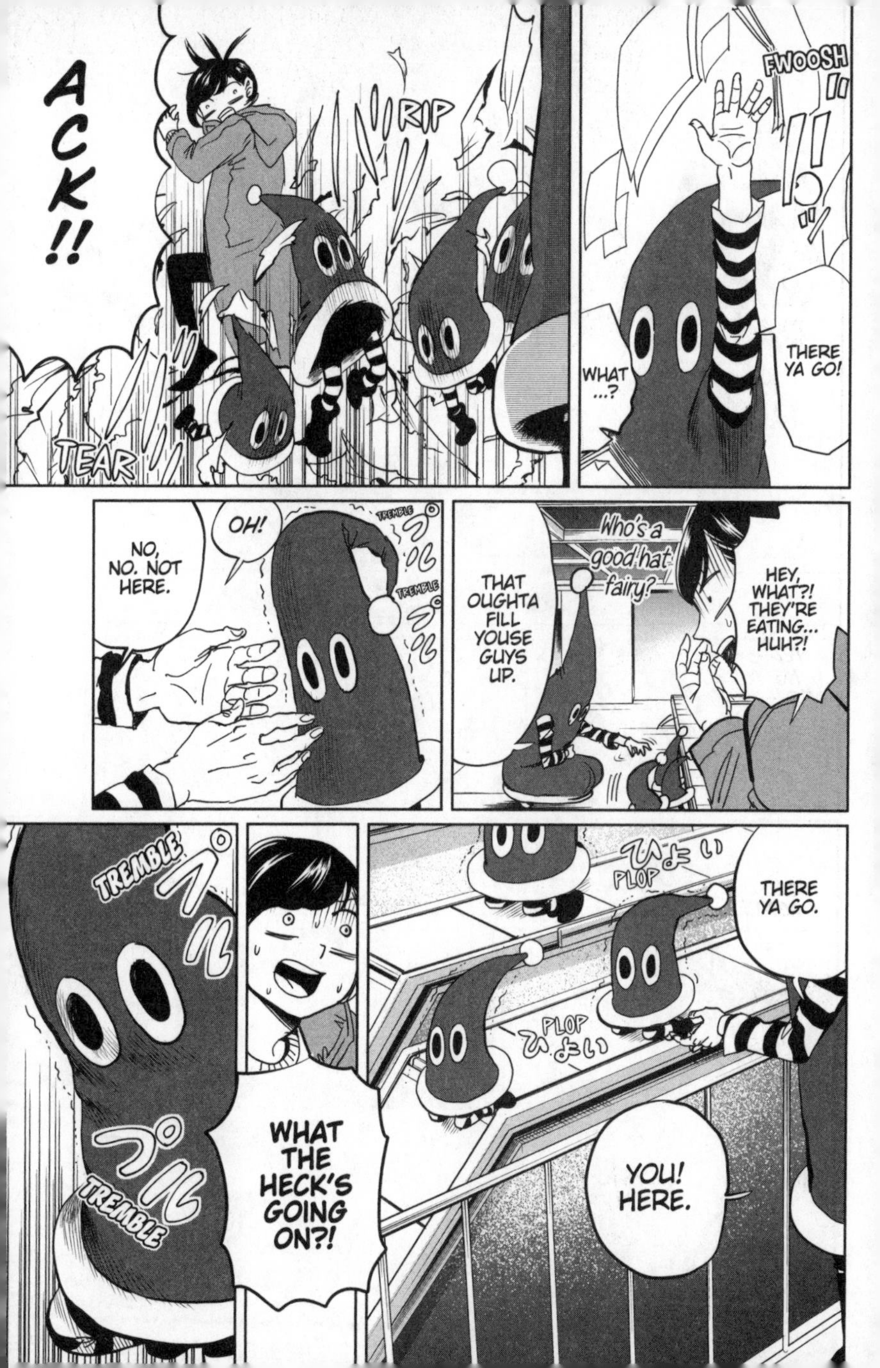
FWOOSH
THERE YA GO!
WHAT ...?
RIP
ACK!!
TEAR
HEY, WHAT?! THEY'RE EATING... HUH?!
Who's a good hat fairy?
THAT OUGHTA FILL YOUSE GUYS UP.
TREMBLE
TREMBLE
OH!
NO, NO. NOT HERE.
THERE YA GO.
PLOP
PLOP
YOU! HERE.
WHAT THE HECK'S GOING ON?!
TREMBLE
TREMBLE

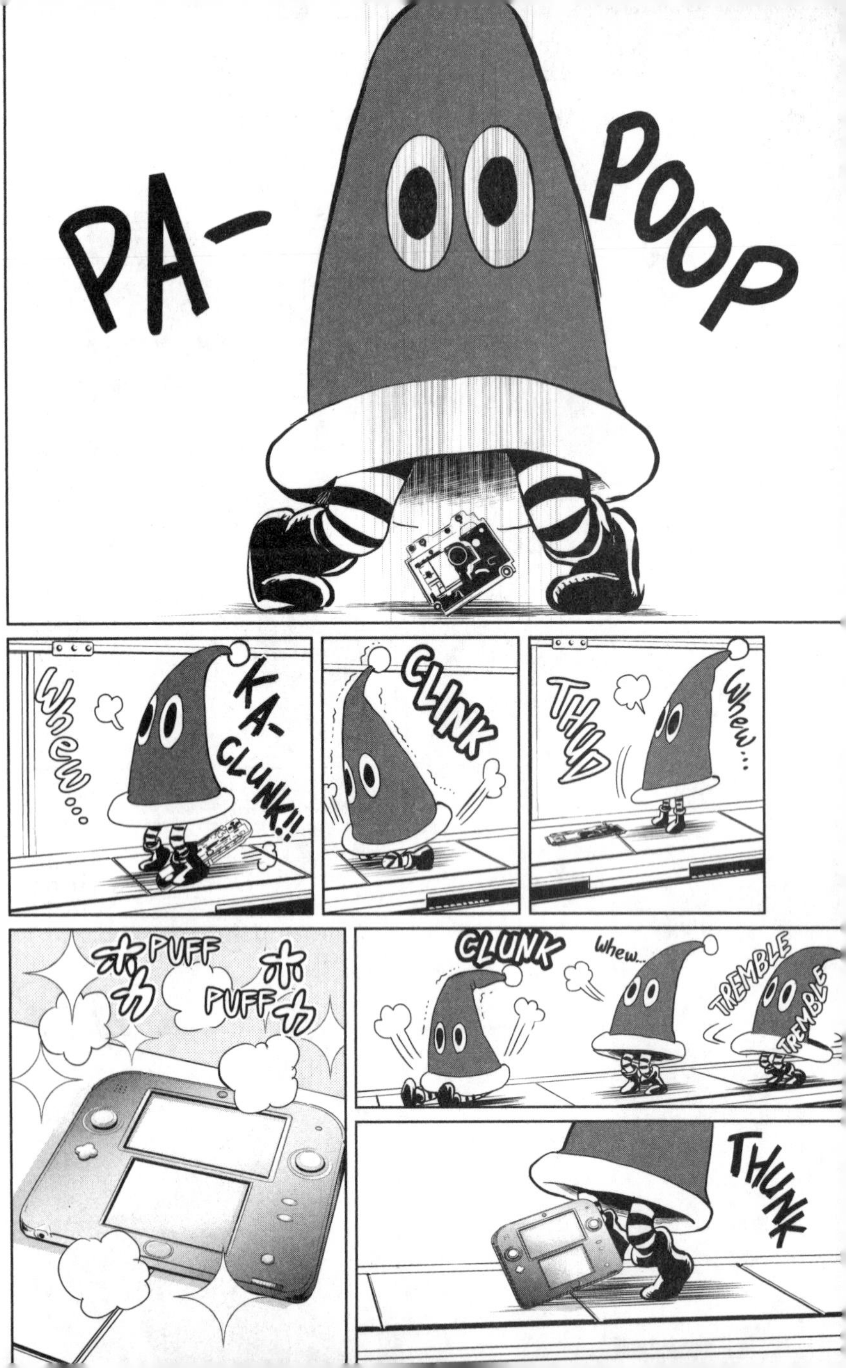
PA-
POOP
Whew...
THUD
CLINK
KA-CLUNK!!
Whew...
TREMBLE
TREMBLE
Whew...
CLUNK
THUNK
ホカ
PUFF
ホカ
PUFF

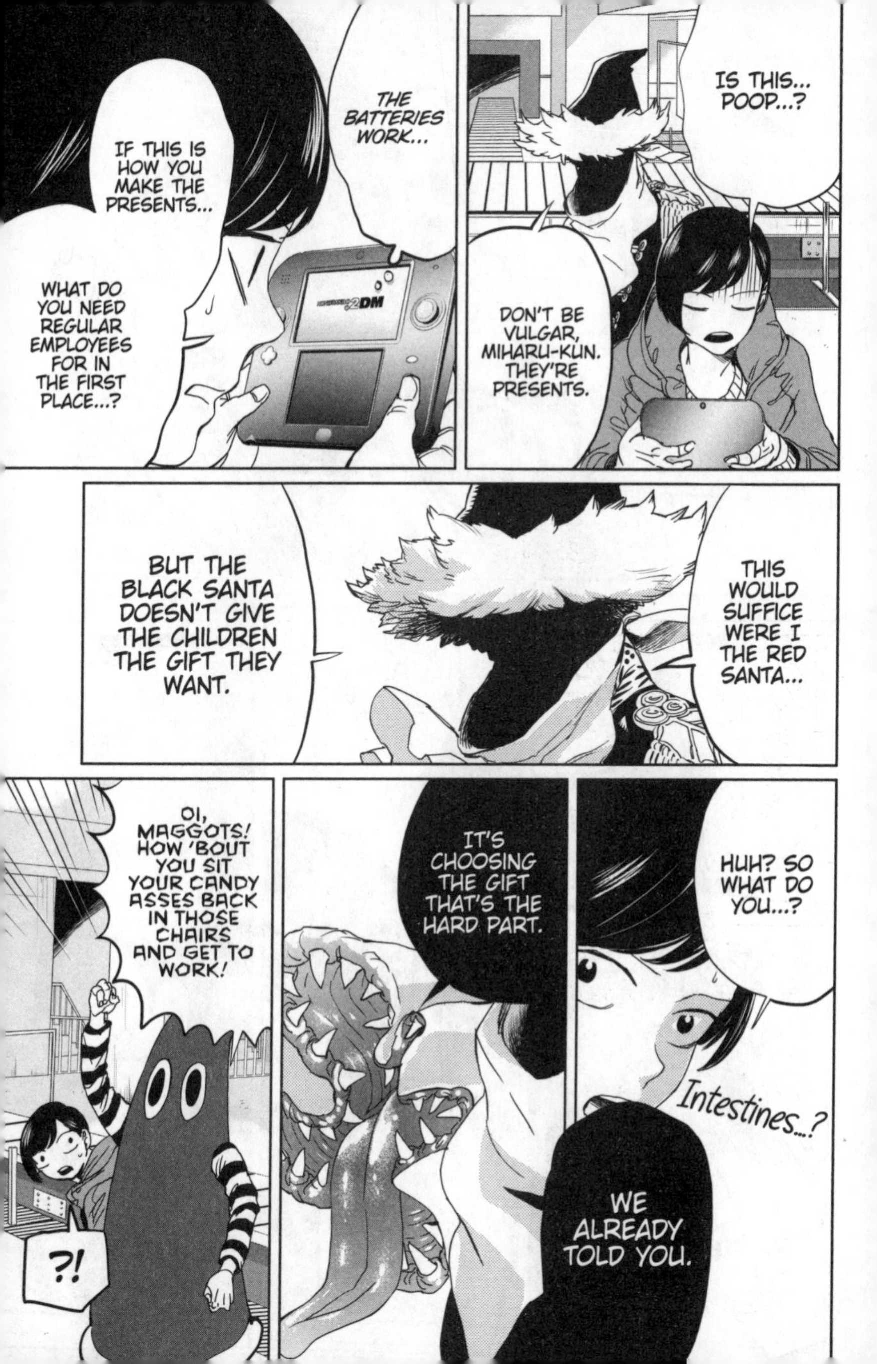

IS THIS... POOP...?
DON'T BE VULGAR, MIHARU-KUN. THEY'RE PRESENTS.
THE BATTERIES WORK...
IF THIS IS HOW YOU MAKE THE PRESENTS...
WHAT DO YOU NEED REGULAR EMPLOYEES FOR IN THE FIRST PLACE...?
THIS WOULD SUFFICE WERE I THE RED SANTA...
BUT THE BLACK SANTA DOESN'T GIVE THE CHILDREN THE GIFT THEY WANT.
HUH? SO WHAT DO YOU...?
Intestines...?
WE ALREADY TOLD YOU.
IT'S CHOOSING THE GIFT THAT'S THE HARD PART.
OI, MAGGOTS! HOW 'BOUT YOU SIT YOUR CANDY ASSES BACK IN THOSE CHAIRS AND GET TO WORK!
?!

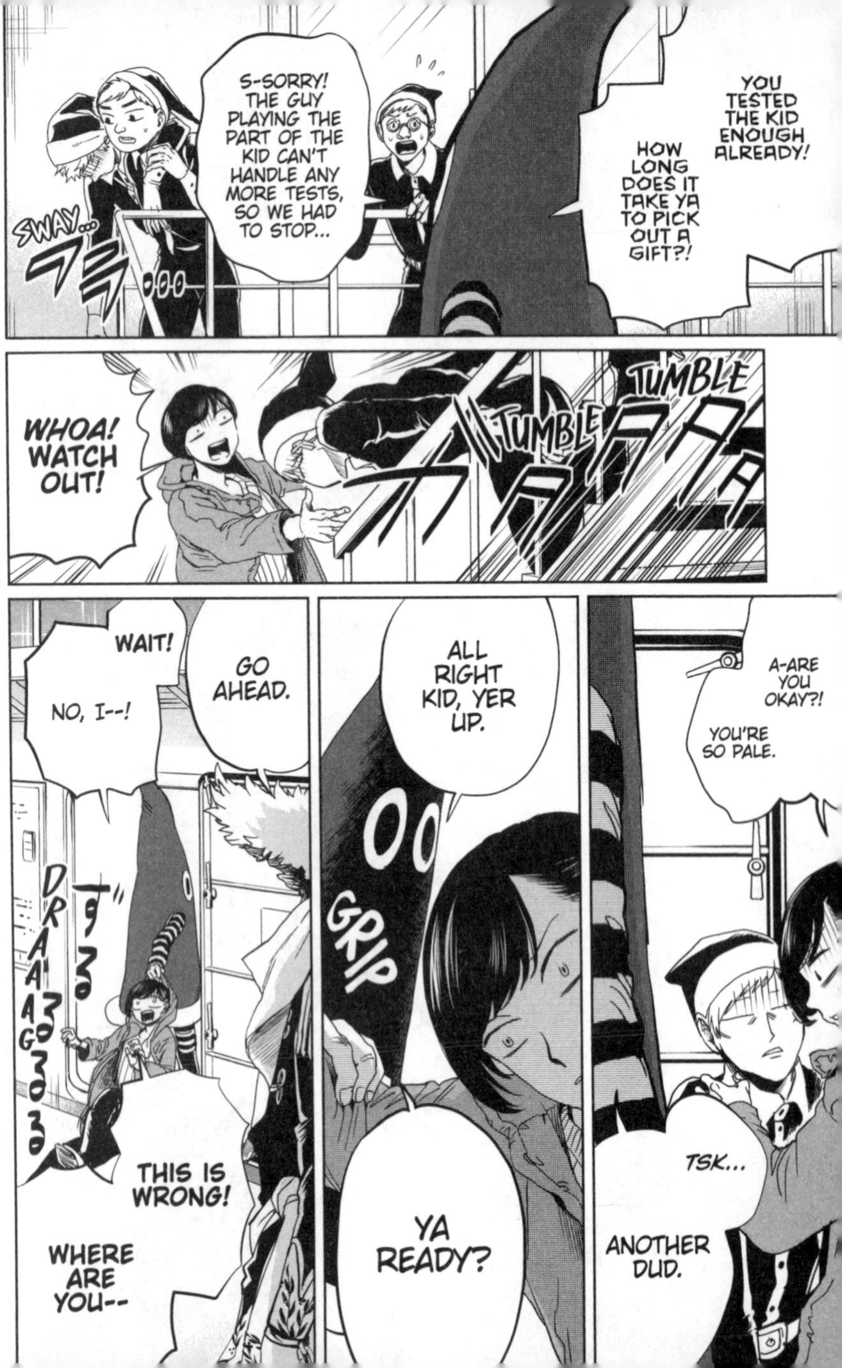
YOU TESTED THE KID ENOUGH ALREADY!
HOW LONG DOES IT TAKE YA TO PICK OUT A GIFT?!
S-SORRY! THE GUY PLAYING THE PART OF THE KID CAN'T HANDLE ANY MORE TESTS, SO WE HAD TO STOP...
SWAY...
TUMBLE
TUMBLE
WHOA! WATCH OUT!
A-ARE YOU OKAY?!
YOU'RE SO PALE.
TSK...
ANOTHER DUD.
ALL RIGHT KID, YER UP.
GRIP
YA READY?
GO AHEAD.
WAIT!
NO, I--!
DRAAAAG
THIS IS WRONG!
WHERE ARE YOU--

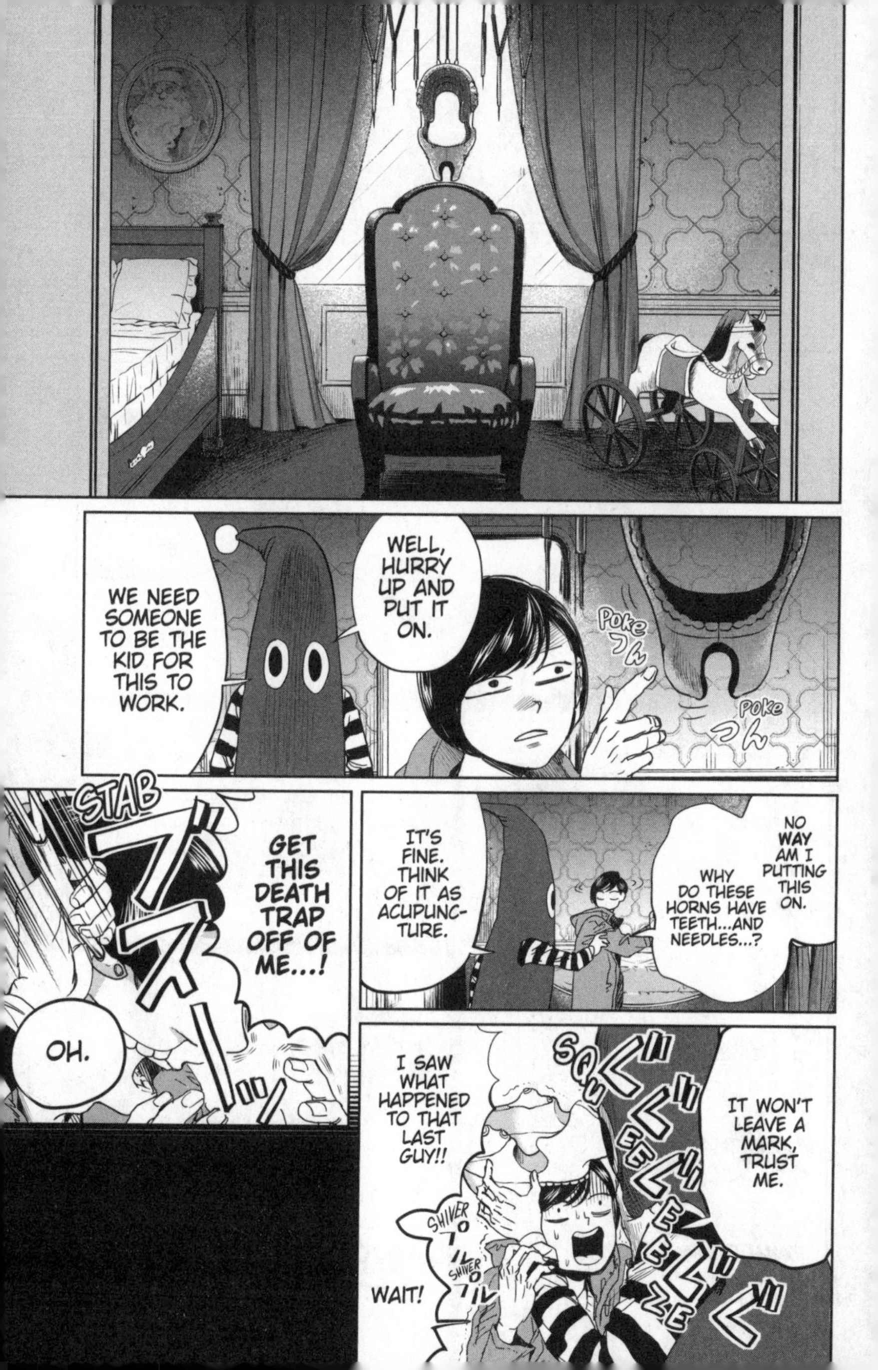
Poke
つん
WELL, HURRY UP AND PUT IT ON.
WE NEED SOMEONE TO BE THE KID FOR THIS TO WORK.
Poke
つん
NO WAY AM I PUTTING THIS ON.
WHY DO THESE HORNS HAVE TEETH...AND NEEDLES...?
IT'S FINE. THINK OF IT AS ACUPUNCTURE.
IT WON'T LEAVE A MARK, TRUST ME.
SQUEEEEZE
I SAW WHAT HAPPENED TO THAT LAST GUY!!
SHIVER
SHIVER
WAIT!
STAB
GET THIS DEATH TRAP OFF OF ME...!
OH.

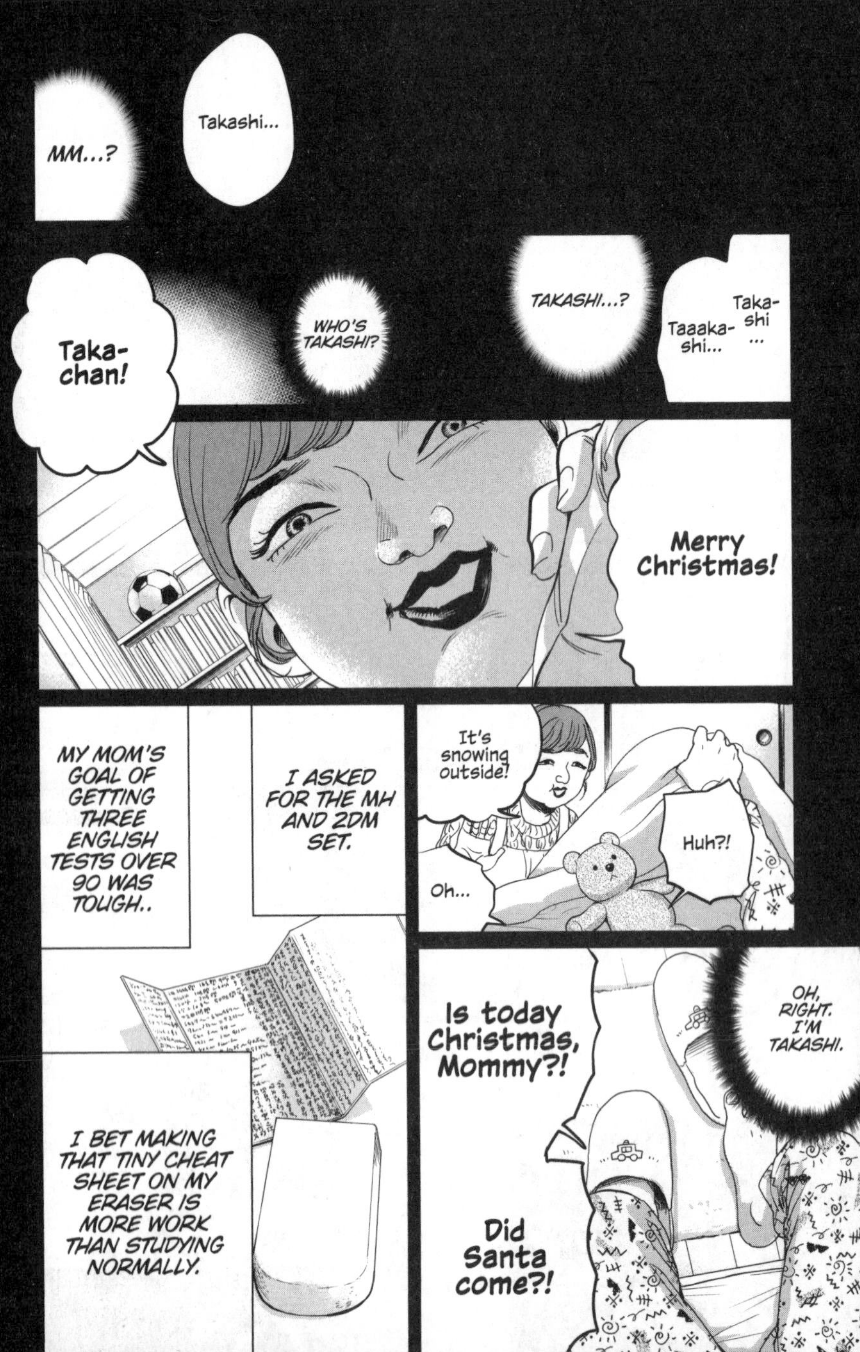
Takashi...
MM...?
Taka-shi...
Taaaka-shi...
TAKASHI...?
WHO'S TAKASHI?
Taka-chan!
Merry Christmas!
Huh?!
It's snowing outside!
Oh...
I ASKED FOR THE MH AND 2DM SET.
MY MOM'S GOAL OF GETTING THREE ENGLISH TESTS OVER 90 WAS TOUGH..
OH, RIGHT. I'M TAKASHI.
Is today Christmas, Mommy?!
Did Santa come?!
I BET MAKING THAT TINY CHEAT SHEET ON MY ERASER IS MORE WORK THAN STUDYING NORMALLY.

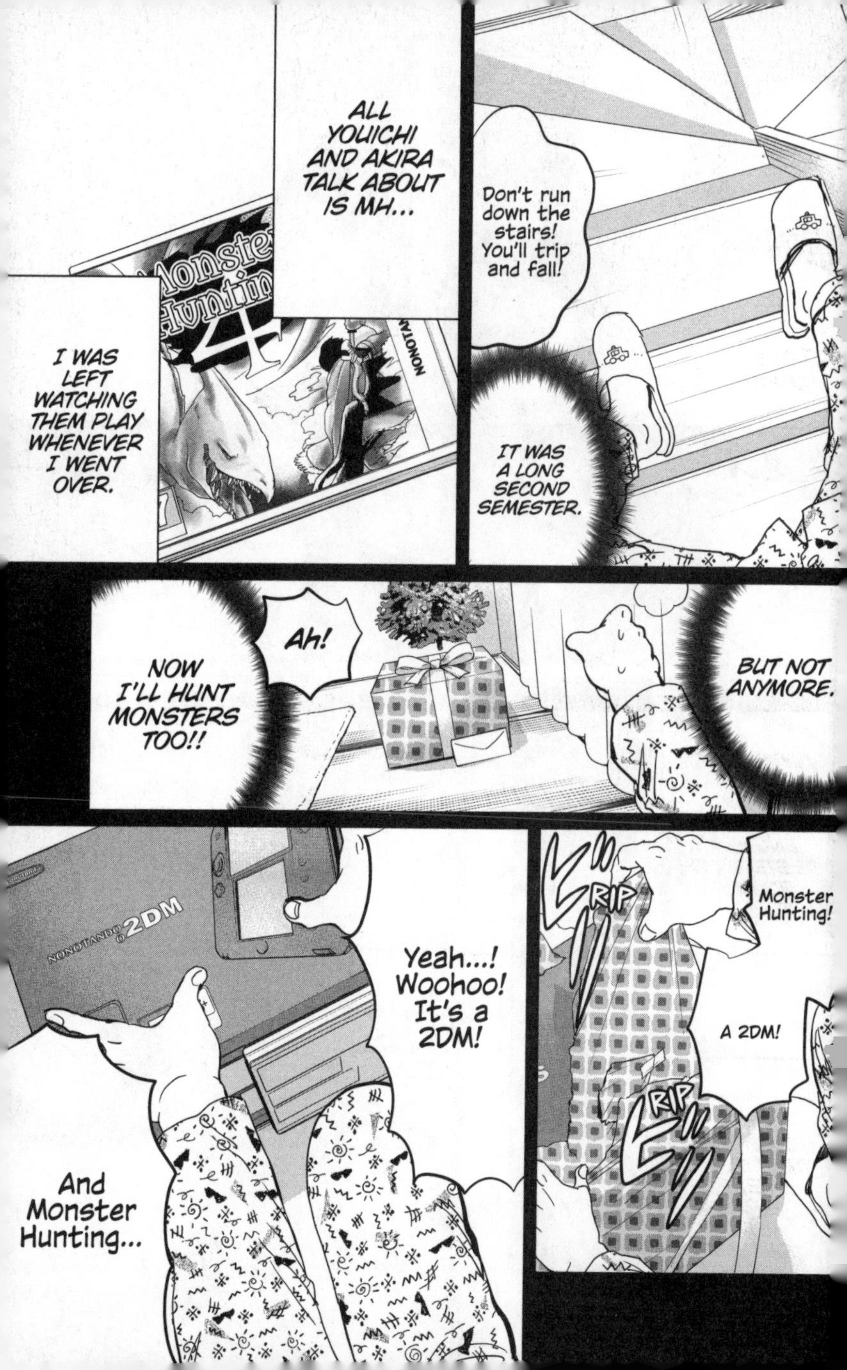

Don't run down the stairs! You'll trip and fall!
IT WAS A LONG SECOND SEMESTER.
ALL YOUICHI AND AKIRA TALK ABOUT IS MH...
I WAS LEFT WATCHING THEM PLAY WHENEVER I WENT OVER.
BUT NOT ANYMORE.
Ah!
NOW I'LL HUNT MONSTERS TOO!!
RIP
Monster Hunting!
A 2DM!
RIP
NONOTANDO 2DM
Yeah...! Woohoo! It's a 2DM!
And Monster Hunting...

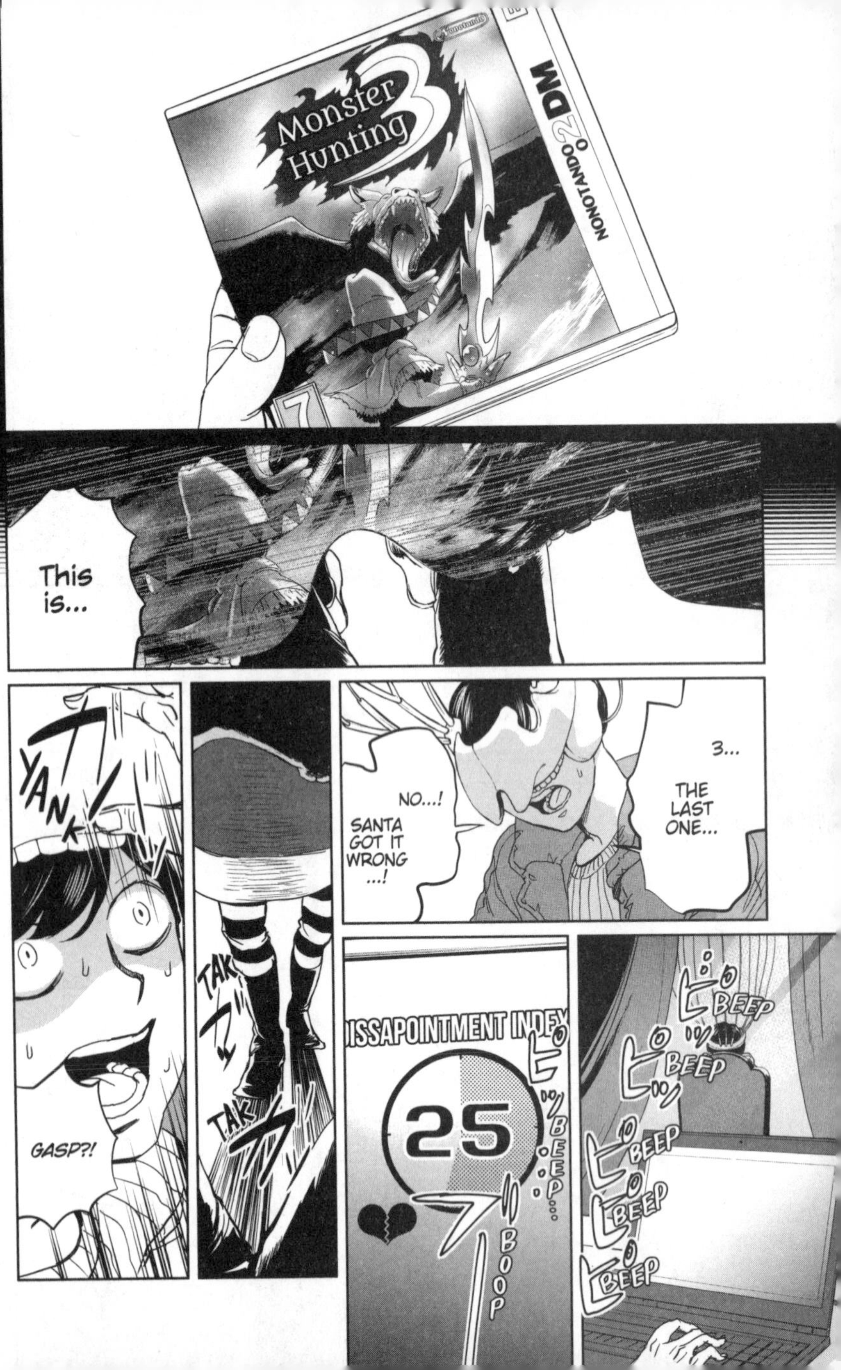
Monster Hunting 3
NONOTANDO 2DM
This is...
3...
THE LAST ONE...
NO...! SANTA GOT IT WRONG...!
BEEP
BEEP
BEEP
BEEP
BEEP
DISSAPOINTMENT INDEX
25
BEEP...
BOOP
TAK
TAK
YANK
GASP?!

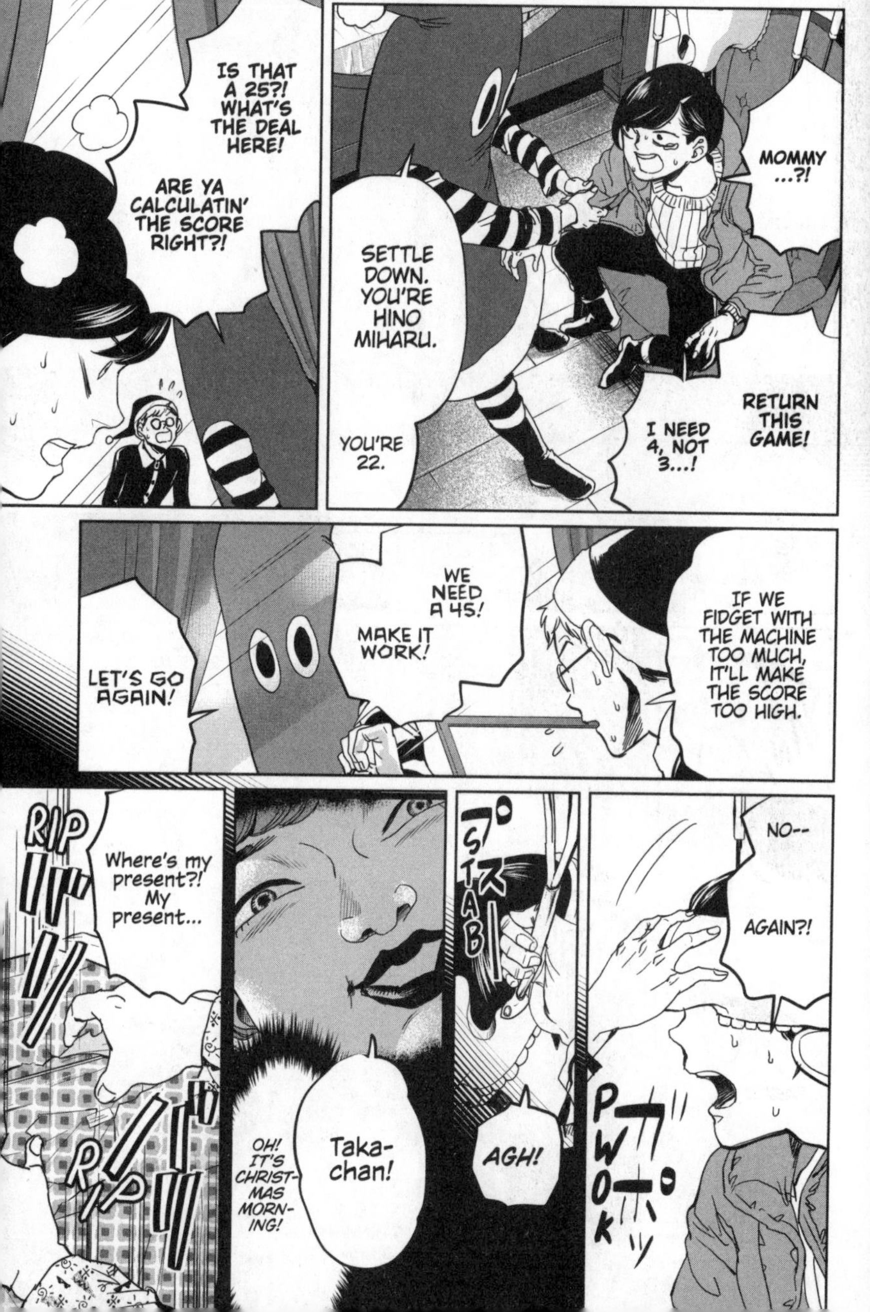
MOMMY ...?!
RETURN THIS GAME!
I NEED 4, NOT 3...!
SETTLE DOWN. YOU'RE HINO MIHARU.
YOU'RE 22.
IS THAT A 25?! WHAT'S THE DEAL HERE!
ARE YA CALCULATIN' THE SCORE RIGHT?!
IF WE FIDGET WITH THE MACHINE TOO MUCH, IT'LL MAKE THE SCORE TOO HIGH.
WE NEED A 45!
MAKE IT WORK!
LET'S GO AGAIN!
NO--
AGAIN?!
PWOK
STAB
AGH!
Taka-chan!
OH! IT'S CHRIST-MAS MORN-ING!
RIP
Where's my present?! My present...
RIP

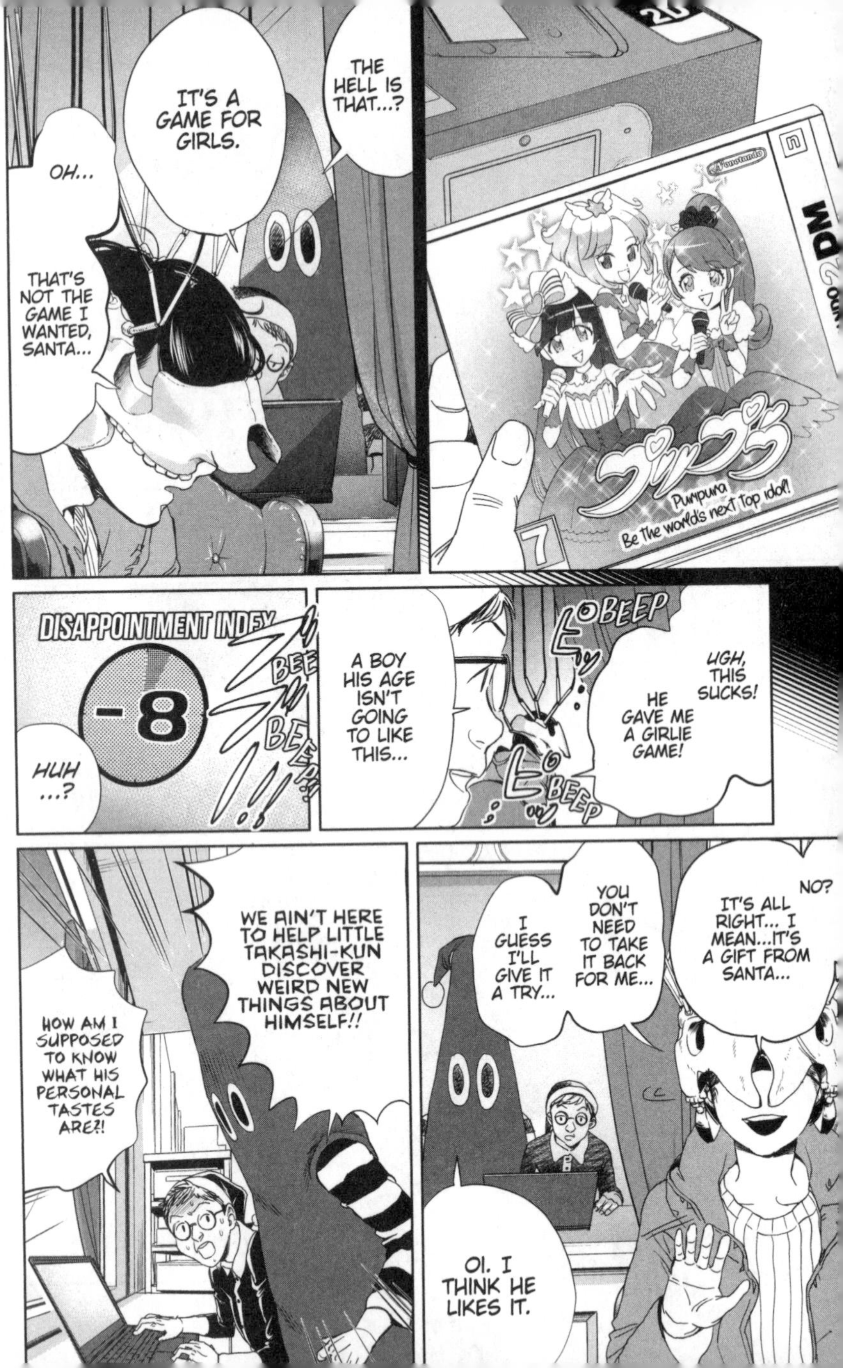

DM
Purupura
Be the world's next top idol!
THE HELL IS THAT...?
IT'S A GAME FOR GIRLS.
OH...
THAT'S NOT THE GAME I WANTED, SANTA...
BEEP
UGH, THIS SUCKS!
HE GAVE ME A GIRLIE GAME!
BEEP
A BOY HIS AGE ISN'T GOING TO LIKE THIS...
DISAPPOINTMENT INDEX
-8
BEEP
BEEP!!
HUH...?
NO?
IT'S ALL RIGHT... I MEAN...IT'S A GIFT FROM SANTA...
YOU DON'T NEED TO TAKE IT BACK FOR ME...
I GUESS I'LL GIVE IT A TRY...
OI. I THINK HE LIKES IT.
WE AIN'T HERE TO HELP LITTLE TAKASHI-KUN DISCOVER WEIRD NEW THINGS ABOUT HIMSELF!!
HOW AM I SUPPOSED TO KNOW WHAT HIS PERSONAL TASTES ARE?!

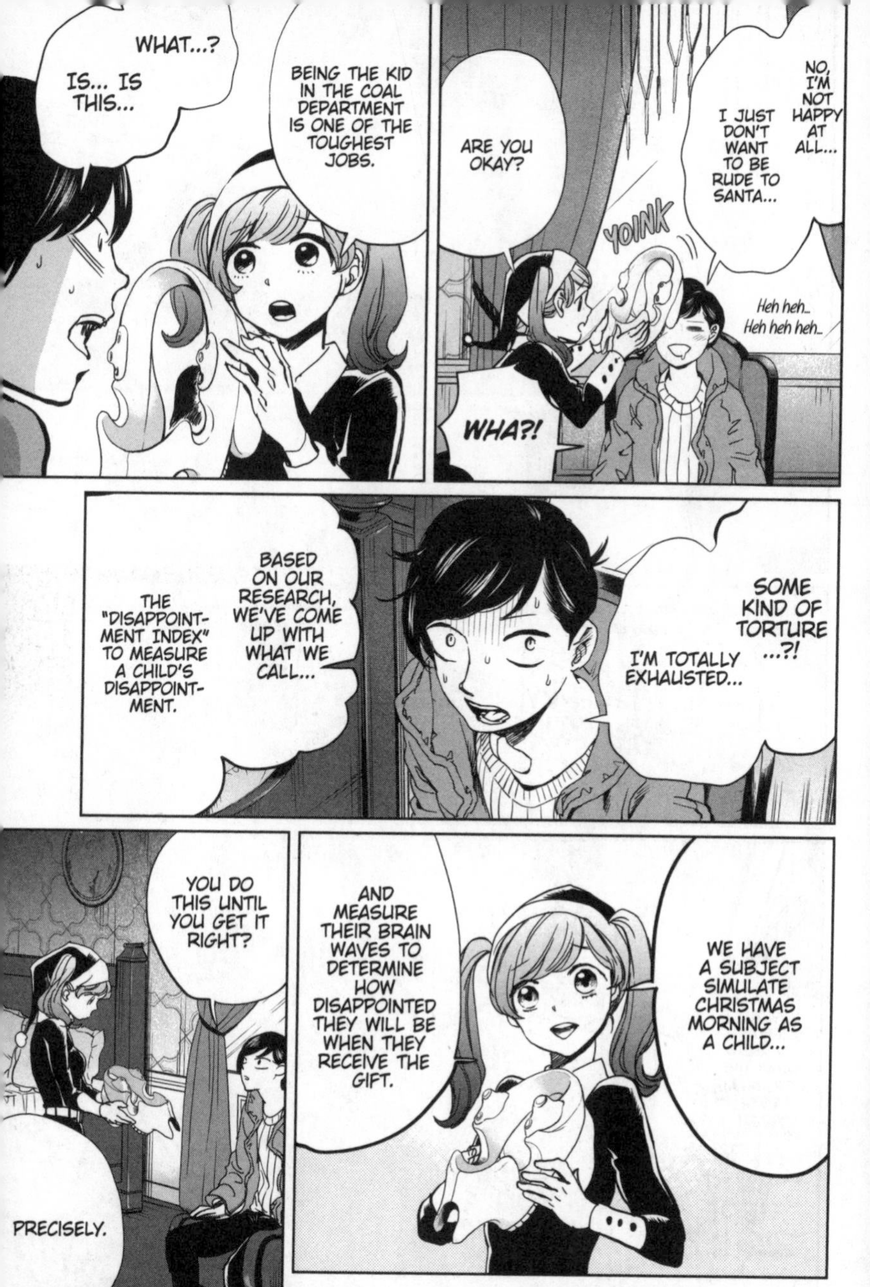
NO, I'M NOT HAPPY AT ALL...
I JUST DON'T WANT TO BE RUDE TO SANTA...
ARE YOU OKAY?
YOINK
Heh heh... Heh heh heh...
WHA?!
BEING THE KID IN THE COAL DEPARTMENT IS ONE OF THE TOUGHEST JOBS.
WHAT...?
IS... IS THIS...
SOME KIND OF TORTURE ...?!
I'M TOTALLY EXHAUSTED...
BASED ON OUR RESEARCH, WE'VE COME UP WITH WHAT WE CALL...
THE "DISAPPOINTMENT INDEX" TO MEASURE A CHILD'S DISAPPOINTMENT.
WE HAVE A SUBJECT SIMULATE CHRISTMAS MORNING AS A CHILD...
AND MEASURE THEIR BRAIN WAVES TO DETERMINE HOW DISAPPOINTED THEY WILL BE WHEN THEY RECEIVE THE GIFT.
YOU DO THIS UNTIL YOU GET IT RIGHT?
PRECISELY.

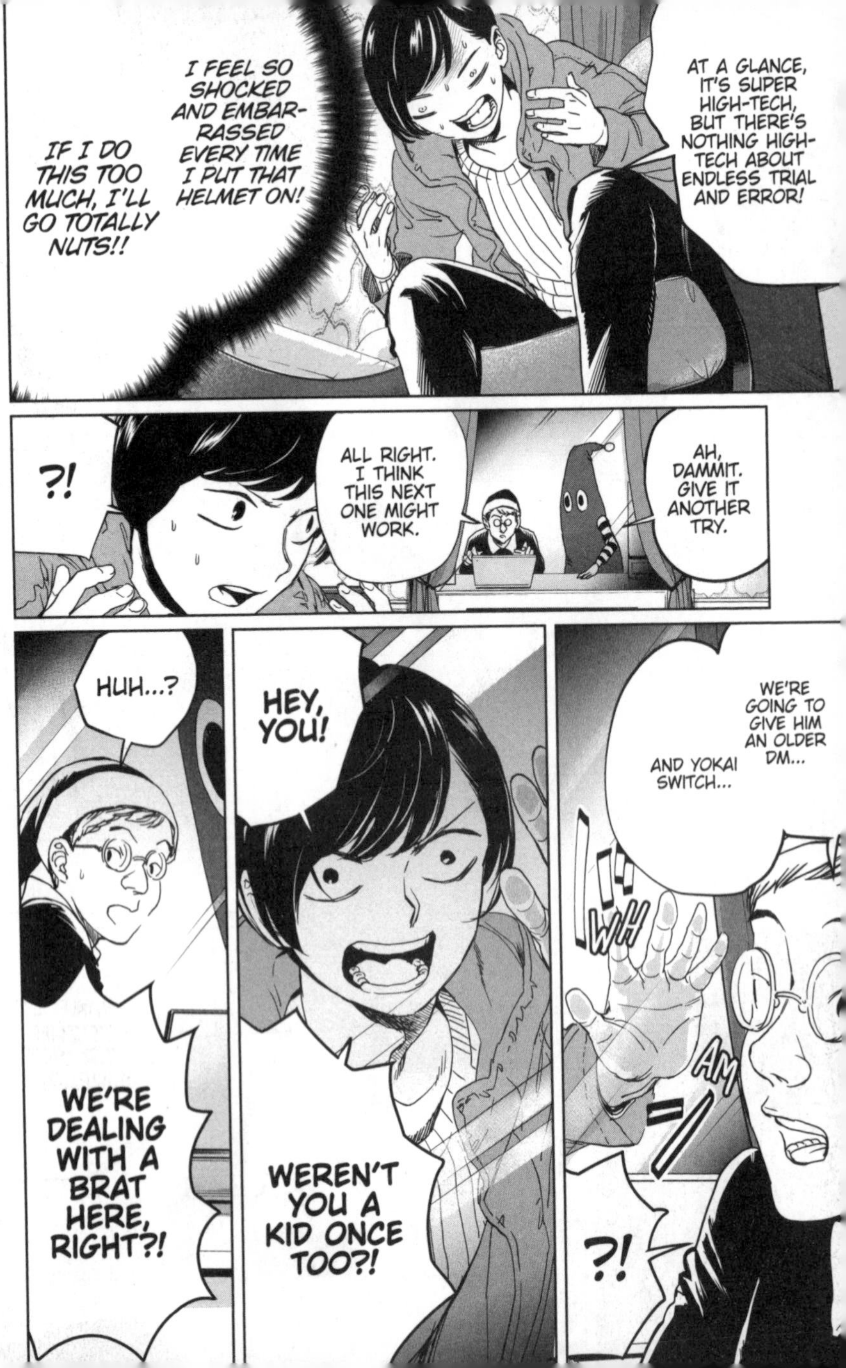
AT A GLANCE, IT'S SUPER HIGH-TECH, BUT THERE'S NOTHING HIGH-TECH ABOUT ENDLESS TRIAL AND ERROR!
I FEEL SO SHOCKED AND EMBARRASSED EVERY TIME I PUT THAT HELMET ON!
IF I DO THIS TOO MUCH, I'LL GO TOTALLY NUTS!!
AH, DAMMIT. GIVE IT ANOTHER TRY.
ALL RIGHT. I THINK THIS NEXT ONE MIGHT WORK.
?!
WE'RE GOING TO GIVE HIM AN OLDER DM...
AND YOKAI SWITCH...
WHAM
?!
HEY, YOU!
WEREN'T YOU A KID ONCE TOO?!
HUH...?
WE'RE DEALING WITH A BRAT HERE, RIGHT?!

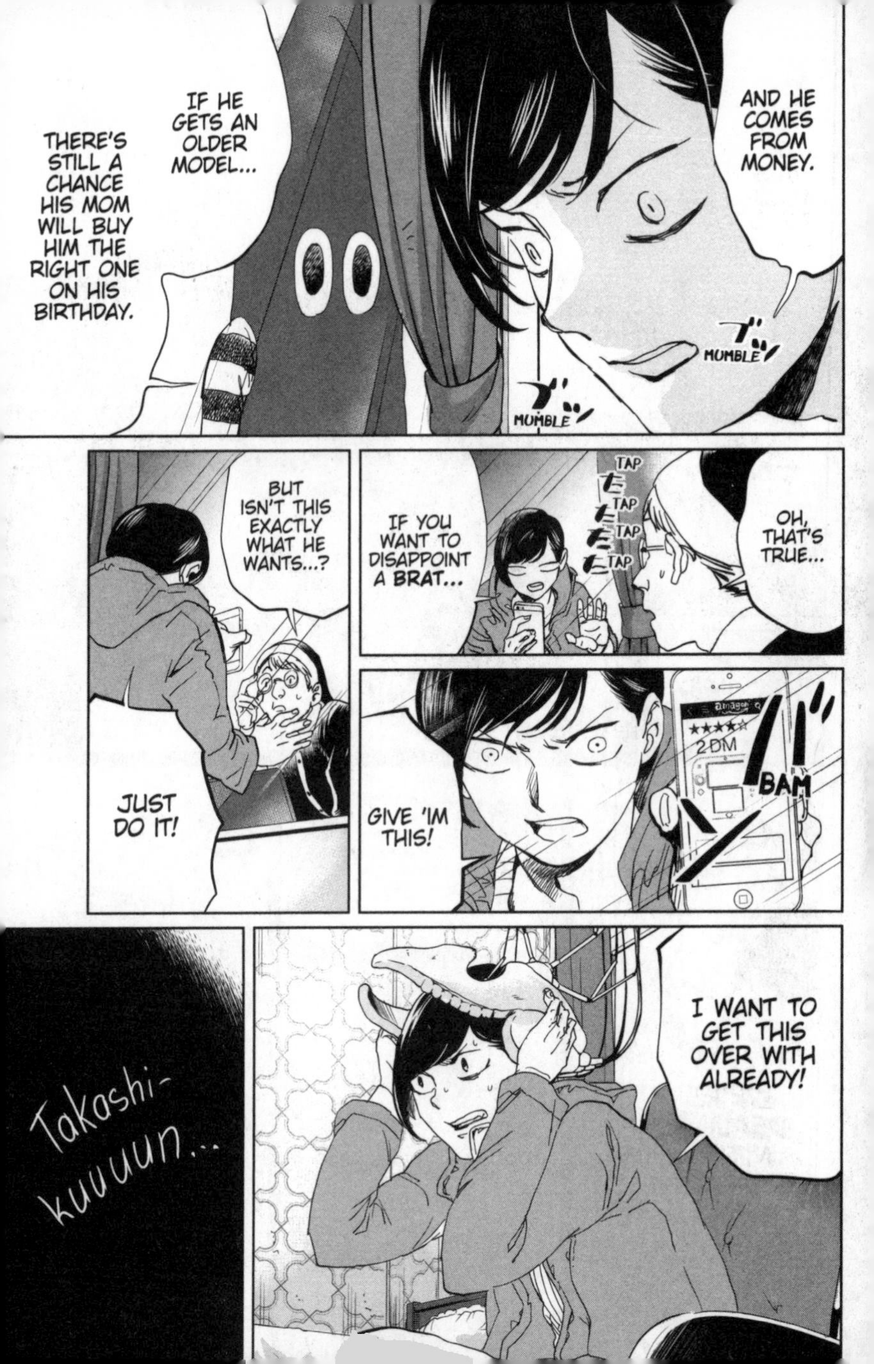
AND HE COMES FROM MONEY.
MUMBLE
MUMBLE
IF HE GETS AN OLDER MODEL...
THERE'S STILL A CHANCE HIS MOM WILL BUY HIM THE RIGHT ONE ON HIS BIRTHDAY.
OH, THAT'S TRUE...
TAP TAP TAP TAP
IF YOU WANT TO DISAPPOINT A BRAT...
BAM
2DM
GIVE 'IM THIS!
BUT ISN'T THIS EXACTLY WHAT HE WANTS...?
JUST DO IT!
I WANT TO GET THIS OVER WITH ALREADY!
Takashi-kuuuun...

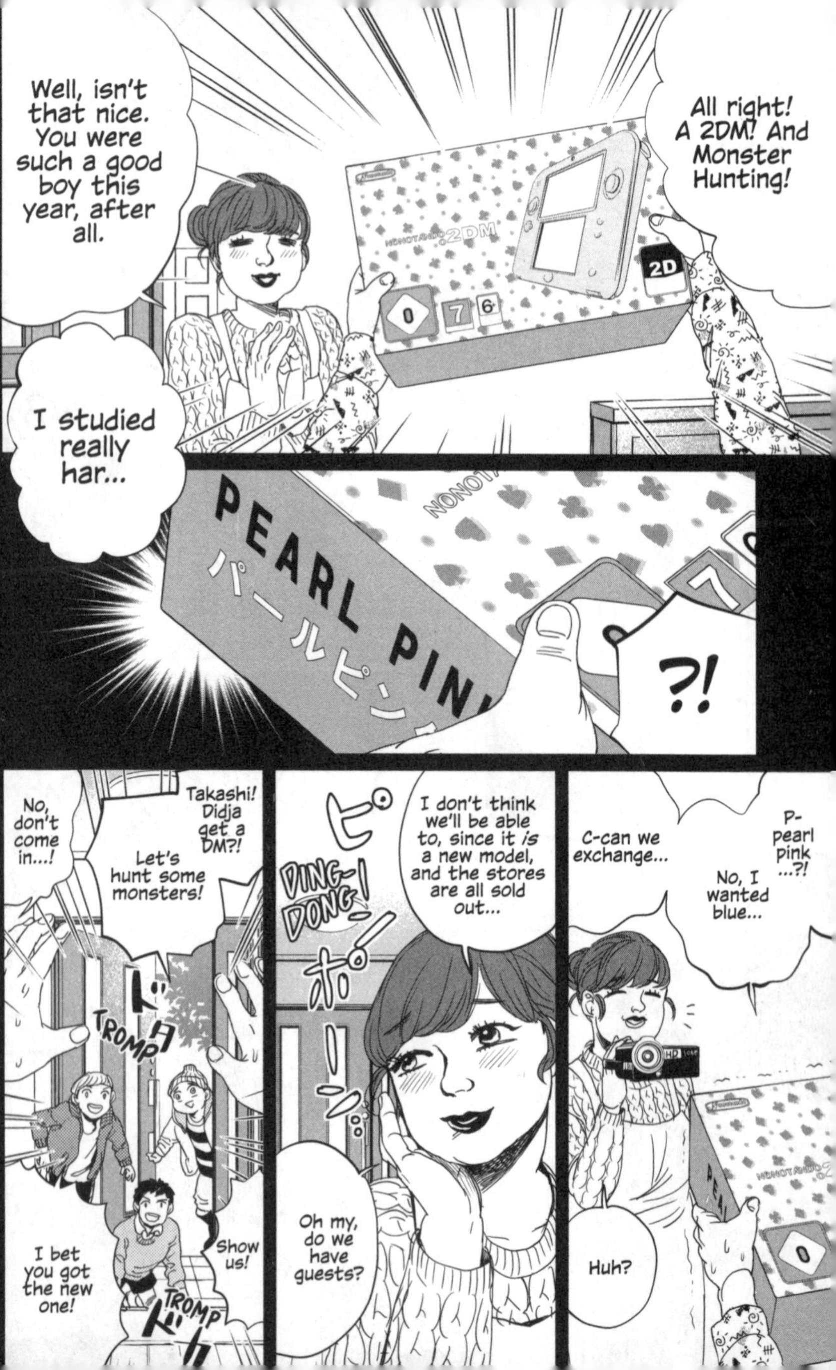
All right! A 2DM! And Monster Hunting!
Well, isn't that nice. You were such a good boy this year, after all.
NONOTANDO 2DM
2D
I studied really har...
PEARL PIN
?!
P-pearl pink...?!
No, I wanted blue...
C-can we exchange...
Huh?
I don't think we'll be able to, since it *is* a new model, and the stores are all sold out...
DING-DONG
Oh my, do we have guests?
Takashi! Didja get a DM?!
Let's hunt some monsters!
No, don't come in...!
TROMP
Show us!
I bet you got the new one!
TROMP

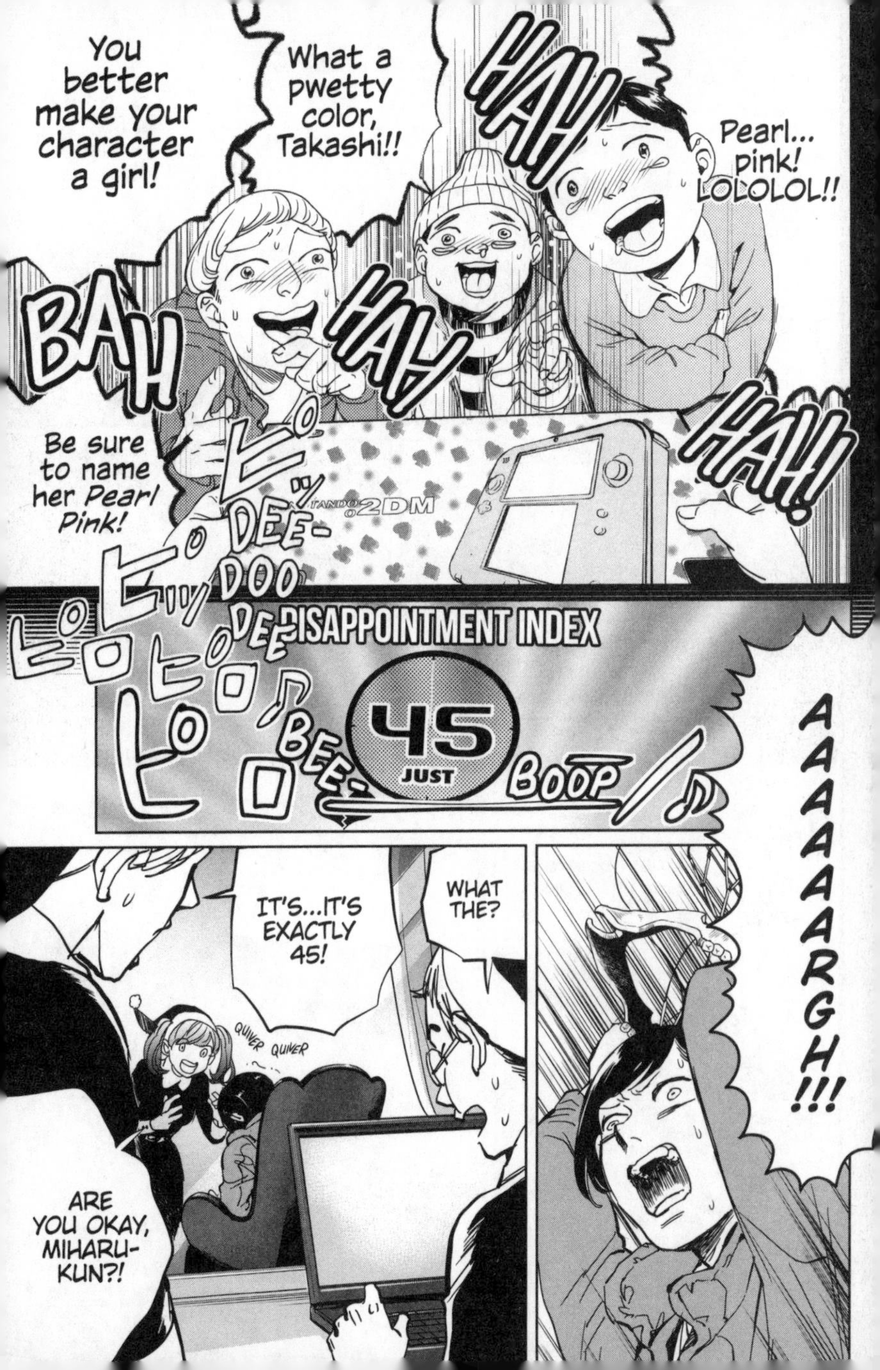

Pearl... pink! LOLOLOL!!
HAH
What a pwetty color, Takashi!!
HAH
You better make your character a girl!
BAH
HAH!!
Be sure to name her Pearl Pink!
TANDO 2DM
DEE-DOO DEE
DISAPPOINTMENT INDEX
45
JUST
BEE-BOOP
AAAAAAAARGH!!!
WHAT THE?
IT'S...IT'S EXACTLY 45!
QUIVER QUIVER
ARE YOU OKAY, MIHARU-KUN?!

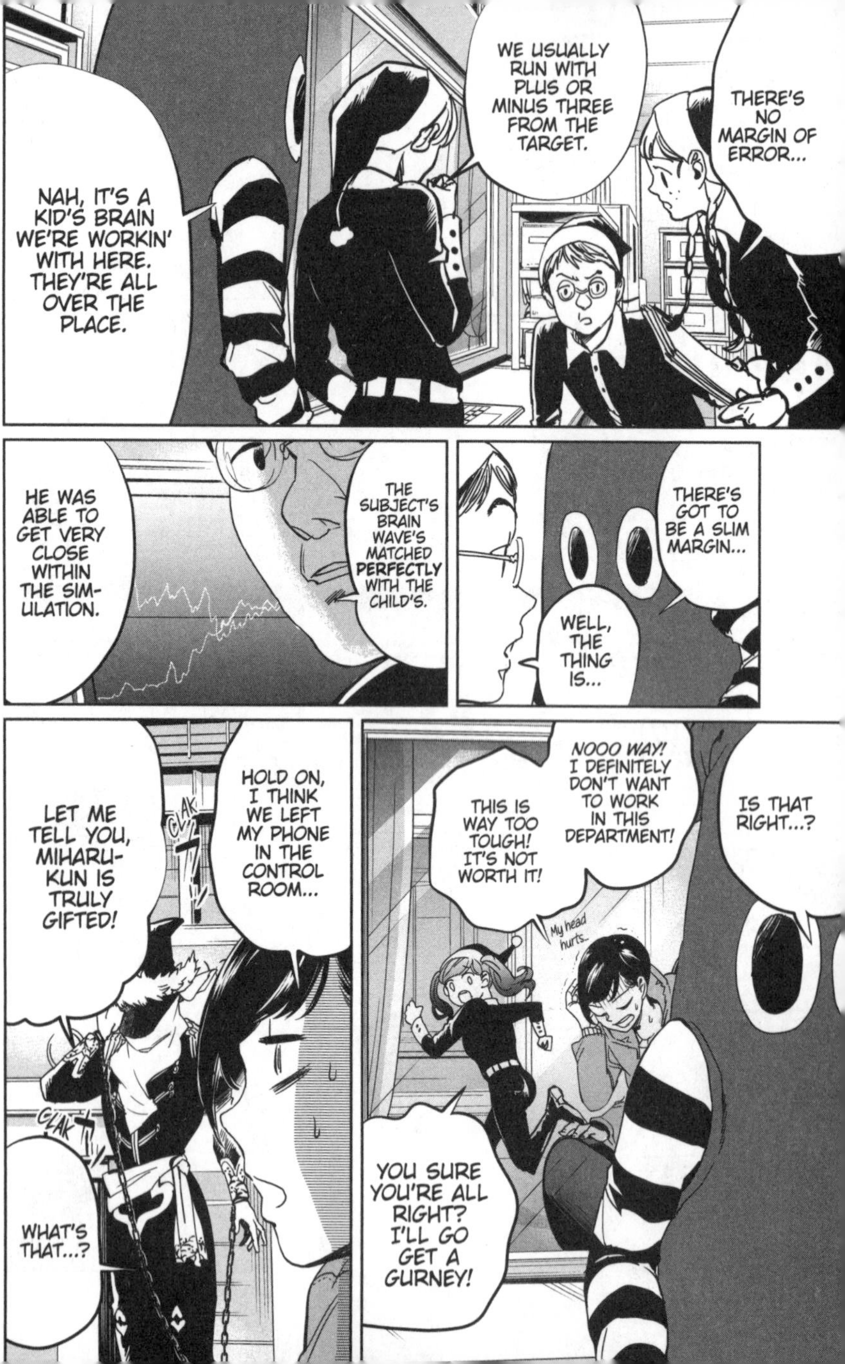
THERE'S NO MARGIN OF ERROR...
WE USUALLY RUN WITH PLUS OR MINUS THREE FROM THE TARGET.
NAH, IT'S A KID'S BRAIN WE'RE WORKIN' WITH HERE. THEY'RE ALL OVER THE PLACE.
THERE'S GOT TO BE A SLIM MARGIN...
WELL, THE THING IS...
THE SUBJECT'S BRAIN WAVE'S MATCHED **PERFECTLY** WITH THE CHILD'S.
HE WAS ABLE TO GET VERY CLOSE WITHIN THE SIM-ULATION.
IS THAT RIGHT...?
NOOO WAY! I DEFINITELY DON'T WANT TO WORK IN THIS DEPARTMENT!
THIS IS WAY TOO TOUGH! IT'S NOT WORTH IT!
My head hurts...
YOU SURE YOU'RE ALL RIGHT? I'LL GO GET A GURNEY!
HOLD ON, I THINK WE LEFT MY PHONE IN THE CONTROL ROOM...
LET ME TELL YOU, MIHARU-KUN IS TRULY GIFTED!
CLAK
CLAK
WHAT'S THAT...?

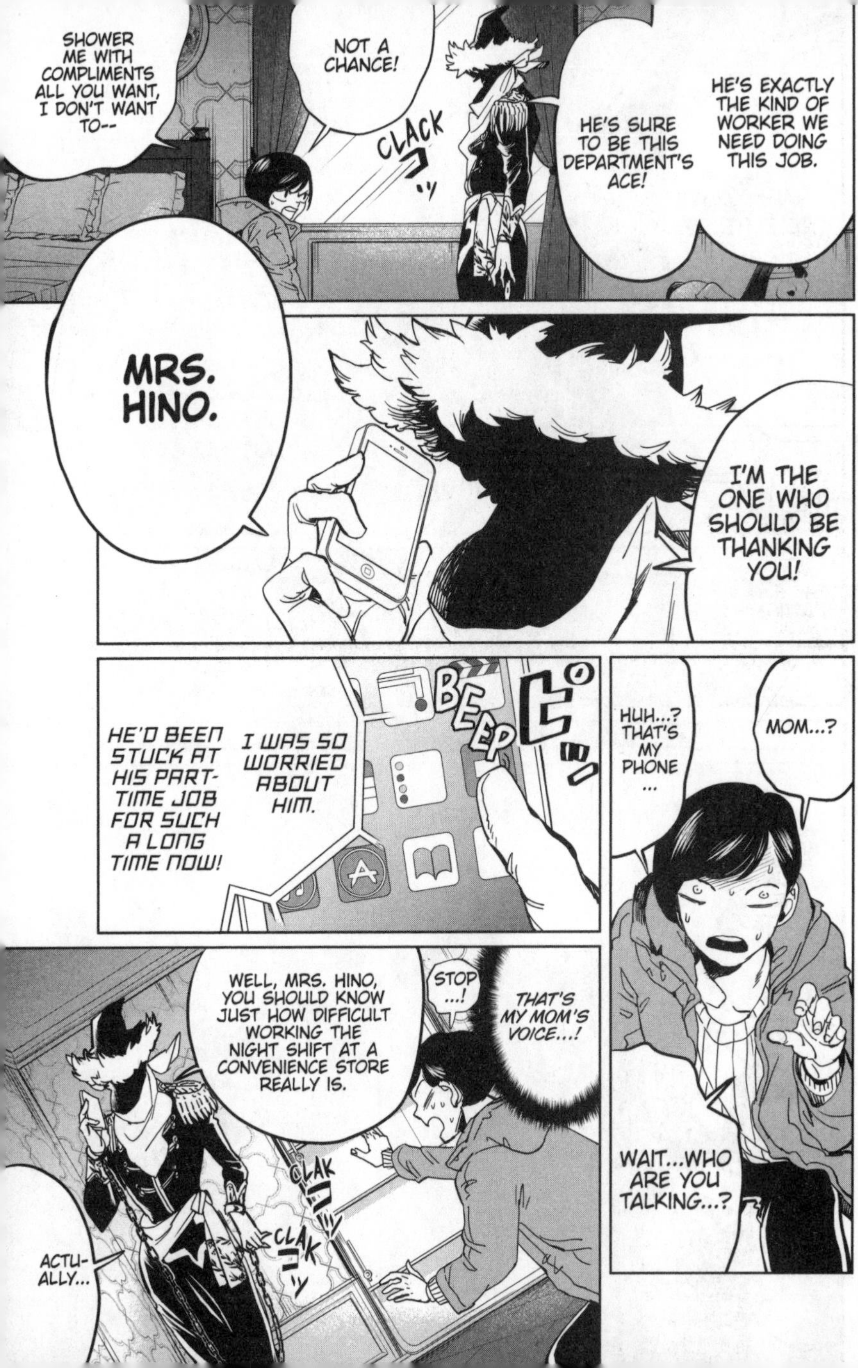
HE'S EXACTLY THE KIND OF WORKER WE NEED DOING THIS JOB.
HE'S SURE TO BE THIS DEPARTMENT'S ACE!
CLACK
NOT A CHANCE!
SHOWER ME WITH COMPLIMENTS ALL YOU WANT, I DON'T WANT TO--
I'M THE ONE WHO SHOULD BE THANKING YOU!
MRS. HINO.
MOM...?
HUH...? THAT'S MY PHONE...
WAIT...WHO ARE YOU TALKING...?
BEEP
I WAS SO WORRIED ABOUT HIM.
HE'D BEEN STUCK AT HIS PART-TIME JOB FOR SUCH A LONG TIME NOW!
THAT'S MY MOM'S VOICE...!
STOP...!
WELL, MRS. HINO, YOU SHOULD KNOW JUST HOW DIFFICULT WORKING THE NIGHT SHIFT AT A CONVENIENCE STORE REALLY IS.
CLAK
CLAK
ACTU-ALLY...

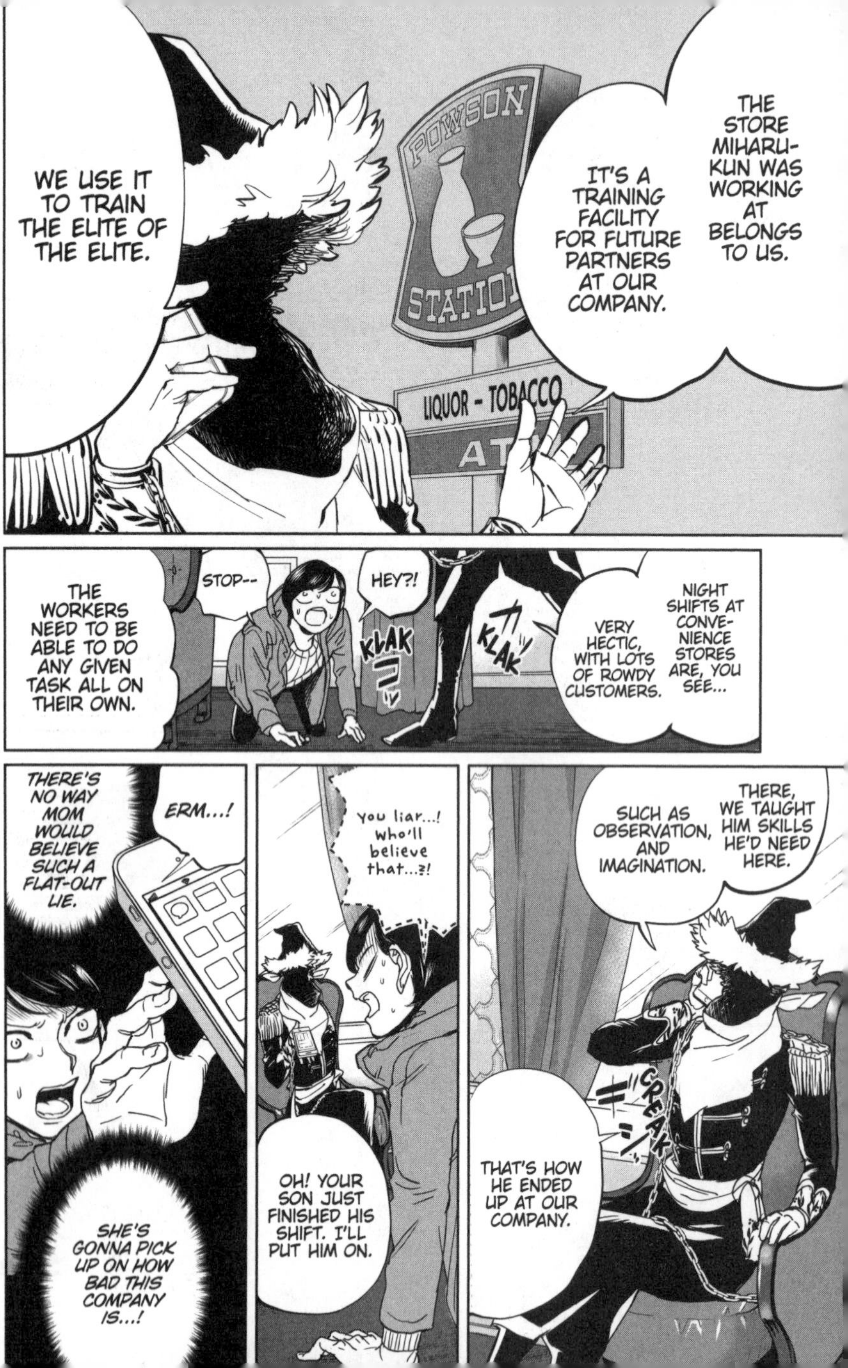
THE STORE MIHARU-KUN WAS WORKING AT BELONGS TO US.
POWSON
LIQUOR - TOBACCO
IT'S A TRAINING FACILITY FOR FUTURE PARTNERS AT OUR COMPANY.
WE USE IT TO TRAIN THE ELITE OF THE ELITE.
NIGHT SHIFTS AT CONVENIENCE STORES ARE, YOU SEE...
VERY HECTIC, WITH LOTS OF ROWDY CUSTOMERS.
KLAK
KLAK
HEY?!
STOP--
THE WORKERS NEED TO BE ABLE TO DO ANY GIVEN TASK ALL ON THEIR OWN.
THERE, WE TAUGHT HIM SKILLS HE'D NEED HERE.
SUCH AS OBSERVATION, AND IMAGINATION.
CREAK
THAT'S HOW HE ENDED UP AT OUR COMPANY.
You liar...! Who'll believe that...?!
OH! YOUR SON JUST FINISHED HIS SHIFT. I'LL PUT HIM ON.
THERE'S NO WAY MOM WOULD BELIEVE SUCH A FLAT-OUT LIE.
ERM...!
SHE'S GONNA PICK UP ON HOW BAD THIS COMPANY IS...!

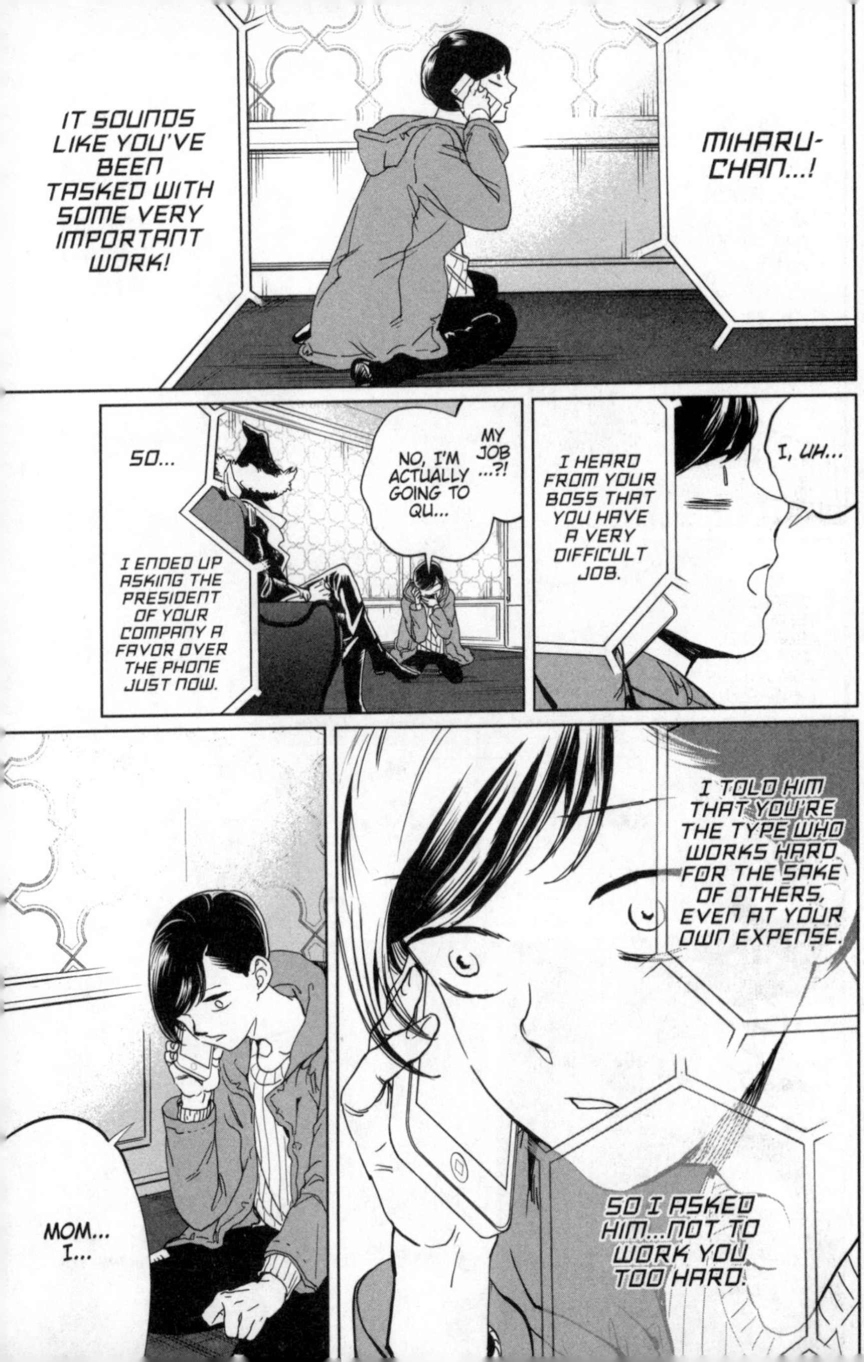
MIHARU-CHAN...!
IT SOUNDS LIKE YOU'VE BEEN TASKED WITH SOME VERY IMPORTANT WORK!
I, UH...
I HEARD FROM YOUR BOSS THAT YOU HAVE A VERY DIFFICULT JOB.
MY JOB ...?!
NO, I'M ACTUALLY GOING TO QU...
SO...
I ENDED UP ASKING THE PRESIDENT OF YOUR COMPANY A FAVOR OVER THE PHONE JUST NOW.
I TOLD HIM THAT YOU'RE THE TYPE WHO WORKS HARD FOR THE SAKE OF OTHERS, EVEN AT YOUR OWN EXPENSE.
SO I ASKED HIM...NOT TO WORK YOU TOO HARD.
MOM... I...

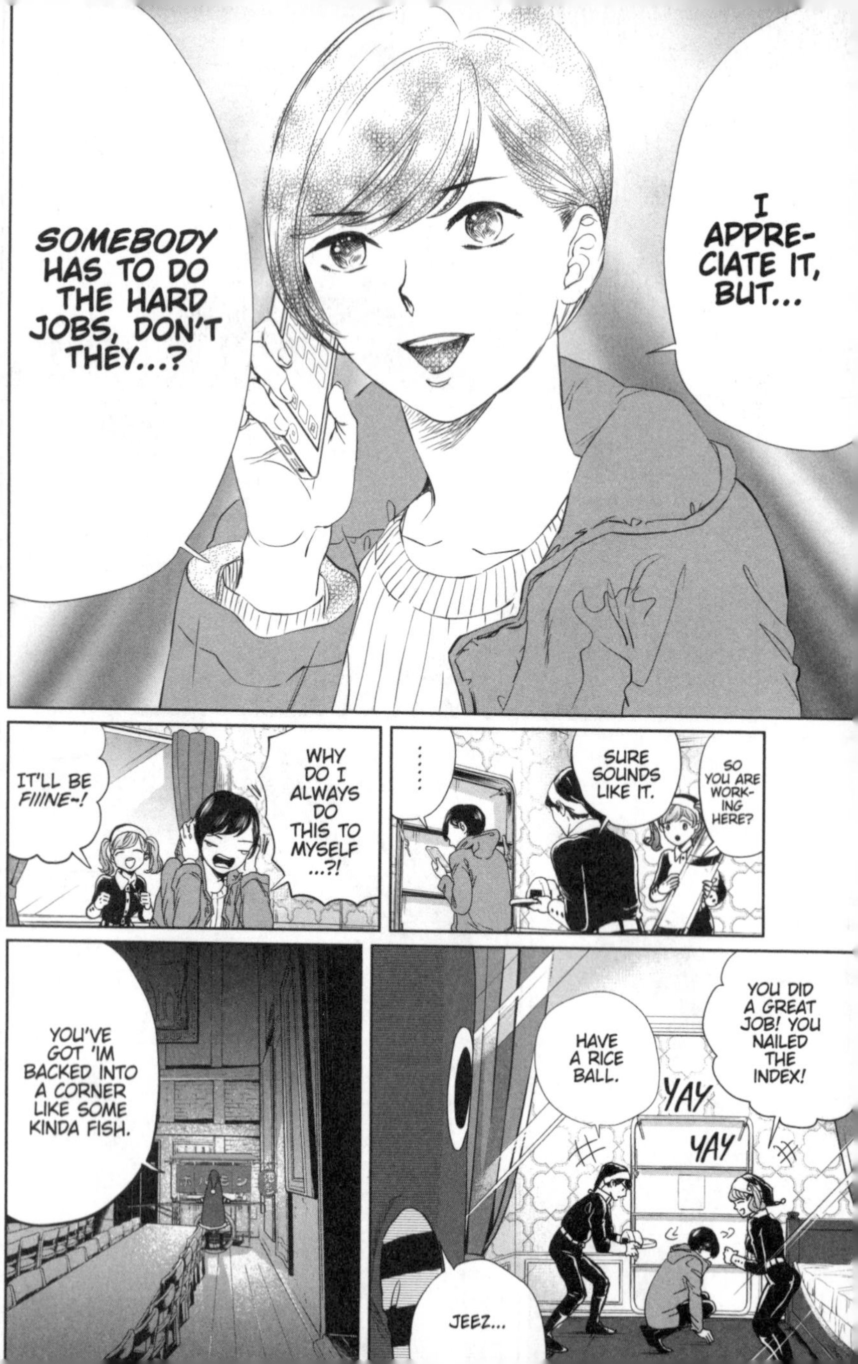
I APPRECIATE IT, BUT...
SOMEBODY HAS TO DO THE HARD JOBS, DON'T THEY...?
SO YOU ARE WORKING HERE?
SURE SOUNDS LIKE IT.
......
WHY DO I ALWAYS DO THIS TO MYSELF...?!
IT'LL BE FIIINE~!
YOU DID A GREAT JOB! YOU NAILED THE INDEX!
YAY
YAY
HAVE A RICE BALL.
JEEZ...
YOU'VE GOT 'IM BACKED INTO A CORNER LIKE SOME KINDA FISH.

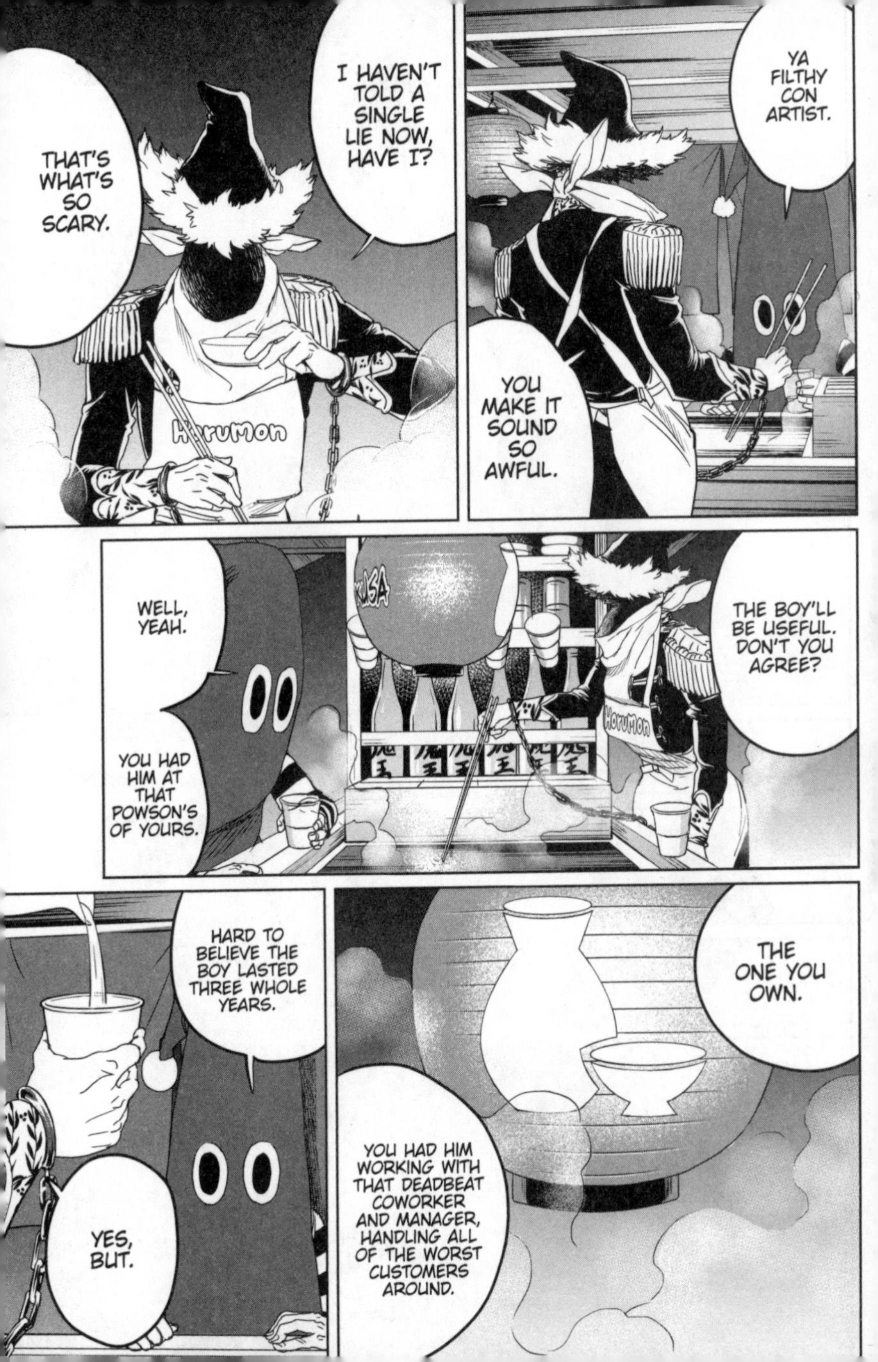
YA FILTHY CON ARTIST.
YOU MAKE IT SOUND SO AWFUL.
I HAVEN'T TOLD A SINGLE LIE NOW, HAVE I?
THAT'S WHAT'S SO SCARY.
THE BOY'LL BE USEFUL. DON'T YOU AGREE?
WELL, YEAH.
YOU HAD HIM AT THAT POWSON'S OF YOURS.
THE ONE YOU OWN.
YOU HAD HIM WORKING WITH THAT DEADBEAT COWORKER AND MANAGER, HANDLING ALL OF THE WORST CUSTOMERS AROUND.
HARD TO BELIEVE THE BOY LASTED THREE WHOLE YEARS.
YES, BUT.

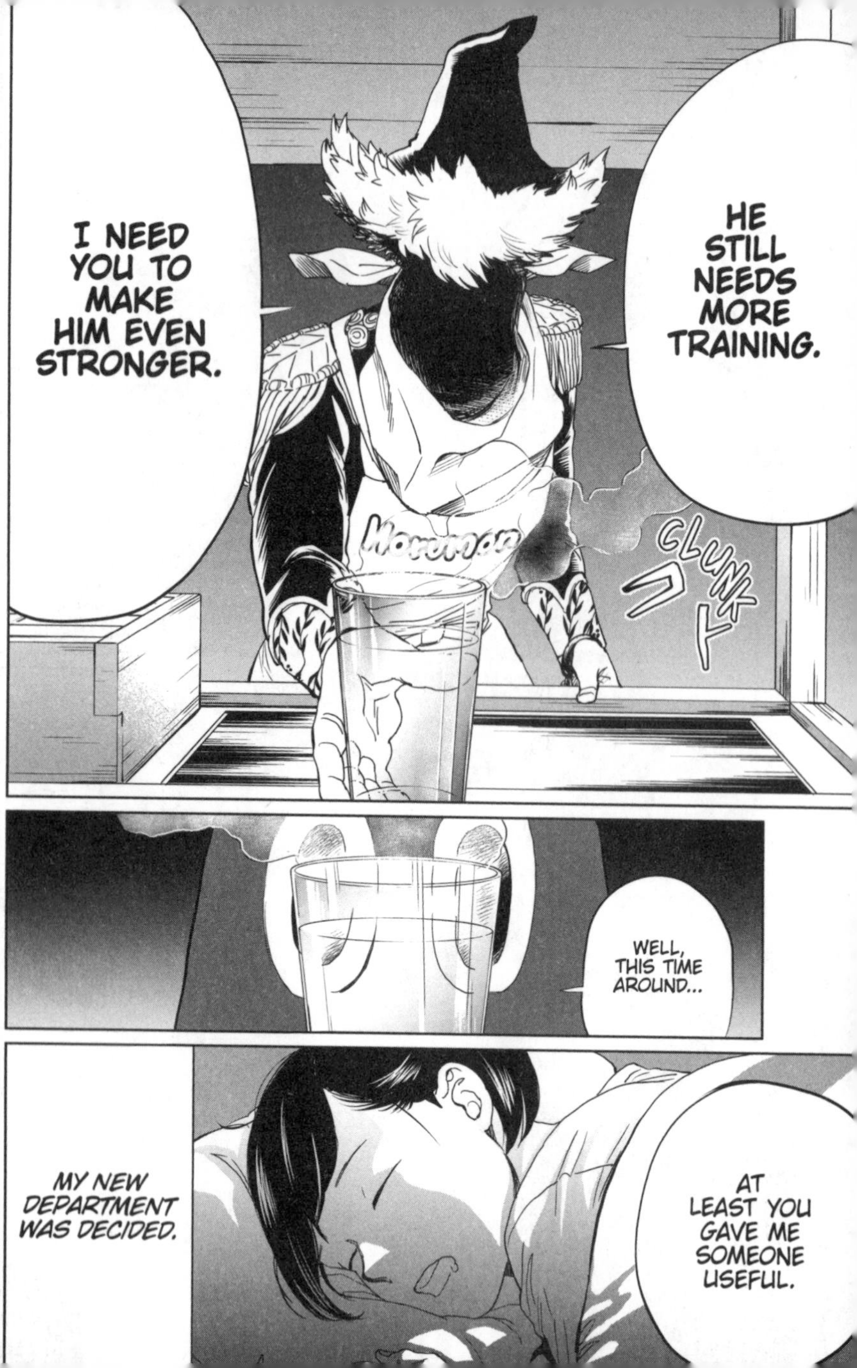
HE STILL NEEDS MORE TRAINING.
I NEED YOU TO MAKE HIM EVEN STRONGER.
CLUNK
コト
WELL, THIS TIME AROUND...
AT LEAST YOU GAVE ME SOMEONE USEFUL.
MY NEW DEPARTMENT WAS DECIDED.

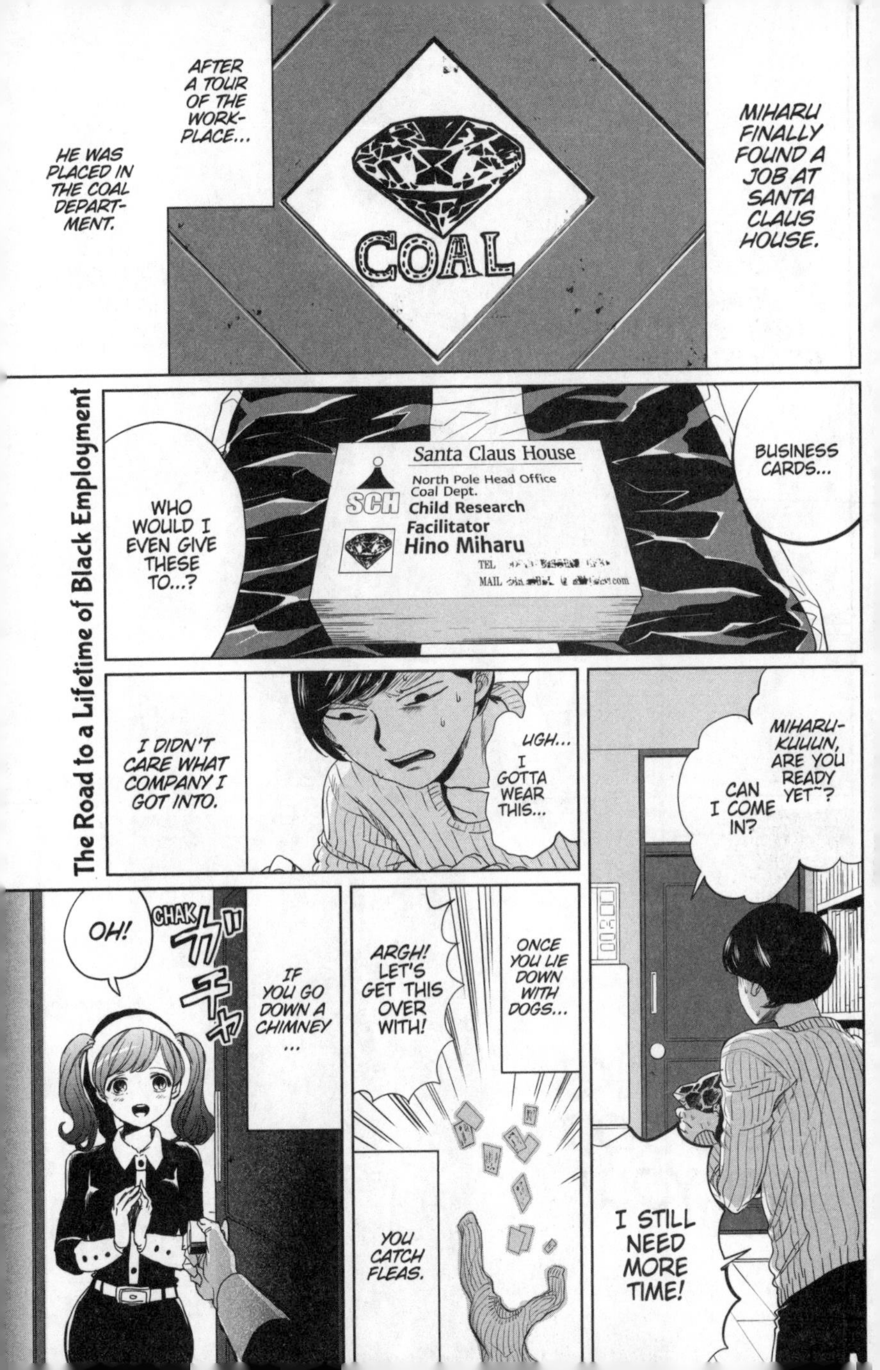
MIHARU FINALLY FOUND A JOB AT SANTA CLAUS HOUSE.
AFTER A TOUR OF THE WORK-PLACE...
HE WAS PLACED IN THE COAL DEPART-MENT.
COAL
BUSINESS CARDS...
Santa Claus House
North Pole Head Office
Coal Dept.
SCH
Child Research
Facilitator
Hino Miharu
TEL
MAIL
WHO WOULD I EVEN GIVE THESE TO...?
MIHARU-KUUUN, ARE YOU READY YET~?
CAN I COME IN?
I STILL NEED MORE TIME!
UGH... I GOTTA WEAR THIS...
I DIDN'T CARE WHAT COMPANY I GOT INTO.
ONCE YOU LIE DOWN WITH DOGS...
ARGH! LET'S GET THIS OVER WITH!
YOU CATCH FLEAS.
IF YOU GO DOWN A CHIMNEY...
CHAK
OH!

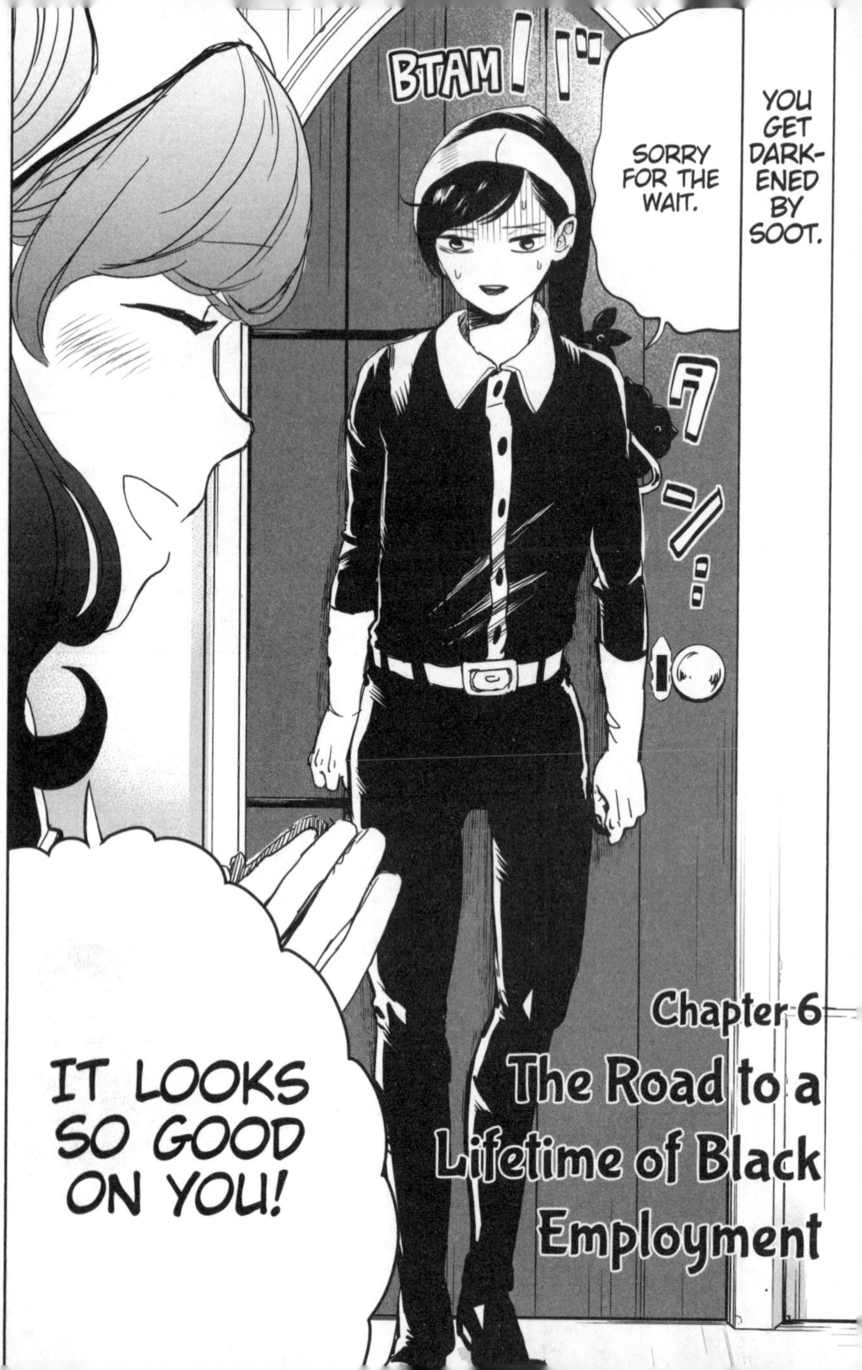
BTAM
SORRY FOR THE WAIT.
YOU GET DARKENED BY SOOT.
Chapter 6
The Road to a Lifetime of Black Employment
IT LOOKS SO GOOD ON YOU!

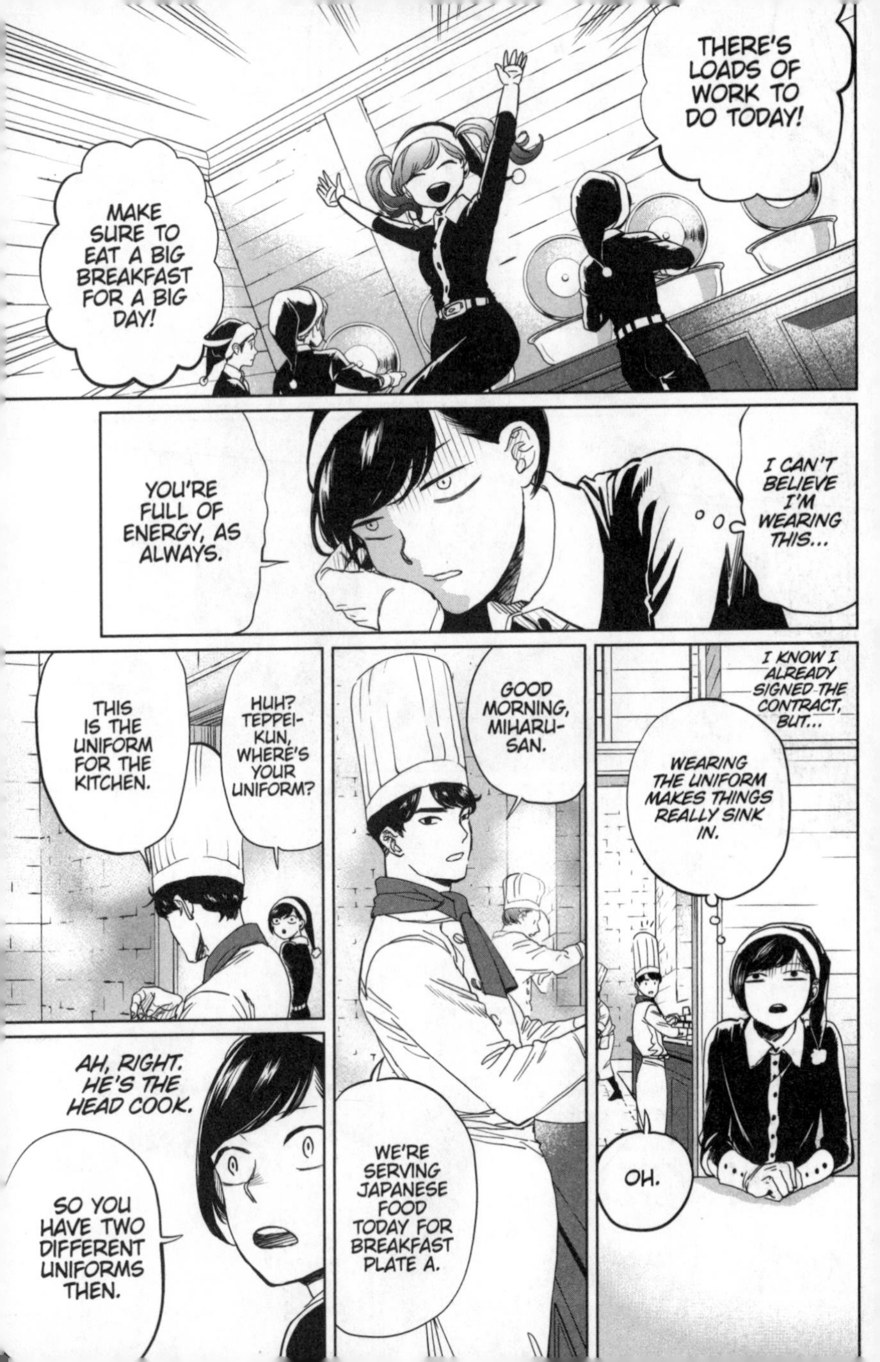
THERE'S LOADS OF WORK TO DO TODAY!
MAKE SURE TO EAT A BIG BREAKFAST FOR A BIG DAY!
I CAN'T BELIEVE I'M WEARING THIS...
YOU'RE FULL OF ENERGY, AS ALWAYS.
I KNOW I ALREADY SIGNED THE CONTRACT, BUT...
WEARING THE UNIFORM MAKES THINGS REALLY SINK IN.
OH.
GOOD MORNING, MIHARU-SAN.
WE'RE SERVING JAPANESE FOOD TODAY FOR BREAKFAST PLATE A.
HUH? TEPPEI-KUN, WHERE'S YOUR UNIFORM?
THIS IS THE UNIFORM FOR THE KITCHEN.
AH, RIGHT. HE'S THE HEAD COOK.
SO YOU HAVE TWO DIFFERENT UNIFORMS THEN.

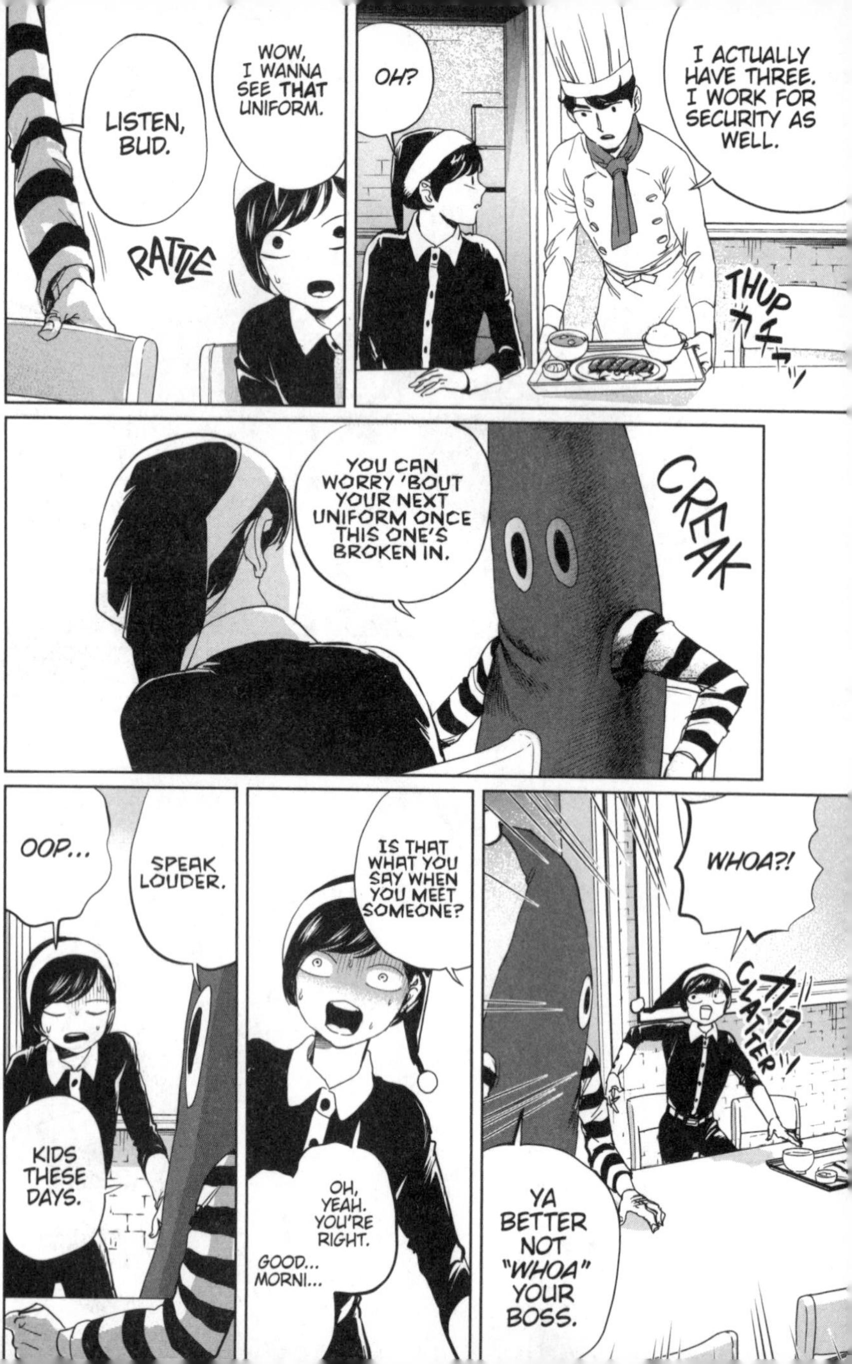
I ACTUALLY HAVE THREE. I WORK FOR SECURITY AS WELL.
THUP
OH?
WOW, I WANNA SEE THAT UNIFORM.
LISTEN, BUD.
RATTLE
CREAK
YOU CAN WORRY 'BOUT YOUR NEXT UNIFORM ONCE THIS ONE'S BROKEN IN.
WHOA?!
CLATTER
YA BETTER NOT "WHOA" YOUR BOSS.
IS THAT WHAT YOU SAY WHEN YOU MEET SOMEONE?
OH, YEAH. YOU'RE RIGHT.
GOOD... MORNI...
SPEAK LOUDER.
OOP...
KIDS THESE DAYS.

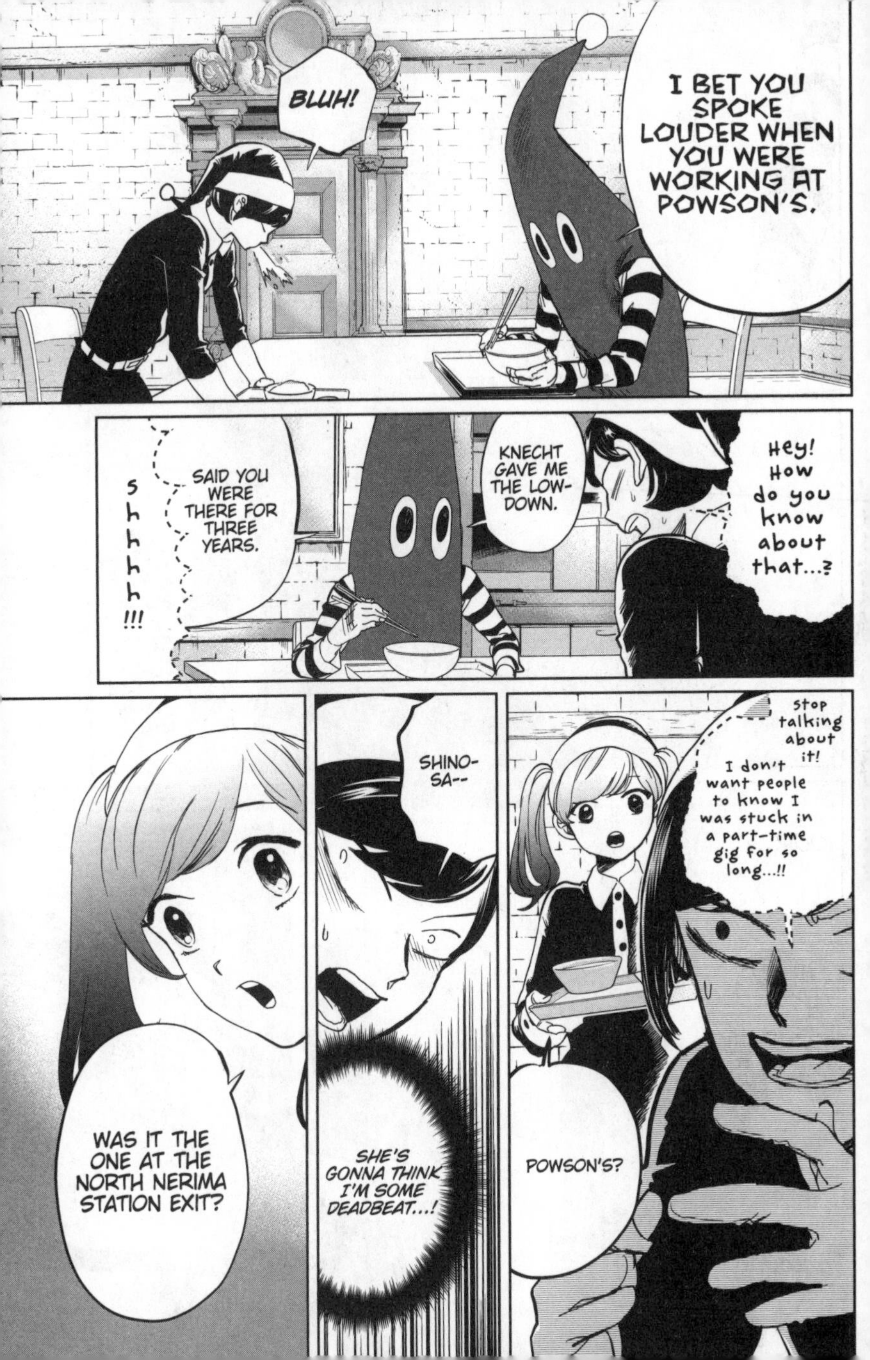
I BET YOU SPOKE LOUDER WHEN YOU WERE WORKING AT POWSON'S.
BLUH!
Hey! How do you know about that...?
KNECHT GAVE ME THE LOW-DOWN.
SAID YOU WERE THERE FOR THREE YEARS.
Shhhhh!!!
Stop talking about it! I don't want people to know I was stuck in a part-time gig for so long...!!
POWSON'S?
SHINO-SA--
SHE'S GONNA THINK I'M SOME DEADBEAT...!
WAS IT THE ONE AT THE NORTH NERIMA STATION EXIT?

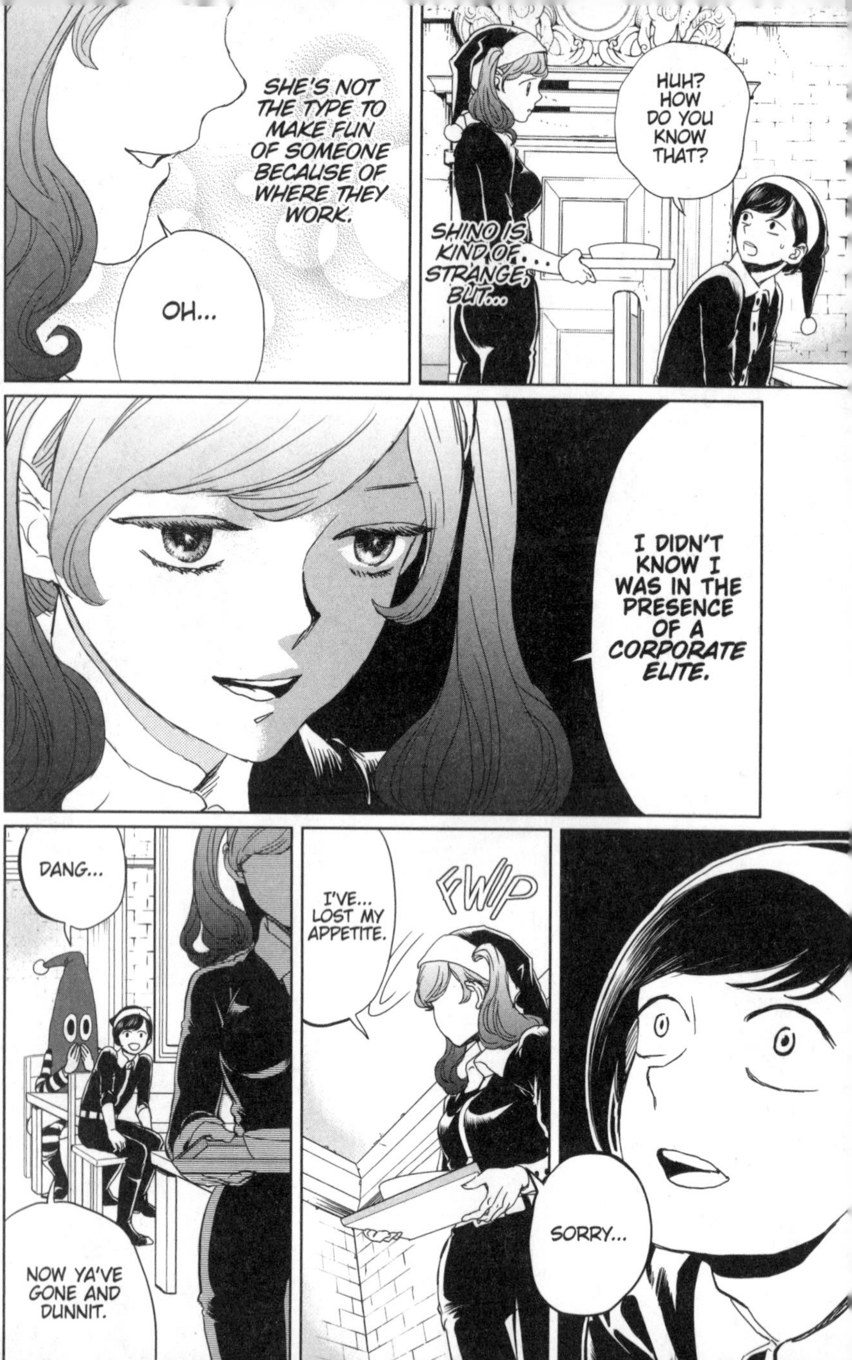
HUH? HOW DO YOU KNOW THAT?
SHINO IS KIND OF STRANGE, BUT...
SHE'S NOT THE TYPE TO MAKE FUN OF SOMEONE BECAUSE OF WHERE THEY WORK.
OH...
I DIDN'T KNOW I WAS IN THE PRESENCE OF A CORPORATE ELITE.
SORRY...
FWIP
I'VE... LOST MY APPETITE.
DANG...
NOW YA'VE GONE AND DUNNIT.

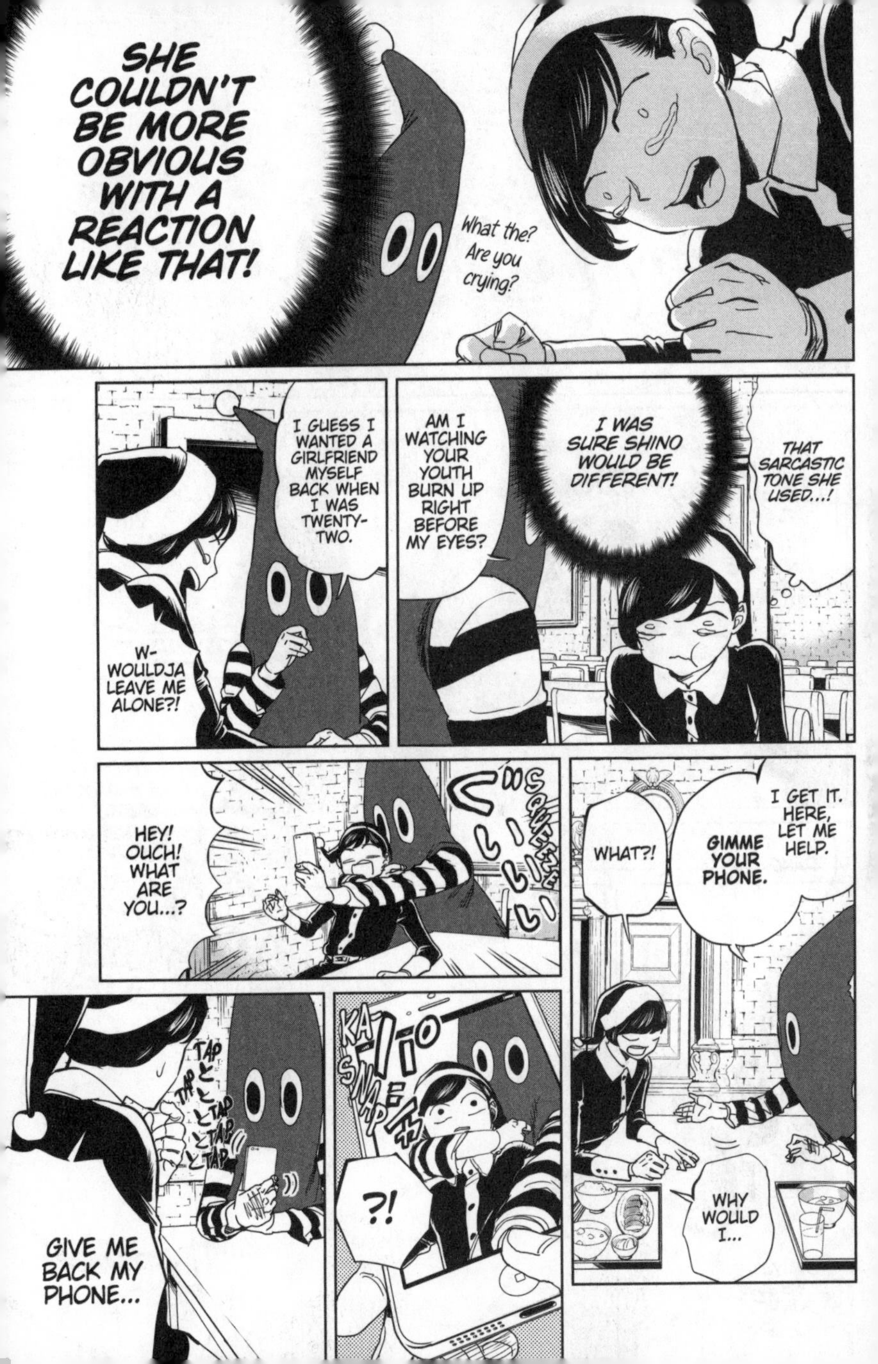
What the? Are you crying?
SHE COULDN'T BE MORE OBVIOUS WITH A REACTION LIKE THAT!
THAT SARCASTIC TONE SHE USED...!
I WAS SURE SHINO WOULD BE DIFFERENT!
AM I WATCHING YOUR YOUTH BURN UP RIGHT BEFORE MY EYES?
I GUESS I WANTED A GIRLFRIEND MYSELF BACK WHEN I WAS TWENTY-TWO.
W-WOULDJA LEAVE ME ALONE?!
I GET IT. HERE, LET ME HELP.
GIMME YOUR PHONE.
WHAT?!
WHY WOULD I...
SQUEEZE
HEY! OUCH! WHAT ARE YOU...?
KA
SNAP
?!
TAP TAP TAP TAP TAP
GIVE ME BACK MY PHONE...

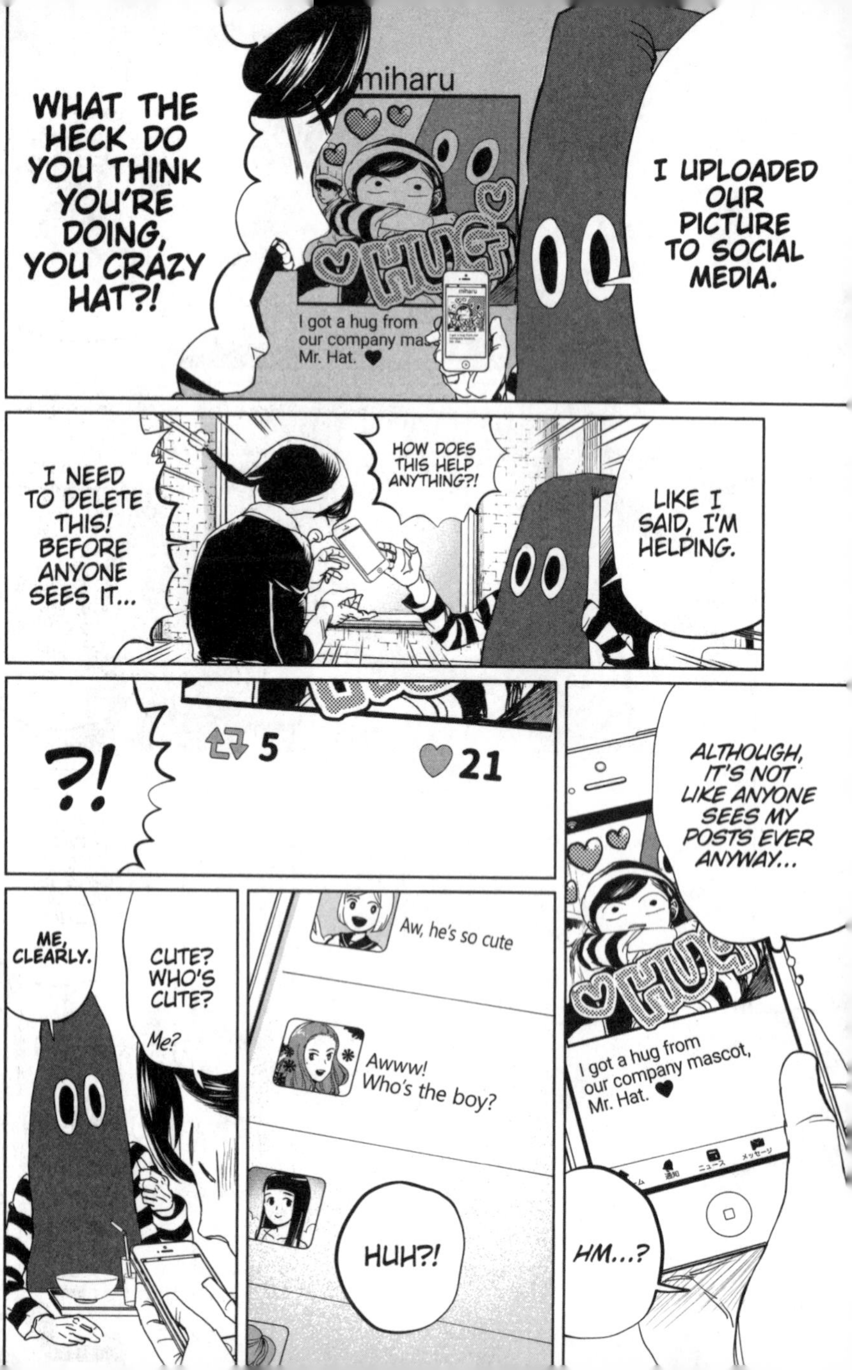
I UPLOADED OUR PICTURE TO SOCIAL MEDIA.
miharu
HUG
I got a hug from our company mas
Mr. Hat.
WHAT THE HECK DO YOU THINK YOU'RE DOING, YOU CRAZY HAT?!
LIKE I SAID, I'M HELPING.
HOW DOES THIS HELP ANYTHING?!
I NEED TO DELETE THIS! BEFORE ANYONE SEES IT...
ALTHOUGH, IT'S NOT LIKE ANYONE SEES MY POSTS EVER ANYWAY...
HUG
I got a hug from our company mascot, Mr. Hat.
HM...?
5
21
?!
Aw, he's so cute
Awww! Who's the boy?
HUH?!
CUTE? WHO'S CUTE?
Me?
ME, CLEARLY.

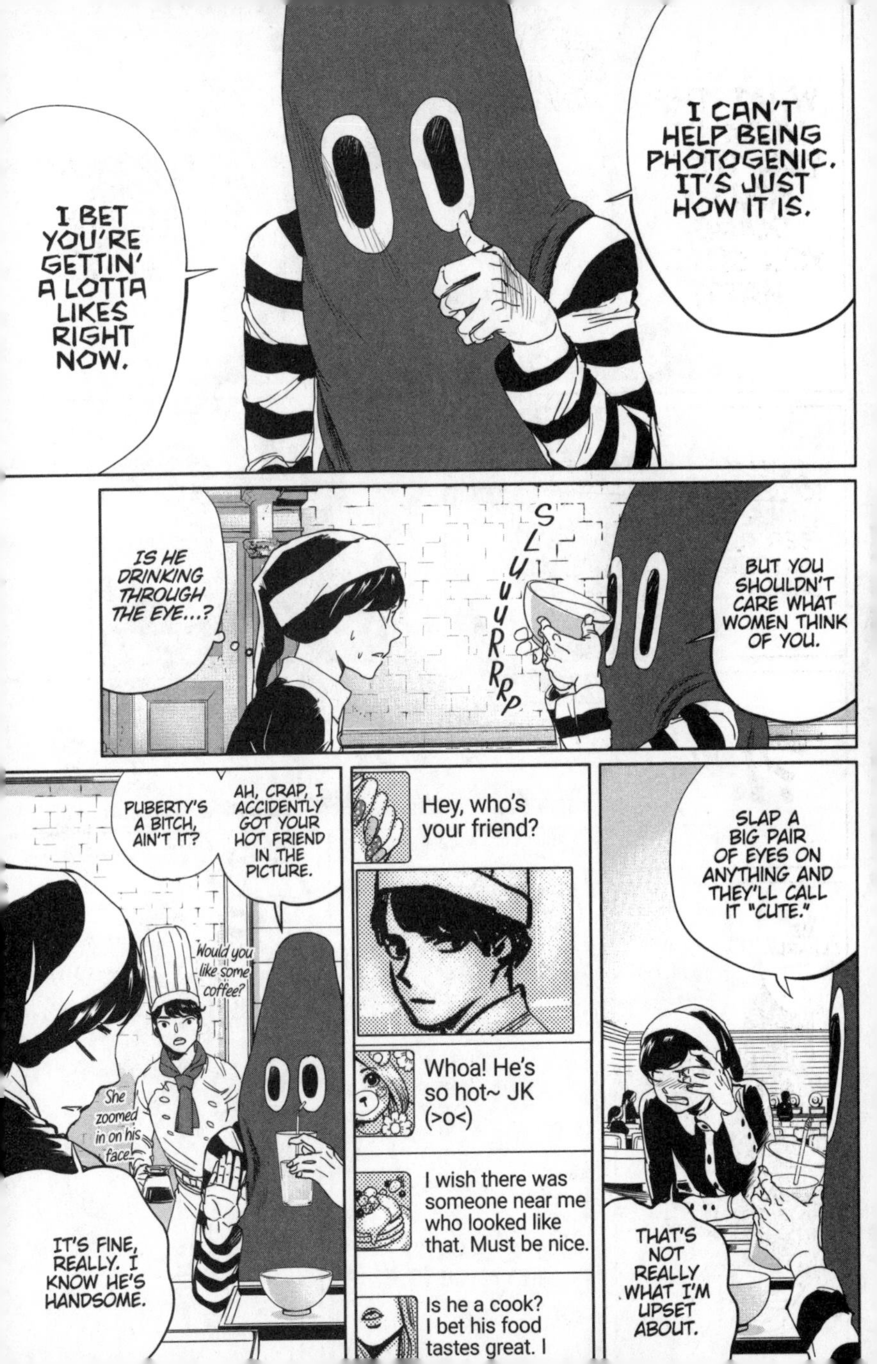
I CAN'T HELP BEING PHOTOGENIC. IT'S JUST HOW IT IS.
I BET YOU'RE GETTIN' A LOTTA LIKES RIGHT NOW.
BUT YOU SHOULDN'T CARE WHAT WOMEN THINK OF YOU.
SLUUUURRRP
IS HE DRINKING THROUGH THE EYE...?
SLAP A BIG PAIR OF EYES ON ANYTHING AND THEY'LL CALL IT "CUTE."
THAT'S NOT REALLY WHAT I'M UPSET ABOUT.
Hey, who's your friend?
Whoa! He's so hot~ JK (>o<)
I wish there was someone near me who looked like that. Must be nice.
Is he a cook? I bet his food tastes great. I
AH, CRAP, I ACCIDENTLY GOT YOUR HOT FRIEND IN THE PICTURE.
PUBERTY'S A BITCH, AIN'T IT?
Would you like some coffee?
She zoomed in on his face.
IT'S FINE, REALLY. I KNOW HE'S HANDSOME.

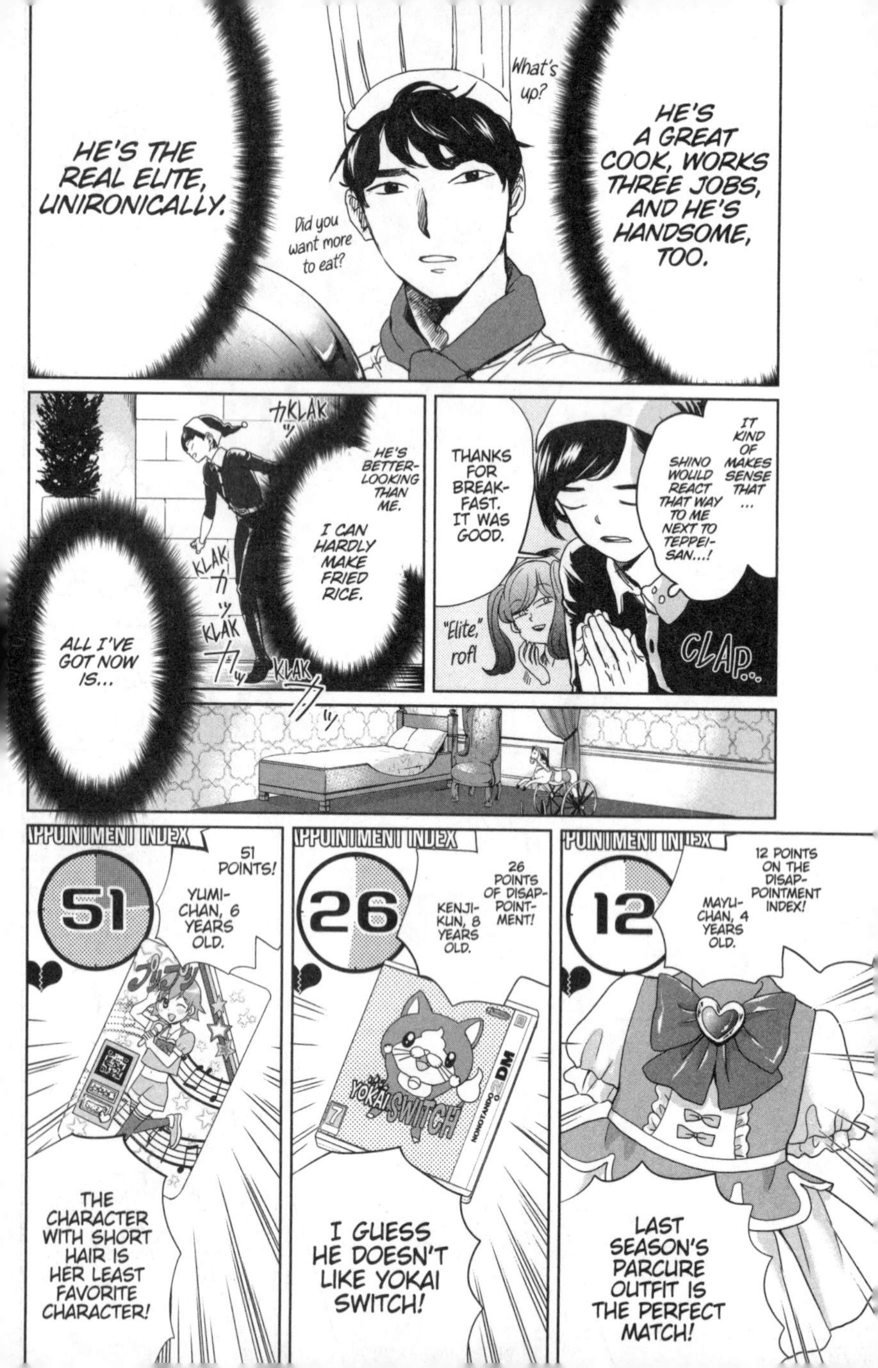

What's up?
HE'S A GREAT COOK, WORKS THREE JOBS, AND HE'S HANDSOME, TOO.
Did you want more to eat?
HE'S THE REAL ELITE, UNIRONICALLY.
IT KIND OF MAKES SENSE THAT ... SHINO WOULD REACT THAT WAY TO ME NEXT TO TEPPEI-SAN...!
THANKS FOR BREAKFAST. IT WAS GOOD.
CLAP...
"Elite," rofl
KLAK
HE'S BETTER-LOOKING THAN ME.
I CAN HARDLY MAKE FRIED RICE.
KLAK
KLAK
KLAK
ALL I'VE GOT NOW IS...
POINTMENT INDEX
12 POINTS ON THE DISAPPOINTMENT INDEX!
12
MAYU-CHAN, 4 YEARS OLD.
LAST SEASON'S PARCURE OUTFIT IS THE PERFECT MATCH!
PPOINTMENT INDEX
26 POINTS OF DISAPPOINTMENT!
26
KENJI-KUN, 8 YEARS OLD.
NONOTANDO 2DM
YOKAI SWITCH
I GUESS HE DOESN'T LIKE YOKAI SWITCH!
PPOINTMENT INDEX
51 POINTS!
51
YUMI-CHAN, 6 YEARS OLD.
THE CHARACTER WITH SHORT HAIR IS HER LEAST FAVORITE CHARACTER!

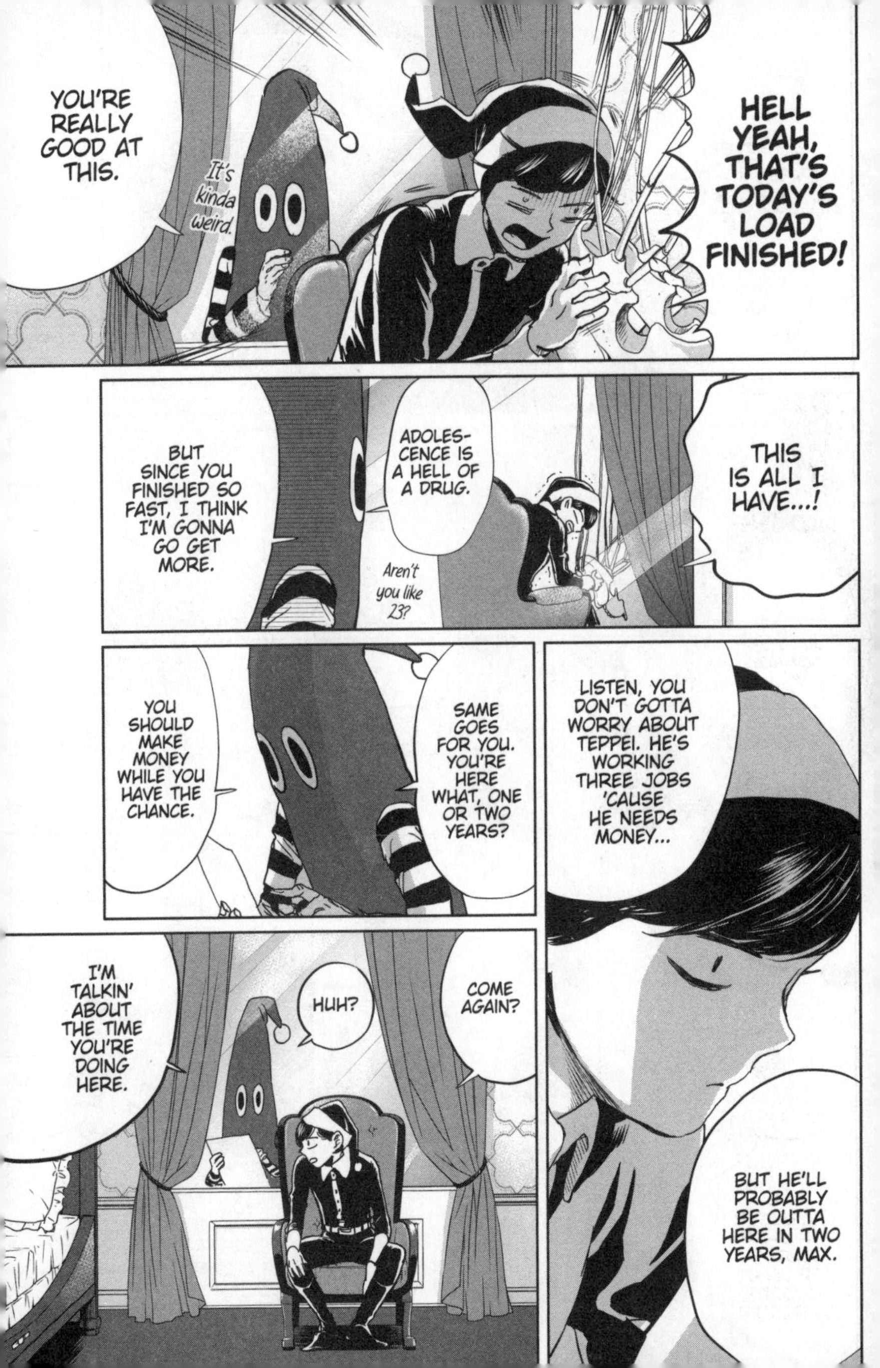
HELL YEAH, THAT'S TODAY'S LOAD FINISHED!
YOU'RE REALLY GOOD AT THIS.
It's kinda weird.
THIS IS ALL I HAVE...!
ADOLES-CENCE IS A HELL OF A DRUG.
BUT SINCE YOU FINISHED SO FAST, I THINK I'M GONNA GO GET MORE.
Aren't you like 23?
LISTEN, YOU DON'T GOTTA WORRY ABOUT TEPPEI. HE'S WORKING THREE JOBS 'CAUSE HE NEEDS MONEY...
BUT HE'LL PROBABLY BE OUTTA HERE IN TWO YEARS, MAX.
SAME GOES FOR YOU. YOU'RE HERE WHAT, ONE OR TWO YEARS?
YOU SHOULD MAKE MONEY WHILE YOU HAVE THE CHANCE.
COME AGAIN?
HUH?
I'M TALKIN' ABOUT THE TIME YOU'RE DOING HERE.

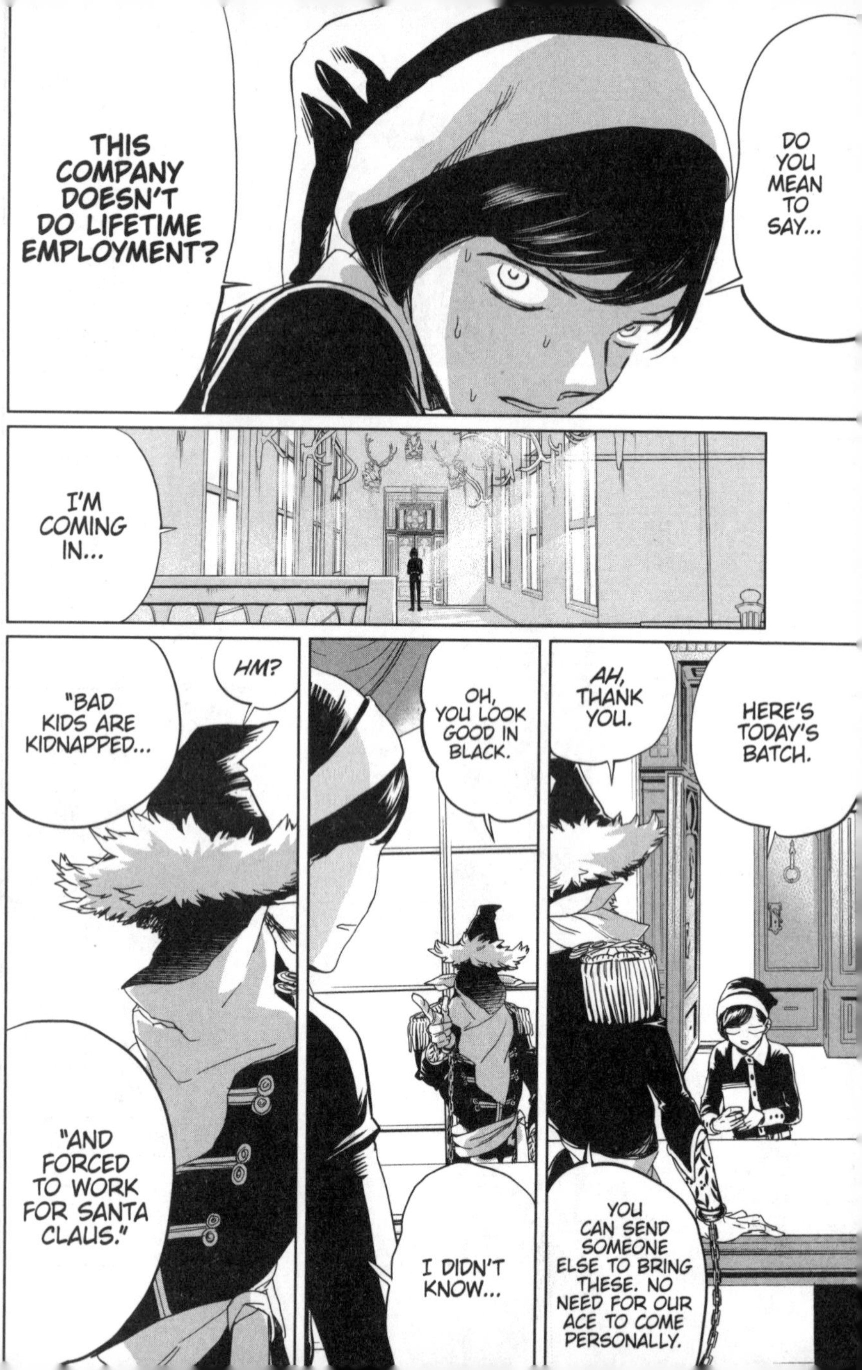
DO YOU MEAN TO SAY...
THIS COMPANY DOESN'T DO LIFETIME EMPLOYMENT?
I'M COMING IN...
HERE'S TODAY'S BATCH.
AH, THANK YOU.
YOU CAN SEND SOMEONE ELSE TO BRING THESE. NO NEED FOR OUR ACE TO COME PERSONALLY.
OH, YOU LOOK GOOD IN BLACK.
I DIDN'T KNOW...
HM?
"BAD KIDS ARE KIDNAPPED...
"AND FORCED TO WORK FOR SANTA CLAUS."

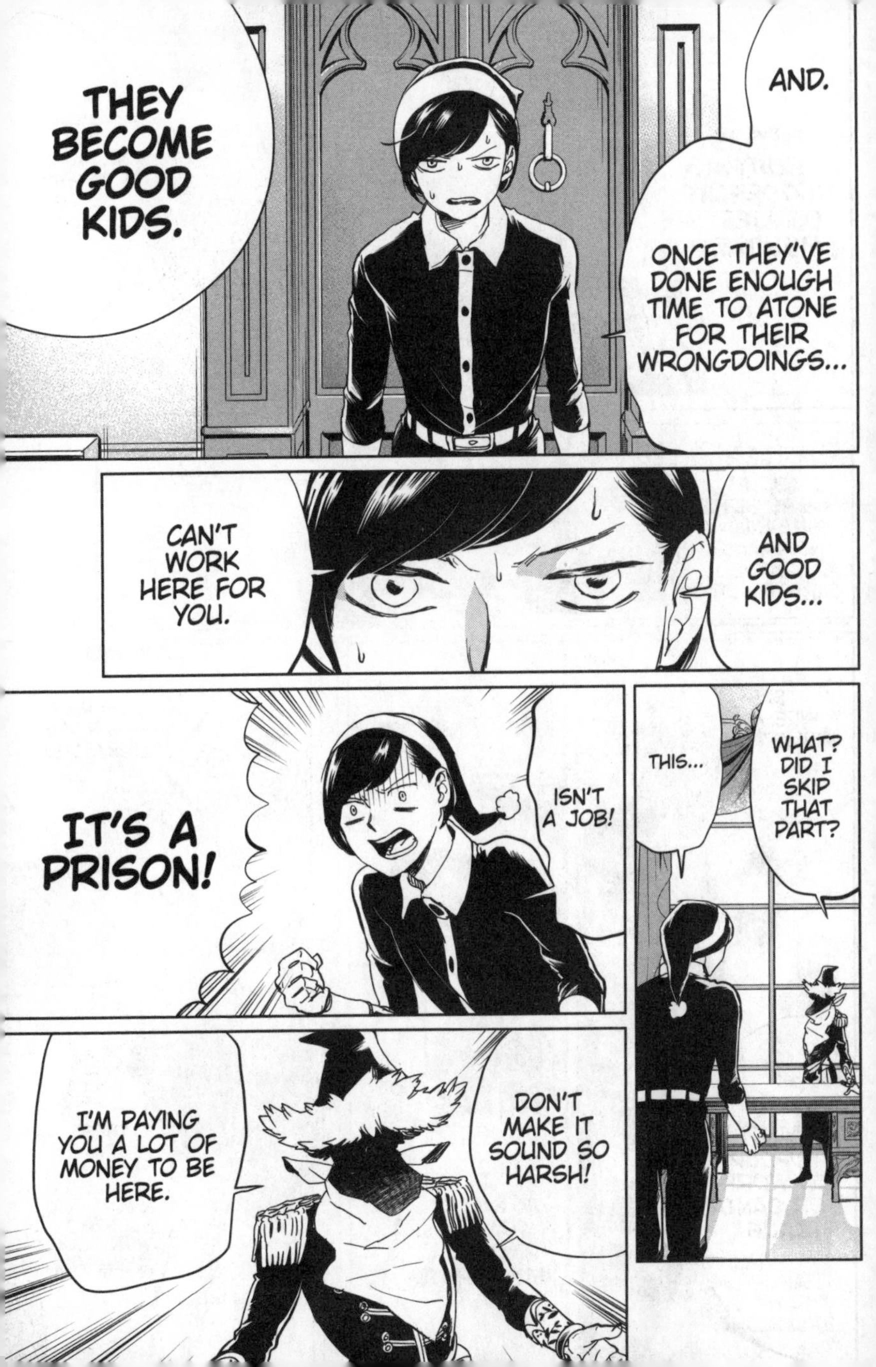
AND.
ONCE THEY'VE DONE ENOUGH TIME TO ATONE FOR THEIR WRONGDOINGS...
THEY BECOME GOOD KIDS.
AND GOOD KIDS...
CAN'T WORK HERE FOR YOU.
WHAT? DID I SKIP THAT PART?
THIS...
ISN'T A JOB!
IT'S A PRISON!
DON'T MAKE IT SOUND SO HARSH!
I'M PAYING YOU A LOT OF MONEY TO BE HERE.

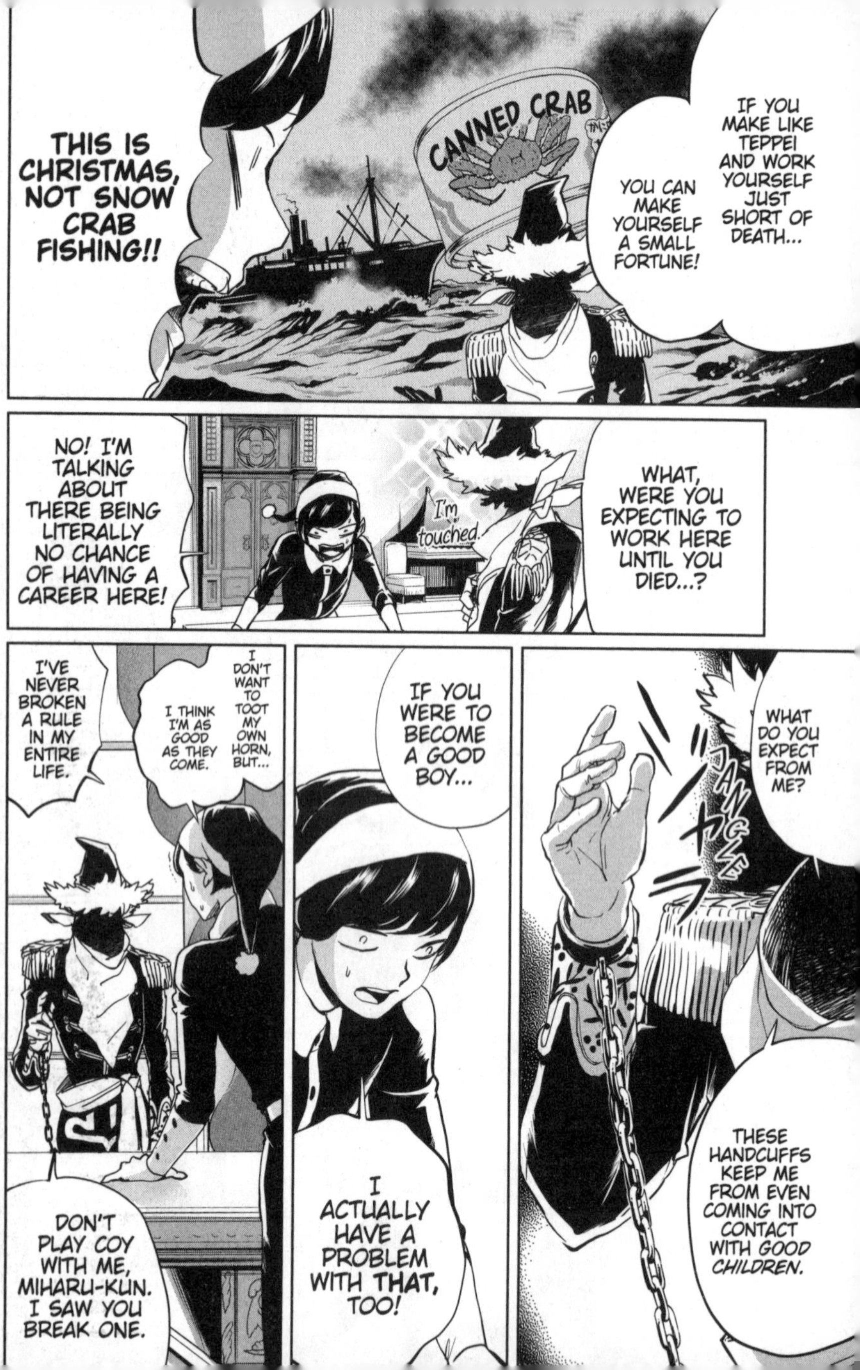
IF YOU MAKE LIKE TEPPEI AND WORK YOURSELF JUST SHORT OF DEATH...
YOU CAN MAKE YOURSELF A SMALL FORTUNE!
CANNED CRAB
THIS IS CHRISTMAS, NOT SNOW CRAB FISHING!!
WHAT, WERE YOU EXPECTING TO WORK HERE UNTIL YOU DIED...?
I'm touched.
NO! I'M TALKING ABOUT THERE BEING LITERALLY NO CHANCE OF HAVING A CAREER HERE!
WHAT DO YOU EXPECT FROM ME?
JANGLE
THESE HANDCUFFS KEEP ME FROM EVEN COMING INTO CONTACT WITH GOOD CHILDREN.
IF YOU WERE TO BECOME A GOOD BOY...
I ACTUALLY HAVE A PROBLEM WITH THAT, TOO!
I DON'T WANT TO TOOT MY OWN HORN, BUT...
I THINK I'M AS GOOD AS THEY COME.
I'VE NEVER BROKEN A RULE IN MY ENTIRE LIFE.
DON'T PLAY COY WITH ME, MIHARU-KUN. I SAW YOU BREAK ONE.

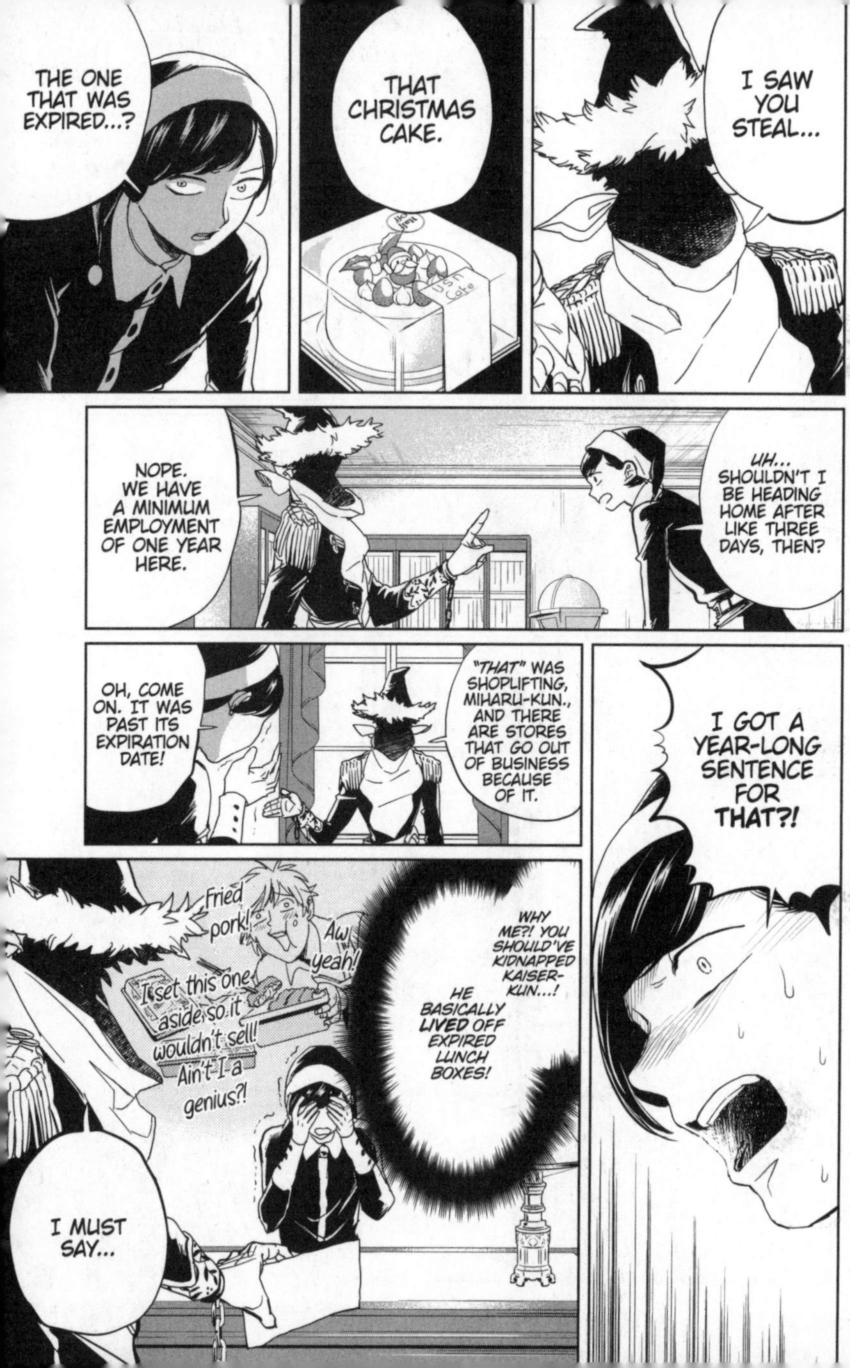
I SAW YOU STEAL...
THAT CHRISTMAS CAKE.
THE ONE THAT WAS EXPIRED...?
UH... SHOULDN'T I BE HEADING HOME AFTER LIKE THREE DAYS, THEN?
NOPE. WE HAVE A MINIMUM EMPLOYMENT OF ONE YEAR HERE.
I GOT A YEAR-LONG SENTENCE FOR THAT?!
OH, COME ON. IT WAS PAST ITS EXPIRATION DATE!
"THAT" WAS SHOPLIFTING, MIHARU-KUN., AND THERE ARE STORES THAT GO OUT OF BUSINESS BECAUSE OF IT.
WHY ME?! YOU SHOULD'VE KIDNAPPED KAISER-KUN...!
HE BASICALLY LIVED OFF EXPIRED LUNCH BOXES!
Aw yeah!
Fried pork!
I set this one aside so it wouldn't sell! Ain't I a genius?!
I MUST SAY...

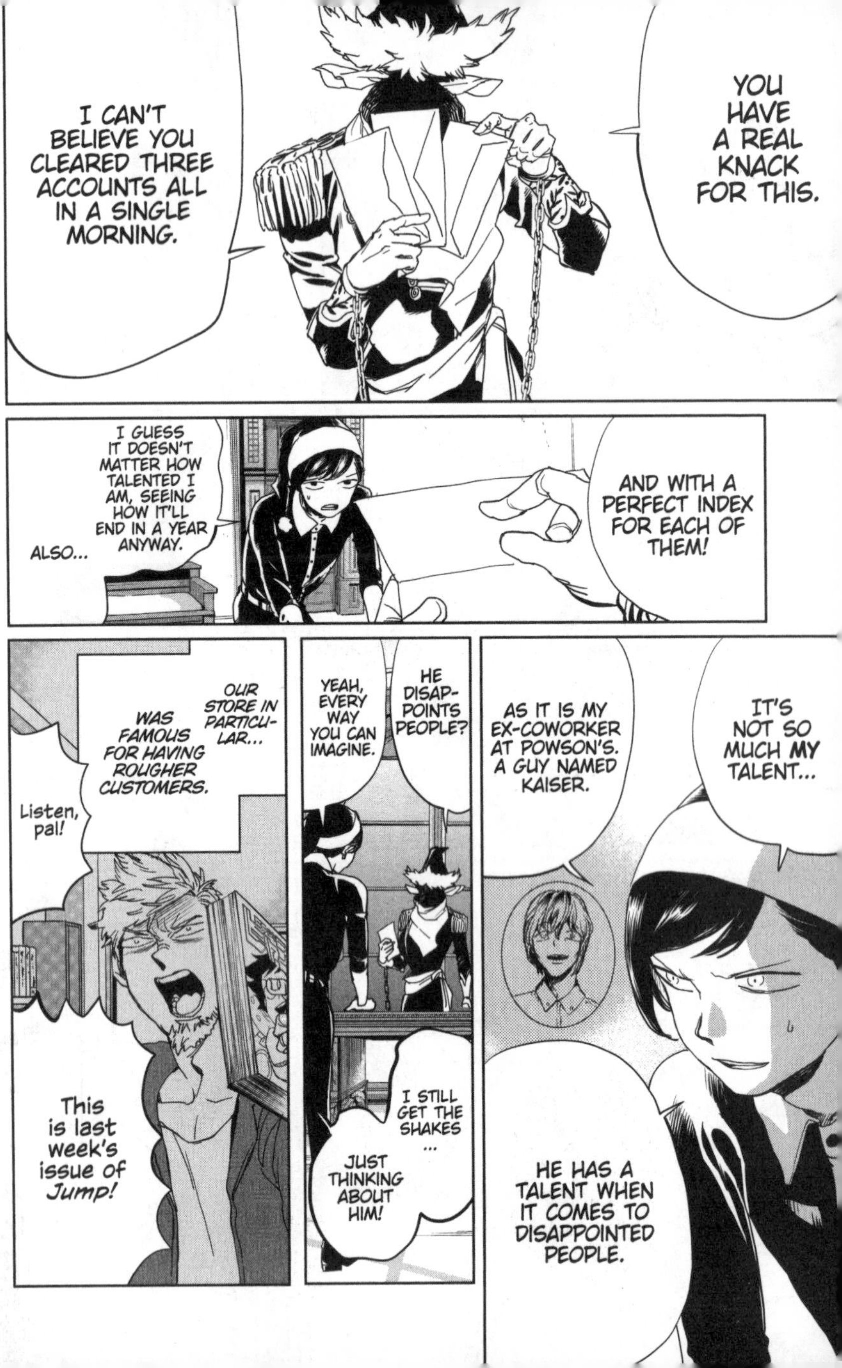
YOU HAVE A REAL KNACK FOR THIS.
I CAN'T BELIEVE YOU CLEARED THREE ACCOUNTS ALL IN A SINGLE MORNING.
AND WITH A PERFECT INDEX FOR EACH OF THEM!
I GUESS IT DOESN'T MATTER HOW TALENTED I AM, SEEING HOW IT'LL END IN A YEAR ANYWAY.
ALSO...
IT'S NOT SO MUCH MY TALENT...
AS IT IS MY EX-COWORKER AT POWSON'S. A GUY NAMED KAISER.
HE HAS A TALENT WHEN IT COMES TO DISAPPOINTED PEOPLE.
HE DISAPPOINTS PEOPLE?
YEAH, EVERY WAY YOU CAN IMAGINE.
I STILL GET THE SHAKES ...
JUST THINKING ABOUT HIM!
OUR STORE IN PARTICULAR...
WAS FAMOUS FOR HAVING ROUGHER CUSTOMERS.
Listen, pal!
This is last week's issue of *Jump!*

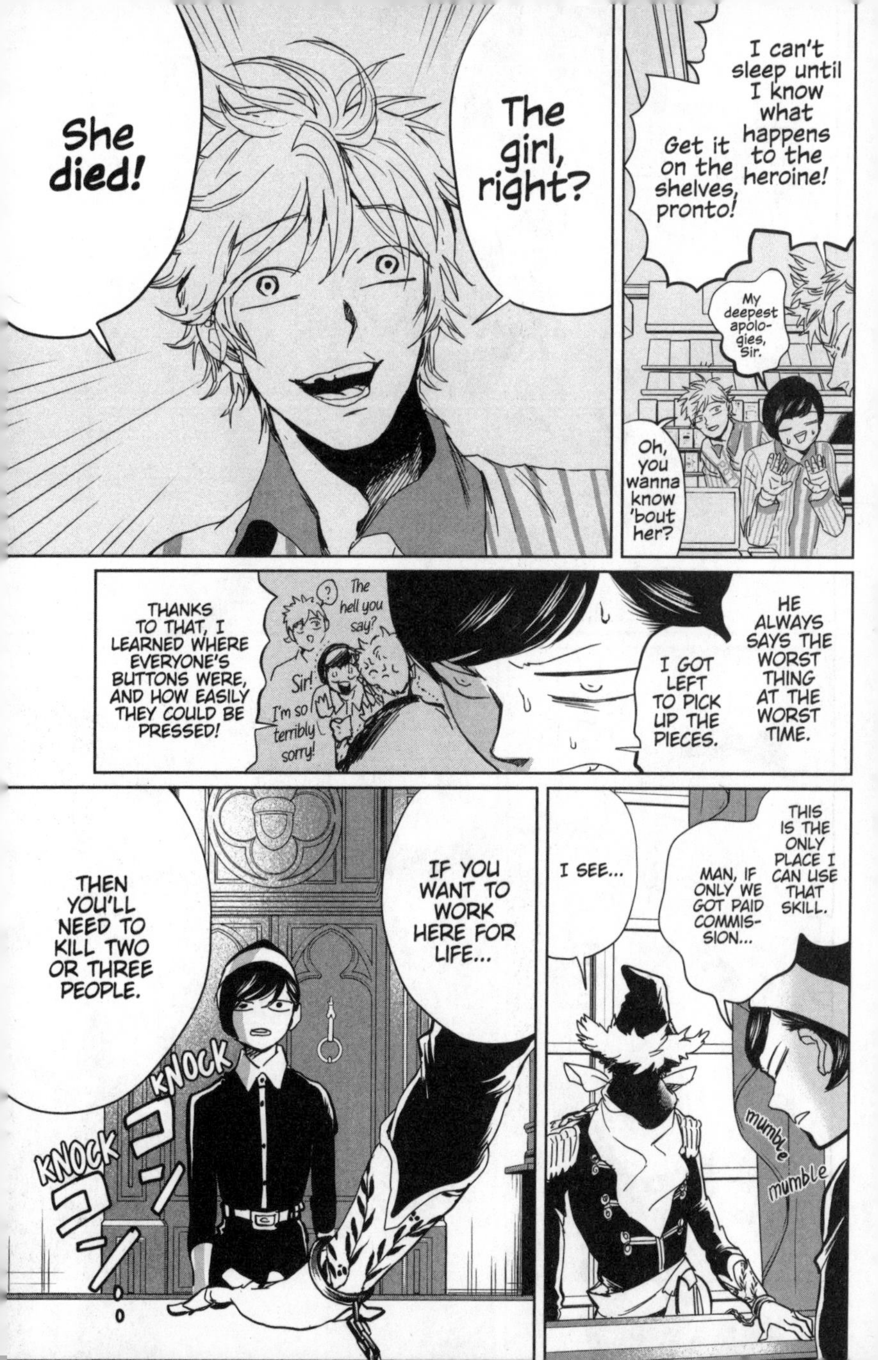
I can't sleep until I know what happens to the heroine!
Get it on the shelves, pronto!
My deepest apolo-gies, Sir.
Oh, you wanna know 'bout her?
The girl, right?
She died!
HE ALWAYS SAYS THE WORST THING AT THE WORST TIME.
I GOT LEFT TO PICK UP THE PIECES.
THANKS TO THAT, I LEARNED WHERE EVERYONE'S BUTTONS WERE, AND HOW EASILY THEY COULD BE PRESSED!
The hell you say?
?
Sir!
I'm so terribly sorry!
THIS IS THE ONLY PLACE I CAN USE THAT SKILL.
MAN, IF ONLY WE GOT PAID COMMIS-SION...
mumble mumble
I SEE...
IF YOU WANT TO WORK HERE FOR LIFE...
THEN YOU'LL NEED TO KILL TWO OR THREE PEOPLE.
KNOCK
KNOCK

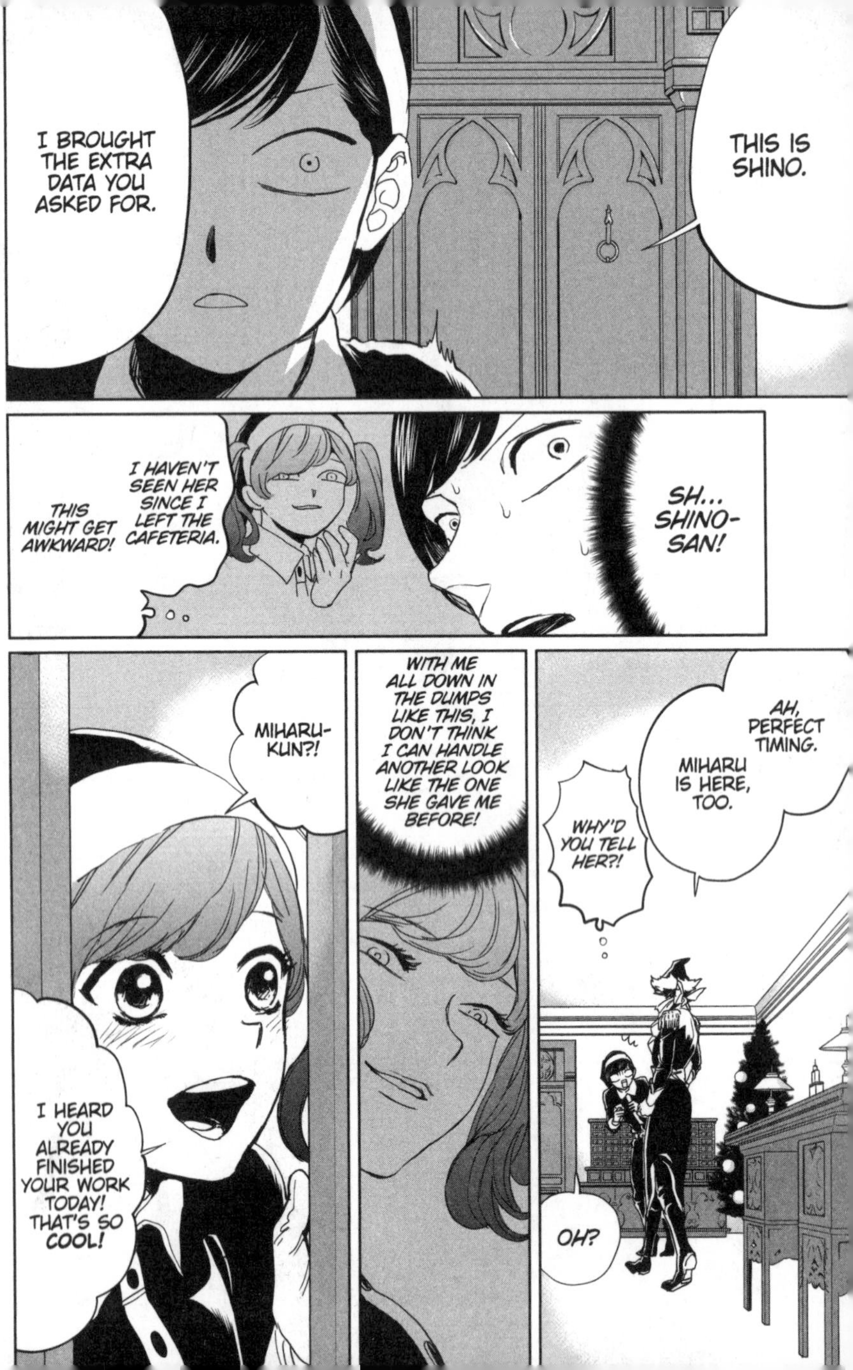

THIS IS SHINO.
I BROUGHT THE EXTRA DATA YOU ASKED FOR.
SH... SHINO-SAN!
I HAVEN'T SEEN HER SINCE I LEFT THE CAFETERIA.
THIS MIGHT GET AWKWARD!
AH, PERFECT TIMING.
MIHARU IS HERE, TOO.
WHY'D YOU TELL HER?!
OH?
WITH ME ALL DOWN IN THE DUMPS LIKE THIS, I DON'T THINK I CAN HANDLE ANOTHER LOOK LIKE THE ONE SHE GAVE ME BEFORE!
MIHARU-KUN?!
I HEARD YOU ALREADY FINISHED YOUR WORK TODAY! THAT'S SO COOL!

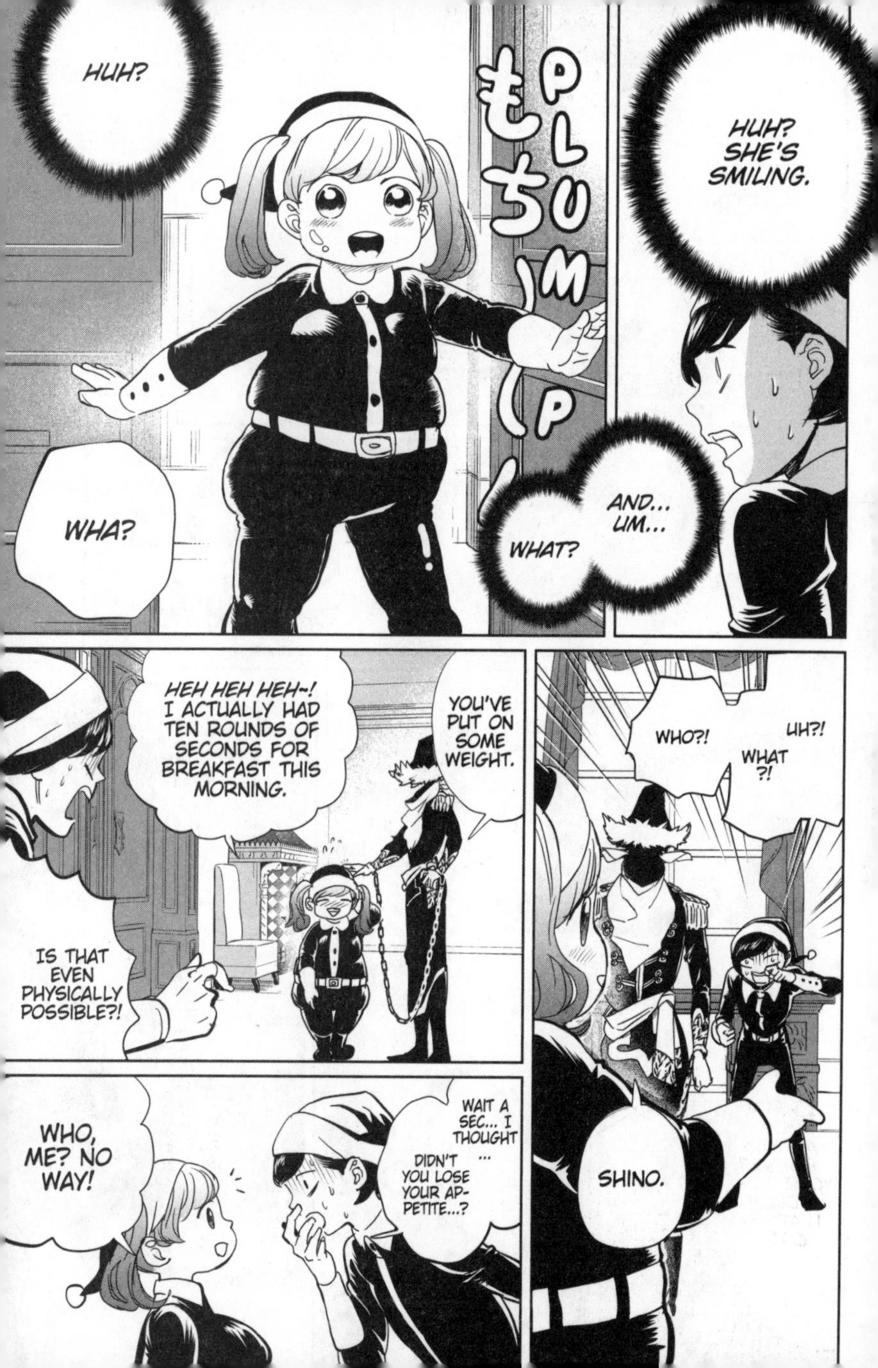
HUH? SHE'S SMILING.
AND... UM...
WHAT?
HUH?
もち
PLUMP
WHA?
UH?!
WHO?!
WHAT ?!
SHINO.
YOU'VE PUT ON SOME WEIGHT.
HEH HEH HEH~! I ACTUALLY HAD TEN ROUNDS OF SECONDS FOR BREAKFAST THIS MORNING.
IS THAT EVEN PHYSICALLY POSSIBLE?!
WAIT A SEC... I THOUGHT...
DIDN'T YOU LOSE YOUR AP-PETITE...?
WHO, ME? NO WAY!

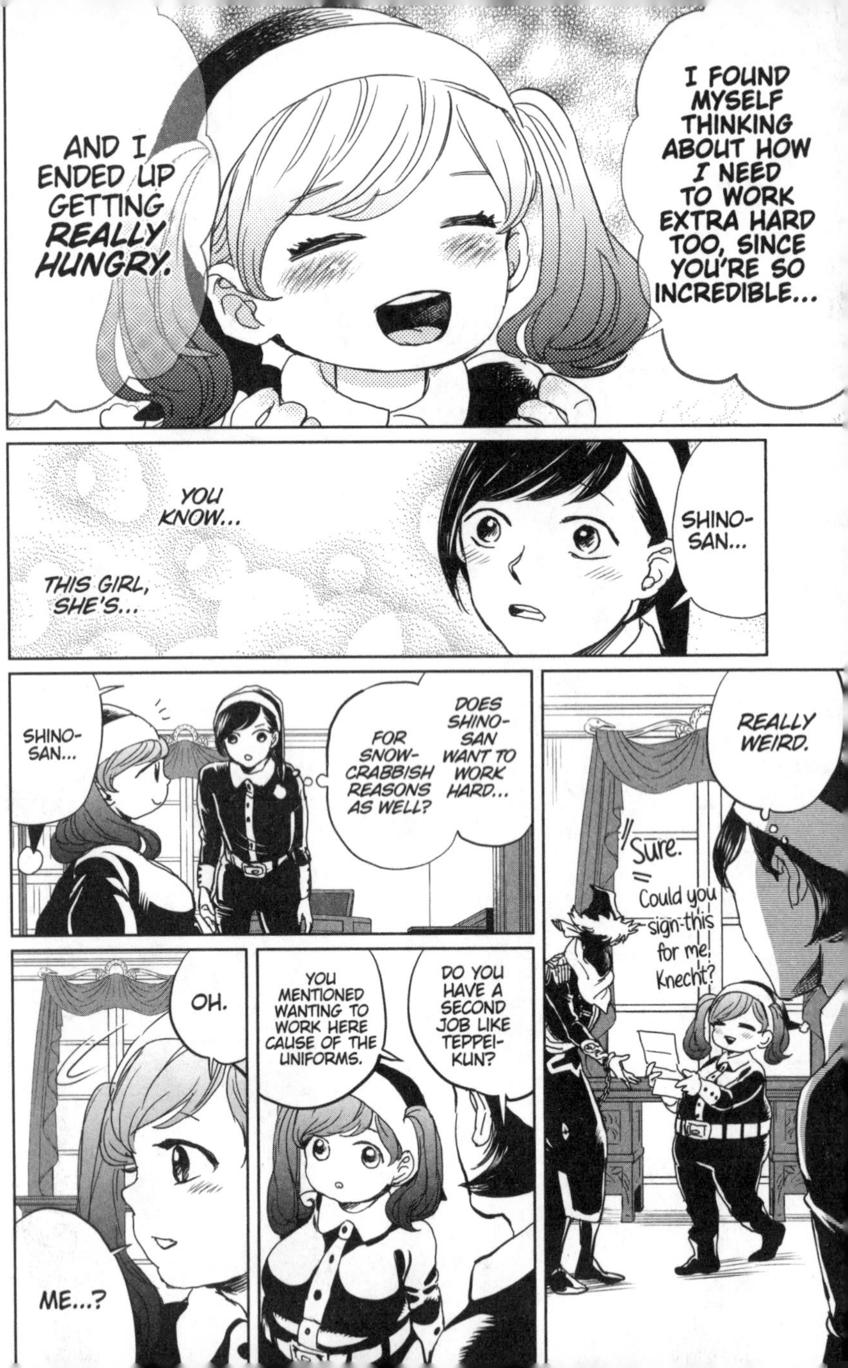
I FOUND MYSELF THINKING ABOUT HOW I NEED TO WORK EXTRA HARD TOO, SINCE YOU'RE SO INCREDIBLE...
AND I ENDED UP GETTING REALLY HUNGRY.
SHINO-SAN...
YOU KNOW...
THIS GIRL, SHE'S...
REALLY WEIRD.
Could you sign this for me, Knecht?
Sure.
DOES SHINO-SAN WANT TO WORK HARD...
FOR SNOW-CRABBISH REASONS AS WELL?
SHINO-SAN...
DO YOU HAVE A SECOND JOB LIKE TEPPEI-KUN?
YOU MENTIONED WANTING TO WORK HERE CAUSE OF THE UNIFORMS.
OH.
ME...?

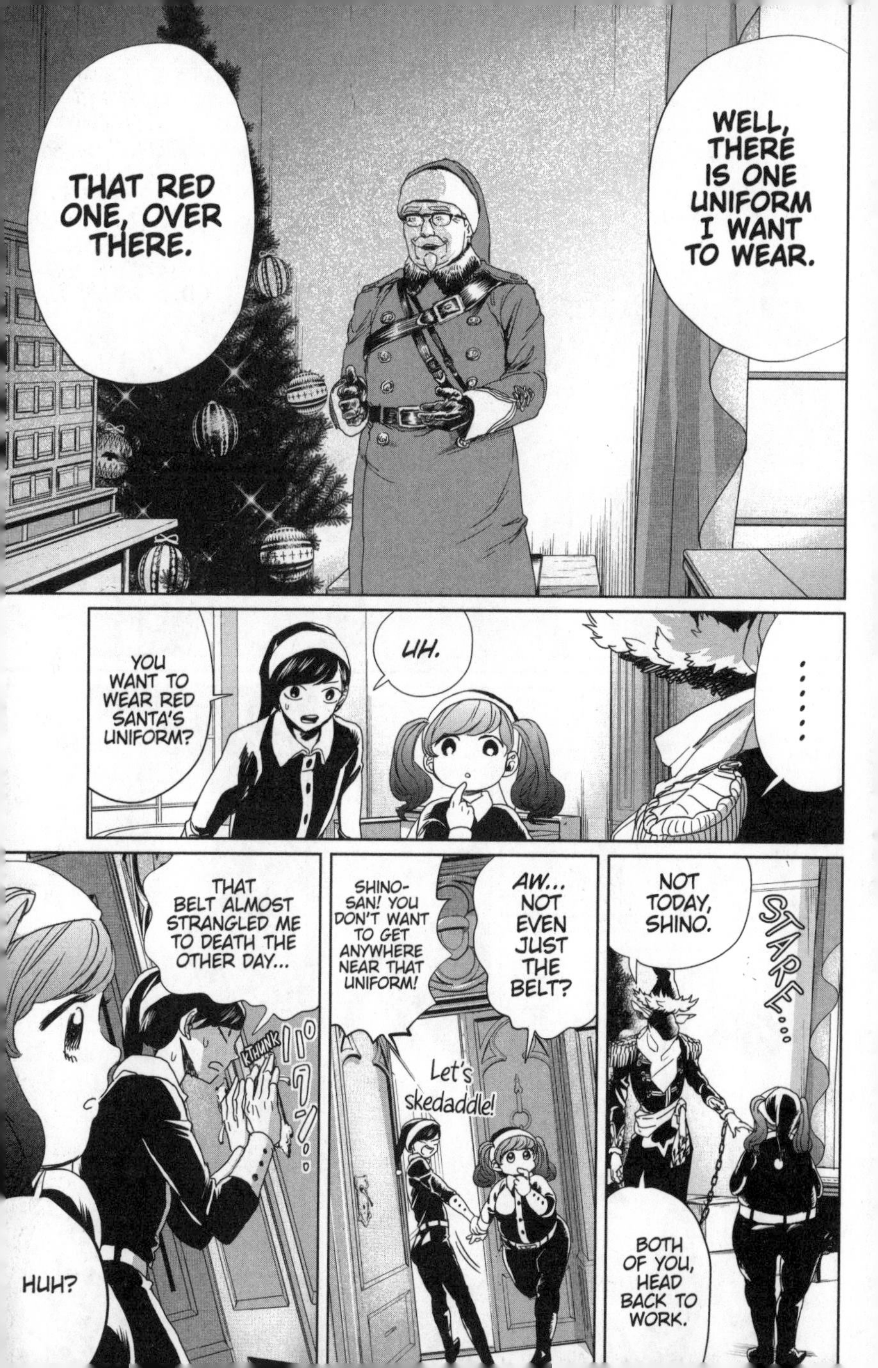
WELL, THERE IS ONE UNIFORM I WANT TO WEAR.
THAT RED ONE, OVER THERE.
......
UH.
YOU WANT TO WEAR RED SANTA'S UNIFORM?
NOT TODAY, SHINO.
STARE...
BOTH OF YOU, HEAD BACK TO WORK.
AW... NOT EVEN JUST THE BELT?
SHINO-SAN! YOU DON'T WANT TO GET ANYWHERE NEAR THAT UNIFORM!
Let's skedaddle!
THAT BELT ALMOST STRANGLED ME TO DEATH THE OTHER DAY...
THUNK
HUH?

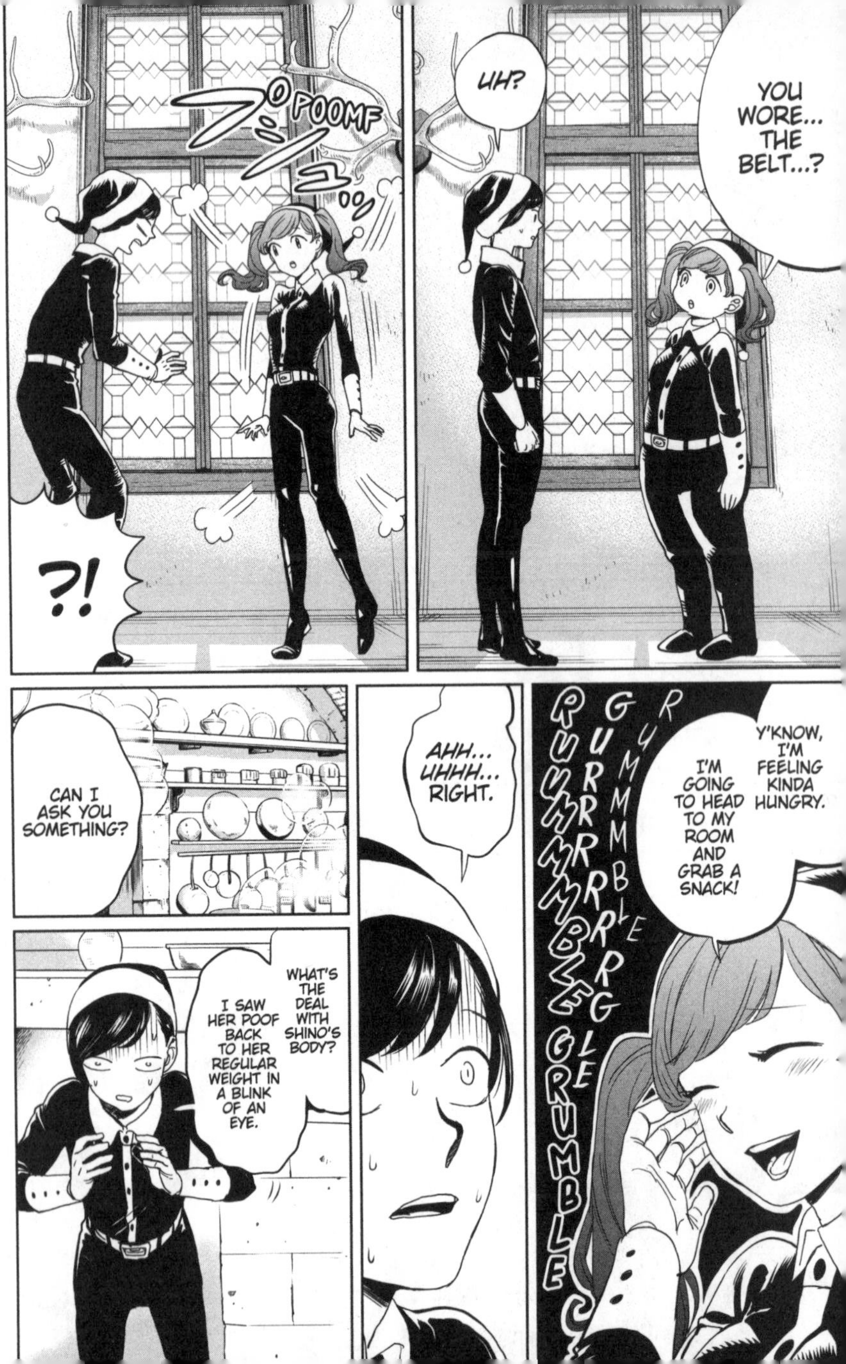
YOU WORE... THE BELT...?
UH?
POOMF
?!
Y'KNOW, I'M FEELING KINDA HUNGRY.
I'M GOING TO HEAD TO MY ROOM AND GRAB A SNACK!
RUMMMBLE
GURRRRRRRGLE
RUUMMMBLE
GRUMBLE
AHH... UHHH... RIGHT.
CAN I ASK YOU SOMETHING?
WHAT'S THE DEAL WITH SHINO'S BODY?
I SAW HER POOF BACK TO HER REGULAR WEIGHT IN A BLINK OF AN EYE.

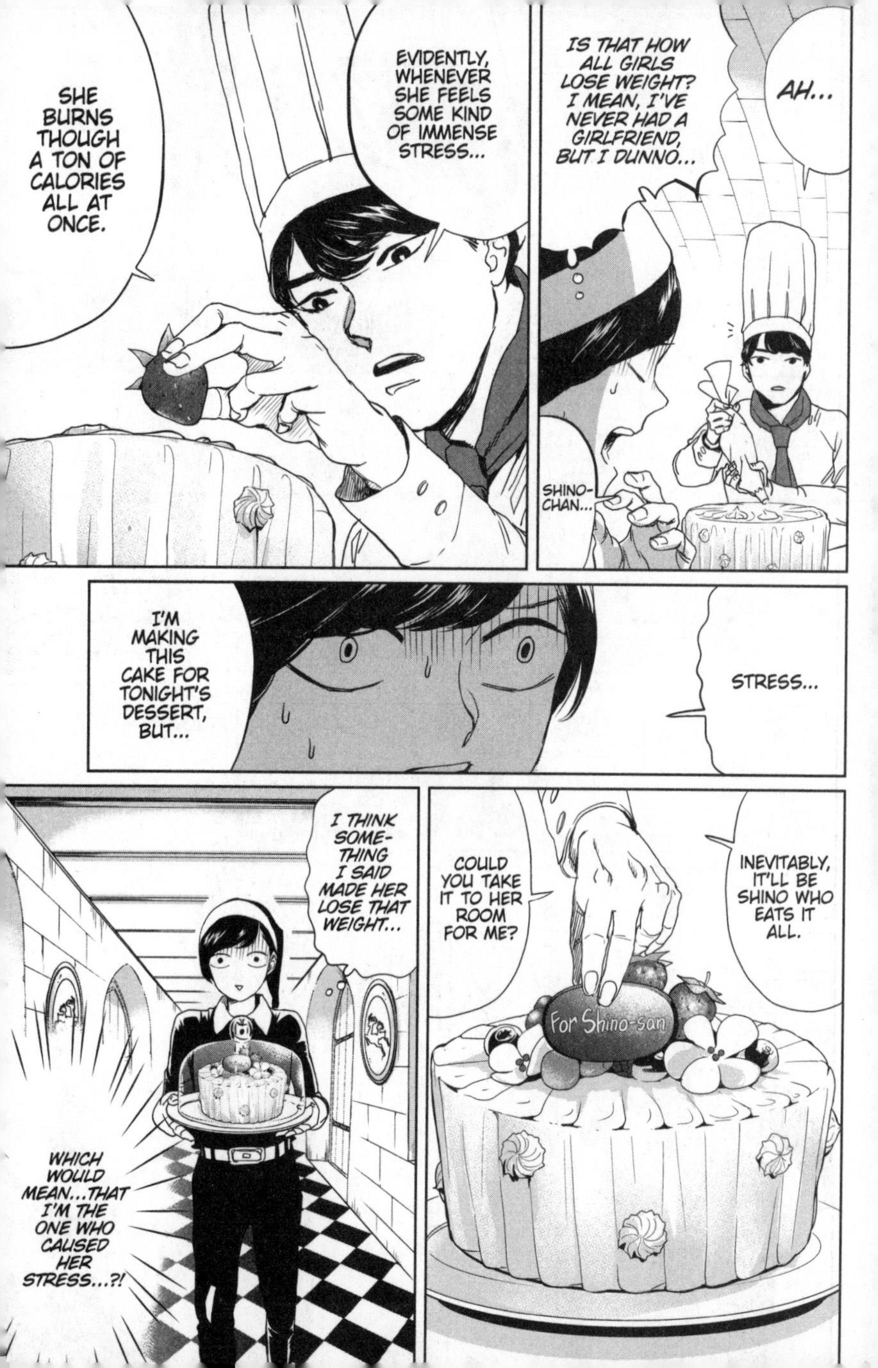
AH...
IS THAT HOW ALL GIRLS LOSE WEIGHT? I MEAN, I'VE NEVER HAD A GIRLFRIEND, BUT I DUNNO...
SHINO-CHAN...
EVIDENTLY, WHENEVER SHE FEELS SOME KIND OF IMMENSE STRESS...
SHE BURNS THOUGH A TON OF CALORIES ALL AT ONCE.
STRESS...
I'M MAKING THIS CAKE FOR TONIGHT'S DESSERT, BUT...
INEVITABLY, IT'LL BE SHINO WHO EATS IT ALL.
COULD YOU TAKE IT TO HER ROOM FOR ME?
For Shino-san
I THINK SOME-THING I SAID MADE HER LOSE THAT WEIGHT...
WHICH WOULD MEAN...THAT I'M THE ONE WHO CAUSED HER STRESS...?!

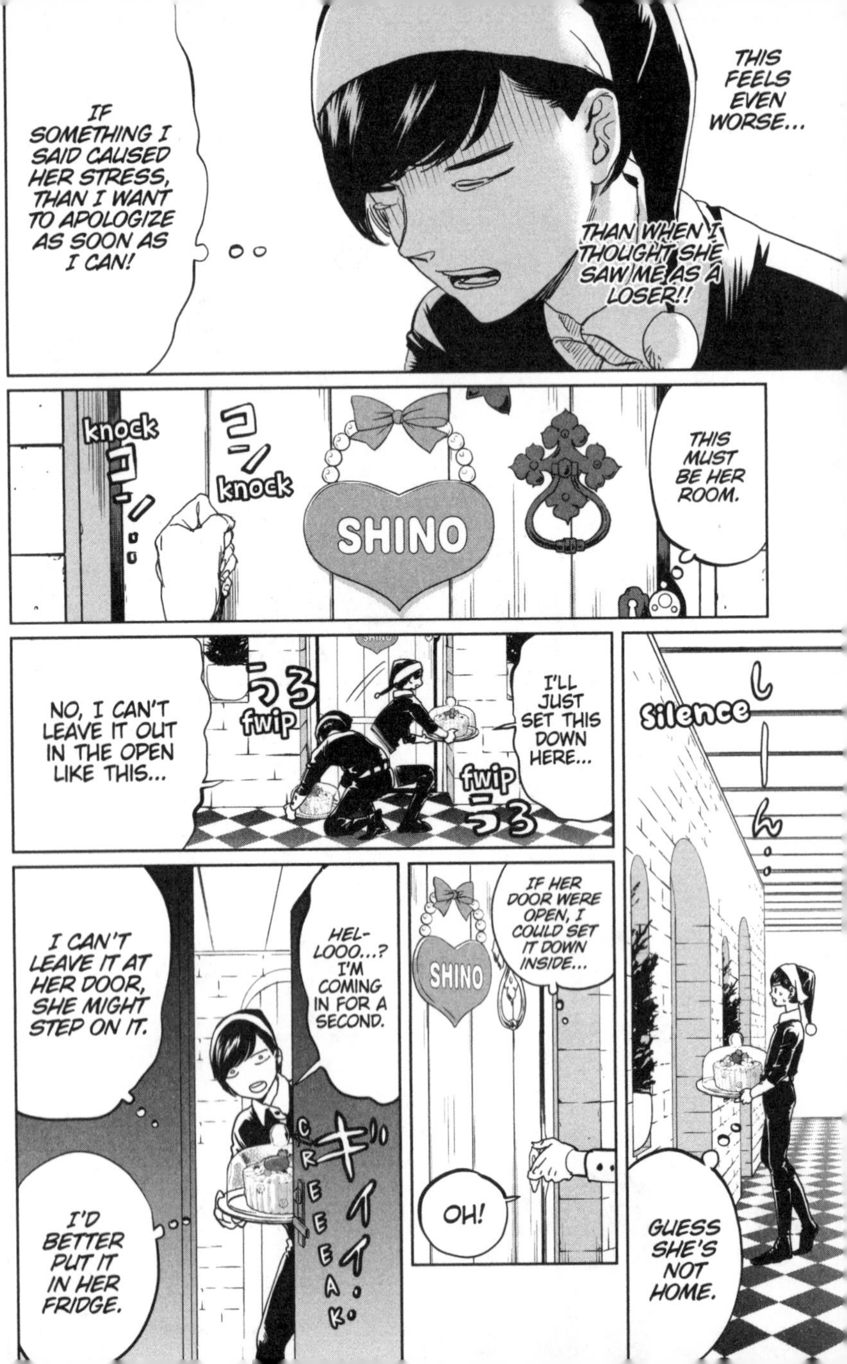

THIS FEELS EVEN WORSE...
THAN WHEN I THOUGHT SHE SAW ME AS A LOSER!!
IF SOMETHING I SAID CAUSED HER STRESS, THAN I WANT TO APOLOGIZE AS SOON AS I CAN!
THIS MUST BE HER ROOM.
SHINO
knock
knock
silence
GUESS SHE'S NOT HOME.
I'LL JUST SET THIS DOWN HERE...
fwip
fwip
NO, I CAN'T LEAVE IT OUT IN THE OPEN LIKE THIS...
SHINO
IF HER DOOR WERE OPEN, I COULD SET IT DOWN INSIDE...
OH!
HEL-LOOO...? I'M COMING IN FOR A SECOND.
CREEEAK
I CAN'T LEAVE IT AT HER DOOR, SHE MIGHT STEP ON IT.
I'D BETTER PUT IT IN HER FRIDGE.

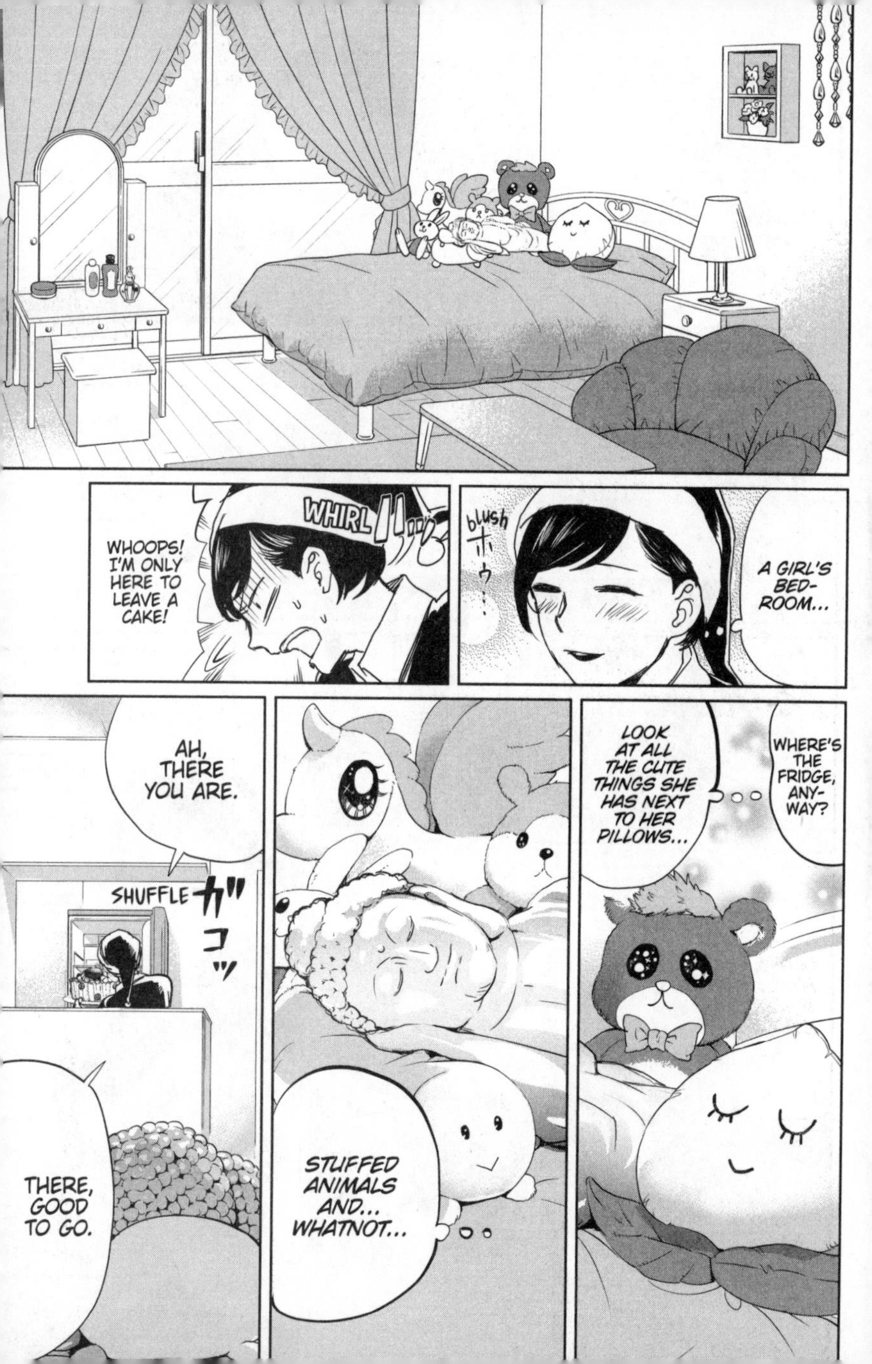
A GIRL'S BED-ROOM...
blush ホゥ…
WHIRL
WHOOPS! I'M ONLY HERE TO LEAVE A CAKE!
WHERE'S THE FRIDGE, ANY-WAY?
LOOK AT ALL THE CUTE THINGS SHE HAS NEXT TO HER PILLOWS...
STUFFED ANIMALS AND... WHATNOT...
AH, THERE YOU ARE.
SHUFFLE ガコッ
THERE, GOOD TO GO.

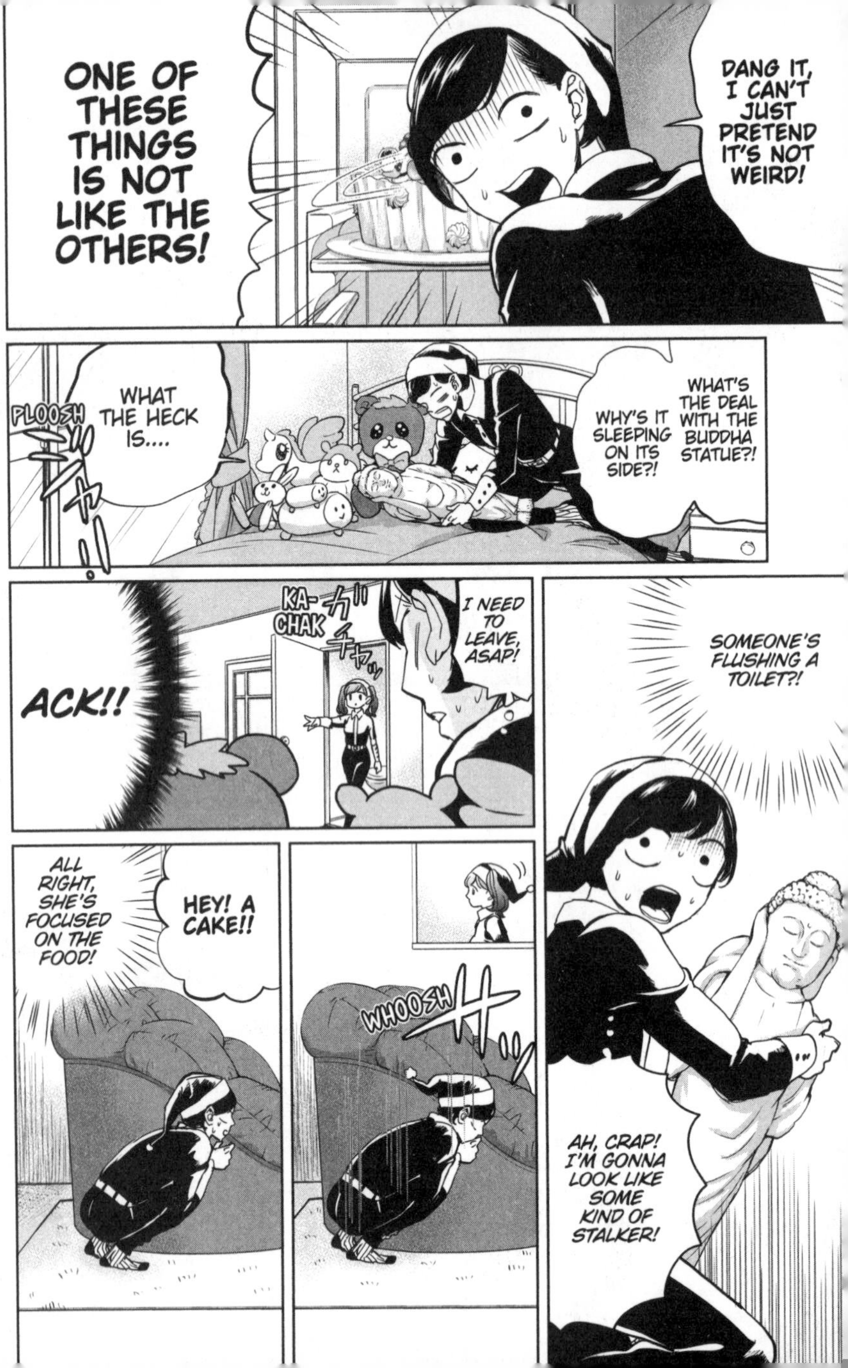
DANG IT, I CAN'T JUST PRETEND IT'S NOT WEIRD!
ONE OF THESE THINGS IS NOT LIKE THE OTHERS!
WHAT'S THE DEAL WITH THE BUDDHA STATUE?!
WHY'S IT SLEEPING ON ITS SIDE?!
WHAT THE HECK IS....
PLOOSH
SOMEONE'S FLUSHING A TOILET?!
AH, CRAP! I'M GONNA LOOK LIKE SOME KIND OF STALKER!
I NEED TO LEAVE, ASAP!
KA-CHAK
ACK!!
WHOOSH
HEY! A CAKE!!
ALL RIGHT, SHE'S FOCUSED ON THE FOOD!

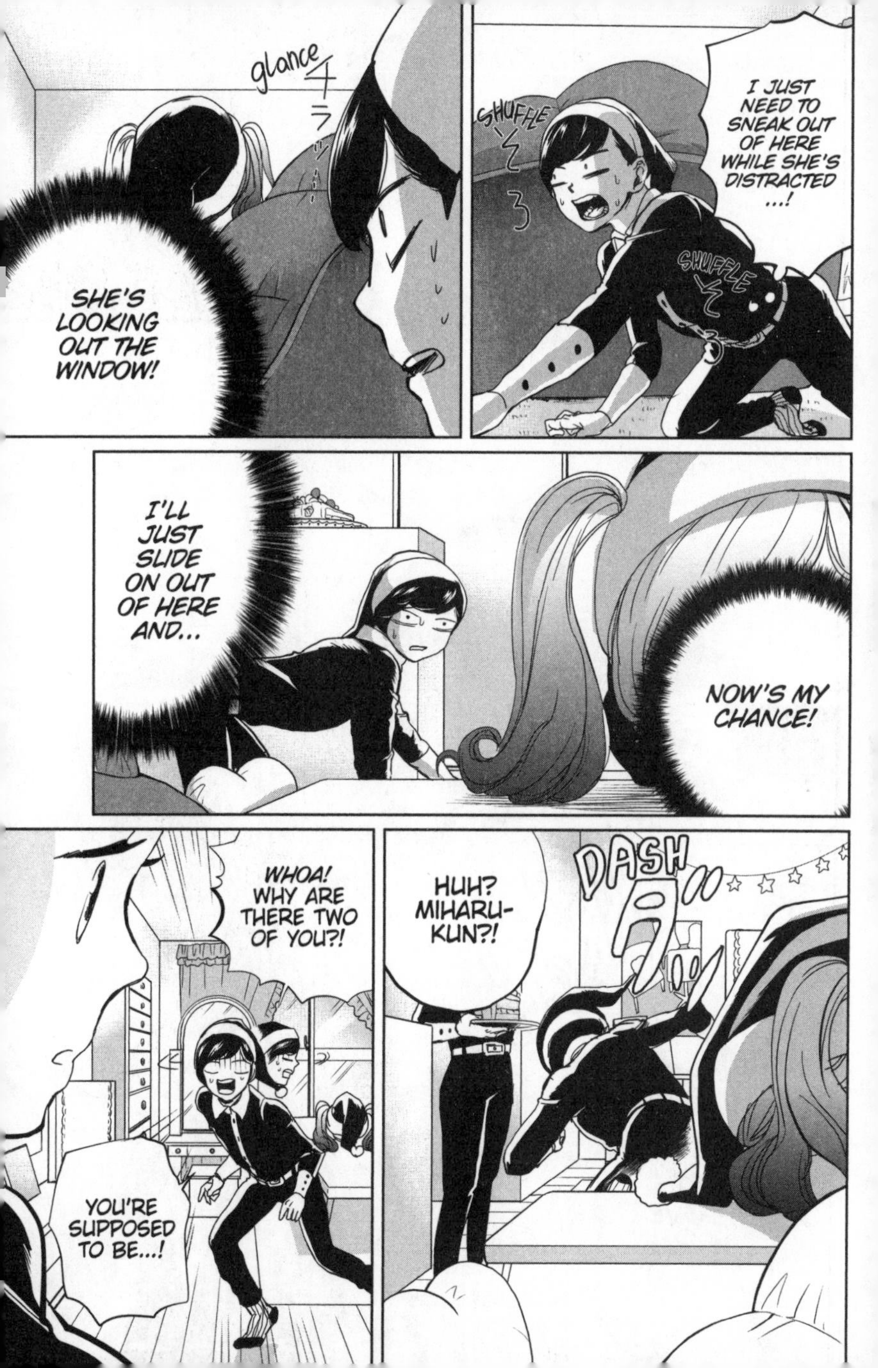
SHUFFLE
I JUST NEED TO SNEAK OUT OF HERE WHILE SHE'S DISTRACTED ...!
SHUFFLE
glance
SHE'S LOOKING OUT THE WINDOW!
NOW'S MY CHANCE!
I'LL JUST SLIDE ON OUT OF HERE AND...
DASH
HUH? MIHARU-KUN?!
WHOA! WHY ARE THERE TWO OF YOU?!
YOU'RE SUPPOSED TO BE...!

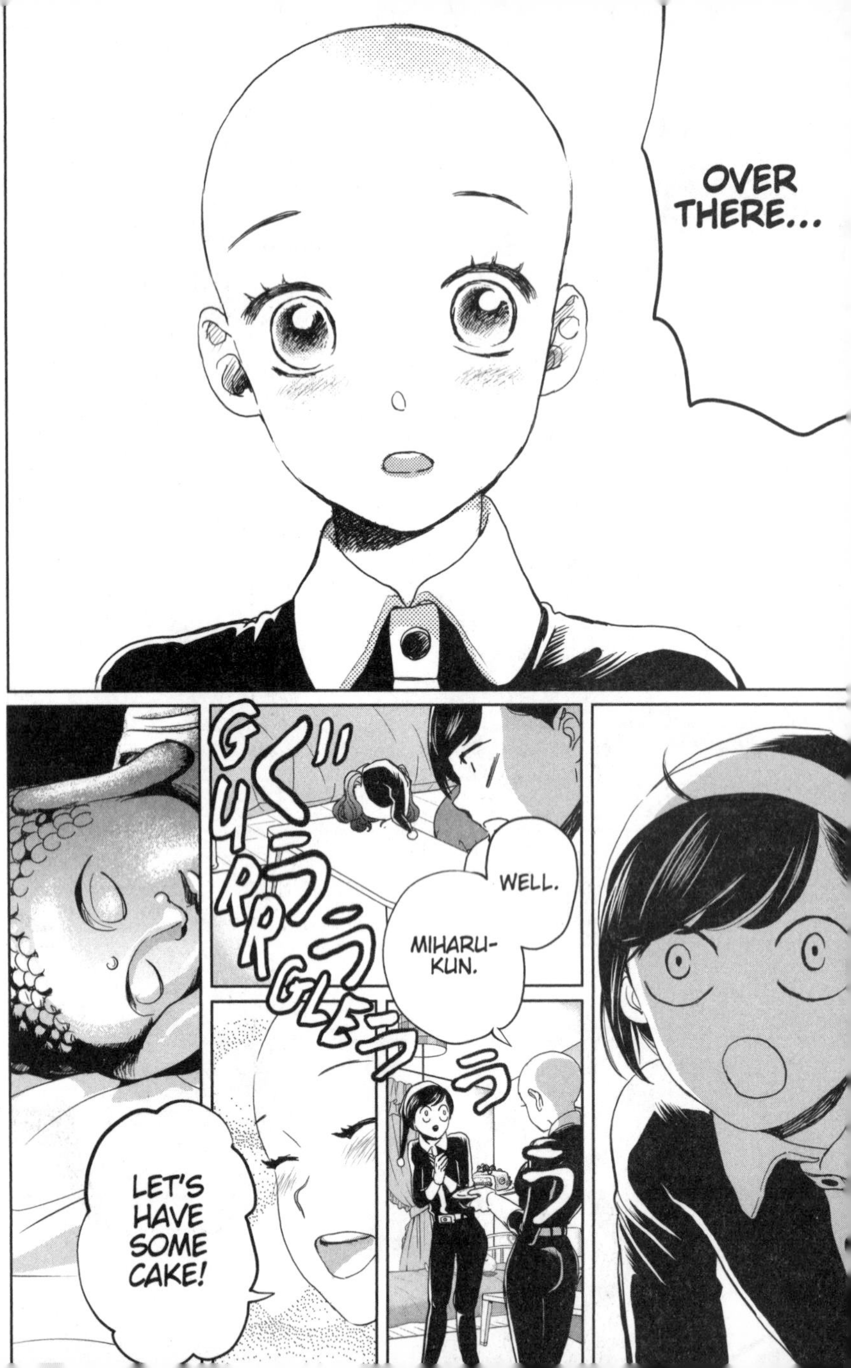

OVER THERE...
GURRRGLE
ぐぅらぅらぅらぅ
WELL.
MIHARU-KUN.
LET'S HAVE SOME CAKE!

Chapter 7: Black Temptation, Red Destiny

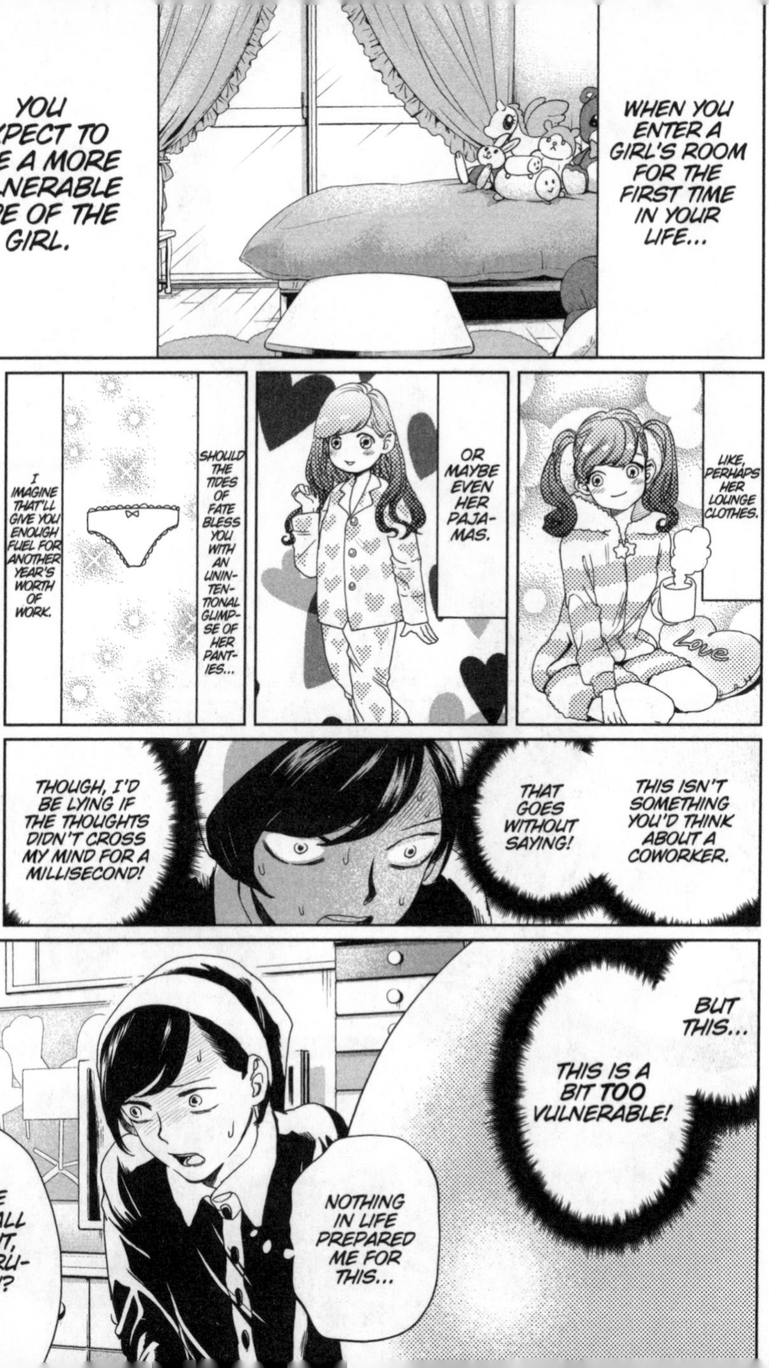
WHEN YOU ENTER A GIRL'S ROOM FOR THE FIRST TIME IN YOUR LIFE...
YOU EXPECT TO SEE A MORE VULNERABLE SIDE OF THE GIRL.
LIKE, PERHAPS HER LOUNGE CLOTHES.
Love
OR MAYBE EVEN HER PAJAMAS.
SHOULD THE TIDES OF FATE BLESS YOU WITH AN UNINTENTIONAL GLIMPSE OF HER PANTIES...
I IMAGINE THAT'LL GIVE YOU ENOUGH FUEL FOR ANOTHER YEAR'S WORTH OF WORK.
THIS ISN'T SOMETHING YOU'D THINK ABOUT A COWORKER.
THAT GOES WITHOUT SAYING!
THOUGH, I'D BE LYING IF THE THOUGHTS DIDN'T CROSS MY MIND FOR A MILLISECOND!
BUT THIS...
THIS IS A BIT TOO VULNERABLE!
NOTHING IN LIFE PREPARED ME FOR THIS...
ARE YOU ALL RIGHT, MIHARU-KUN?

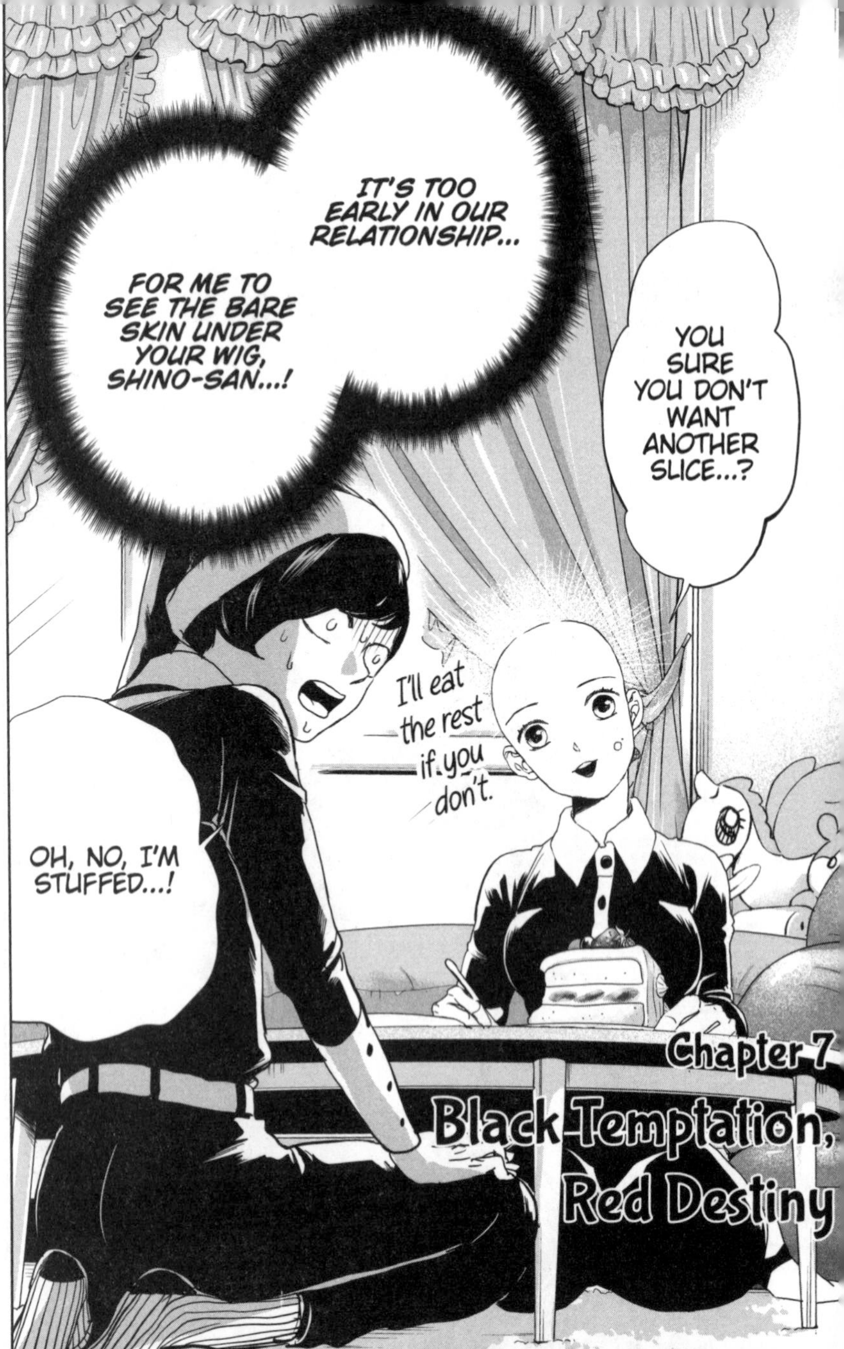
YOU SURE YOU DON'T WANT ANOTHER SLICE...?
I'll eat the rest if you don't.
OH, NO, I'M STUFFED...!
IT'S TOO EARLY IN OUR RELATIONSHIP...
FOR ME TO SEE THE BARE SKIN UNDER YOUR WIG, SHINO-SAN...!
Chapter 7
Black Temptation, Red Destiny

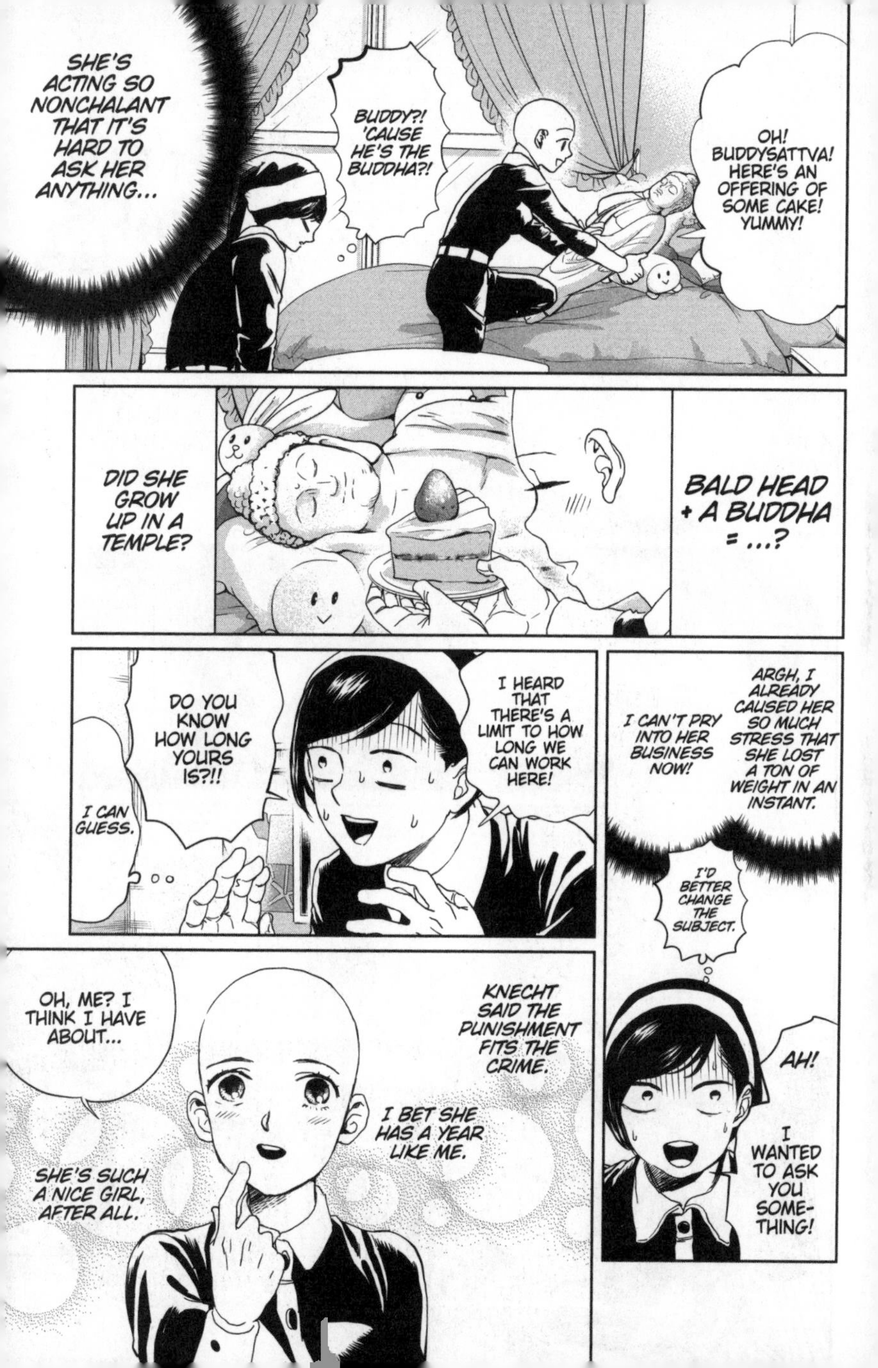
OH! BUDDYSATTVA! HERE'S AN OFFERING OF SOME CAKE! YUMMY!
BUDDY?! 'CAUSE HE'S THE BUDDHA?!
SHE'S ACTING SO NONCHALANT THAT IT'S HARD TO ASK HER ANYTHING...
BALD HEAD + A BUDDHA = ...?
DID SHE GROW UP IN A TEMPLE?
ARGH, I ALREADY CAUSED HER SO MUCH STRESS THAT SHE LOST A TON OF WEIGHT IN AN INSTANT.
I CAN'T PRY INTO HER BUSINESS NOW!
I'D BETTER CHANGE THE SUBJECT.
AH!
I WANTED TO ASK YOU SOME-THING!
I HEARD THAT THERE'S A LIMIT TO HOW LONG WE CAN WORK HERE!
DO YOU KNOW HOW LONG YOURS IS?!!
I CAN GUESS.
OH, ME? I THINK I HAVE ABOUT...
KNECHT SAID THE PUNISHMENT FITS THE CRIME.
I BET SHE HAS A YEAR LIKE ME.
SHE'S SUCH A NICE GIRL, AFTER ALL.

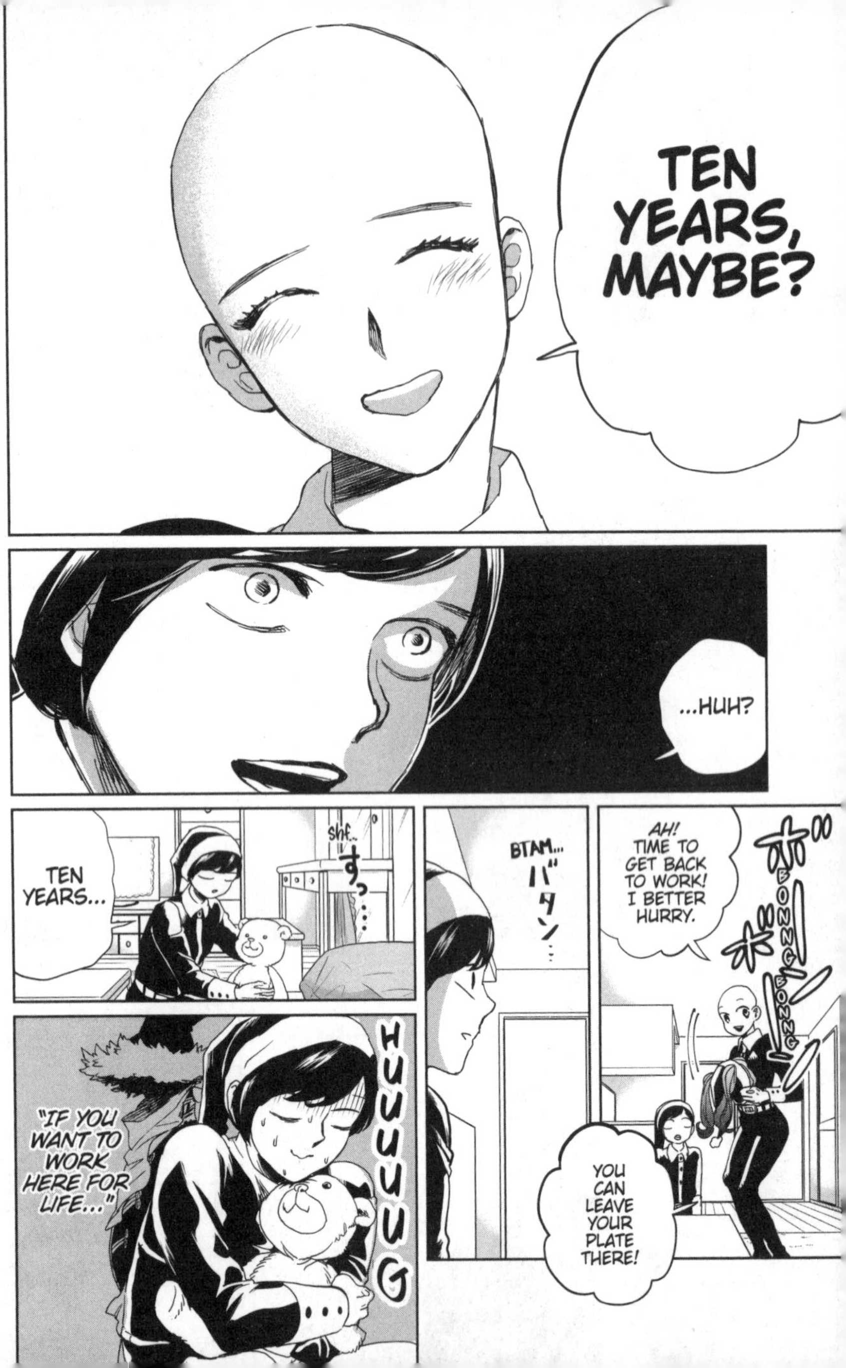
TEN YEARS, MAYBE?
...HUH?
AH! TIME TO GET BACK TO WORK! I BETTER HURRY.
BONNG
BONNG
YOU CAN LEAVE YOUR PLATE THERE!
BTAM...
バタン...
TEN YEARS...
shf..
すっ...
HUUUUUG
"IF YOU WANT TO WORK HERE FOR LIFE..."

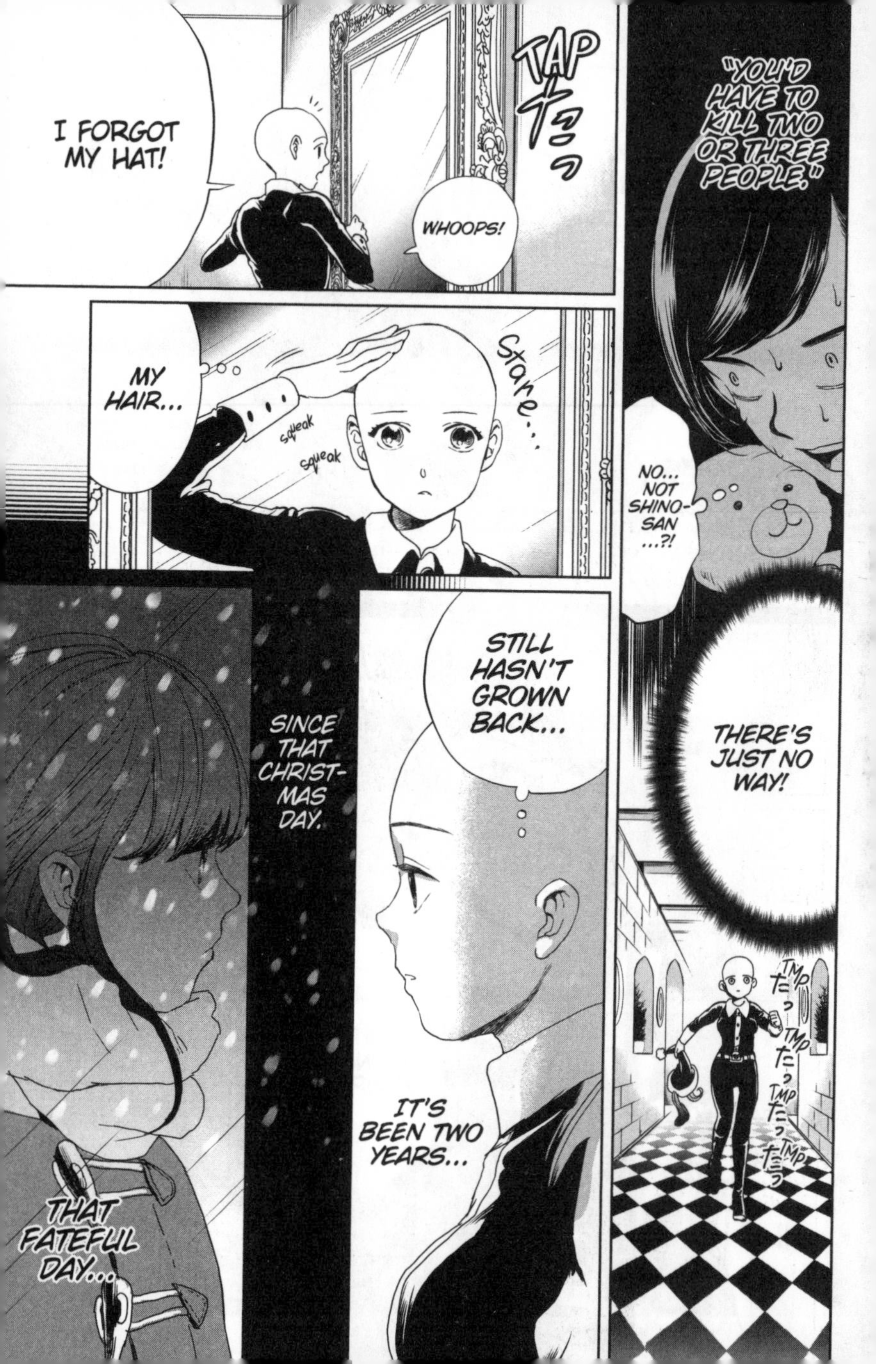
"YOU'D HAVE TO KILL TWO OR THREE PEOPLE."
NO... NOT SHINO-SAN ...?!
THERE'S JUST NO WAY!
TMP TMP TMP TMP
TAP
WHOOPS!
I FORGOT MY HAT!
Stare...
squeak squeak
MY HAIR...
STILL HASN'T GROWN BACK...
IT'S BEEN TWO YEARS...
SINCE THAT CHRIST-MAS DAY.
THAT FATEFUL DAY...

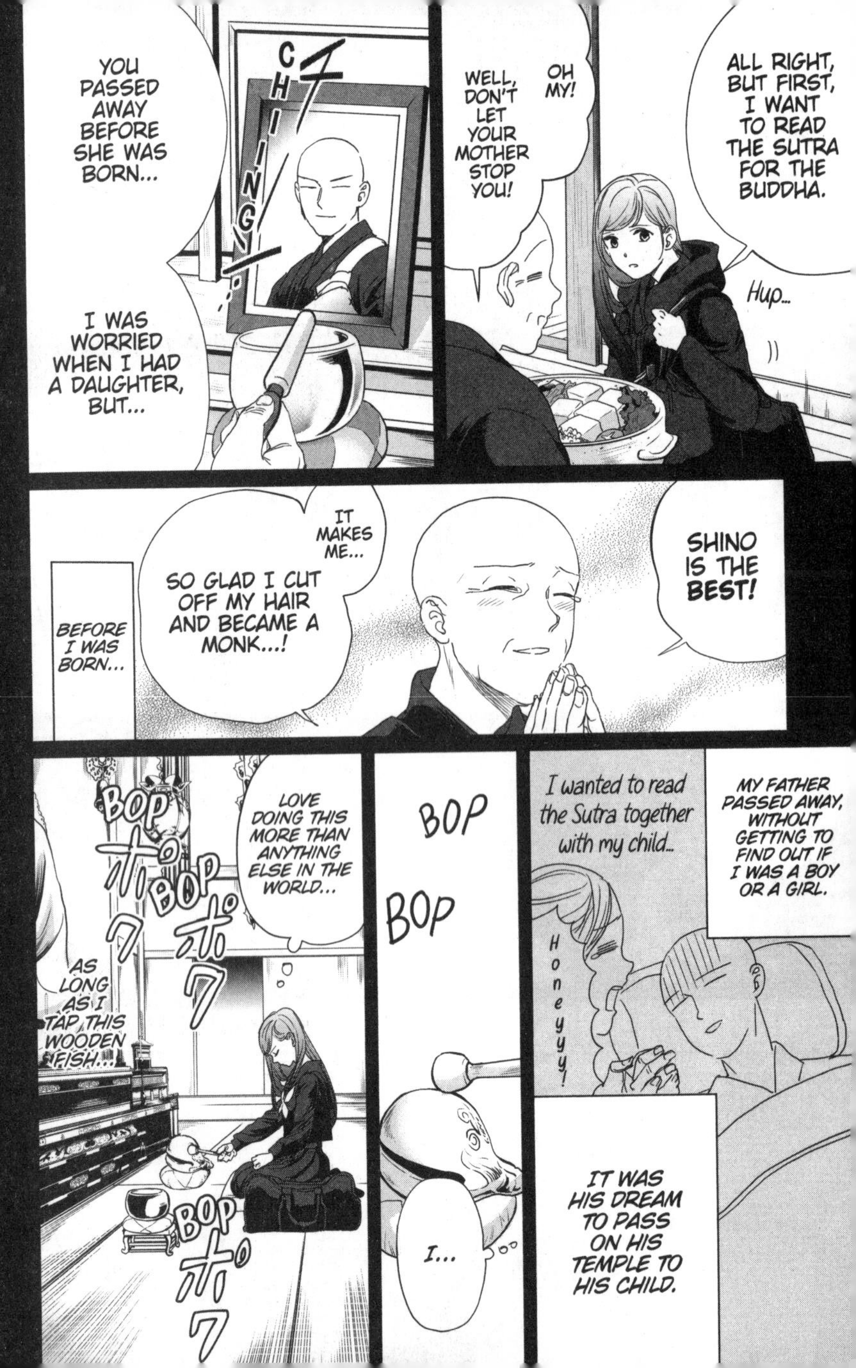
ALL RIGHT, BUT FIRST, I WANT TO READ THE SUTRA FOR THE BUDDHA.
Hup...
OH MY!
WELL, DON'T LET YOUR MOTHER STOP YOU!
CHIIING
YOU PASSED AWAY BEFORE SHE WAS BORN...
I WAS WORRIED WHEN I HAD A DAUGHTER, BUT...
SHINO IS THE BEST!
IT MAKES ME...
SO GLAD I CUT OFF MY HAIR AND BECAME A MONK...!
BEFORE I WAS BORN...
MY FATHER PASSED AWAY, WITHOUT GETTING TO FIND OUT IF I WAS A BOY OR A GIRL.
I wanted to read the Sutra together with my child...
Honeyyy!
IT WAS HIS DREAM TO PASS ON HIS TEMPLE TO HIS CHILD.
BOP
BOP
I...
LOVE DOING THIS MORE THAN ANYTHING ELSE IN THE WORLD...
BOP ポク
BOP ポク
AS LONG AS I TAP THIS WOODEN FISH...
BOP ポク

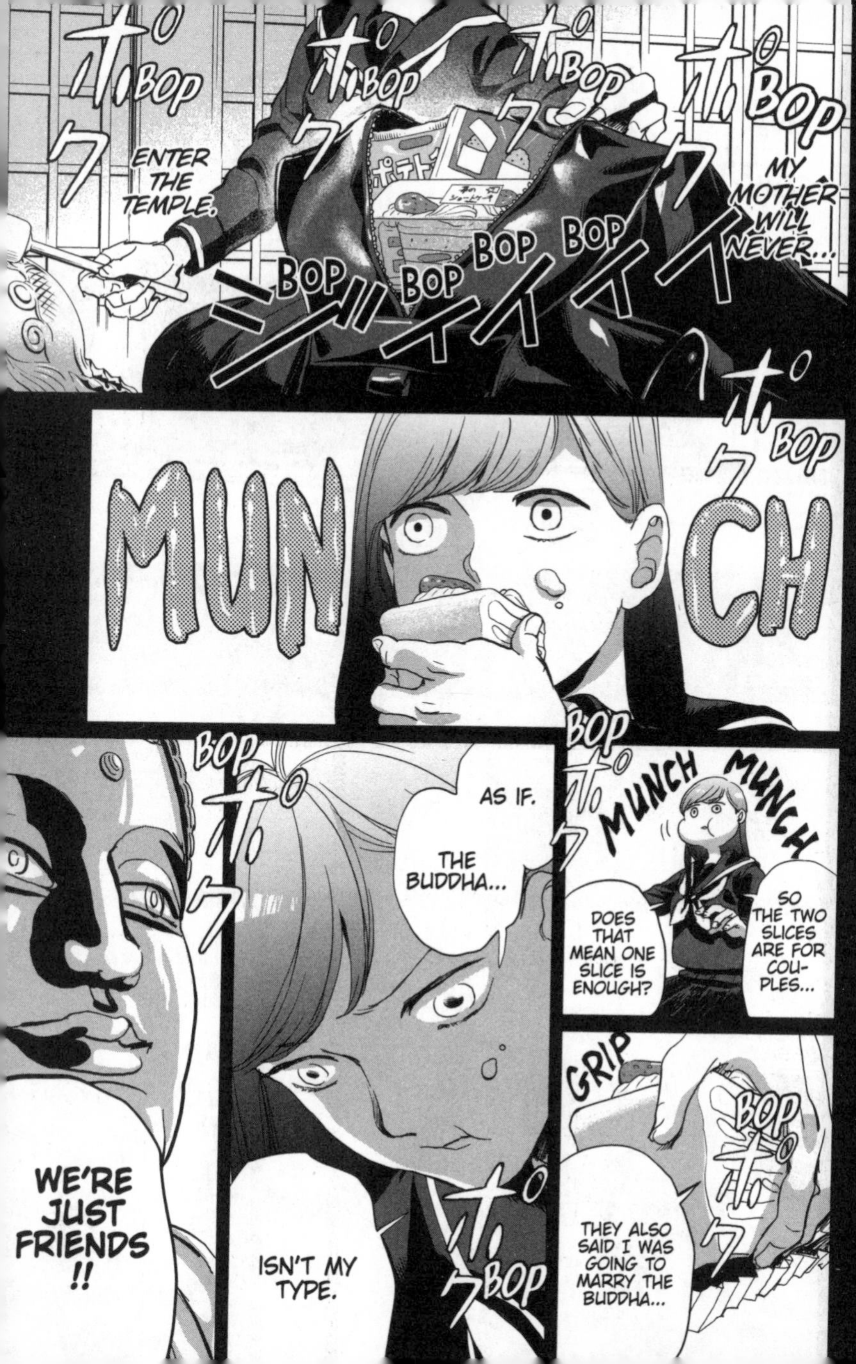
BOP BOP BOP BOP
MY MOTHER WILL NEVER...
ENTER THE TEMPLE.
BOP BOP BOP BOP
BOP
MUNCH
MUNCH MUNCH
SO THE TWO SLICES ARE FOR COUPLES...
DOES THAT MEAN ONE SLICE IS ENOUGH?
BOP
GRIP
BOP
THEY ALSO SAID I WAS GOING TO MARRY THE BUDDHA...
AS IF.
THE BUDDHA...
ISN'T MY TYPE.
BOP
BOP
WE'RE JUST FRIENDS!!

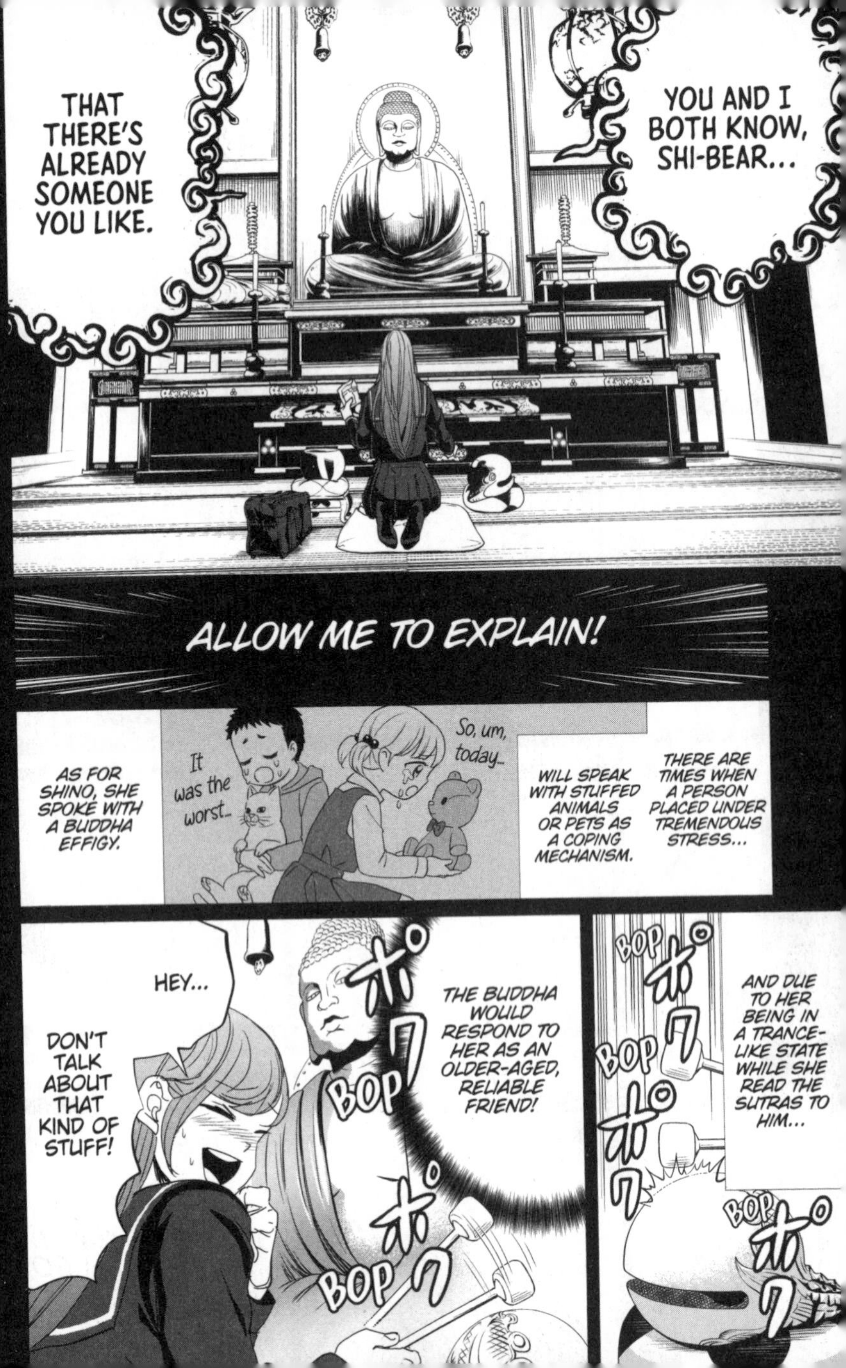
YOU AND I BOTH KNOW, SHI-BEAR...
THAT THERE'S ALREADY SOMEONE YOU LIKE.
ALLOW ME TO EXPLAIN!
THERE ARE TIMES WHEN A PERSON PLACED UNDER TREMENDOUS STRESS...
WILL SPEAK WITH STUFFED ANIMALS OR PETS AS A COPING MECHANISM.
So, um, today...
It was the worst...
AS FOR SHINO, SHE SPOKE WITH A BUDDHA EFFIGY.
AND DUE TO HER BEING IN A TRANCE-LIKE STATE WHILE SHE READ THE SUTRAS TO HIM...
BOP
BOP
BOP
THE BUDDHA WOULD RESPOND TO HER AS AN OLDER-AGED, RELIABLE FRIEND!
BOP
BOP
HEY...
DON'T TALK ABOUT THAT KIND OF STUFF!

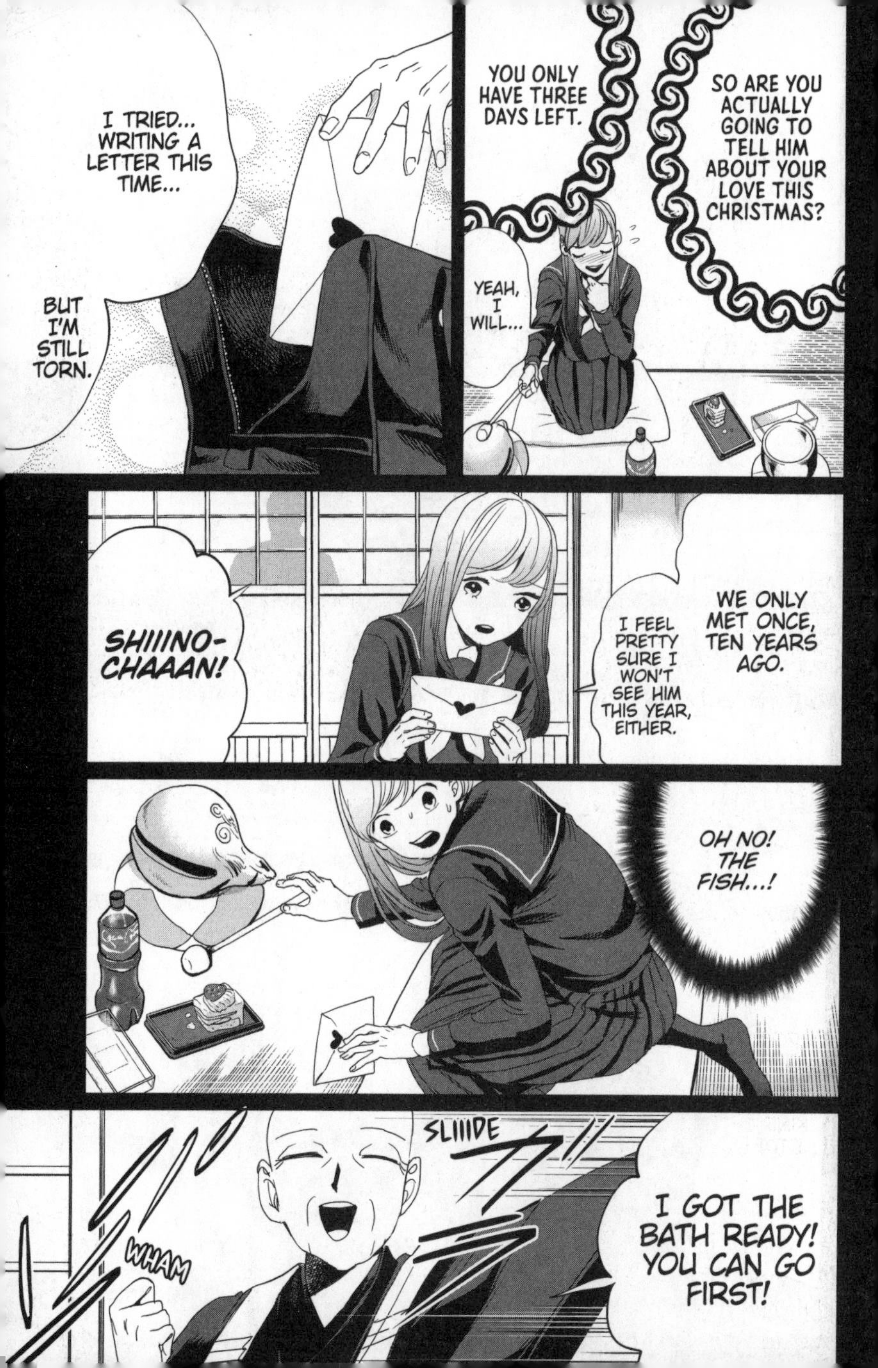
SO ARE YOU ACTUALLY GOING TO TELL HIM ABOUT YOUR LOVE THIS CHRISTMAS?
YOU ONLY HAVE THREE DAYS LEFT.
YEAH, I WILL...
I TRIED... WRITING A LETTER THIS TIME...
BUT I'M STILL TORN.
WE ONLY MET ONCE, TEN YEARS AGO.
I FEEL PRETTY SURE I WON'T SEE HIM THIS YEAR, EITHER.
SHIIINO-CHAAAN!
OH NO! THE FISH...!
SLIIIDE
I GOT THE BATH READY! YOU CAN GO FIRST!
WHAM

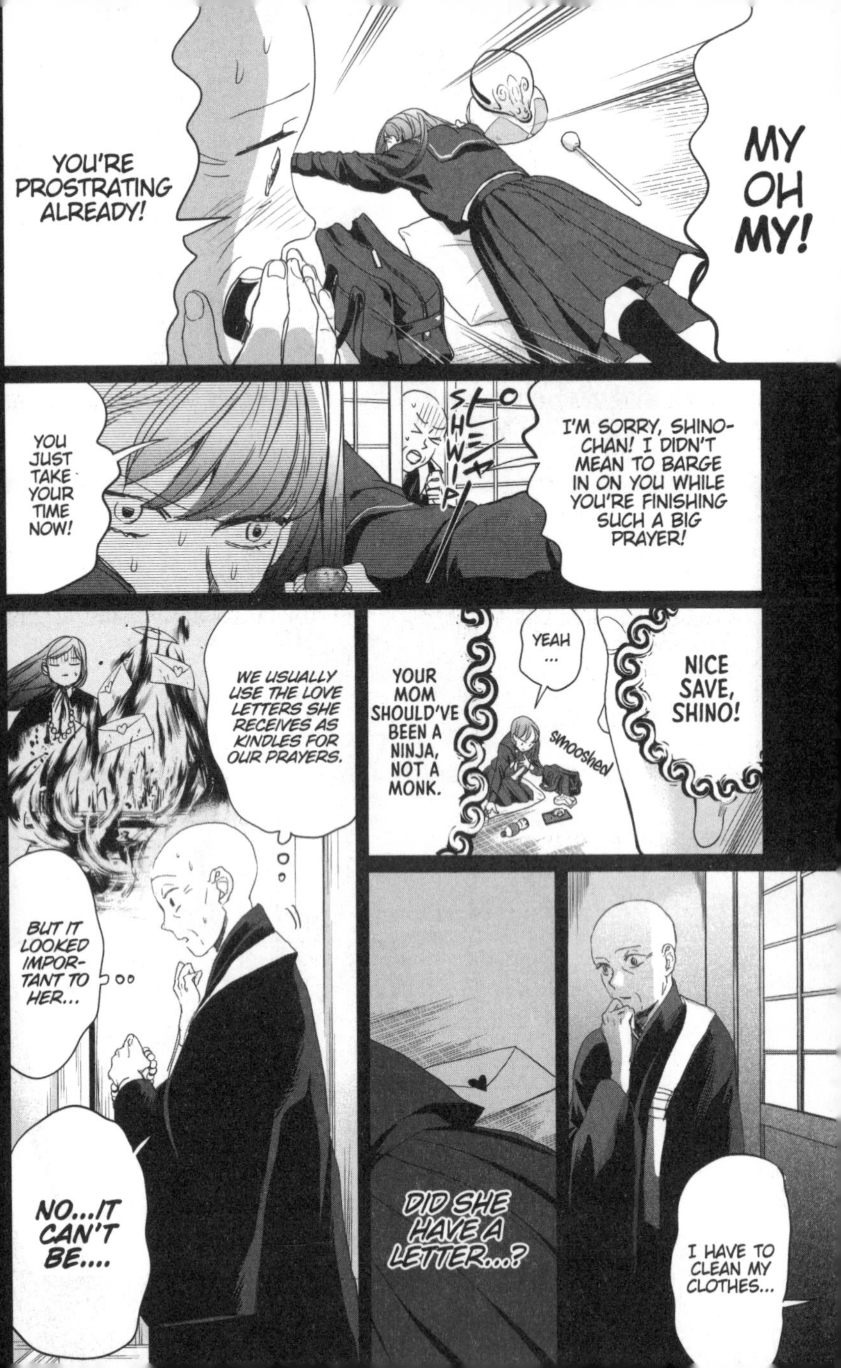
MY OH MY!
YOU'RE PROSTRATING ALREADY!
I'M SORRY, SHINO-CHAN! I DIDN'T MEAN TO BARGE IN ON YOU WHILE YOU'RE FINISHING SUCH A BIG PRAYER!
SHWIP
YOU JUST TAKE YOUR TIME NOW!
NICE SAVE, SHINO!
YEAH ...
YOUR MOM SHOULD'VE BEEN A NINJA, NOT A MONK.
smooshed
I HAVE TO CLEAN MY CLOTHES...
DID SHE HAVE A LETTER...?
WE USUALLY USE THE LOVE LETTERS SHE RECEIVES AS KINDLES FOR OUR PRAYERS.
BUT IT LOOKED IMPORTANT TO HER...
NO...IT CAN'T BE....

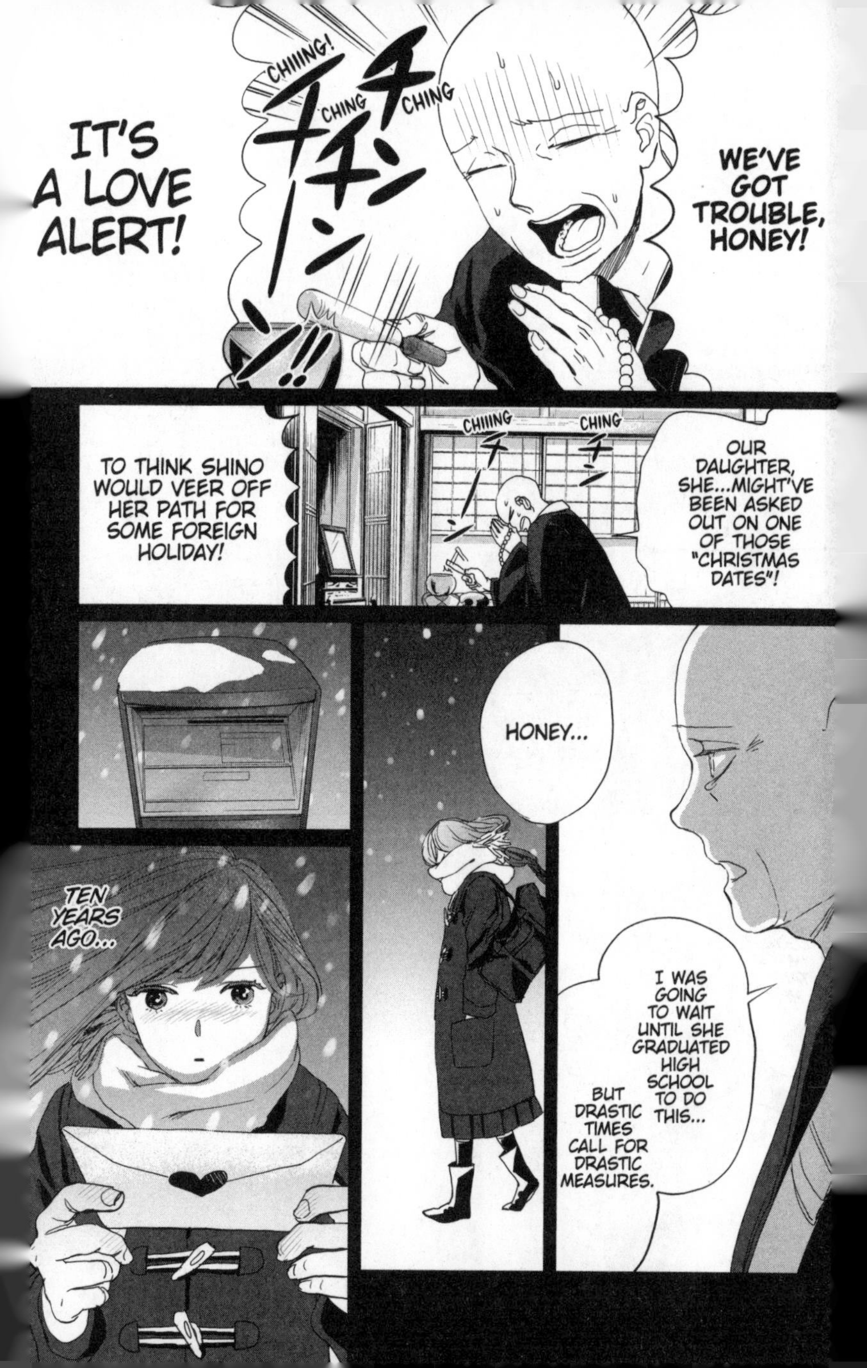
WE'VE GOT TROUBLE, HONEY!
CHIIING! CHING CHING
IT'S A LOVE ALERT!
OUR DAUGHTER, SHE...MIGHT'VE BEEN ASKED OUT ON ONE OF THOSE "CHRISTMAS DATES"!
CHIIING CHING
TO THINK SHINO WOULD VEER OFF HER PATH FOR SOME FOREIGN HOLIDAY!
HONEY...
I WAS GOING TO WAIT UNTIL SHE GRADUATED HIGH SCHOOL TO DO THIS...
BUT DRASTIC TIMES CALL FOR DRASTIC MEASURES.
TEN YEARS AGO...

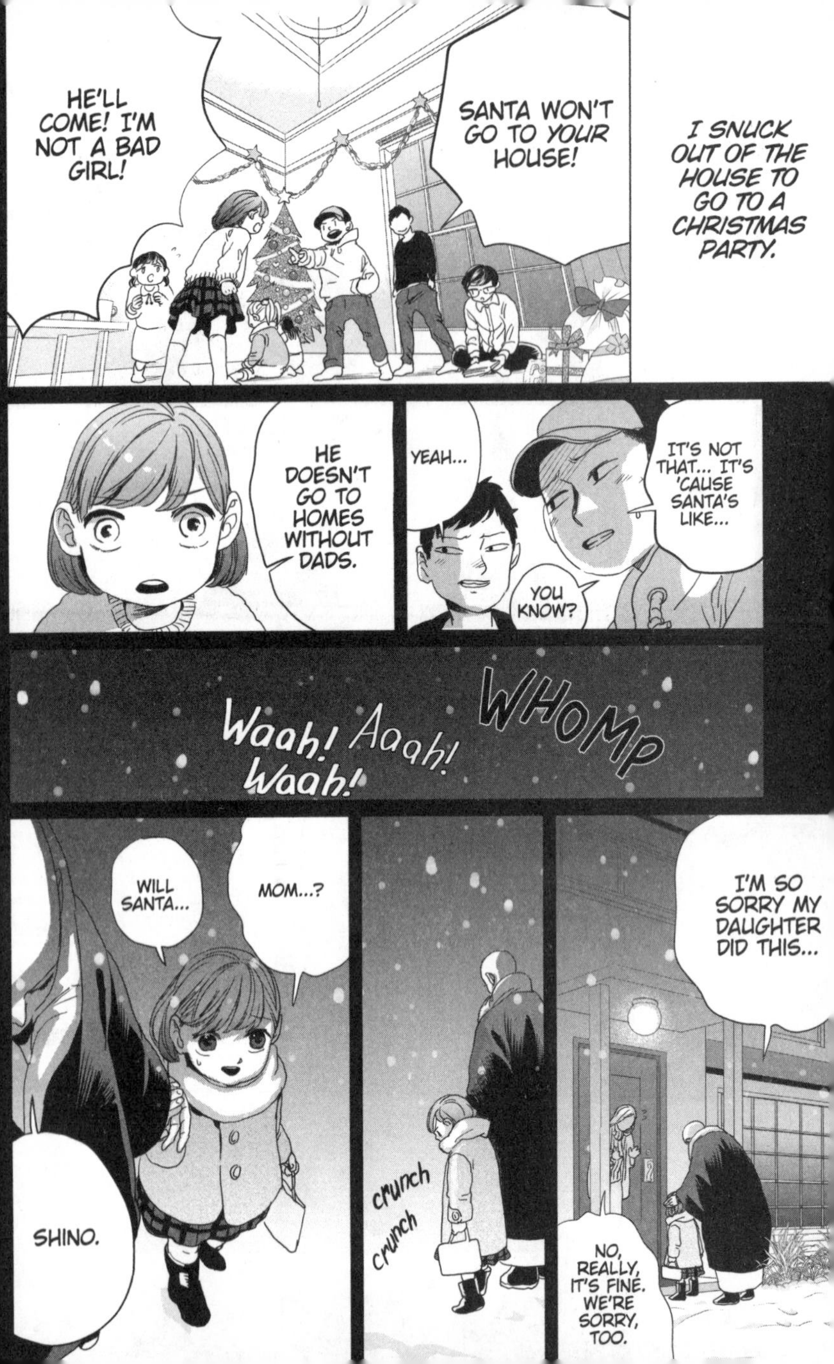
I SNUCK OUT OF THE HOUSE TO GO TO A CHRISTMAS PARTY.
SANTA WON'T GO TO YOUR HOUSE!
HE'LL COME! I'M NOT A BAD GIRL!
IT'S NOT THAT... IT'S 'CAUSE SANTA'S LIKE...
YEAH...
YOU KNOW?
HE DOESN'T GO TO HOMES WITHOUT DADS.
WHOMP
Waah! Aaah!
Waah!
I'M SO SORRY MY DAUGHTER DID THIS...
NO, REALLY, IT'S FINE. WE'RE SORRY, TOO.
crunch
crunch
MOM...?
WILL SANTA...
SHINO.

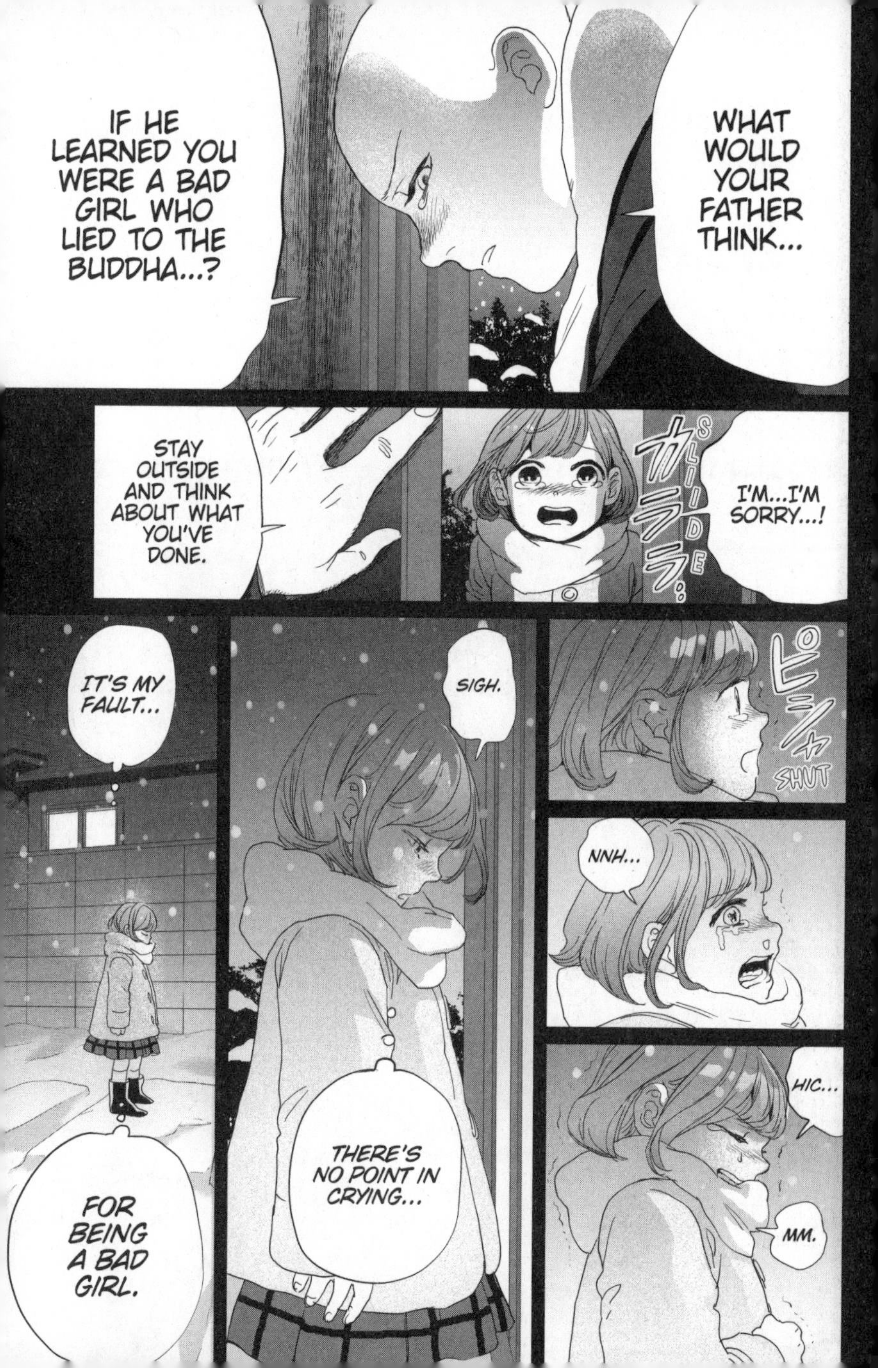
WHAT WOULD YOUR FATHER THINK...
IF HE LEARNED YOU WERE A BAD GIRL WHO LIED TO THE BUDDHA...?
カララ
SLIIIDE
I'M...I'M SORRY...!
STAY OUTSIDE AND THINK ABOUT WHAT YOU'VE DONE.
ピシャ
SHUT
NNH...
HIC...
MM.
SIGH.
THERE'S NO POINT IN CRYING...
IT'S MY FAULT...
FOR BEING A BAD GIRL.

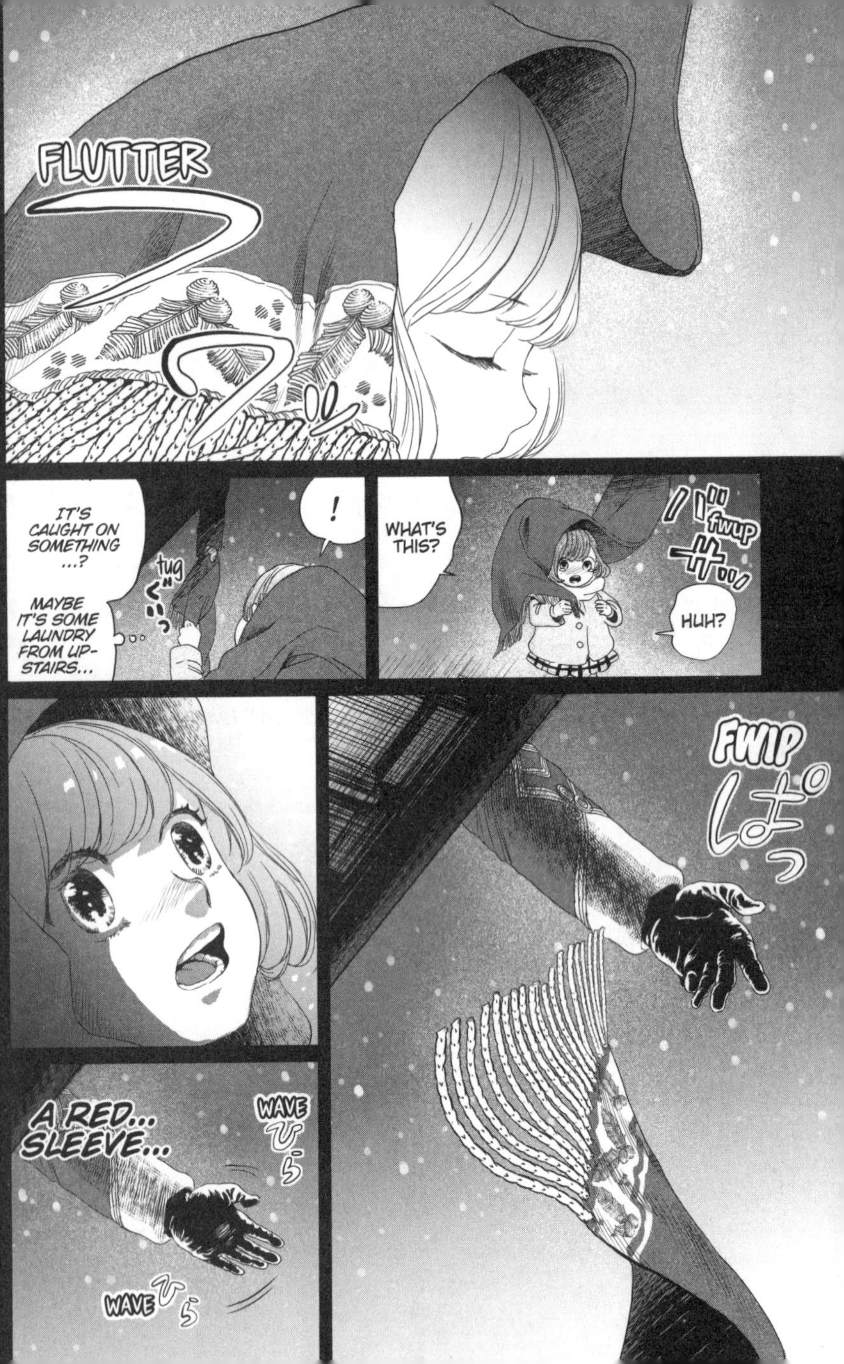

FLUTTER
fwup
HUH?
WHAT'S THIS?
!
tug
ぐいっ
IT'S CAUGHT ON SOMETHING ...?
MAYBE IT'S SOME LAUNDRY FROM UP-STAIRS...
FWIP
ぱっ
A RED... SLEEVE...
WAVE
ひら
WAVE
ひら

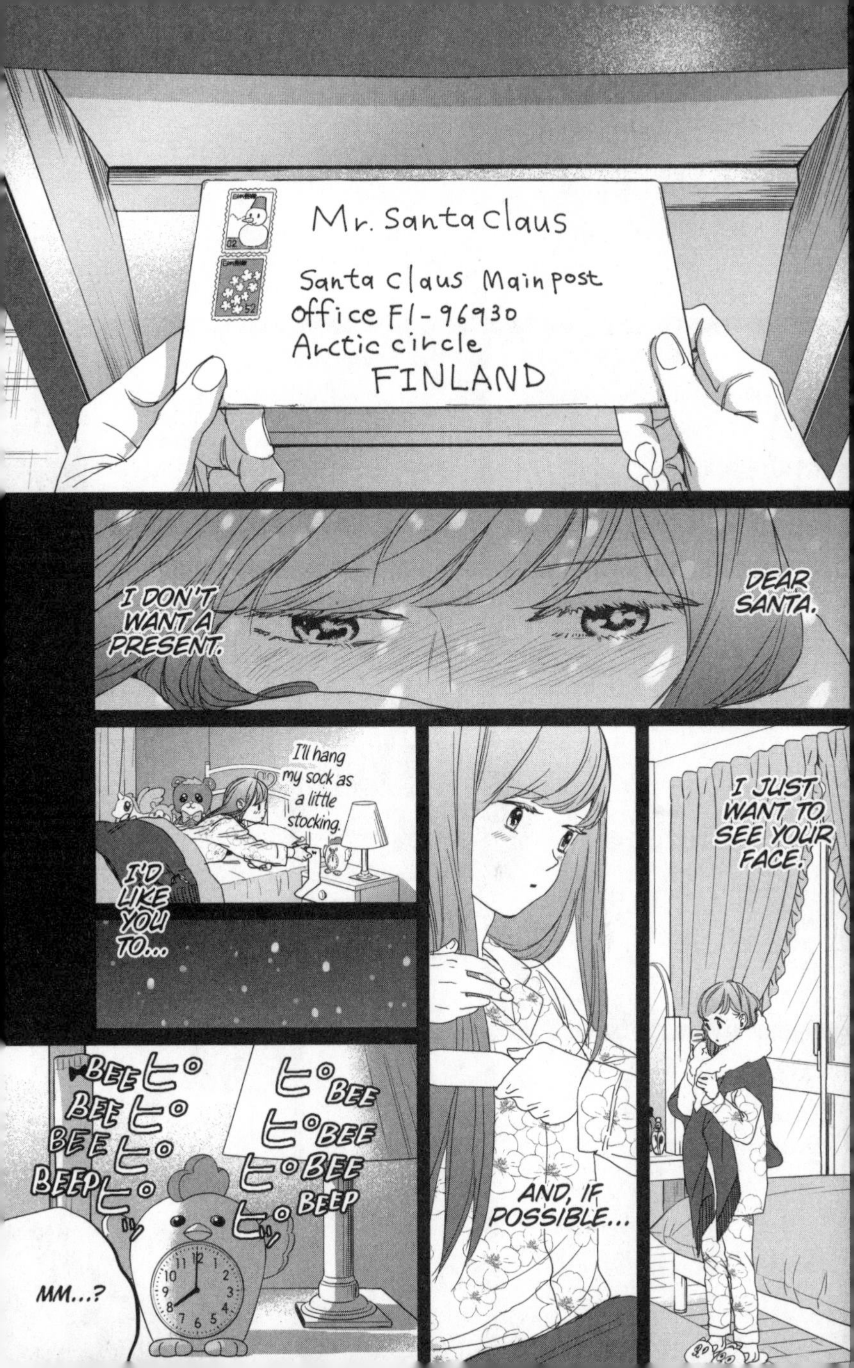

Mr. Santa claus
Santa claus Main post
office FI-96930
Arctic circle
FINLAND
DEAR SANTA.
I DON'T WANT A PRESENT.
I JUST WANT TO SEE YOUR FACE.
AND, IF POSSIBLE...
I'll hang my sock as a little stocking.
I'D LIKE YOU TO...
ピBEE ピBEE ピBEE ピBEEP
BEEピ BEEピ BEEピ BEEPピ
MM...?

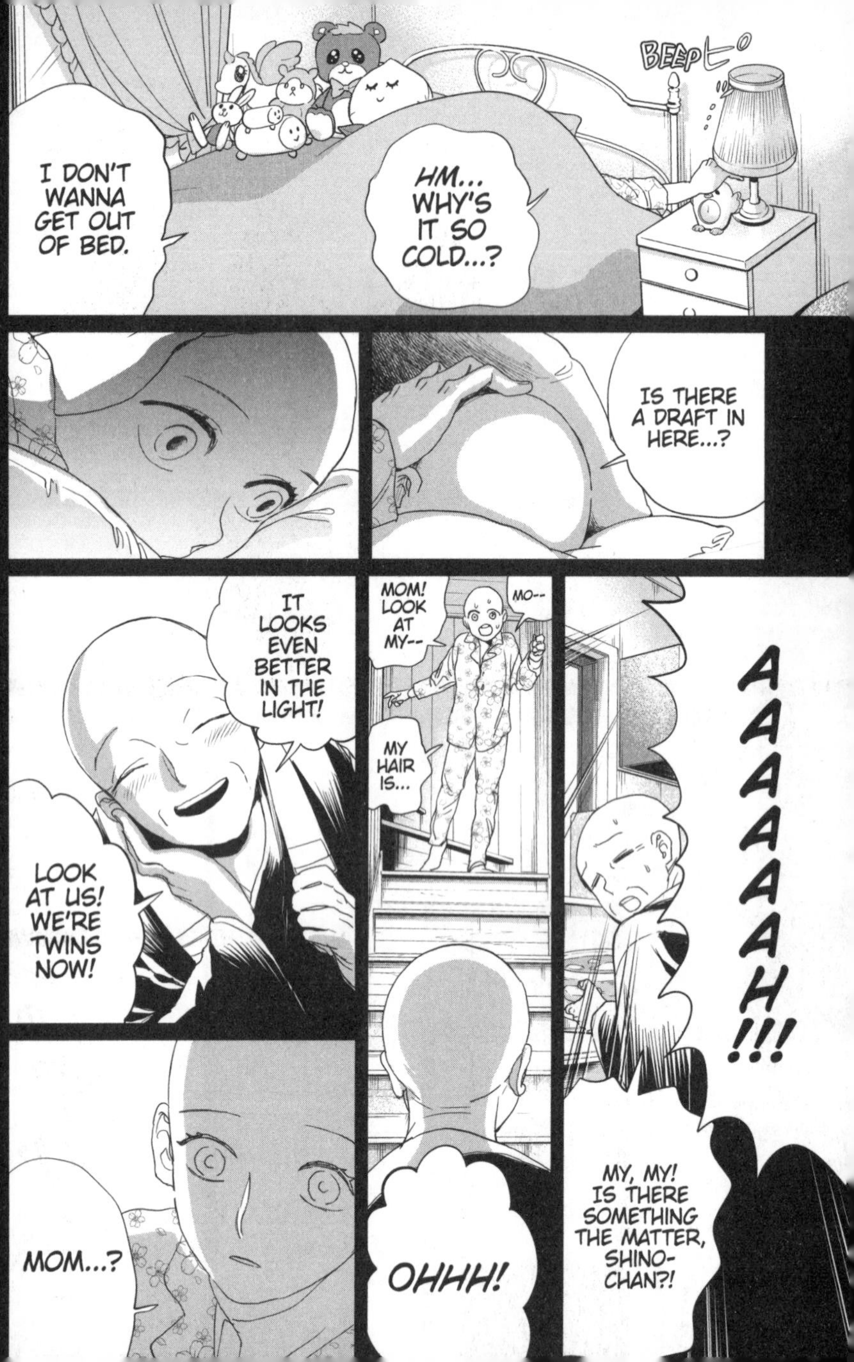
BEEP ピ
HM... WHY'S IT SO COLD...?
I DON'T WANNA GET OUT OF BED.
IS THERE A DRAFT IN HERE...?
AAAAAAH!!!
MY, MY! IS THERE SOMETHING THE MATTER, SHINO-CHAN?!
MO--
MOM! LOOK AT MY--
MY HAIR IS...
OHHH!
IT LOOKS EVEN BETTER IN THE LIGHT!
LOOK AT US! WE'RE TWINS NOW!
MOM...?

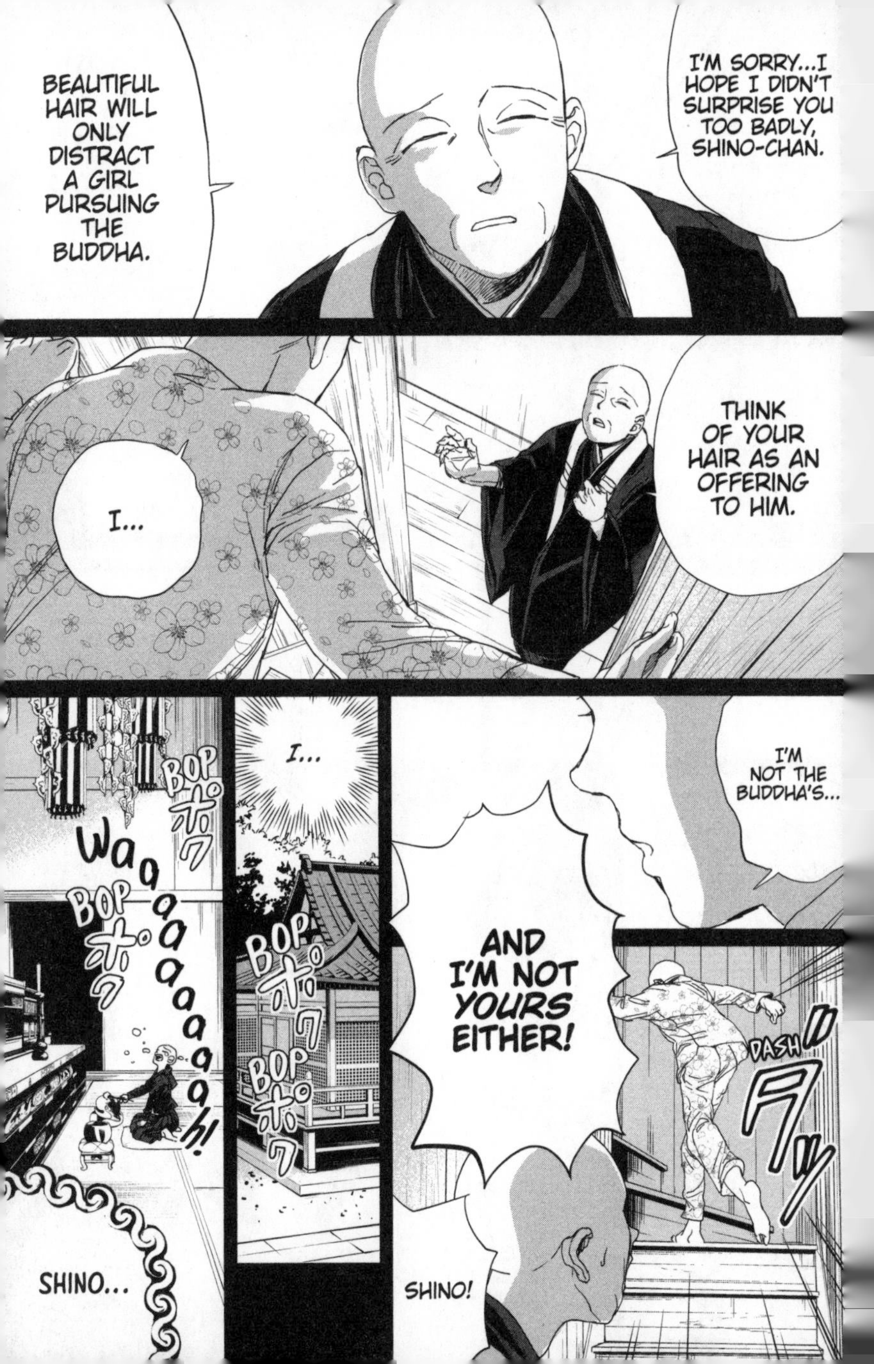
I'M SORRY...I HOPE I DIDN'T SURPRISE YOU TOO BADLY, SHINO-CHAN.
BEAUTIFUL HAIR WILL ONLY DISTRACT A GIRL PURSUING THE BUDDHA.
THINK OF YOUR HAIR AS AN OFFERING TO HIM.
I...
I'M NOT THE BUDDHA'S...
AND I'M NOT YOURS EITHER!
DASH
SHINO!
I...
BOP
BOP
BOP
BOP
Waaaaaaaaaaah!
BOP
SHINO...

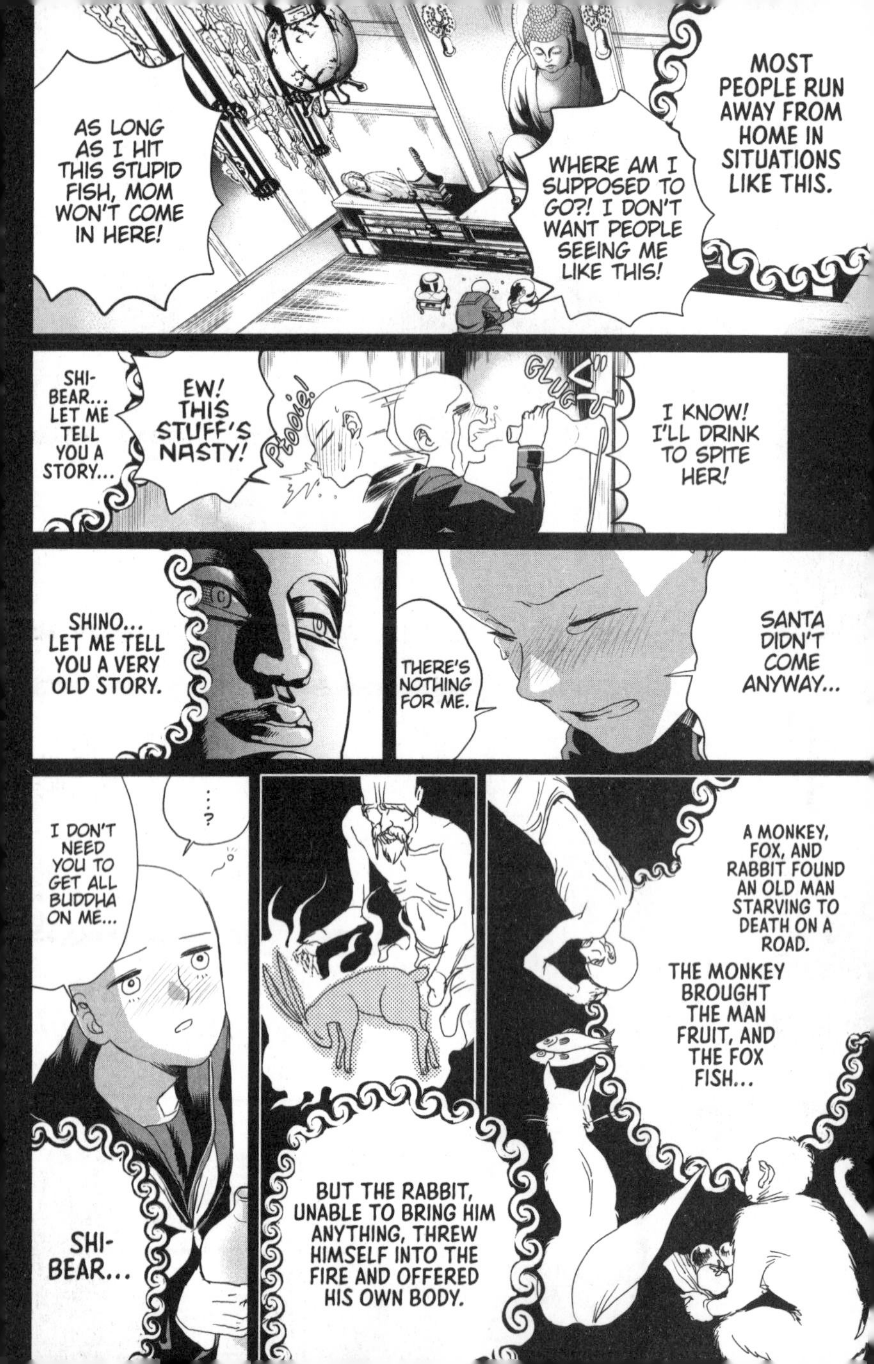
MOST PEOPLE RUN AWAY FROM HOME IN SITUATIONS LIKE THIS.
WHERE AM I SUPPOSED TO GO?! I DON'T WANT PEOPLE SEEING ME LIKE THIS!
AS LONG AS I HIT THIS STUPID FISH, MOM WON'T COME IN HERE!
I KNOW! I'LL DRINK TO SPITE HER!
GLUG
Ptooie!
EW! THIS STUFF'S NASTY!
SHI-BEAR... LET ME TELL YOU A STORY...
SANTA DIDN'T COME ANYWAY...
THERE'S NOTHING FOR ME.
SHINO... LET ME TELL YOU A VERY OLD STORY.
A MONKEY, FOX, AND RABBIT FOUND AN OLD MAN STARVING TO DEATH ON A ROAD.
THE MONKEY BROUGHT THE MAN FRUIT, AND THE FOX FISH...
BUT THE RABBIT, UNABLE TO BRING HIM ANYTHING, THREW HIMSELF INTO THE FIRE AND OFFERED HIS OWN BODY.
...?
I DON'T NEED YOU TO GET ALL BUDDHA ON ME...
SHI-BEAR...

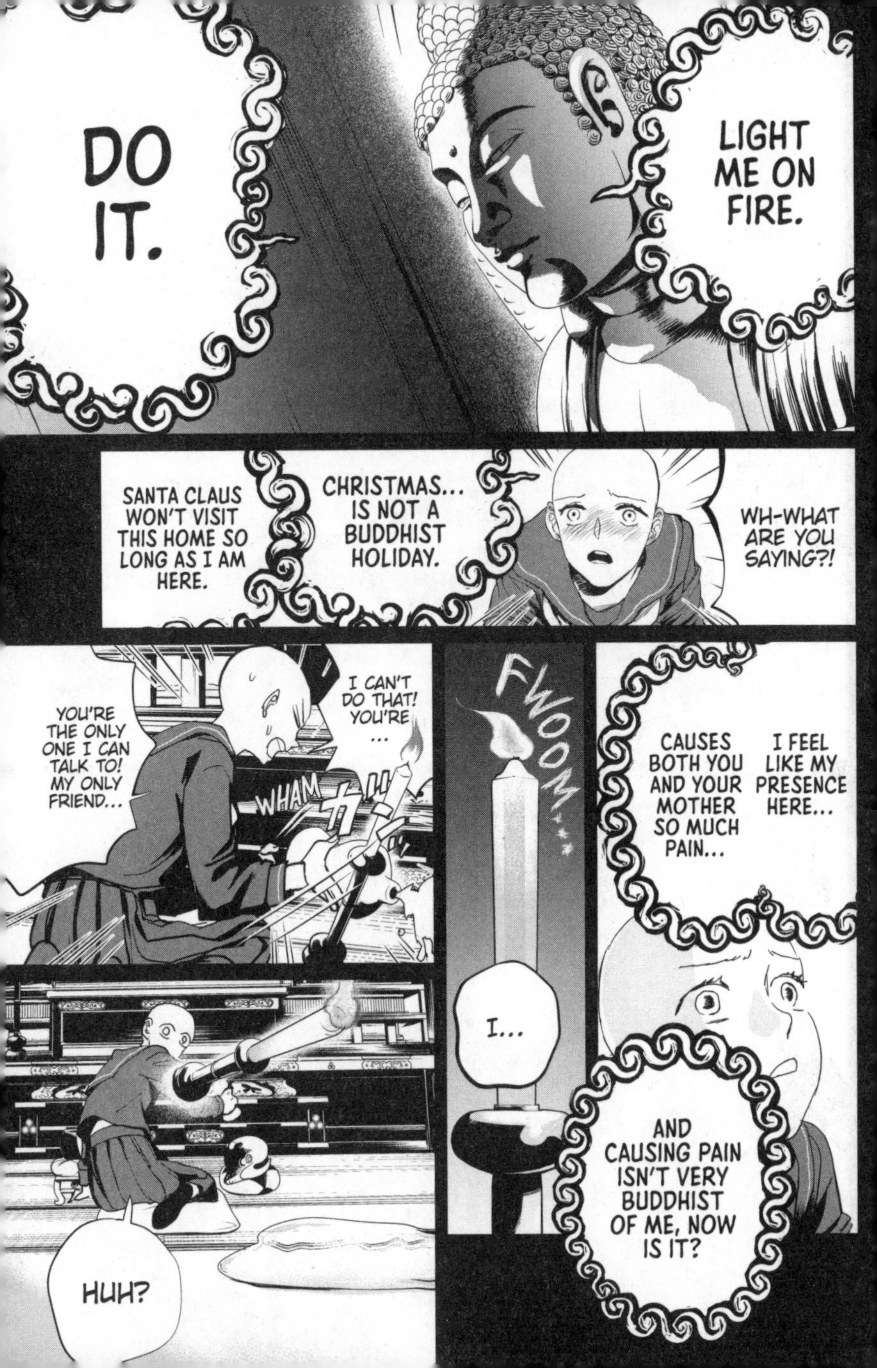
LIGHT ME ON FIRE.
DO IT.
WH-WHAT ARE YOU SAYING?!
CHRISTMAS... IS NOT A BUDDHIST HOLIDAY.
SANTA CLAUS WON'T VISIT THIS HOME SO LONG AS I AM HERE.
I FEEL LIKE MY PRESENCE HERE...
CAUSES BOTH YOU AND YOUR MOTHER SO MUCH PAIN...
AND CAUSING PAIN ISN'T VERY BUDDHIST OF ME, NOW IS IT?
FWOOM...
I...
I CAN'T DO THAT! YOU'RE ...
YOU'RE THE ONLY ONE I CAN TALK TO! MY ONLY FRIEND...
WHAM
HUH?

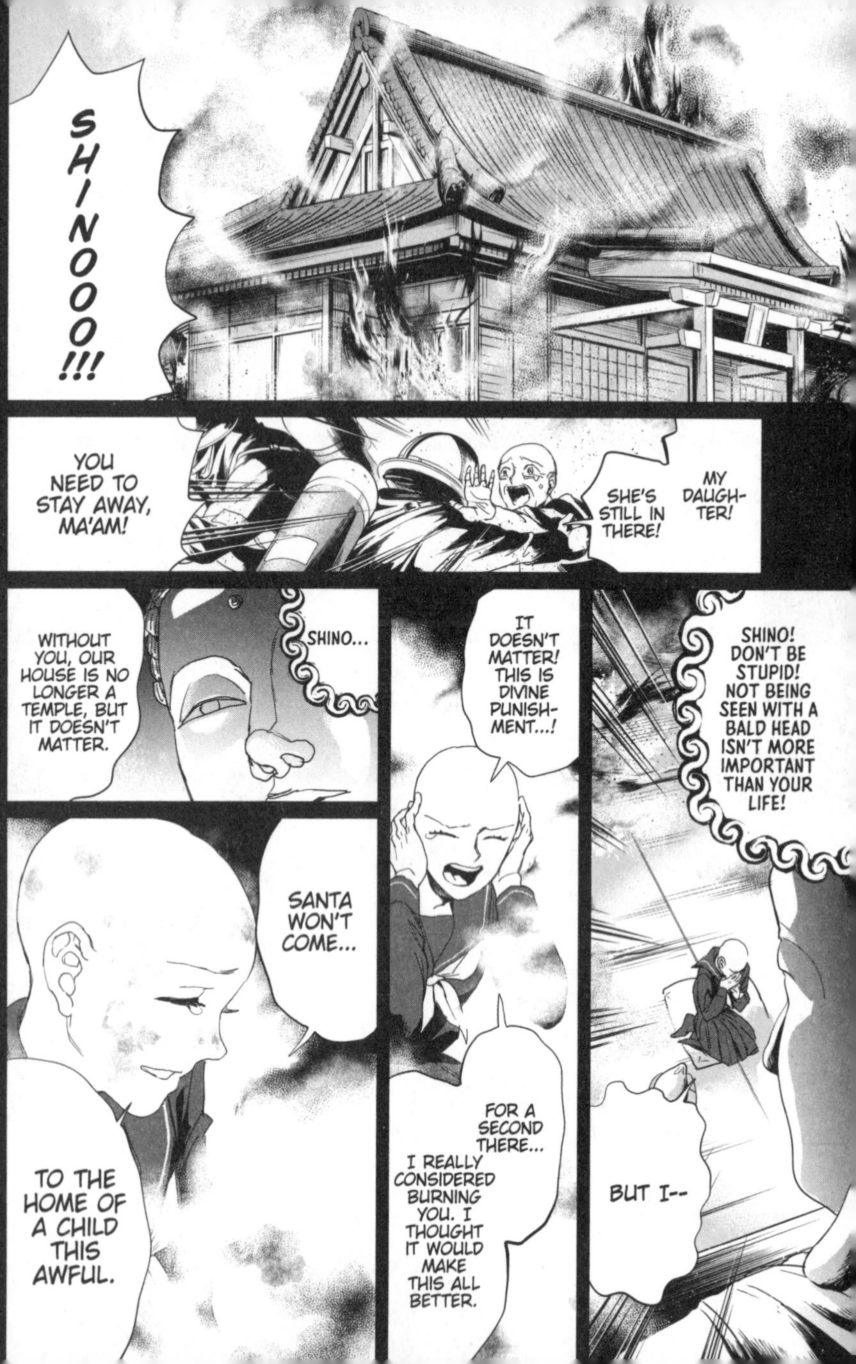
SHINOOOO!!!
MY DAUGHTER!
SHE'S STILL IN THERE!
YOU NEED TO STAY AWAY, MA'AM!
SHINO! DON'T BE STUPID! NOT BEING SEEN WITH A BALD HEAD ISN'T MORE IMPORTANT THAN YOUR LIFE!
BUT I--
IT DOESN'T MATTER! THIS IS DIVINE PUNISHMENT...!
FOR A SECOND THERE... I REALLY CONSIDERED BURNING YOU. I THOUGHT IT WOULD MAKE THIS ALL BETTER.
SHINO...
WITHOUT YOU, OUR HOUSE IS NO LONGER A TEMPLE, BUT IT DOESN'T MATTER.
SANTA WON'T COME...
TO THE HOME OF A CHILD THIS AWFUL.

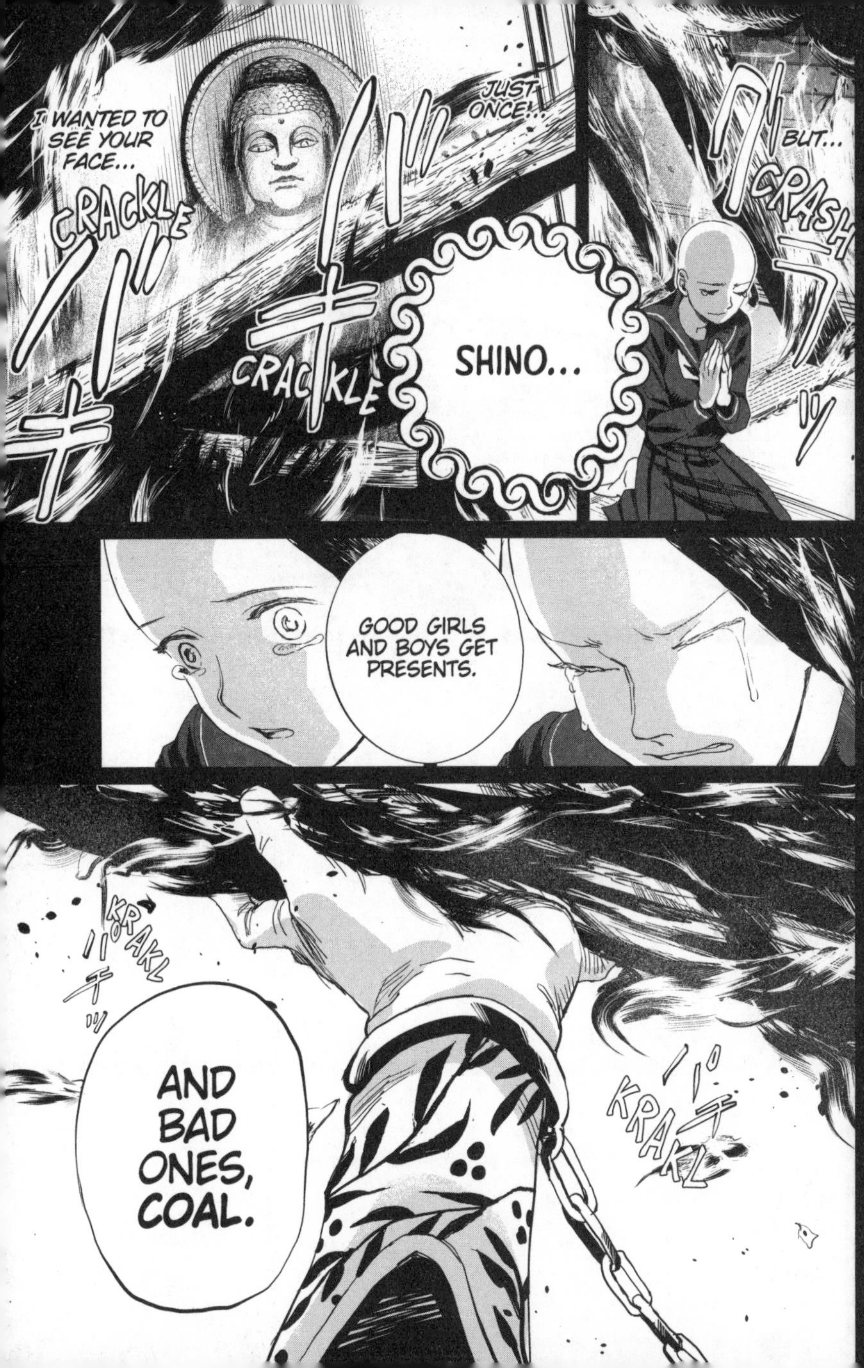
BUT...
CRASH
I WANTED TO SEE YOUR FACE...
JUST ONCE!...
CRACKLE
CRACKLE
SHINO...
GOOD GIRLS AND BOYS GET PRESENTS.
KRAKL
KRAKL
AND BAD ONES, COAL.

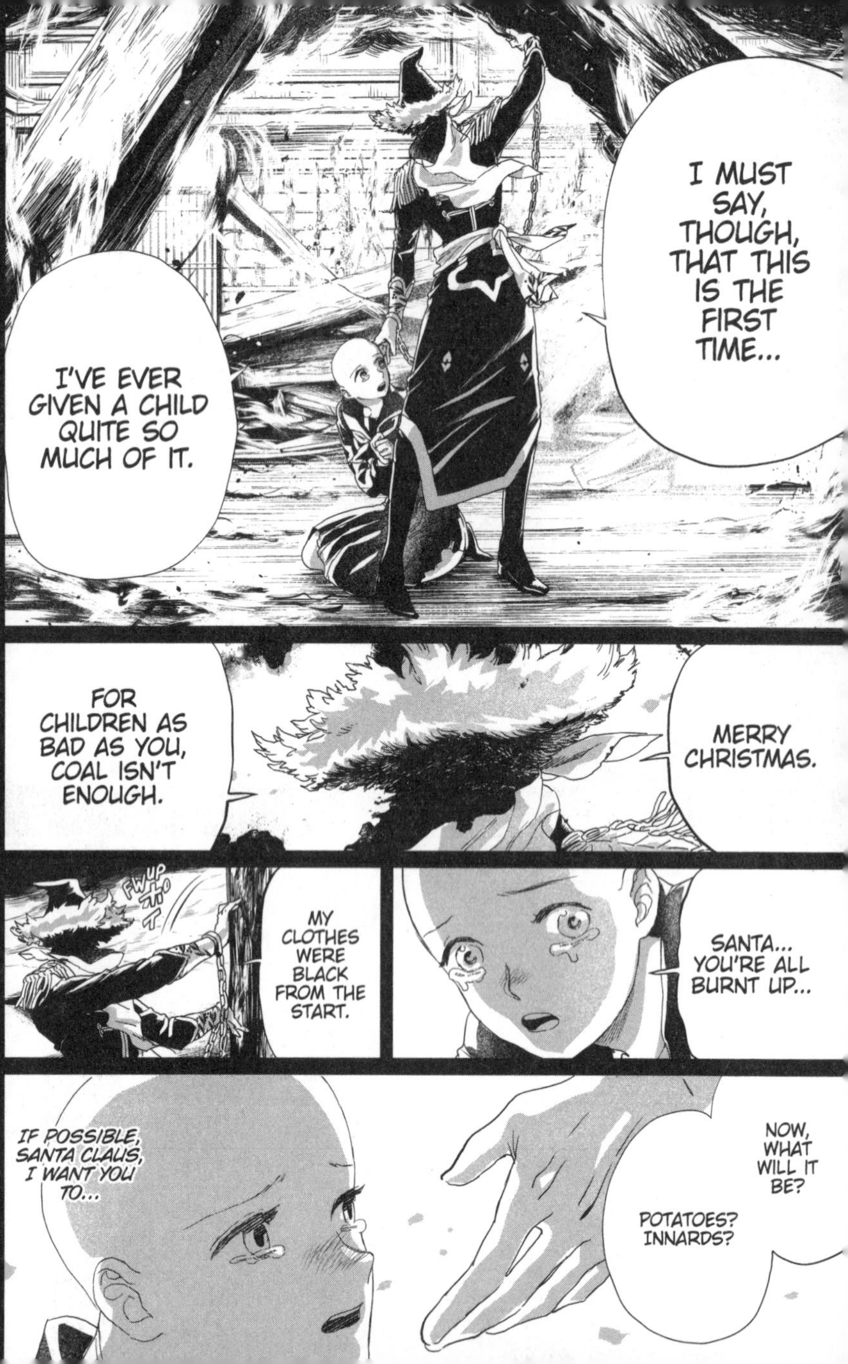
I MUST SAY, THOUGH, THAT THIS IS THE FIRST TIME...
I'VE EVER GIVEN A CHILD QUITE SO MUCH OF IT.
MERRY CHRISTMAS.
FOR CHILDREN AS BAD AS YOU, COAL ISN'T ENOUGH.
SANTA... YOU'RE ALL BURNT UP...
MY CLOTHES WERE BLACK FROM THE START.
FWUP
NOW, WHAT WILL IT BE?
POTATOES? INNARDS?
IF POSSIBLE, SANTA CLAUS, I WANT YOU TO...

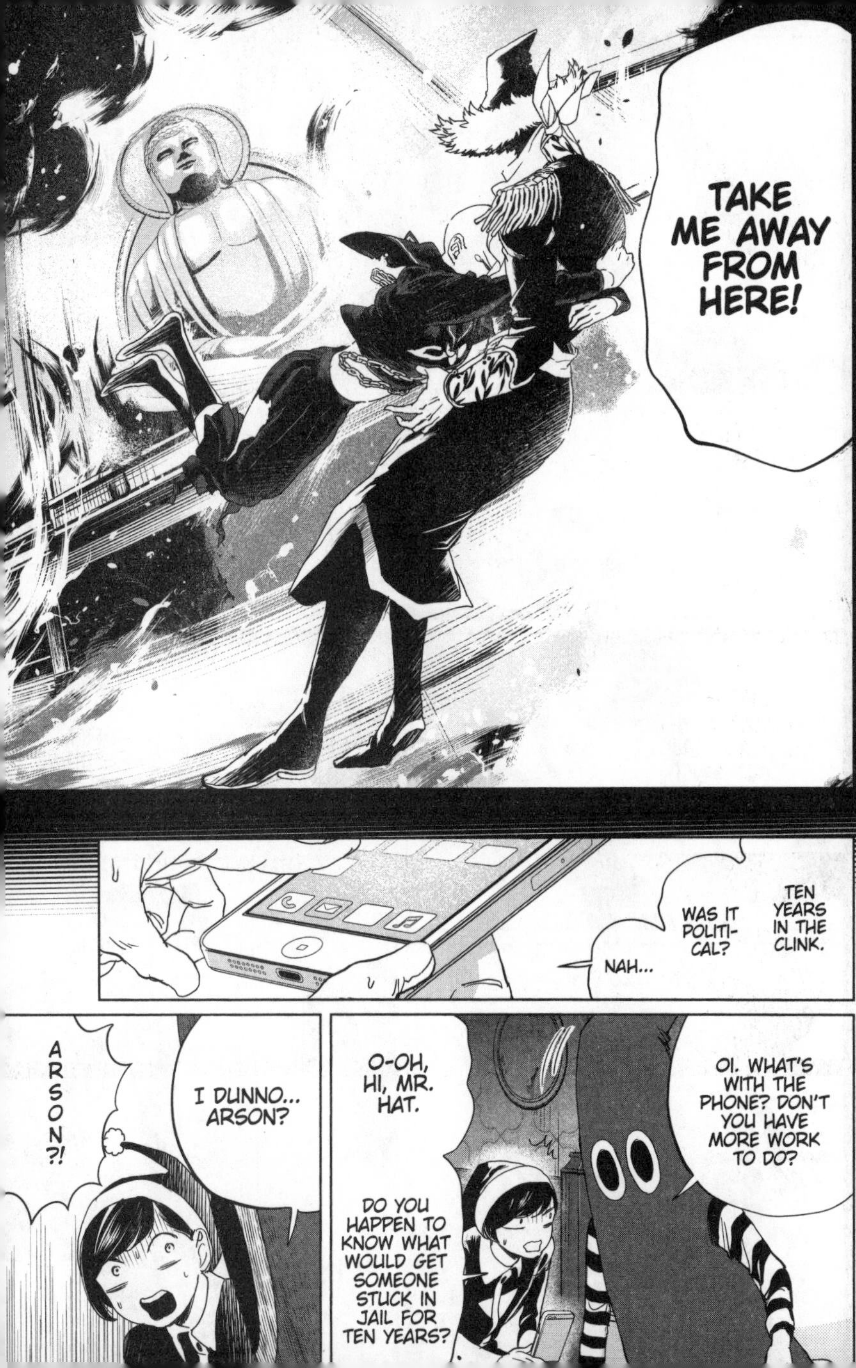
TAKE ME AWAY FROM HERE!
TEN YEARS IN THE CLINK.
WAS IT POLITI-CAL?
NAH...
OI. WHAT'S WITH THE PHONE? DON'T YOU HAVE MORE WORK TO DO?
O-OH, HI, MR. HAT.
DO YOU HAPPEN TO KNOW WHAT WOULD GET SOMEONE STUCK IN JAIL FOR TEN YEARS?
I DUNNO... ARSON?
ARSON?!

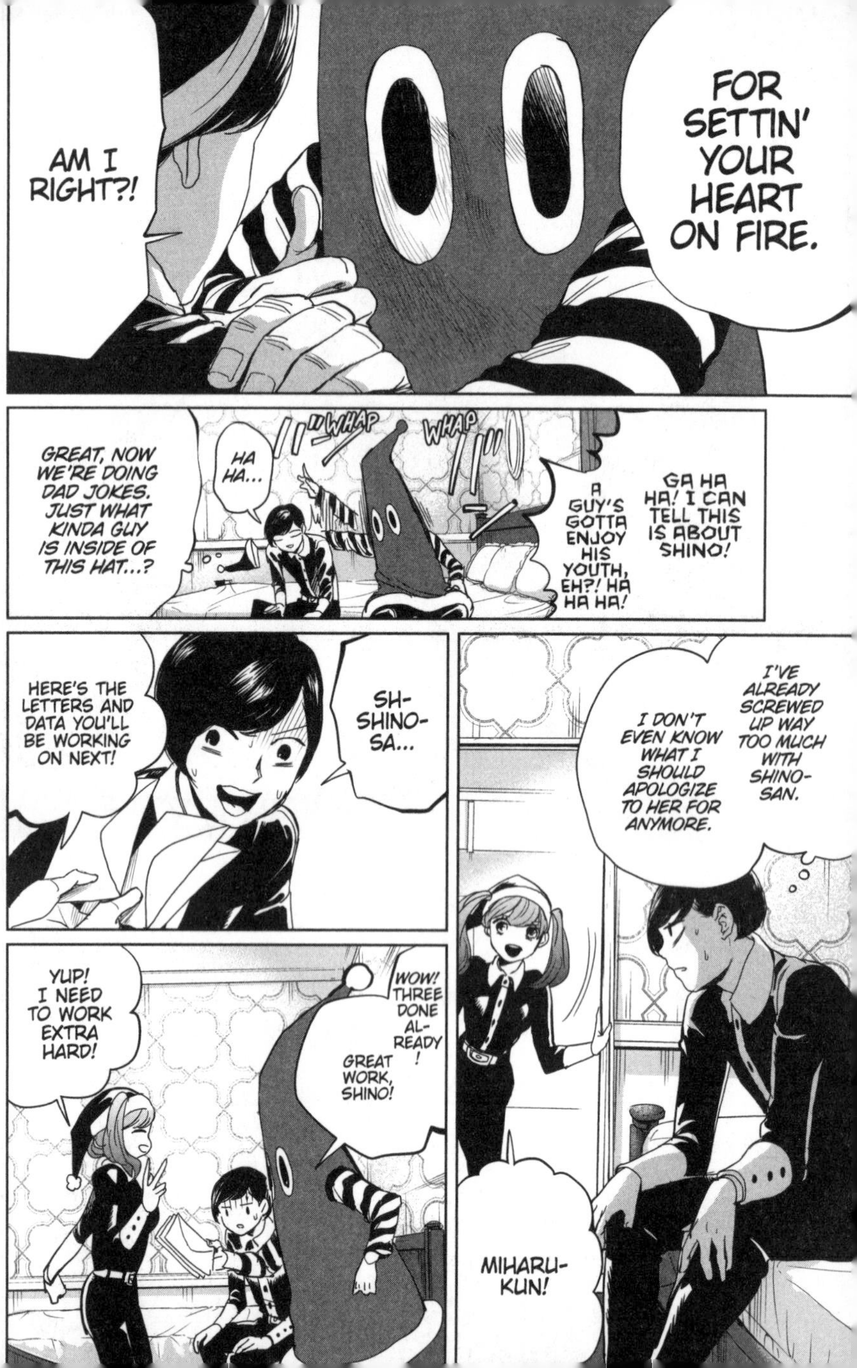
FOR SETTIN' YOUR HEART ON FIRE.
AM I RIGHT?!
GA HA HA! I CAN TELL THIS IS ABOUT SHINO!
A GUY'S GOTTA ENJOY HIS YOUTH, EH?! HA HA HA!
WHAP
WHAP
HA HA...
GREAT, NOW WE'RE DOING DAD JOKES. JUST WHAT KINDA GUY IS INSIDE OF THIS HAT...?
I'VE ALREADY SCREWED UP WAY TOO MUCH WITH SHINO-SAN.
I DON'T EVEN KNOW WHAT I SHOULD APOLOGIZE TO HER FOR ANYMORE.
MIHARU-KUN!
SH-SHINO-SA...
HERE'S THE LETTERS AND DATA YOU'LL BE WORKING ON NEXT!
WOW! THREE DONE AL-READY!
GREAT WORK, SHINO!
YUP! I NEED TO WORK EXTRA HARD!

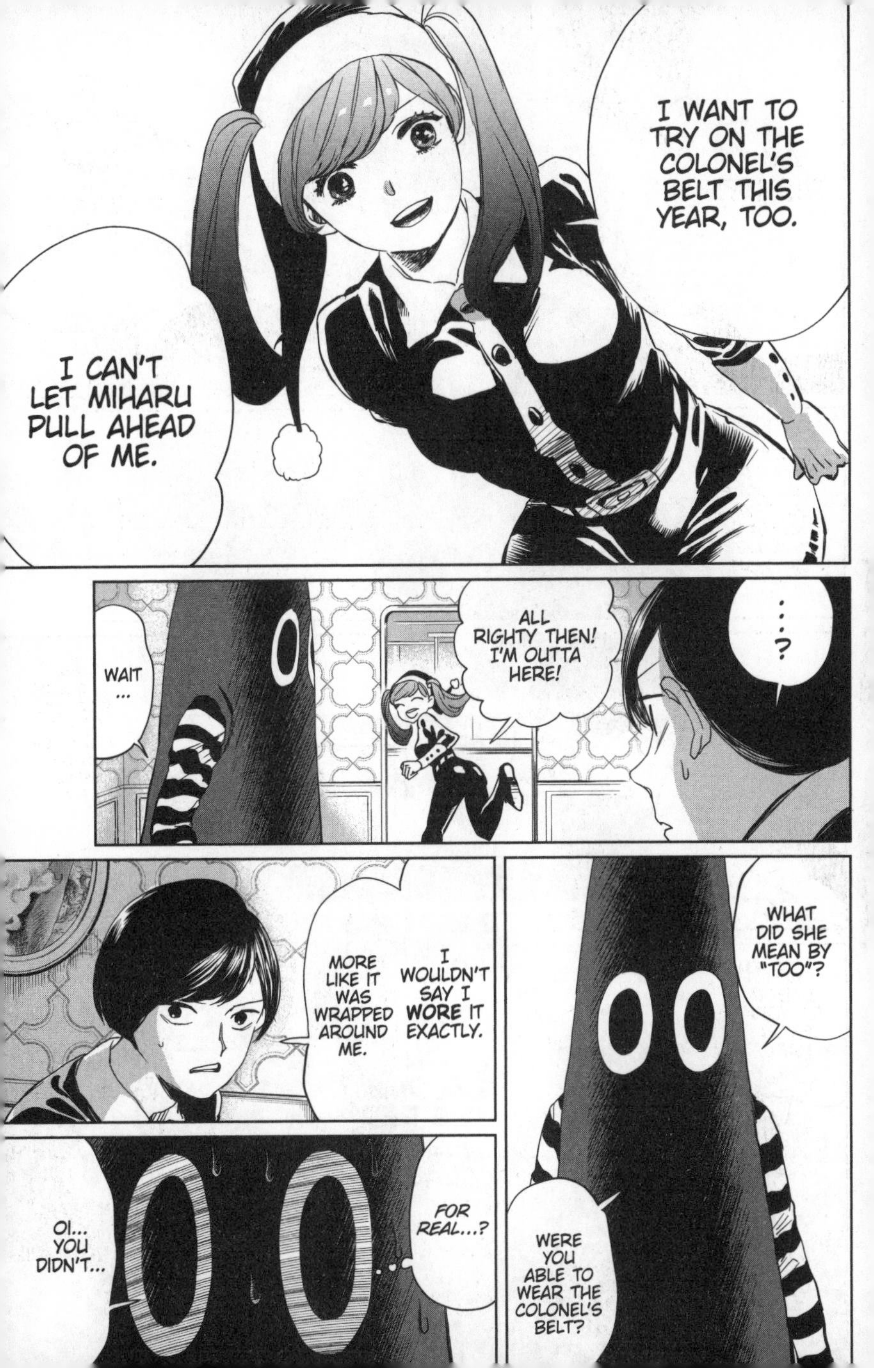
I WANT TO TRY ON THE COLONEL'S BELT THIS YEAR, TOO.
I CAN'T LET MIHARU PULL AHEAD OF ME.
...?
ALL RIGHTY THEN! I'M OUTTA HERE!
WAIT ...
WHAT DID SHE MEAN BY "TOO"?
WERE YOU ABLE TO WEAR THE COLONEL'S BELT?
I WOULDN'T SAY I **WORE** IT EXACTLY.
MORE LIKE IT WAS WRAPPED AROUND ME.
FOR REAL...?
OI... YOU DIDN'T...

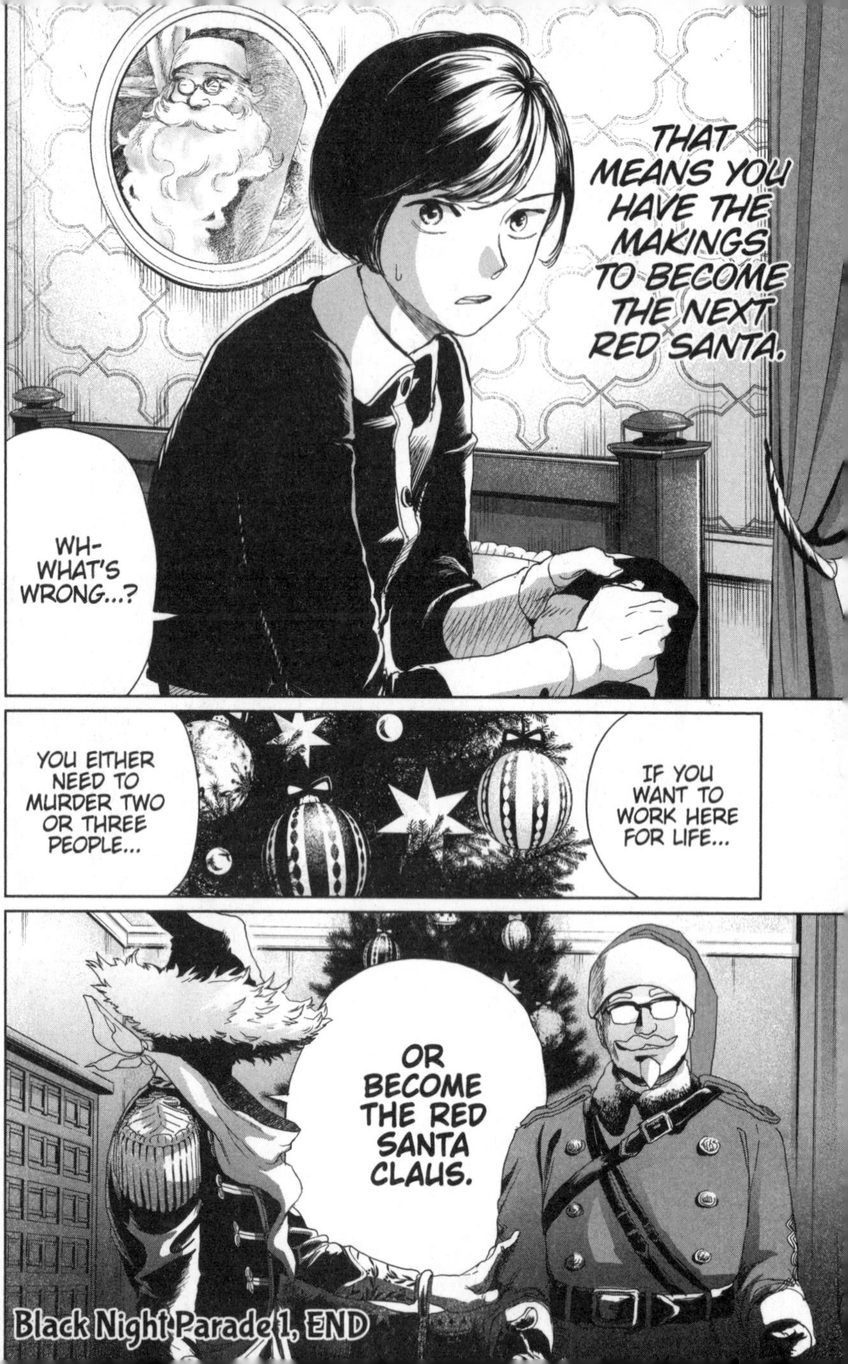
THAT MEANS YOU HAVE THE MAKINGS TO BECOME THE NEXT RED SANTA.
WH- WHAT'S WRONG...?
IF YOU WANT TO WORK HERE FOR LIFE...
YOU EITHER NEED TO MURDER TWO OR THREE PEOPLE...
OR BECOME THE RED SANTA CLAUS.
Black Night Parade 1, END

SEVEN SEAS ENTERTAINMENT PRESENTS

BLACK NIGHT PARADE VOL. 1

story & art by HIKARU NAKAMURA

TRANSLATION
Richard Tobin

LETTERING AND RETOUCH
Viet Phuong Vu

COVER DESIGN
H. Qi

PROOFREADER
Dave Murray

COPY EDITOR
Leighanna DeRouen

EDITOR
Linda Lombardi

SENIOR EDITOR
J.P. Sullivan

PREPRESS TECHNICIAN
Melanie Ujimori
Jules Valera

PRODUCTION DESIGNER
Stevie Wilson

PRODUCTION MANAGER
Lissa Pattillo

EDITOR-IN-CHIEF
Julie Davis

ASSOCIATE PUBLISHER
Adam Arnold

PUBLISHER
Jason DeAngelis

First published in Japan in 2016 by SHUEISHA Inc., Tokyo.
English translation rights arranged by SHUEISHA Inc.
through TOHAN CORPORATION, Tokyo.

Seven Seas press and purchase enquiries can be sent to Marketing Manager Lianne Sentar at press@gomanga.com. Information regarding the distribution and purchase of digital editions is available from Digital Manager CK Russell at digital@gomanga.com.

ISBN: 979-8-88843-189-4
Printed in Canada
First Printed: November 2023
10 9 8 7 6 5 4 3 2 1

READING DIRECTIONS

This book reads from ***right to left***, Japanese style. If this is your first time reading manga, you start reading from the top right panel on each page and take it from there. If you get lost, just follow the numbered diagram here. It may seem backwards at first, but you'll get the hang of it! Have fun!!

1
2
3
4
5
6
7
8
9

Follow us online: www.SevenSeasEntertainment.com

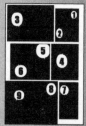